Guerrilla Strategies

Other Publications by Gérard Chaliand

Armed Struggle in Africa
New York: Monthly Review Press, 1969.

Peasants of North Vietnam
Baltimore: Penguin, 1969.

The Palestinian Resistance
Baltimore: Penguin, 1972.

Revolution in the Third World
Baltimore: Penguin, 1977.

People without a Country: The Kurds and Kurdistan
London: Zed Press, 1980.

The Struggle for Africa
London: Macmillan, 1982.

Food without Frontiers
London: Pluto Press, 1981.

Report from Afghanistan
Baltimore: Penguin, 1982.

Guerrilla Strategies

An Historical Anthology
from the Long March
to Afghanistan

Edited, with an introduction, by
GÉRARD CHALIAND

University of California Press *Berkeley   Los Angeles   London*

University of California Press
Berkeley and Los Angeles, California

University of California Press, Ltd.
London, England

© 1982 by
The Regents of the University of California

Library of Congress Cataloging in Publication Data
Main entry under title:

Guerrilla strategies.

Bibliography: p.
1. Guerrilla warfare—Addresses, essays,
lectures.   2. Counterinsurgency—Addresses, essays,
lectures.   3. Military history, Modern—20th cen-
tury—Addresses, essays, lectures.   4. Revolutions—
History—20th century—Addresses, essays, lectures.
I. Chaliand, Gérard, 1934–   .
U240.G8234   355′.02184   81-16347
ISBN 0-520-04444-4   AACR2
ISBN 0-520-04443-6 (pbk.)

Printed in the United States of America

1 2 3 4 5 6 7 8 9

This book is dedicated
to the United States of America,
my second home.

Contents

viii   Contents

Acknowledgments

This research has been done without the support of any grant or organization. I want to thank the following for their help: the Library of Congress (Washington, D. C.), la Bibliothèque Nationale (Paris), and the British Museum (London). Christoph Bertram, Director of the International Institute for Strategic Studies, London, and his staff have provided invaluable assistance, for which I extend my warmest thanks. I would also like to thank my translator, Mike Pallis, and, at the University of California Press, my friend Alain Hénon for his enthusiastic support of the project and Rebecca Stein for her fine editorial work.

Finally, many thanks to the original publishers of the works that follow for their permission to reprint.

Abbreviations

A.N.C.	African National Congress
A.R.V.N.	Revolutionary Army of Vietnam
A.V.N.O.J.	Anti-Fascist Council of the National Liberation of Yugoslavia
C.I.A.	Central Intelligence Agency
E.L.A.S.	National Popular Liberation Army
E.L.F.	Eritrean Liberation Front
E.L.N.	National Liberation Army
E.O.K.A.	National Organization of Cypriot Fighters
E.P.L.F.	Popular Liberation Front of Eritrea
E.R.P.	People's Revolutionary Army
F.A.R.C.	Colombian People's Revolutionary Armed Forces
F.A.R.P.	Armed Revolutionary Forces of the People
F.E.U.	Federation of University Students
F.L.I.N.G.	Front for the National Liberation of Guinea-Bissau
F.L.N.	National Liberation Front
F.L.Q.	National Liberation Front of Quebec
Frelimo	Mozambique Liberation Front
Frolinat	National Liberation Front

H.M.B.	Hukbalahuks
I.R.A.	Irish Revolutionary Army
L.E.H.I.	Lohami Herut Israel (Stern Gang)
M.I.R.	Movement of the Revolutionary Left
N.L.F.	National Liberation Front
O.A.S.	Secret Army Organization
O.A.U.	Organization of African Unity
O.L.A.S.	Organization of Latin American Solidarity
O.P.A.	Administrative and Political Organization of the Front
P.A.I.G.C.	African Party for the Independence of Guinea-Bissau and Cabo Verde
P.L.O.	Palestinian Liberation Organization
R.A.R.	The Rhodesian African Rifles
R.O.T.C.	Reserve Officers' Training Corps
S.A.S.	Special Administrative Section
U.P.C.	Union of Cameroonian Peoples
Z.A.N.U.	Zimbabwe African National Union
Z.A.P.U.	Zimbabwe African People's Union

Introduction

Guerrilla warfare has been particularly important ever since the Second World War. This book is concerned less with the history and more with the strategy of this kind of war, analyzing its underlying principles and their connection with the ultimate goal, political change. This is not to say that guerrilla techniques and tactics are a new phenomenon. On the contrary, they go back to the dawn of history. Guerrilla warfare has consistently been the choice of the weak who oppose the strong, for it enables them to avoid direct decisive confrontations and rely on harassment and surprise.

Guerrilla techniques are recorded in ancient Egypt and China. They are mentioned in the Bible and described, sometimes at length, by classical historians, notably Polybius, Appius, Plutarch, Flavius Josephus, Herodotus, and Tacitus. While Rome was still expanding its empire, in the two centuries before Christ, there were long and bitter guerrilla wars in Spain and, later, during the first century A.D., in North Africa. Throughout the Middle Ages and afterward, religious movements made use of guerrilla techniques, as did the peasants who fought in innumerable revolts, the classical example being the peasant war in sixteenth-century Germany. In the Ottoman-dominated Balkans, from the fifteenth to the nineteenth century, socially or nationally oriented bandit groups and movements were based entirely on guerrilla tactics. The most famous guerrilla war, fought by the Albanians against the authority of the Turkish sultan, was simply on a much larger scale.

This type of warfare has been characteristic of social and religious movements and has even enabled people to avoid taxation, but it has also been one of the most important forms of resistance to aggression and foreign occupation, notably during the expansion of the Roman, Ottoman, and Napoleonic empires and during the European expansion in the nineteenth century. Guerrilla tactics played a not unimportant role in the American War of Independence, as fought by Marion, also known as the Swamp Fox. Apart from the Vendée uprising during the French Revolution, however, the real "classics" of this period were the wars of national resistance in the Tyrol (1809), in Russia (1812), and in Spain (1808–1813)—giving us the term "guerrilla." More than any other ideology, modern nationalism managed to extend guerrilla warfare beyond regional or local confines.

Military theoreticians, particularly French and German, have not overlooked the peculiarities of the "little war." It was analyzed as early as the eighteenth century, but there was no treatment of the subject as a whole until Le Mière de Corvey wrote his *Des partisans et des corps irréguliers*. The two great theoreticians of the nineteenth century, Clausewitz and Jomini, gave it some attention. For Clausewitz, influenced as he was by the emergence of nationalism, popular warfare was a war of peasant resistance to a foreign aggressor. Several other theoreticians of the period just preceding the 1830s, notably the Italians, wrote on the subject, sometimes displaying an appreciation of its political potential. But, at the time, guerrilla warfare was quite rightly regarded as only a minor technique that could not carry the day and that was best used to back up a regular army.

In fact, if one leaves aside the Carlist Wars of Succession in Spain and the Italian Risorgimento, guerrilla warfare was a minor and very marginal feature of the post-Napoleonic period, the main examples having been the Polish insurrections and the Greek War of Independence. Indeed, from 1830 until the end of the nineteenth century, as socialism became more influential, urban insurrection came to be considered a better means of gaining power. Rapid urbanization, mass proletarianization, the conservatism of the peasantry, and the increasing centralization of the state apparatus within the capital all seemed to confirm this viewpoint, which found explosive expression in 1830, 1848, and 1871. It was only the Italians and the Poles who felt that studies on guerrilla warfare were particularly relevant. As in the United States, Latin America's Wars of Independence, led by Bolivar and San Martín, were essentially fought by regular armies. The exceptions were in Mexico, in Venezuela (where the *Llaneros* gave considerable support to Bolivar), and in the Plata (especially in Uruguay, where the *montoneros* were active). In Peru (1809–1816) a major insurrection was crushed. The astonishing saga of Toussaint L'Ouverture in Haiti provides another instance of guerrilla activity in Latin America.

A little later, two major guerrilla offensives against Spanish domination were launched in Cuba (particularly in Oriente) from 1863 to 1878 and from 1895 to 1898. The outcome was that the island ceased to be a Crown dependency; in the process, the Spanish General Weyler learned to take the technique of counterinsurgency farther than ever before.

European Expansion and Guerrilla Resistance

The longest, most numerous, and most important guerrilla wars were fought in response to European colonial expansion in Asia and Africa. Examples of such struggles against the British include the bitter, long drawn-out campaigns in Burma (1824–1825, 1852, 1885), the endless wars fought by the Afghans, the Sierra Leone Campaign, the Boer War (1899–1902), and the Somalia Campaigns that dragged on from the turn of the century until just after the First World War. The French fought in Algeria from 1830 to 1847. The conquest of Vietnam took them ten years. Gradually, they perfected political and military counterinsurgency techniques, and they fought on, in Madagascar (1844–1895) and in West Africa, where they encountered stiff opposition (1882–1898). Bitter campaigns were fought by the Dutch in Java and by the Germans against the Herreros of South West Africa. The Portuguese Wars in Angola and Guinea-Bissau continued for more than half a century. The Russians had to overcome the guerrilla forces led by Sheikh Shamyl before they could control the Caucasus (1836–1859). American colonization of the Philippines was bitterly resisted. Finally, full-scale guerrilla struggles erupted repeatedly in nineteenth-century China.

Guerrilla operations nonetheless remained marginal in the eyes of Western strategists. Military writing around the end of the nineteenth century and immediately after was still concerned almost exclusively with regular armies and mastery of the seas, as can be seen from the works of Moltke and von der Goltz (German); Ardant du Picq and Foch (French); and Mahan (American). The orientation was justified, for the ensuing First World War was fought almost entirely with conventional forces. Guerrilla operations played no part in that conflict, with two minor exceptions: Lawrence's campaign in Arabia, which owes its reputation more to his remarkable talent as an author than to its military importance, and the exploits of General von Lettow Vorbek, who opposed the British Army in Tanganyika from 1915 to 1918 with a few thousand African soldiers and a handful of German officers. The latter struggle is less well known as Vorbek was no writer and, after all, was on the losing side.

Apart from the Irish National Movement (1916–1920) and the activities of the Macedonian Internal Revolutionary Organization, which has been fighting since the beginning of the century to reintegrate a community split between three states, the main theater of guerrilla activity following the First World War was the Soviet Union. The Soviet authorities found themselves under attack by irregulars almost immediately after the revolution. Some had a left-wing orientation, such as Makhno's irregulars in the Ukraine; others were simply adventurers, like Ungern-Sternberg in the marches of Mongolia. In the early 1930s the Basmatchi Muslims of Central Asia also took up arms against the Soviet state, and the technique of counterinsurgency ironically found itself enriched by a few texts from General Tukhatchevski. And after the defeat of the Second Reich, German volunteer brigades fought on for years against the Red Army in the Baltic countries. One should never forget that guerrilla warfare is only a technique and is in itself neither left wing nor right wing, as countless examples from the past clearly illustrate.

In the colonies, calm prevailed during the period following the First World War. The established order was contested by only an extremely small elite, and European public opinion remained convinced of the validity of the West's civilizing mission. The major outbreaks of guerrilla warfare occurred in Morocco against the successive Spanish and French occupiers (1925–1927) and in Libya against the Italians (1922–1932). In British-mandate Palestine, the Palestinian guerrillas' struggle against the influx of Jewish settlers continued unsuccessfully from 1936 to 1939. In Latin America, throughout this period, there was only one guerrilla war worth noting: after six years of struggle (1927–1933), the left populist forces of Sandino won the day in Nicaragua. In China, after suffering terrible defeats in the cities, the communists were withdrawing to the countryside. Having survived the five Kuomintang attempts to encircle them, they organized an orderly retreat and by 1935–1936 had already established a solid base in the Yenan.

The Second World War was about to start.

Partisan Campaigns During the Second World War

During the Second World War, partisan campaigns were fought against both the Germans and the Japanese. In Greece, Albania, and the U.S.S.R., this type of warfare achieved substantial, if not always decisive, results. It was also a factor in France, Italy (after 1943), and especially Yugoslavia.

In the U.S.S.R., Stalin appealed to the people to form partisan groups as early as July 1941. The mobilization was conducted from above, and in less than two years their number grew from 30,000 to more than 250,000; these men were state irregulars following in the classical tradition of earlier armies. To counter the partisan menace, both in the Soviet Union and in the Balkans, the Germans organized specialized troops called *Jagdkommandos* (hunting commandos); these combatants operated at night and had no contact with the local population. Generally speaking, because the communists already had a political infrastructure that could be adapted to armed struggle, they were the most easily organized. Indeed, as soon as the U.S.S.R. was invaded, resistance movements were mobilized. But the Communist Party of Yugoslavia, led by an exceptional man and a group of remarkable cadres, was the only organization that presented a platform of demands common to all the ethnic and religious groups in the country. The inactivity of the communists' immediate rival, Mikhailovitch, along with the tremendously repressive and confining character of A. Pavelitch's pro-Nazi regime, gave them plenty of recruits, whom they were able to organize without external aid (1941–1943). In spite of very different circumstances, the partisans were able to elude all German offensives intended to encircle them. Under similar conditions (tempered slightly by the country's geographic isolation), the Albanians, like the Yugoslavs, were able to seize power at the end of the war.

In Greece, the communists participated actively in the Nazi resistance. Having held onto the weapons left over from the previous war, they resumed hostilities from 1946 until 1947, inflicting severe defeats on a poorly organized and unmotivated regular army. Because they controlled the northern area that bordered Yugoslavia and Albania (encompassing Mt. Vitsi and Mt. Grammos), their logistical position was ideal. However, their situation soon began to deteriorate. In July 1948, the Cominform expelled Tito. Markos and many other Greek leaders were replaced by cadres whose approach was more closely in keeping with Stalin's. Yugoslavia closed its frontier. Internal dissension spread through the communist movement, and eventually a new strategy of frontal confrontation was substituted for guerrilla operations. The moment was particularly ill chosen. The Greek Army, recently reorganized by General Papagos and fully reequipped by the United States, crushed the divided and logistically isolated movement in the major August 1949 offensive against the communist bases.

That same year, however, one of the most important events in postwar history occurred: the Chinese communists came to power. One fourth of the world's population came under the sway of a radically different kind of regime. From 1937, when Mao Tse-tung and Chu Teh commanded only 80,000 men, to 1945, when their forces had grown ten times over, the communists had been busily organizing the vast northern areas, extending their control over more than 20 percent of the Chinese population. Their military potential had increased in all respects. They managed to survive the Japanese extermination campaigns, reinforce their positions, and steadily prepare themselves for the decisive postwar confrontation with the Kuomintang, which lasted from 1946 to 1949 and ended in the complete military victory of the communist forces.

The campaign in China was based on a remarkable innovation. Until the Second World War, the military doctrine of both right and left treated guerrilla operations as purely secondary. The main concerns were, quite rightly, aviation and mechanical forces. Although they contain nothing new in terms of technique, Mao Tse-tung's writings, which deal with revolutionary war rather than with guerrilla operations per se, constitute a major breakthrough. It is quite meaningless to isolate the strictly military element in his writing, as certain authors have been tempted to do, for what matters is the close link between the political and the military that characterizes Mao's thinking. The point is that *guerrilla warfare is a military tactic aimed at harassing an adversary, whereas revolutionary war is a military means whereby to overthrow a political regime.*

What was Mao saying that was new? Not unlike his predecessors, he considered guerrilla warfare more than a mere backup for the regular army, although Mao did not in fact write about guerrilla war. What he was concerned with was revolutionary war, in which regular army units employ the tactics of irregulars, partisan units fight in parallel to the regular forces (with their actions sometimes considered most important), and classical full frontal assaults are launched only when the situation demands them. Mao's real innovation lay elsewhere, in the field of politics. His political insight was special, for he was a specific and unforeseen avatar of Leninism.

Mao's great political breakthrough was his unorthodox and unexpected application of Lenin's theory of the vanguard party to the peasantry. For the intellectuals, semi-intellectuals, and other more or less enlightened, humiliated, patriotic, and radical elements in the dominated countries, Leninism appeared as a tool, a solution to their immediate problems.

Leninism, the political innovation that made the October revolution possible, opened the way for the creation of new regimes in Europe (Yugoslavia and Albania) and Asia (China and Indochina), wherever the vanguard party could count on the support of a large part of the population. The Vietnamese and Chinese approaches, which are in fact very similar, both stem from Leninism: they rely on generalized propaganda, mass organization (noncombatants and combatants being given equal importance), and a vanguard party that functions as the instrument for political mobilization and military leadership. But all this resulted in a truly effective operational force in Asia only

when the full consequences had been drawn from the discovery
that the peasantry had revolutionary potential.[1]

Historical Factors in Popular Warfare

Purposefully or not, the movements that have engaged in
armed struggle during the last four decades each fit a particular
framework. This framework did not automatically determine
each movement's chances of success or failure, but it did provide
a number of favorable or unfavorable reference points according
to which a definite process was either accelerated or slowed
down. Three historical forces helped shape revolutionary warfare
and guerrilla techniques in the contemporary period.

The first influence we have already mentioned: the emergence,
on a national scale, of the peasant question and, more generally,
the participation of peasants in armed struggle, either as a combat force or as an underground political structure. A vanguard
organization leads the struggle, and its mobilizatory ideology elic-
its a spirit of self-sacrifice, discipline, and cohesion. Such an organization tends to ensure that it enjoys substantial support
among the population by a process of education/politicization and
selective use of terror.

The second important influence is the Second World War. The
Japanese and German attempt at securing world hegemony broke
the international equilibrium and opened the way for the successful Chinese, Vietnamese, Albanian, and Yugoslav campaigns as
well as for the abortive ones in Malaysia, the Philippines, and
Greece.

The third influence stems from the second and is the gradual
breakdown and eventual disappearance of the European colonial
empires. The colonial powers were seriously weakened by the
partial defeat the Japanese wrought in Asia. The colonial administrations had collapsed under the Japanese thrust. Japanese fascism preached its own version of "Asia for the Asians" as it
vanguished the whites; the Western powers fought back in the
name of democracy and freedom—but for whom? As the colonial
wars continued, European public opinion, once frankly imperialist, gradually began to discover the colonized peoples' right to

[1] Cf. Mao Tse-tung, *An Inquiry on the Hunan Peasantry* (Peking, 1957).

liberty and independence. The colonized peoples began to see that what they had once regarded as a fact of life was actually quite unacceptable. As a result, many armed liberation movements in colonized or semicolonized countries did not have to fight on till they had secured a military victory, which in many cases was quite beyond their reach. By dint of their determination and tenacity—aided by the weariness of Western public opinion, the high cost of war, and the impossibility of any military solution—many of these movements achieved what was primarily a political victory.

This third factor has two major consequences. First, given that European colonialism has almost disappeared from the Third World (except in Namibia), the armed national liberation movements must have reached their zenith during the 1950s and 1960s. With the collapse of Portuguese colonialism in 1974, an era came to an end. Second, it is important to note that *political* victories are only possible in struggles directed against the Western democracies that do not use *all* the means at their disposal; these regimes, sensitive to public opinion at home, will often consent to negotiate, especially since a political defeat carries no serious consequences for them. But dictatorial regimes, whether totalitarian or not, never consider negotiating with a weaker adversary (consider Budapest, 1956) and are certainly not concerned about domestic public opinion. (International opinion is the public opinion of the dictatorships.) To this day, there is practically no example of a struggle waged against this sort of regime that has achieved even a few of its aims without first securing a complete military victory. In Latin America, Asia, and Africa, secessionist or social movements can have only one hope: to win by force of arms.

The Lessons of Revolutionary Warfare

The lessons that can be drawn from the experience of revolutionary war during the past half century can be reduced to two fundamental points.

- The conditions for the insurrection must be as ripe as possible, the most favorable situation being one in which foreign domination or aggression makes it possible to mobilize broad support for a goal that is both social and national. Failing this, the ruling stratum should be in the middle of an acute political crisis and popular discontent should be both intense and wide ranging.

- The most important element in a guerrilla campaign is the *underground political infrastructure*, rooted in the population itself and coordinated by middle-ranking cadres. Such a structure is a prerequisite for growth and will provide the necessary recruits, information, and local logistics.

There have been several armed movements that at least superficially owed little to Leninism, notably General Grivas' E.O.K.A. in Cyprus and the Mau Mau in Kenya. Although ideologically not "communist," very few modern nationalist movements of the past thirty years have been able to avoid using the Leninist organizational apparatus. They have had to rely on a mobilizatory political organization; propaganda has been an important aspect of their struggle; cohesion on a national scale has been crucial; and unity has stemmed from a definite ideology, be it nationalism with a populist connotation or something radically revolutionary. Leninism, originally a technique developed to bring about internationalist proletarian revolutions, has clearly undergone strange and unforeseen evolutions.

By contrast, the class struggle, that ideology which grew from revolutionary Marxism and was propagated by Leninism, has been rejected by many national liberation movements, wherever such a struggle seemed incompatible with the idea of common opposition to a foreign invader or occupier. Not all elites have been collaborationist—far from it. In the Far East, the Vietnamese consistently managed to set up united fronts dominated by the communists. But elsewhere, notably in the Middle East, the various communist movements, and the other more or less important followers of Marxism-Leninism in a postwar period dominated by the Cold War, were incapable of using the national question to their advantage and generally seemed to be appendages of the Soviet Union.

Nature and Typology of Armed Movements

The useful but rather vague term "guerrilla war" encompasses a varied range of armed activities, including:

- very sophisticated popular wars that may well lead to military victory;
- armed national liberation movements conducted on a national or local level but controlling and organizing at least a significant part of the country;
- regionally isolated embryonic guerrilla movements that pose no direct threat to the established authorities and whose main problems are usually simple survival and preventing a lapse into mere banditism;
- commando actions launched from a neighboring frontier at the behest of a leadership in exile; and
- militarily impotent struggles amounting to little more than headline-grabbing terrorism.

These forms of struggle, clearly differentiated by the level of action each involves, are not, in principle, necessarily characteristic of any particular ideological movement.

A rough typology of the armed conflicts in the Third World over the past decade enables us to distinguish three main categories:

- national liberation movements fighting against a colonial power, an aggressor, or a foreign occupier;
- revolutionary struggles based on social demands in independent countries (civil wars);
- struggles waged by ethnic, religious, or ethnic-religious minorities, either with a more or less openly declared secessionist aim or with lesser ambitions.

Each of the three categories of insurgency has a markedly different probability of success. The first kind of armed conflict is the most likely to arouse mass popular support within the country and to benefit from international backing. Since the Second World War, the following wars of national liberation have fallen within this category: Vietnam (until 1954); Indonesia (1945–1949); Malaysia; the traditionally oriented Mau Mau in Kenya; the Union of Cameroonian Peoples (1957–1960); General Grivas' E.O.K.A. in Cyprus; Algeria; and the former Portuguese colonies of Guinea-Bissau, Angola, and Mozambique. Examples of conflicts in which foreign occupation/aggression and the national question are of critical importance include the Zionist movement in Palestine (1946–1947); the South Vietnamese N.L.F. (once the

Americans had committed their own troops); the Palestinian national movement; the struggle against the British and then the Iranians in Oman (Dhofar); the national liberation movements in southern Africa (Zimbabwe, Namibia, and South Africa); the activities of the Provisional I.R.A. in Ulster; and the Polisario in the ex-Spanish Sahara.

The second category, encompassing those struggles aiming to overthrow the established regime in an independent state, includes all the struggles in Latin America, notably in Cuba, Venezuela, Guatemala, Colombia, Uruguay, Nicaragua, and El Salvador. In Asia, the struggles of the Pathet Lao and the Khmer Rouge fall within this category. In Africa, struggles of this kind broke out in Zaire (1961–1966) and in Chad. Finally, in Europe, there was the case of postwar Greece.

In the third category, covering secessionist struggles or struggles for autonomy conducted by ethnic or ethnic-religious minorities, we can place Biafra (more like a conventional war than a guerrilla campaign), the Kurds of Iraq (1961–1970 and 1974–1975), and southern Sudan (1965–1972), where a black non-Muslim minority fought an Arab Muslim majority. More recently, movements of this kind have developed among the Baluchis in Pakistan and the Kurds in Iran. This sort of struggle will inevitably become increasingly widespread.

Before we analyze these struggles, the general laws that pertain to them, and their particular characteristics, it is worthwhile to try to answer the most complex question that arises: under what conditions will an insurrection break out and what determines its efficacy? There is no single model of armed struggle and no classical situation that invariably precedes it, so there are necessarily several different answers. The simplest insurrection is that directed against a foreign occupier, preferably white and Western (given the contemporary context). Minority movements, especially when they openly proclaim separatist aims—as, for example, the Eritreans do—are by definition in a less favorable position. Furthermore, the wave of anti-Western feeling that grew out of the anticolonial struggles in Africa and Asia has until recently hidden the fact that states in these two continents can have an imperialistic policy toward weaker groups or nations, both within and without its frontiers. Nonetheless, such minority struggles will often manage to mobilize a considerable number of the population concerned, provided both that the injustices at issue are keenly felt and that a capable leadership emerges (which is not always so simple, given that the minorities are often backward compared to the group oppressing them). It is nearly always far more difficult to launch an insurrection based on class conflict, unless of course the state under attack has already been largely undermined.

It is a rare tyranny that is so unpopular and so poorly defended by those who benefit from it that it collapses without a fight to the finish; Cuba under Batista was an unusual exception. It is also rare for an insurrectionary movement to find a provisional common denominator that unites the diffuse discontent of the various strata of the population, each with its own aspirations and motives. The Shah of Iran did manage to alienate most of the population. His program of rapid growth made wide sectors of the population economically marginal and dislocated their traditional universe; he shocked the masses by proclaiming himself Shah of the Aryans, thereby identifying himself with a pre-Islamic Iranian past that was meaningless to a population firmly committed to an identity based on Shia Islam; finally, his tyranny weighed heavily on various sections of the middle classes.

The actual *catalyst* of insurrection can vary, although certain classical factors, such as excessive taxation, prohibitive tariffs, religious or ethnic oppression, and so on, frequently reappear. But the catalyst itself is often the result of a particular spirit of the age—a specific international situation or a combination of characteristic local features.

In Iran, the catalyst was an increasingly aggressive religious zeal that developed within a few months in the context of the urban insurrections. It provided a focus for the suburban masses, the far-left movements that sought to keep in touch with the people, and the more liberal political aspirations of the middle classes. In Cuba this focus was provided by a group of a dozen men with a program based on the struggle against tyranny and a demand for "bread and freedom." In Algeria, a few hundred militants who had broken away from the reformist secret organization of the National Movement were crucial. In Kenya, traditionalist tribal elements regrouped around the issue of foreign control of lands.

The general tendency of the period, nonetheless, is one of the organizational volunteerism of a movement or party that wishes to catalyze the destruction of a situation deemed unacceptable or potentially revolutionary.

Reduced to its fundamentals, the first objective of an avant-garde group is to make already sensitized elements—trade unionists, semiintellectuals, marginalized and rebellious youth, the unemployed—aware of oppression. These people, the middle-level cadre, will then be able to enlighten the more passive sectors of the population. The degree to which the masses are oppressed is less significant than how they perceive their oppression. It is critical that leaders of the mobilized group seek to understand the society. However, for the past thirty years many revolutionary groups have been unable to reach this stage of development.

Without doubt, during a movement's initial development nothing is more important than achieving a correct understanding of the social situation one seeks to alter. Such careful analysis would have led numerous Latin American groups to the conclusion that the likelihood of a victorious end to armed struggle was minimal if not zero. In order for the directing core to develop a successful strategy, the leaders must properly evaluate both the economic dependency and social composition of the area and the availability of sensitized and easily mobilized ranks (these could be composed of either rural or urban populations, ethnic or religious groups, or people of a particular age). Viewed in this light, once its initial errors of urban strategy have been rectified, Amilcar Cabral's analysis of the society of Guinea-Bissau as it relates to national liberation is most interesting. It consists of determining the sociological imbalances within a society,[2] its revolutionary potential, the political and military weaknesses of the opponent, and the relevant regional and international support available.

The formation of a middle-ranking cadre structure is another essential step. The middle-ranking cadres must be drawn from the people and must speak the people's language if they are to bring about a mass mobilization. The lack of such cadres has proved disastrous for many revolutionary groups, notably in Latin America. Che Guevara's failure in Bolivia is a striking example.

[2] Cf. Amilcar Cabral, *Unity and Struggle: Speeches and* Writings (New York, 1980) for a brief analysis of the social situation in Portuguese Guinea.

In the early stages, the aim of a vanguard movement is to secure the effective support of a substantial portion of the population. This requires a propaganda effort on two levels: indoctrinating the population and accomplishing successful armed actions that demonstrate the opponent's vulnerability and one's own strength. Terrorism may be used both against those who collaborate politically with the enemy and against the actual enemy. This mobilizatory propaganda should lead to organization—another stage many movements never reached, having confused it with agitation. The point is not merely to break the population's passive respect for the established order: a new underground political infrastructure must be constructed and built up patiently by the middle-ranking cadres at a village and neighborhood level. Agitation may produce explosions of support when circumstances are favorable, but organization makes it possible to hold on and even advance when times are hard, as they nearly always are. When control of specific areas has been established, new administrative, political, social, and economic structures must be set up within them, so that a break can be made with the old order and the framework of the new can actually be developed.

The essential elements of this process are absolutely central to a popular war. It is difficult to carry out guerrilla warfare on a national rather than regional scale, but, when the rebellion has wide support, counterinsurrection becomes an arduous task. The problem is that the general level of consciousness is usually low, and the oppressed will fight only when their backs are to the wall. Armed struggle is thus an acceptable course only when there is simply no other way to resolve the crisis within a society; only then is national support possible. Too many Latin American armed movements have initiated armed struggle without considering the situation and the possibility of legal and semilegal action.

In some cases, an existing organization having some links with the population may benefit from a revolutionary situation or an unexpected explosion. This happened in Russia between February and October 1917. Although a theory of the accidental is by definition impossible, it is clear that wars, more than anything else, have made many historical accidents—and much guerrilla activity—possible.

In all mobilizations, the motivations at work are enormously varied. Psychological factors, such as feelings of humiliation and hatred (channeled and cultivated by the organization), a thirst for dignity, and the quest for identity, are fairly fundamental and play a far more important role than the hope of economic change, especially among the young people who usually do most of the fighting.

It becomes very difficult to eradicate an insurrectional movement once its large-scale underground political infrastructure has been set up. Many other factors can still tip the balance, of course. The quality of a fighting movement is often determined by its historical heritage, but a mobilizatory ideology can greatly increase the frequency of successful combat. The level of mobilization/organization of the troops is critical: those people actively engaged in the struggle must be thoroughly convinced of the cause, since there will be no shortage of reasons to doubt the possibility of victory. Also, the average age of guerrillero troops in the Third World (15 to 25 years) is much lower than is usual in conventional armies, and this extreme youth often results in the boldest action. Suicide commandos, whose intervention may prove decisive at a critical moment, are usually composed of these young guerrilleros. But the calibre of the leader is as important as, and in some circumstances more important than, the quality of the troops (consider Mao, Tito, Castro, and Cabral). The leader's strategic, political, and military savvy has consistently been as crucial as popular support. It is not enough to have a following: one must also know how to get to where one wants to go. Finally, the existence of a *sanctuary* just over the border is almost essential and always highly desirable. Few popular wars did not rely on such sanctuaries. Only China, Yugoslavia, and Cuba lacked them, but the rebel forces in these countries were able to set up bases that more or less served as sanctuaries.

Historical Experiences and What They Teach Us

The revolutionary wars in China and Vietnam were exemplary in many ways. The reasons for their success are varied and include:
- the existence of a party that managed to secure a broad popular base and set itself up as the uncontested champion of both patriotism and social change; and

• the Japanese aggression that decisively weakened the established authorities and fired the patriotism of the Vietnamese and Chinese people.

In both countries, guerrilla techniques were only a means to build up and then defend the basis on which a popular war could be conducted, and the struggle eventually turned into an offensive fought on classical but not conventional lines.

Guerrilla tactics were introduced after the Long March, but it was really only after the Japanese invasion that priority was given to partisan activities. On the military level, the fundamental points stressed by Mao include the following: the need for firm bases (sanctuaries) from which to wage prolonged offensives (this is particularly important given China's size and demography); the importance of mobile fronts and articulation between partisan forces and the regular army; and, finally, the human factor, or the motivation of the troops. At the end of the Long March (1935), the Chinese communists had about 35,000 men left (they started with 100,000), yet their numbers had grown to over a million by 1945, when the Japanese were defeated. Their main efforts during those years were more political than military and were geared to the political end of building a broad popular base in well-organized areas (this in contrast to the mismanagement and corruption of the Kuomintang). In the end, the Kuomintang lost because they had no real will to fight.

In September 1945, Ho Chi Minh proclaimed the independence of Vietnam, seizing the opportunity presented by the prevailing political vacuum: the Japanese had been evacuated, the Kuomintang Chinese occupied only the north, the colonizing power had not yet reasserted itself, and the British were far to the south. The French did not return in force to repossess their colony until ten months later and in doing so committed two major errors, one military and the other political:

• first, they thought they could fight communism without offering an alternative that would satisfy national aspirations (a fallacy noted by General Leclerc); and
• second, they were misled by a colonialist (and racist) underestimation of their adversary and his particular form of combat.

The Vietnamese modernizing elites had in fact drawn a great deal on European military thought and technology and were thus able to break free from the West.

The Vietnamese organized their military forces on the basis of local militias that evolved into regional forces and, finally, into the national popular army.

In the course of the war, the Vietminh also made mistakes, but only military ones that were not repeated—for example, Giap's frontal assaults in late 1950 and early 1951. The French troops were very well equipped and initiated some interesting new tactics, such as the use of *Dinassauts* (small gunships) on the navigable waterways, a technique the Americans did not rediscover until much later. But right up to the fall of Dien Bien Phu, the French General Staff continued to underestimate their opponents. According to a widespread belief, Dien Bien Phu fell because it was in a geographical basin. In fact it would have fallen whatever the terrain, for it was far from the French logistic bases and, above all, the French General Staff—not their reconnaissance services—underestimated their adversary's military capacity, artillery, and logistics. Some brilliant senior officers in the Algerian war (Ximenes, J. Hogard, Souyris, and L. Poirier, for example) used the lessons of Indochina to achieve a clear military victory. The victory turned into a frustrating political defeat, which was quite predictable, given the parameters of the problem. It was obviously impossible to "integrate" ten million Muslims, and, since the F.L.N. was nationalist rather than communist, there was no way of playing off one force against another within the overall perspective of a move toward independence.

The United States sent half a million troops into Vietnam when the Saigon regime it had been actively supporting was about to collapse under the assault of the N.L.F. Despite all its technological might, the United States proved incapable of beating its opponents. When the Tet offensive was launched in February 1968, General Westmoreland boasted that the Vietcong were effectively finished. Although the N.L.F. suffered high losses, Tet turned out to be a psychological Dien Bien Phu for the United States.

However, in spite of its eventual political defeat following the military intervention of the North Vietnamese Army, the United States did manage to conduct a reasonably successful two-pronged policy of counterinsurrection from 1968 to 1972. Its main planks were, first, the physical liquidation of many N.L.F. cadres during

Operation Phoenix (in which they combed village after village in all the infiltrated areas) and, second, the economic reinforcement of a strongly anticommunist urban stratum that was committed to resisting a communist takeover.

Other guerrilla wars are obviously minor when compared with these two "classics," but it is nonetheless interesting to briefly examine the reasons why some succeeded and, even more so, why some failed.

Asia: Two Major Failures

Having already fought the Japanese, the communists in Malaysia went to war again in 1948, and it took the British about eight years to defeat them. Here, too, colonial authority had been weakened by the Japanese occupation. But the mainly Chinese insurgents were operating within a bi-ethnic society; 35 percent of the population was Chinese and 65 percent Muslim Malays. Although the Chinese controlled an important part of the economic activity, they were not really integrated into the society, for the British made it quite difficult to obtain Malaysian citizenship— the more so because the Muslims mistrusted the Chinese. The half a million Chinese squatters who had sought refuge in the jungle after the Japanese occupation formed the base of the insurgency and exacerbated the problem of Muslim-Chinese relations. Certain of the support of the Muslim Malays in general and of the feudal class in particular (whom they promised independence), the British were able gradually to respond to the state of emergency and develop a counterinsurgency plan. This plan later served as a model in Kenya, Cyprus, Oman, and other countries.

In the Philippines, which had been an American colony until 1946, the Huk communist forces had been fighting the Japanese since 1942. They decided to resume the armed struggle, even though the United States had granted them a potentially immobilizing independence. The struggle was initially successful (1948–1950), but then in 1950 roughly half the political leaders of the movement were arrested in an ambush in Manila, and the struggle remained regionally circumscribed (regionalism is endemic to the Philippines). Isolated and on the defensive, the movement crumbled under the blows of a reorganized counterinsurgency, which also promised amnesty to defectors and mollified the population by offering agrarian reform.

Meanwhile, in Indonesia, the Dutch were faced with armed struggle and abandoned the country after attempting to reconquer it by force (1949). The British withdrew from India and Burma without a fight, having created all the conditions for a partition of the Indian Union. Their departure was of course enormously accelerated by the intense campaign of passive resistance organized by Gandhi.

Both in Laos and Cambodia, the various forms of insurgent movements over the past several decades have always been closely linked to what was happening in Vietnam. The emergence of the Pathet Lao and the Khmer Rouge in 1975 was inseparable from the American withdrawal from the area.

Anticolonial Struggles in Africa

The Challe plan (1958–1959) facilitated the military victory of the French troops in the Algerian war, a victory that was wiped out by complete political defeat when the myth of French Algeria collapsed before the will of the overwhelming majority of the Muslim population to be Algerians. Repression in Algeria in 1945 and in Madagascar in 1947, struggles in Tunisia from 1952 to 1955, the situation in Morocco, Dien Bien Phu in Vietnam, the U.C.P. operations from 1957 to 1960, and above all the Algerian war itself had shaken France's hold on its empire. Eventually, nearly all the French colonies attained independence without major confrontation.

In the British empire, the Mau Mau insurrection in Kenya, poorly organized and lacking a modernist elite, was eventually crushed after a bitter struggle.

Most of the guerrilla wars in Africa remained on a fairly low level, notably in Zaire from 1960 to 1966 and in the Cameroons from the 1960s on. The struggles were regionally circumscribed and were often ephemeral efforts by small isolated groups, such as the Sawaba in Niger and the African Independence Party in Senegal. From the 1960s until 1974, when Fascism was overthrown in Portugal, the most serious struggles in the continent were fought in the Portuguese colonies. The campaign organized by the P.A.I.G.C. and led by the most remarkable of African revolutionary leaders, Amilcar Cabral, was quite exemplary. Angola, however, was riven by the ethnic polarization of its three rival movements, and it was only in 1971–1972 that Frelimo in Mozambique was able to penetrate the central provinces.

In Chad, despite internal dissension, the Frolinat managed to resist the specialized French forces from 1966 to 1979. The insurrection was essentially based on regional, ethnic, and religious alliances (among Northern Muslims) but managed to chip away at the area controlled by the central authorities, who were themselves associated with the regional, ethnic, and religious base that reflects the historical heritage of the Sahel area. The southward push by Muslim elements that are linked in varying degrees to the Arab and Muslim world seems likely to continue in the Sahel. However, the political errors of Colonel Khadafy, who is pursuing an annexationist policy, may yet contribute to the development of a currently nonexistent nationalism.

Unlike all African colonies except Eritrea, the ex-Spanish Sahara was not granted independence but was simply attached to Morocco by fiat. This outcome could not but anger the Algerians, who had decided to help set up the Polisario and had worked actively to support it. Disregarding the role played by competing national interests, the struggle, which continues with considerable success, can only reinforce the sense of indentity of the Sahravis (inhabitants of the ex-Spanish Sahara). The use of motorized forces by the Polisario (and by the Eritreans) is incidentally a new and notable feature of guerrilla war.

Secessionist Struggles

Minority struggles are a growing issue in Africa and, given the continent's colonial heritage, will continue to be so unless federal solutions, regional reorganizations, and measures to promote ethnic equality are applied in time. Biafra's attempted secession does not fall within the scope of this essay, since the war there was essentially fought on conventional lines. In southern Sudan, a black non-Muslim group rose up against a central authority that the Arab and Muslim majority controlled. The struggle, activated by ethnic, religious, economic, and cultural forces, eventually made the authorities grant a level of autonomy they would not otherwise have conceded. The Eritrean national movement, and particularly the E.P.L.F. (militarily and politically the most well organized group within the movement), also warrants consideration.

Eritrea, an Italian colony from 1890 to 1941, was federated to the Ethiopian Empire in 1952 at the request of Emperor Haile Selassie. British support and the offices of the United Nations assisted. Then in 1962 the negus annexed Eritrea as the fourteenth province of his empire.

The armed struggle waged by the E.L.F., an essentially Muslim movement that enjoys the support of the Arab countries, developed quite slowly until about 1967–1968. A split then occurred, and Christian elements set up the E.P.L.F. The population as a whole is about 50 percent Muslim and 50 percent Christian, but the Muslims are divided, and the Christians, all of whom speak the same language, make up the largest single ethnic group. After the civil war with the E.L.F. (1971–1974), the E.P.L.F. emerged as undoubtedly the most well organized armed movement in the continent. This achievement was largely due to the fact that the movement's leadership and cadre structure within the country based itself on a very strict revolutionary ideology. The negative aspects of such rigor are well known, but it does confer certain advantages in the course of an armed struggle. The troops will be more highly motivated and more willing to risk their lives than troops lacking a strong ideology; equally important, an exceptional level of discipline and organizational efficiency can be imposed. The urban background of the higher cadres, the cultural level of the middle cadres, and the warlike traditions of the society undoubtedly also contributed to the movement's achievements. In 1977, the E.P.L.F. successfully conducted a campaign that has no parallel in Africa. They managed to seize several towns, including Keren, the third largest town in Eritrea and the strategic strongpoint of the country. They besieged Asmara and took control of large sections of Massawa, an important port. These exceptional military successes would surely have led to complete military victory had it not been for the shift in Soviet-Cuban policy vis-à-vis Somalia. Thanks to Cuban and Soviet support, the Ethiopian offensive launched in Autumn 1978 broke the E.P.L.F.'s hold both on the towns and on the strategic roads; by 1979, the E.P.L.F. was forced to fall back on guerrilla tactics. However, as long as the Sudanese frontier remains open to E.P.L.F. logistics, the guerrillas will be able to continue fighting.

None of these secessionist struggles is supported by the Organization of African Unity, which opposes all territorial changes, even those that are both historically legitimate and consistent with the aspirations of the population, as was the case with the Somalians in the Ogaden.

The Weaknesses of the African Movements

The specific conditions that characterize African armed movements south of the Sahara and that determine their main weaknesses can be summarized as follows:

- The absence of a nation exacerbates the ethnic rivalries and divisions that are often behind proclaimed ideologies. South of the Sahara, only Somalia and the Somalians form a homogeneous ethnic group, speaking one language and sharing one religion; even there, clan differences are significant.

- Revolutionary leaderships in exile often become disconnected from the struggle itself and get bogged down in rivalries revolving around control of the organizational apparatus. Their failure to intervene actively in the struggle usually stems from a misperception of local realities and a fear of taking risks that might jeopardize their subsidized life-style.

- Aberrant strategies that rely on commando operations without establishing any real links with the local population usually result in an unstaunchable hemorrhage of troops and middle-level cadres.

- Throughout the continent, with only three or four exceptions, no country has a sufficient level of population density for large-scale military operations to be feasible.

Finally, the backwardness of the societies concerned is ill suited to guerrilla warfare and its demands (attitude toward time, coordination of activities, and so on). Any insurgent movement must constantly struggle against various magical and religious beliefs and attempt to change prevailing ways of thought.

The Near East

One of the first major postwar struggles in the Near East was waged by Zionist organizations against the British in British-mandate Palestine as part of their effort to establish a Jewish state. The British, worn down by the Second World War and facing a difficult moral dilemma in the wake of Nazi genocide, gave in fairly easily to the determined Jewish settlers, who were backed by the terrorism of the Irgun and L.E.H.I. (the Stern Gang). A few years later, in Cyprus, terrorist operations conducted from 1955 to 1958 by a few hundred individuals under General Grivas culminated in independence for the island, even though these actions represented only one of the island's two communities, the Greek majority. The fact that in both Israel and Cyprus the organizations concerned were purely nationalist and firmly anticommunist helps explain why political success came relatively easily. The opposite was true in Dhofar (in Oman), where both the British and the Iranians did everything in their power to crush a Marxist-Leninist revolutionary movement.

In military terms, the major armed insurrection in the Near East of the past twenty years was that of the Kurds in Iraq, led by Mustafa Barzani (1961–1970 and 1974–1975). The Kurdish minority, at one point backed by the Soviet Union and militarily powerful enough to cause the collapse of several Iraqi regimes, eventually obtained a promise of autonomy in 1970. In the meantime, however, the Iraqi state changed its alliances. The form of autonomy actually granted the Kurds seemed inadequate to General Barzani, who now enjoyed the support of the Shah and the C.I.A. The Kurdish struggle continued until 1975, when it collapsed, partly as a result of the treaty between Iraq and Iran but also because the Kurdish leadership (in this case, Barzani) abandoned guerrilla tactics in favor of conventional warfare, which requires very different logistics. Furthermore, the movement never generated the kind of modernizing elites that could have made the best of the situation. The Kurdish national movements in Turkey and Iran as well have constantly been one step behind the national movements of the dominant majority in the area. The Kurdish leadership in Iraq failed for want of modernity and revolutionary ideology. [3]

The Palestinian national movement imitated all the other national liberation movements from 1967 to 1977 (up to the period

---

[3] Cf. Gérard Chaliand (ed.), *People without a Country: The Kurds and Kurdistan* (London, 1980), introduction.

of military collapse in Lebanon) without ever managing to grasp the real parameters of its own specificity. The autocriticism developed by Abu Iyad, [4] one of Al Fatah's main leaders, came ten years too late. The Palestinian leadership failed to create a united and independent national movement of Arab states, failed to understand that its immediate strategic enemies in Jordan and Lebanon were, respectively, the Hashemite monarchy and Syria, and failed to build an underground infrastructure in the West Bank and Transjordan. The Palestinian organization can claim only one major success, but it is a crucial one. It has simultaneously returned to the Palestinians their sense of national identity and shown the world that the Palestinian national question is at the core of the Arab-Israeli conflict. The Israelis, for their part, have managed to break up the Palestinian underground in Gaza in an operation led by General Sharon. A relative economic and political liberalism has made it possible to defuse the vicious circle of repression and insurrection, although Israel's recent adoption of the death penalty for terrorist offences may contribute to the intensification of conflict that is already manifest in Palestinian mass demonstrations within the occupied territories. The Israeli dilemma, given that country's annexationist policies, is accentuated by the rapid demographic growth of the Arab population and by the steady development of nationalism, a force difficult to repress in today's world.

The Palestinians have displayed a love of overblown language and an absence of lucidity, rigor, and, ultimately, efficiency; its negative characteristics are reminiscent of those of most Latin American movements. There may well be more in common between Arab societies and Hispanic societies of Latin America than one would think.

Latin America

The Cuban Revolution is the classical example of a militarily weak guerrilla campaign, launched without any political preparation. It nonetheless won the struggle in less than two-and-a-half years and was by far the shortest of all guerrilla wars. Batista's unpopular tyranny finally collapsed without much resistance, and

---

[4] See the essay by the Abu Iyad in this volume.

urban strikes, demonstrations, and sabotage played a considerable role in this way. The struggle was above all populist, waged in the name of "bread and freedom."

Eighteen months after the seizure of power, the radicalization of the regime, which was soon to proclaim itself "Marxist-Leninist," surprised and appalled large sections of the middle classes that had supported the overthrow of Batista but in no way desired the instauration of communism; the benevolent neutrality of the United States turned into active hostility. Surprises and accidents of this sort can occur only once.

Most of the insurrections that broke out after the successful Cuban revolution collapsed or made little headway; in most countries they were unable to secure the support of the population. The theory of the *foco* [5] (mobile strategic base), which involves launching armed struggle without preparatory political work among the peasantry, has led most Latin American movements straight into the grave. Disgusted with the Latin American Communist Parties' generally reformist strategy, many urban groups, including students, trade unionists, intellectuals, and semi-intellectuals retired to the maquis and attempted to repeat the Cuban "exploit." At least twenty *focos* appeared and disappeared between 1960 and 1967, notably in Peru (1965) and Bolivia (1967), where Che Guevara, operating in total isolation, was finally killed and became one more revolutionary myth. The only sizable rural guerrilla campaigns were in Colombia and Guatemala. In Colombia *violencia* prevailed, and the peasantry had already begun to rebel when the revolutionaries came in and attempted to direct the revolt. In 1964–1965, a counterinsurgency offensive destroyed the "independent republics" of Marquetalia and Samapaz. In the period that followed, various revolutionary movements, such as the Colombian Revolutionary Armed Forces (initially aligned with the Communist Party) and the National Liberation Army (originally claiming a Castroist orientation), were successfully confined to four or five provinces. In Guatemala, despite initial successes from 1963 to 1966, the revolutionary movements never managed to mobilize the Indian peasants who make up most of the rural population. In the meanwhile, the ruling regime became more and more repressive.

[5] Cf. Gérard Chaliand, *Revolution in the Third World* (Baltimore, 1977).

These repeated failures led some groups to adopt an urban strategy, both in Brazil, where the campaign (led by Marighella) was relatively insignificant, and in Uruguay, where the Tupamaros had profound impact but remained essentially "focoist" and never managed to develop a real mass organization. The only other important armed movements in Latin America of the past two decades were in Argentina, where the E.R.P. was decimated by an intense repression, and in Nicaragua, where the Sandinista Front triumphed over an unpopular dictatorship that had allowed the economy to stagnate.

Weaknesses of the Latin American Movements

Why did the Latin American movements fail, even when circumstances—a social crisis, economic stagnation, or obvious agrarian problems—seemed to favor their projects? In every case except Santo Domingo in 1965 (where the U.S. Marines were sent in), the stimulus of nationalism was lacking because there was no obvious foreign military intervention or occupation. This handicap cannot be underestimated. The theory of the *foco* was of no help. Without political preparation, the support of the masses, and an underground political infrastructure, the weaker guerrilla movements often found themselves in the position of an isolated gang, easy prey for a mobile counterinsurgency force perfected by experts in Fort Bragg and Panama.

The more sophisticated guerrilla campaigns enjoyed a period of ephemeral successes as long as they had the advantage of surprise, but the insurrections themselves remained regionally confined. The substantial Indian minorities were never mobilized except by Hugo Blanco in Peru (1963). Even in countries where Indians form a majority of the population, the Guerrilleros could rarely speak their language.

The Latin American guerrilla groups in fact spent most of their usually short lives merely fighting for survival, growing weaker and weaker in the process. They were riven by serious internal dissension and lacked the middle-level cadres who might have been able to mobilize the population. Of course this did not prevent them from using overblown rhetoric to inflate their importance abroad.

Tenacity was not one of their strong points. The slogan adopted by most of the Latin American groups, "Victory or

Death," implied that the alternatives they really envisaged were either a quick victory or a glorious death. This fascination with death, rooted in hispanic machismo and accentuated by their organizational fragility, explains why so few of the Latin American guerrilla leaders of the past twenty years are still alive.

The Importance of History and of Cultural Traditions

The desire to avoid being accused of racism is often used as an excuse for ignoring broad cultural differences that result from different societies' histories. Is it not striking that for more than a century the major social metamorphoses—whether capitalist or not—have occurred in sinicized Asia: in Japan, China, North and South Korea, Vietnam, Singapore, and Taiwan? Can one overlook the fact that, compared to what prevails in the rest of Asia, in Africa, and in Latin America, the national sentiment in this sinicized Asia is extraordinarily strong? Is there any question that these societies more than others have remained true to their own culture? Loss of culture has clearly been one of the main sources of tension in, for example, the Arab countries, where the problem of identity has long been and continues to be central.

The profound nationalism, the village-level solidarity and communal institutions, the thousand-year-old habits of collective work, and the patient and precise labor of a rice-growing peasantry with intense ties to the soil are clearly characteristic of Vietnamese society. Such characteristics, which are so important, are nowhere to be found in Latin America or the Middle East. Egyptian peasantry does have a strong attachment to the soil, but, even there, the people have not been hardened by a millenarian battle with the rivers for subsistence. Furthermore, sinicized Asia, unlike Egypt, has a military tradition of conquest and resistance that has never been allowed to fall dormant.

National cohesion, a capacity for prolonged effort, experience with the sort of secret societies that can be the crux of a resistance movement that foster the ability to keep secrets (an ability rare in Latin America and the Middle East), and the existence of cultural traditions favoring adaptation (notably Confucianism) must all be taken into account in any comparative evaluation of the peoples of Asia, Africa, and Latin America.

Sinicized Asia's various attempts to cope with the challenge of the West were manifest decades before anything similar occurred in the rest of Asia. And Marxism was introduced into the area some thirty years before it reached the Arab world. In China, Vietnam, and to some extent Korea, Marxist-Leninist revolutionaries managed to take the reins of the national movement. This revolutionary current, active for half a century, has produced great leaders who were fully aware of the national realities of their countries, as well as many middle-level cadres who managed to establish themselves within the populations. Radical and revolutionary processes are of course feasible in the Middle East, Latin America, and Africa, but it would be absurd to invoke some abstract universalism in order to pretend that the economic and military successes of sinicized Asia were not partly due to historical and cultural traditions.

Counterinsurgency

The technique of counterinsurgency has been extensively perfected over the past twenty-five years, primarily due to the efforts of the British, the French, and the Americans.The main developments can be summarized as follows:

- Organization of "parallel hierarchies" within the opposing forces; resettlement of the local populations to control them better and to block the insurgents' support.
- Reliable analysis of local data and of the social strata; development of mobile and aggressive specialized forces.
- Above all, development of intelligence techniques, including torture, aimed at breaking up underground political structures through the liquidation of the opposition's most precious and irreplaceable asset, its cadres.
- Finally, a subtle approach that is not widely practiced: detection and liquidation of an insurrectionary organization that is just beginning and is therefore most fragile. In many countries this has not been a preoccupation of the dominant classes, who seem more concerned with short-term profit than with long-term prospects.

Terrorism and Propaganda Terrorism

For at least ten years, terrorism has been headline news: hijackings, kidnappings, and assassinations have repeatedly made the front page. In most cases, both in Latin America and in the Middle East, terrorism has been a *substitute* for classical guerrilla operations. In the industrialized countries, such as the United States, Quebec, Germany, and Italy, it has been a futile attempt to destabilize the state and sensitize public opinion to some real or assumed oppression.

Tyrannicide was probably the first terrorist act. In this sense, the Russian *Narodniks* are the direct heirs of a tradition as old as despotism itself. The first modern act of terrorism was probably the seizure of the Ottoman Bank of Constantinople in 1896 by an Armenian Dashnak (Socialist Party) commando who was seeking to draw the attention of the Western chancelleries to the situation of the Armenians within the Ottoman Empire. Terrorism was widespread at the turn of the twentieth century, employed first by the various anarchist currents and then by the Irish national movement and the revolutionaries in Macedonia. Like guerrilla war, terrorism in itself has no specific political connotations. It is a weapon the weak use who seek to have an effect on public opinion and has in recent times been used by both right and left. The Algerian F.L.N. and E.O.K.A. in Cyprus resorted to terrorism in the colonial struggle, whereas the O.A.S. in Algeria and the Death Squads in Brazil used it to preserve the status quo. It was a feature of the battle against foreign occupation in Europe during the Second World War, but it was also used by the Fascists and Nazis to destroy democratic institutions and to seize power.

The main characteristic of contemporary terrorism, however, is that what was once only a last resort is now systematically adopted as a means of expression. The use of terrorism as propaganda stems largely from the attitude of the media in the Western democracies, which accord an often disproportionate amount of attention to spectacular acts of violence. The prevailing attitude toward information is so perverse and twisted that a gang of hijackers can draw far more attention from the world press than struggles that are operating efficiently on the real battlefield. The media never accorded the campaign led by Amilcar Cabral and the P.A.I.G.C. the importance it warranted, even though for ten years it was the most significant struggle in Africa.

Terrorism is an essentially urban technique, and its impact can vary. It is never more efficacious than when it is used as a specialized branch of military activity within the overall struggle of a political movement backed or actively supported by a large portion of the population. Terrorism obeys the same laws as contemporary guerrilla war: it can win political victories only when aimed at a liberal democracy (e.g., the E.O.K.A. campaign against Britain in Cyprus), and its chances of military victory depend on the organizational support it can elicit. The latest avatar of terrorism, the attempt to turn it from a backup technique into a strategy for seizing power in the context of an "urban guerrilla war," has produced nothing but failure. Urban insurrection is a classical phenomenon, the last major example taking place in Budapest in 1956. The "urban guerrilla warfare" in Latin America was simply an urban version of the *foco*. Terrorism that is not correlated with a major political organization suffers from a severe handicap: it must remain completely underground and must operate within a very close-knit group and therefore essentially cannot organize the masses. Unless the state apparatus in question is practically impotent or the terrorist group is enjoying a wave of mass popular support, the fate of urban terrorists is to be eliminated one by one. However, the acceleration of urban warfare during the past two decades is a phenomenon that cannot be neglected by contemporary strategists.

In industrialized countries, left-wing terrorism, be it the Weathermen in the United States, the F.L.Q. in Quebec, the Red Army Faction (Baader-Meinhof group) in Germany, or even the Red Brigades in Italy, cannot hope to win mass support. The thoroughly marginal character of terrorist groups is hardly surprising: only the Provisional I.R.A. is made up of popular elements rather than of students and *déclassés*.

Terrorism, especially the more spectacular versions thereof, will continue to be a serious problem. In terms of efficacy, it is possible that in the coming years some small groups will achieve significant results by means of such tactics, but the most likely form of terrorism in the future is *state terrorism*. In the industrialized countries, given the extreme vulnerability of vital sectors, it seems reasonable to assume that sabotage, carried out by professionals on a national scale, will be used as a prelude to foreign aggression.

This anthology strives to reflect the most striking struggles of the past fifty years. It is not quite comprehensive but certainly covers most varieties of the guerrilla experience. I have deliberately left out texts both on the European resistance movements of the Second World War and on the kind of urban terrorism that has developed in industrialized countries.

My selection was determined by the quality of the essays and by the availability of material on particular movements. Theoretical texts analyzing how, for example, the struggle in southern Sudan was conducted simply do not exist. There are also essentially no accounts of the Algerian war written from a military point of view by the Algerian F.L.N. I have tried to avoid over-ideological analyses, rhetorical proclamations, and journalistic pieces that do not transcend the limitations of journalism. The book is the result of many years of reading and reflection. It is also the product of the concrete interest I have had in the subject for over fifteen years, during which time I have frequently spent periods of up to a year and a half in areas where guerrilla and popular warfare was being waged—in Asia, Latin America, and Africa; in Guinea-Bissau, Colombia, Vietnam, Jordan, Eritrea, Iranian Kurdistan, and Afghanistan.

I felt that the best structure for a book of this sort was division into parts. The accounts by participants in the struggles illustrate from the inside the particular characteristics of a conflict at a given stage or in an especially revealing light. The analyses drawn up by combatants and witnesses establish a straightforward balance sheet from which certain theoretical and practical conclusions flow.

With the exception of a few classic pages, the texts that follow are generally not very well known. Many are published here for the first time in English. I have sought to present as rigorous as possible a survey and to elucidate in this introduction the lines of force and the political and military lessons to be drawn from the armed struggles of the contemporary era. In the past four decades, guerrilla warfare, more than anything else, has reshaped the map of the world.

Gérard Chaliand

PART ONE

Stories

I.

The Historical Dimension of Guerrilla Warfare

CAMILLE ROUGERON

Camille Rougeron, one of the major
French theoreticians of the past few
decades, examines the historical evolution
of guerrilla warfare from the Napoleonic
Wars to the Second World War.

. . . The fact that the origins of both guerrilla warfare and the term applied to it are usually traced back to the Spanish uprising against Napoleon may not be significant in itself. But when one considers that this popular reaction occurred repeatedly in that period, during military operations that had nothing in common, it seems clear that the times were favorable to the emergence of a new type of war.

There has never been a satisfactory explanation for the failure of the Duke of Brunswick's 1792 campaign in France. Prussia may well have had good reasons for not getting involved in lengthy confrontations in the west when she had more important matters to deal with in the east, but this only explains the decision to retreat, not what happened before and during the battle of Valmy. How was it possible for a handful of untrained volunteers under Dumouriez and Kellerman to bring down the more numerous forces of what was at the time the best regular army in Europe?

What was left of the soldiers of the French Republic eventually became the war-hardened troops of the Napoleonic Grande Armée. The Russian and Spanish peasants who defeated them did not do so in pitched battles. What was it about Valmy that

From Camille Rougeron, *La prochaine guerre* (Paris: Berger-Levrault, 1948). Reprinted by permission of Berger-Levrault.

makes it the first exception to a rule that, until then, had been consistently validated? We know the details of the encounter; some authors even refuse to dignify it by calling it a battle, since no real fighting took place. The role played by the peasants of Argonne and Champagne in the preliminary operations is much less well documented, however. This is how it appeared to Lombart, the king's secretary, who was traveling with the Prussian Army: "Not one Frenchman was coming forward to engage us, and the viciousness of the local inhabitants was proving a major obstacle to all our plans. The peasants would flee into the woods when we approached. They hid everything they owned and gave it all to the French, whom they were helping to spy on us and harass our supply trains." The Prussian Army set out with 42,000 men. When it returned home, having failed to obtain any supplies either on the spot or by convoy, only 20,000 were left to cross the frontier. The others were in French hospitals or lay slain on French soil.

A few years later, the same methods were turned against the Republic in western France and almost brought it to its knees during the Vendée campaign. The guerrilla tactics employed attained a level of perfection that would certainly have been decisive had it not been for quarrels between the royalist leaders. (This problem has remained one of the strategy's weak points; it reemerged in Yugoslavia, with Tito and Mikhailovitch, and in China, where some partisans supported Chiang-Kai-shek and others recognized only the communist leadership.)

The same form of resistance to an occupying army recurred during certain insurrections in the Kingdom of Naples, seriously worrying Napoleon, who wrote several letters advising his generals on how to deal with the problem.

But in Spain, from 1807 onward, the new form of war finally proved itself conclusively. The Spanish campaigns were the real beginning of Napoleon's downfall. Guerrilla operations took an annual toll of about 100,000 French soldiers—more men were lost there than in all the emperor's campaigns against Prussia and Austria, and almost as many as in Russia. His best troops and his best generals exhausted themselves to no avail: Spain was truly the grave of the Grande Armée.

The Russian guerrilleros were not the only force opposing the French in the 1812 campaign. The regular army also fought courageously, and although it won no victories it inflicted severe losses on the Grande Armée. However, it was the partisans rather than Kutosov's army that engineered Napoleon's supply problem, a problem that cost him first his convoys, then his cavalry, and finally even his infantry, who at the end simply had nothing to eat.

Russian historians of the 1812 campaign, especially the more recent writers, have illustrated the partisans' role and methods very clearly. As Tarlé, a professor of French at Leningrad University, puts it,

> It was the Russian peasant who annihilated Murat's magnificent cavalry. The peasants would set fire to the hay and oats sought by Murat's foragers, and in many cases the foragers themselves were thrown into the blaze. . . . On first sight, this may seem strange; the peasants hated their serfdom and had repeatedly protested against it through revolts and by assassinating their masters; only thirty-seven years earlier they had threatened the whole system of serfdom. Yet now these same peasants greeted Napoleon as their worst enemy, set fire to wheat, hay, and oats, even burned down their own isbas when they could kill French quartermasters by doing so.

Perhaps Tarlé is letting himself be overinfluenced by some preconceived notion of the people's capacity to save themselves despite the unworthiness of their leaders. However, the same observations figure in Milioukov's accounts of the period (Milioukov was an emigré Russian and onetime professor at the Imperial University in Petrograd).

Confronted with a lack of food, Napoleon understandably hastened back to France, leaving Murat with the job of bringing back what was left of his army.

One may ask why guerrilla warfare made so successful an appearance at the beginning of the 19th Century. Nowadays, when an ideology backed by skillful propaganda is quite capable of launching both a guerrilla offensive and a conventional war, one might easily be tempted to attribute this direct intervention by a people defending their own land to the Revolution and to the principles it propagated. In fact, the principles of 1789 had nothing whatsoever to do with the insurgency of the times. Revolutionary enthusiasm may have disrupted Kant's early morning constitutional or inspired Goethe to utter prophetic words, but it had certainly not trickled down to the peasants in the poorest and most backward regions of Europe, Estremadura, and White Russia. Furthermore, the revolts were directed precisely against those who were importing the revolutionary ideology.

The "patriotism" of the Spanish or Russian people is the reason most frequently advanced by historians in the countries themselves. Both the Peninsular War and the 1812 campaign are referred to as "the patriotic war" by local historians. The invaders prefer to see what happened in Spain as an explosion of "fanaticism," whipped up by priests and monks; events in Russia, where the popes played a very minor role, are explained away either as the predestined end of an adventure that had already gone on too long or as a conjunction of mishaps, according to whether the authors prefer to give general or specific reasons for disasters.

Neither of these very similar explanations, fanaticism or patriotism, is at all convincing. They have the disadvantage of not being specific to the events of 1807 and 1812 and of not telling us anything about why those events took the form they did. It is hard to imagine a more patriotic revolt than the uprising in the Netherlands against Spanish domination, yet it never turned into a guerrilla campaign. The Wars of Religion, in which fanaticism certainly was a major factor, also never took on the aspect of a guerrilla war. In any case, religious arguments were not what motivated the Spanish peasantry during the Peninsular War.

The immediate cause of guerrilla warfare and the explanation for its emergence in Spain and Russia is much more down to earth. It was no accident that guerrilla warfare broke out in those provinces of the Spanish interior where, a century later, travelers were still warned that they could eat in the inns only if they brought their own food; and in the marshy forests of White Russia, which were even poorer. Relations between a starving soldier and a peasant who will starve if he feeds him naturally tend to become tense. Indeed, the fanaticism of the Spanish monk was less a matter of religious orthodoxy than a reaction to the pillage of his monastery's last resources.

. . . Guerrilla warfare is the reaction of the peasant who is not paid when his cow or his wheat is taken from him. When the nation sounds a call to arms, he may be willing to risk his life and that of his children for the cause, without grumbling too much in the process; but there are limits to his forbearance. It is not just in the songs that he prefers his two red-daubed white oxen to his wife: he is willing to die defending them and will fight for them with an ardor that no patriotism could elicit. This peasant attitude was perfectly familiar to the generals at the time. It was not unheard of for soldiers to be brought before a firing squad for having taken a few cherries from a nearby tree during a break in a march.

The German authorities during the 1940–1945 occupations took all this very much into account. They managed to avoid a peasant upheaval by tolerating enormous price increases for the products they bought from the local farmers, at a time when they were being extremely strict with their own peasants and when, throughout Europe, industrial wages had been frozen. The same preoccupation was a central aspect of American psychological warfare. U.S. troops were fed out of tins even in areas where fresh food was abundant, so as to avoid even the appearance of starving the local population.

One may ask why this immediate cause of guerrilla outbreaks did not appear during the many previous occasions when the military was either forced or allowed to live at the expense of the local inhabitants. Over time, the local inhabitants developed a status at least equal to that of the military—even as, paradoxically, armaments and military organization became more complex.

When individual armaments became increasingly portable and easy to hide, regular armies benefited less than their adversaries. When armor was a luxury only a few warriors could afford, it conferred such superiority that the warrior had nothing to fear from the wrath of the locals. The advent of the crossbow and, even more so, of firearms turned the tables in favor of those who could set an ambush: the emergence of new weaponry was bitterly resented by the regular forces and aroused much protest; there were even attempts to ban it. "As long as we still have one soldier to wield a sword or one peasant to wield a scythe, we must not give up," said Joan of Arc when she called on the people to revolt. But a scythe was not much use against armor. The chorus of a popular song at the time of the Vendée uprising, *"Prend ton fusil, Gregoire"* (Take up your rifle, Gregory), expressed the great change that had taken place in the positions of rebel and master. The submachine gun, the hand grenade, and the bits of plutonium that planes may tomorrow deliver by parachute to allies below, instead of Sten guns and plastic explosives, all give the partisan a strength he has never had before.

As the development of weaponry for individuals conferred a greater and greater advantage on would-be troublemakers, the evolution of collective armaments and the organizational changes implied increased the vulnerability of the regular army.

There is, however, a whole category of troops proved by history to be quite unaffected by the use of guerrilla tactics: troops organized so as to be independent of their lines of communication. When Alexander set off to conquer Asia Minor with an infantry 32,000 strong and with 5,000 cavalrymen, each soldier carried his own kit and his own supplies; in each phalanx there was only one orderly for ten fighting men. The Roman legions carried the principle even further, turning the soldier into a beast of burden who carried his weaponry, several weeks' supply of food, and even the mobile fortification to be erected around the camp he built every night. Thus equipped, the legionnaire could cross hundreds of miles of hostile territory. Horses need not always be excluded from this kind of venture: the Mongol and Arab invasions that used horses were no more vulnerable to guerrilla harassment than were the Roman legions. However, in areas where there is no grazing, reliance on horses can lead to complete disaster, as happened in Spain and Russia, where Junot's troops and the Grande Armée learned to their cost that horses are even less capable than men when it comes to carrying their own food over great distances.

The two profound changes that made modern armies so vulnerable to guerrilla tactics were the increased use of military hardware and the massive growth in the number of troops deployed. The main advances in these areas were brought about by the French Revolution, and countervailing weaknesses emerged immediately.

The new stress on military hardware began with Napoleon, who in effect doubled the relative importance of artillery. This approach remained more or less unchanged until the First World War. When artillery was first introduced it did not hamper the mobility of the troops, as one might have expected, for it was preceded by a complete transformation of the way armies were kept supplied in the field. Armies had previously subsisted on food carried by their baggage train and their convoys; after the French Revolution, they began to live off the land. The enormous reduction in the amount of supplies thay had to carry amply compensated for the increased length of the artillery train: in fact, this new mobility was decisive in enabling Napoleon to outmaneuver his opponents, whose adherence to the old system slowed their progress and forced them to spend far more energy than the emperor did in defending their lines of communication.

Living off the land did not mean turning one's soldiers loose on the countryside without bothering to worry about how they and their horses would feed themselves: such an approach would have been as bad for discipline as for the likelihood of winning the support of the invaded populations. On the contrary, Napoleon's forces were kept supplied by quartermasters, who bought foodstuffs and forrage on the spot. They negotiated their purchases as amicably as possible and paid in cash. Everybody was satisfied. The peasants were well pleased to get such good prices for their produce, the middlemen were happy with their profits, the officials whose job it was to arrange the deals found all sorts of opportunities to pad out their fee, and, according to Bonaparte's accounts of his first campaigns, so did the Italian actresses who accompanied the regiment. If the venture was successful, the spoils of victory amply covered the costs incurred.

The difficulties began when there was nothing to buy. Having benefited from the advantages of the new system in Italy and central Europe, Napoleon discovered its drawbacks in Spain and Russia. A return to a strategy based on stores and convoys proved essential but insufficient in Spain, where the small staff detached to obtain supplies could not counterbalance the several years' absence of a government acceptable to the people. In the 1812 campaign in Russia, however, stores and convoys should have been entirely suitable. Clausewitz, who was following the operations from the Russian side, has conclusively shown that Napoleon's preparations for the expedition were inadequate. Stores built up in towns during the advance would have saved the Grande Armée during the retreat. The French forces either could have withdrawn successively from various positions as the stores ran down or could have set up winter quarters and withstood a siege. Clausewitz's argument is unfortunately not very well known, since it appears in his history of the 1812 campaign rather than in his major work. Hitler, however, was well aware of it and organized his winter campaigns and eventually the general withdrawal from the eastern front accordingly. The stand at Storaia-Roussa in the winter of 1941–1942 is the best known example of Hitler's use of the technique.

In the early nineteenth century, the food problem was compounded by the enormous increase in the number of troops deployed, first under the Republic and then under Napoleon. Conscription was all very well in Frederick's small Prussia, where it offered only advantages. But when it was extended to the whole of France in 1792–1815, the number of men in an army already swollen by big foreign contingents reached such a level that it was practically impossible to provide the transport that could keep them fully provisioned when operating in a poor country.

Vulnerability to guerrilla warfare is a weakness particular to modern armies. Indeed, this weakness emerged during the very period when the two main characteristics of modern armies first became apparent and in the regions that favored their development.

How are we to explain that a technique as powerful as guerrilla warfare then remained dormant for more than a century? The main reasons seem to have been, first, the relative tranquility of those hundred years and, second, the attitude of military men and administrators toward the new tactics, a point we shall return to later. Guerrilla war reemerged in China in 1937 and in various European countries from 1940 to 1945, but on these occasions the circumstances were as artificial as those that had prevailed at its birth were natural.

Guerrilla tactics were first employed in a modern world conflict during the Chinese resistance to the Japanese invasion. Was the best strategy to defend the coasts against the invader? Or was it better to let him forge his way into vast tracts of territory where he could then be worn down bit by bit and to gradually break his lines of communication and his ability to administer the occupied areas. Chiang Kai-shek opted for the latter and gained the time he needed, for he was expecting eventual support from the western nations, especially the United States.

It is not generally realized that the Chinese leadership only chose this tactic, after several months of hesitation and many defeats in conventional confrontations, at the insistence of the German general who was responsible for military organization. He formulated a set of rules that codified his doctrine; the idea was to organize genuine "soldier-peasant" armies behind the Japanese lines. The Japanese advance columns would be incapable of identifying their opponents, who would re-form and concentrate on cutting lines of communication once the columns had passed. This method was so successful that Hitler had to recall his overconscientious mission commander, after repeated pleas by Japan, Germany's new ally. But the damage had been done.

The German regulations that follow were not really an innovation in terms of how to conduct a guerrilla campaign.

> Guerrilla warfare [kleiner Krieg, little war] is a method of supporting the operation of friendly forces and hampering those of the enemy through a variety of small, secondary actions.
> Guerrilla warfare is mainly conducted behind enemy lines. Its main objectives are to harass the adversary, cause losses, divert his forces . . . , and disrupt all his operations, especially those concerned with supply. . . . Blocking and mining lines of communication is particularly recommended, [1] in order to hamper the enemy's movements on roads and tracks as much as possible. Similarly, destruction of bridges and tunnels disrupts supply lines.
> Small irregular corps are the most suitable executors of such missions. Their actions should rely on the element of surprise. Trickery and cunning should be their main assets.

The principles outlined for campaigns against guerrilleros were not new either. Naturally, the recommendations included "surprising and surrounding them," but a certain pessimism as to the ease with which such actions could be executed was ever present: " . . . The use of special forces may prove necessary behind the front lines. . . . A methodical step-by-step cleaning up operation may be essential but will usually require the deployment of a substantial number of troops."[2]

The success of the German regulations in China was quite prodigious. Throughout the war, Japan, although theoretically controlling vast territories, could actually hold only a few main channels of communication, two or three big rivers, and a few

---

[1] This action (Sperren) included planting antipersonnel mines, mining roads and railways, and, generally, introducing obstacles to free circulation.
[2] Truppenführung, October 17, 1933, Art. 642–647.

railway lines crisscrossing several hundred square miles. The rest of the country was controlled by guerrilla leaders loyal to Tchung-King or the communist authorities, who were thus free to levy taxes, recruit troops, and organize manufacture of munitions in most of China.

Guerrilla warfare alone proved sufficient to make the Japanese Army's position in China untenable. It would have taken massive numbers of troops to occupy the provinces in which the guerrilleros prevailed. The Japanese made over half a dozen attempts to establish a firm link between their forces in Canton and those in central China: each attempt cost them a few divisions and ended in complete failure. And meanwhile, the U.S. Navy and Air Force were cutting off the Japanese sea-lanes. Japanese expeditions starting out from Burma finished as disastrously as did those from Canton.

In eight years, during four of which the Japanese were free to concentrate exclusively on the "liquidation" of the Chinese problem, they just barely managed to cut themselves a few routes through some of the more accessible areas. The Japanese commanders were fully aware of the difficulties involved and of the consequences of failure; they committed all their country's energies to the effort. Finally, in desperation, they threw themselves into a war with the western nations that was clearly suicidal from the beginning. A few Chinese or Manchu "bandits" managed to stand up to an army that claimed, probably correctly in at least the early days of the war, to be the greatest in the world. Guerrilla warfare had won its most resounding victory ever.

In China, guerrilla tactics were coordinated with the operations of Chinese front line troops that represented a serious, albeit flexible, obstacle to the Japanese advance. By contrast, in Yugoslavia, from 1941 to 1945, the "interior front" alone caused the German and Italian General Staff many problems. In Spring of 1941, 20 divisions had swept into Yugoslavia, and the Greek and Yugoslav regular armies were broken within a few weeks. But then, for four years, 30 Italian divisions, backed by a few Bulgarian divisions and some forces sent by the Serbian and Croatian "governments," failed to maintain the authority of the Axis. Mikhailovitch and then Tito repeatedly gained control of an area in the middle of Yugoslavia as large as Belgium. The insurrection spread to Greece and then to Albania. German troops had to be called in at regular intervals to prevent the area controlled by the guerrillas from expanding too dramatically. From 1941 to 1945, Yugoslavia was to Mussolini what Spain had been to Napoleon. In April 1943, shortly after capture of the two Italian expeditionary forces on the Don and in Tunisia had freed Italy from the need to concern itself with distant matters, Guglielmotti, a member of the National Council, described what was happening in the Balkans on a Radio-Rome Broadcast:

> It is time the Italians appreciated what is going on there. . . . Our units are kept constantly on the alert. Our supply columns are frequently ambushed and destroyed. The situation is very difficult. Everybody feels threatened. To tell the truth, it is a cruel and exhausting war.

Fascist vainglory, which had once threatened Europe with its "eight million bayonnets," collapsed before one hundred thousand Yugoslav peasants.

In the U.S.S.R., guerrilla operations were neither the entire defence as in Yugoslavia, nor even predominant, as in China. The outcome of the war was decided on the front lines. But action behind the lines helped both wear down and immobilize the German forces. Extensive areas, especially in the marshy forests, remained practically impenetrable to the Germans. Those who found refuge in these forests would make expeditions to cut nearby lines of communication. Sometimes a few civilians would set an ambush; sometimes several battalions of regular Red Army troops would be involved.

. . . By the time guerrilla warfare had indisputably proved effective, it had lost its original spontaneity. Conventional war had also changed. A modern army going to war backed by the full industrial might of a country has little in common with the call to arms of a clan or tribe. Contemporary guerrilla war is organized and deploys all the resources of modern propaganda: people must be made to see their own unhappiness. Guerrilla activity springs up in the fresh footsteps of the enemy, provided the allied commanders decide it is an indispensable part of their strategy. If they choose to rely on other operations, the guerrilla offensive may be held in reserve for a few months or even a few years, depending on how much time is required before the main offensive that it is designed to support can be launched. Guerrilla activity has become an integral aspect of modern warfare and is as important as artillery emplacements, strategic bombardments, peace offensives, and nuclear warfare. But it has inconveniences, and both administrators and career officers are still debating its appropriateness to various situations.

. . . Considering the cavalryman's disdain for tanks and the sailor's dislike of airplanes, it is not difficult to imagine the instinctive reaction of the regular military to organizations that are in a sense the antithesis of their own yet that often obtain far superior results. As General von Rustow puts it, "Partisan forces are generally seen as the armed populace; hardly surprising then that they should be viewed with ill favor by regular armies." The regular military still does not fully accept guerrilla warfare, just as for over a century it refused to accept the replacement of the professional soldier by conscripts and reservists. Very few agree with the opinion expressed by Clausewitz as he returned from Russia along a road littered with the corpses of soldiers from the Grande Armée: "The immensity of the Russian landscape prevents the assailant from occupying and holding the country strategically. He simply moves forward, without being able to secure his rear. Having thought on the matter at length, I am now convinced that a great civilized European country cannot be conquered unless there is dissension within it."

The first complaint about guerrilla warfare concerns its effectiveness. The cavalryman with his sabre has made similar complaints about the tank for over twenty years; the sailor with his 406 cannon is equally bitter about the airplane.

Although Clausewitz was alone in his thorough grasp of the consequences of the effectiveness of guerrilla warfare, those who did the fighting shared his opinion on the facts themselves. In the preface to his *Guerra de la Independencia,* the Spanish General Arteche gives a much more satisfactory explanation of Wellington's successes than that advanced by Napier, who speaks of disjointed and pointless maneuvers by the Spanish armies. Arteche points out that "all the French armies were fully occupied containing the general insurrection in the provinces, and nobody could divert troops to any other end. The French forces that opposed the allied armies were exhausted by the constant clash with the Spanish and were always numerically inferior as a result of constant detachments. The real resistance, the efficacious resistance, the one that discouraged the invaders, the one that they could not repress, was the national resistance." On this point, the Spanish historian is in complete agreement with the superlative leader Marshal Suchet, who declared in his memoirs that "this new system of resistance did far more to defend the country than the ordered campaigns of the regular armies."

One hundred and thirty years later, in 1943 and 1944, 100,000 Yugoslav peasants were able to immobilize more German troops than could the entire Anglo-American war effort on the Italian front, to which the Germans committed only a dozen divisions. What gives the partisan his advantage over the regular soldier is the simplicity of his needs, which have remained unchanged over one hundred and fifty years, unlike those of the regular armies, which have become more and more complex. As early as 1808–1809, Gouvion Saint-Cyr pointed out in his *Journal des opérations de l'armée de Catalogne* that the partisans were "willing to make every sacrifice, free of any craving for the soft life, untramelled by military form and regimental tradition. They would form irregular corps, choose their own commanders, operate according to whim, attack wherever they enjoyed some advantage, and flee without shame whenever they were not sure that theirs was the superior strength."

People sometimes express surprise that the one million Germans that occupied France did not succeed in eliminating a resistance movement of only a fifth or a tenth as many people. But such a comparison is not valid, even in terms of numbers. Like any modern army, the *Wehrmacht* had at least as many men in its rear guard as in its line regiments. Perhaps half the fighting men assigned to France had to guard the coasts, leaving the rest to maintain order within the country itself. How many of the latter were available for operations against partisans in the countryside? Artillery and service corps must be discounted, and only about half a division is composed of infantrymen. And then within the infantry, ordnance corporals, telephonists, *minenwerfer* teams, and mule drovers could not be sent out to fight the resistance. Once the apparently imposing occupation army has thus been halved four times over, the numbers committed to fighting the resistance seem far less daunting.

Guerrilla warfare retains its effectiveness against modern weapons because it can avoid their full impact. An army equipped with sabres and machine guns may be unable to do much against an attack by tanks and airplanes, but a catapult, a box of matches or even a stick may be effective against the crew of those tanks and planes when they are in the barracks. *Wehrmacht* volunteer legions recruited for the battles on the eastern front were reported by accompanying journalists to feel naively indignant at the tactics employed against them; the peasants would return to the isbas (log huts) from which they had been displaced by the occupying forces and set them alight, shooting any Germans who escaped from the flames. It was their way of economizing on ammunition. Had they been equipped with planes and tanks they could have machine-gunned refuge columns or finished off the wounded under their caterpillars, as their opponents did.

Neither heavy artillery nor the air force is much use against partisans who are careful to avoid frontal confrontations. Tanks may be helpful in mop-up operations, since they protect the crew from snipers' bullets, but cannot by themselves enforce repression. A tank is hardly suitable for searching abandoned villages, woods, rough terrain, or fields crisscrossed with hedges. Such missions call for foot soldiers, who must operate unprotected and exposed to the fire of those they are pursuing. On many levels, guerrilla forces have benefited more from advances in armaments and methods of combat than have their adversaries. Parachute drops make it possible for guerrilla offensives to be launched wherever and whenever the leadership decides. Radio links and airborne supplies ensure coordination and continuity. Generalized and improved camouflage techniques and anti-personnel and antivehicle mines are even more effective in the hands of guerrilla forces than when used by regular soldiers. Soviet tank columns suffered terrible losses in Finland during the winter of 1939–1940 when partisans would immobilize the first tank along the only road through difficult terrain. The Red Army adopted the same tactics against the *Panzerdivisionen* which they bottled up on the wooded slopes of the Caucasus near Ordzhonikidze.

The enormous quantities of war material that armies trail along with them often provides an excellent target for guerrilla operations. These operations are aimed particularly at communications, and modern warfare relies more than ever before on its transport facilities, not only to move goods and materials up to the front but also to keep the whole machinery of wartime production turning.

Rail and road communications offer endless opportunities to the ill-intentioned passerby: oil gauges can be tampered with, gearboxes gritted up, wheels unscrewed, garages burned down, and so on. To keep all relevant installations under surveillance at all times requires extensive personnel.

. . . Guerrilla warfare of today is "directed." The original tactics have been retained, but the technique has been developed to include bombs under trains, assassination from bicycles, radio contact, and underground newspapers. Spontaneous uprisings no longer provide the cadres and militants.

. . . What territory is appropriate for a guerrilla offensive? Any region is suitable, not just those that are inaccessible or where guerrilla warfare has been waged in the past. Marshall Tito, who had some considerable experience with the subject and who did not restrict his operations to the mountains of Yugoslavia, makes this point quite categorically. In an article written in 1943 concerning the fifth major German offensive against his strongholds, he states that, "although many people believe that the difficulty of the terrain and natural obstacles are crucial assets in our struggle, this is not so."

The idea that guerrilla warfare is best suited to areas that are difficult to reach is based on confusing such areas with impoverished areas. Poverty and inaccessibility generally go together, but, historically speaking, it is only the first characteristic that correlates with the origins of guerrilla warfare. In any case, the whole question is relatively unimportant, since modern transport facilities make it reasonably easy to keep armies supplied—the problem is obtaining war material in the first place. Indeed, recent experience confirms Marshall Tito's assertion. The Chinese resistance movement was equally effective in every area of the country. The French *Résistance*, when it became generalized, was not restricted to the maquis in the mountains or forests. The Palestinian resistance movement inevitably operated in the areas settled by Israelis, which were the richest in the country and particularly well served by road and rail. Indeed it seems that the most appropriate areas for guerrilla activities are heavily populated urban areas and sprawling suburbs.

In the past, when an occupying force deemed it too costly to hold a whole territory, it would seek refuge behind the walls of a town and seal the gates, thereby attaining an acceptable level of security in exchange for sacrificing its communications. This was precisely how Napoleon's troops held Spain. But how can one lock oneself behind the walls of a town today? Where are the walls; where is the boundary between town and countryside?

. . . The main target continues to be transport systems, especially rail transport, which is particularly vulnerable to mines timed to explode as the train passes.

. . . Road communications are also easily mined, but the anti-tank gun may in some cases be preferable.

. . . Domestic navigation is another key target. Ships are fragile, take a long time to unload, and are often docked for long periods. Locks and weirs are also susceptible: repeated destruction of their gates will cause sufficient loss of water to dry up most canals during the summer.

. . . It is always important that the belligerents who benefit from guerrilla operations put as much effort into studying, making, and supplying the specialized material required for unusual actions as they devote to keeping their regular troops provided with appropriate weaponry. The links between the British and the French resistances show that an "interior front" can be maintained at a far smaller cost in effort and casualties than would be incurred were the air force to attempt to wreak a similar level of havoc. For one tenth of the entire expense involved in strategic bombardment during the Second World War, Yugoslavia was able to completely counteract all its antagonist's efforts to conquer and occupy the area.

Guerrilla warfare waged on this scale runs the risk of exhausting a population that may well be more concerned with immediate inconvenience than with future benefits. Among those who are forced to guard trains and travel in them as hostages or who suffer reprisals for guerrilla actions, there will always be some who find the price too high, even if as a result of their efforts the occupying force must forgo the advantages it might otherwise draw from the country it supposedly dominates, even if it must let the peasants get on with their agricultural work. In such cases, support for the partisans can take the form of small, airborne commando groups. British leaders were the first to attempt such tactics, in Calabria. The experiment failed, but they had sent British soldiers in full uniform. Similar operations conducted by regular Soviet troops behind the German lines on the eastern front proved completely successful. The most suitable candidates for such missions are of course people who come from the territory in which one is attempting to trigger and sustain revolt. During the war, "displaced persons" were recruited in great numbers for precisely this purpose.

The effectiveness of guerrilla warfare is incontestable. The only thing that prevents administrators and military men from recognizing and exploiting it is that it seems to favor social and political doctrines not to their liking. Guerrilla warfare is assumed to be "left wing," just as the regular army is supposedly on the right. Such a conclusion, based entirely on recent examples, ignores important precedents in which established authorities used guerrilla tactics against troublemakers. During the Napoleonic Wars, it was the emperor who represented the "left"; neither his territorial ambitions nor the pragmatic necessity for authority that every revolution faces can hide the underlying meaning of his actions. The Spanish peasant and the Russian serf refused to believe that they had "nothing to lose but their chains." They defended those chains, which were reimposed upon them with a severity that should be remembered by anybody who fears to see a people benefit from its own military successes.

The revolt of the occupied against the occupiers is the closest thing there is to pure patriotism: the nature of the ideologies involved is largely irrelevant. Should the Soviet grasp on half of Central Europe extend to the other half and to Western Europe, there would be as much discontent with the order imposed by the "left" as is expressed against the "right-wing" order of today. For nearly a century the supporters of the two ends of the political spectrum have balanced each other out, with neither able to establish lasting domination. Dissident forces, suddenly finding themselves reinforced and equipped with parachute-dropped plastic explosives and machine guns, would be able to act with a level of determination they have so often lacked in the past. Those who echo the call of Marx and Engels for workers of the world to unite would discover the truth of a less eloquent but more universal maxim: "The master is always the enemy."

II.

The Red Phalanx

AGNES SMEDLEY

*An American, Agnes Smedley spent many
years in China. In her biography of
Marshall Chu Teh, who with Mao
Tse-tung headed the Red Army for twenty
years, she recounts the history of the
Chinese revolution. The following passages
concern the organizational Yenan period
between the Japanese invasion in 1937 and
1944–1945, when the Red Army achieved
full strength.*

. . . When Japanese imperialism began its attempted conquest of
China by striking at the Twenty-ninth Route Army near Peking
on July 7, 1937, the united front had still not been consolidated
and Chiang Kai-shek had still not made up his mind to fight.
Despite this, the Special Administrative Border Region was put
on a war footing, and within twenty-four hours the commanders
who had been studying in Kangta began marching southward to
rejoin their troops, while other hundreds left their units and
marched to Yenan.

Ten days after Japan began the invasion of China, Chiang
Kai-shek finally issued a proclamation calling for resistance and
stating that there could be no turning back. By then the Japanese
had occupied Hopei Province and were pouring into northwest
China. By August 13 their armies began the campaign that led to
the fall of Shanghai and, by December, of Nanking.

Only at Shanghai did Chiang Kai-shek's armies really begin to

From Agnes Smedley, *The Great Road: The Life and Times of Chu Teh* (New
York and London: Monthly Review Press, 1956). Copyright 1956 by the Estate of
Agnes Smedley. Reprinted with permission of Monthly Review Press.

fight, and only when Nanking was menaced did the Kuomintang agree to active cooperation with the Red Army. On August 9, General Chu Teh and Chou En-lai, with a group of Red Army and Communist Party representatives, flew to Nanking for a conference of the National Military Defense Council.

On September 6, three divisions of the Red Army were reorganized into the National Revolutionary Eighth Route Army, with General Chu Teh as commander in chief and Peng Teh-huai as vice-commander. Not one new gun was given the three divisions—the 115th, 120th, and the 129th—and the only medical supplies issued to them consisted of three pounds of iodine crystals and two pounds of aspirin tablets. They were, however, supplied with ammunition and money for three divisions.

These three divisions, forty-five thousand men strong, left at once for the front in Shansi Province. They still wore their old Red Army uniforms and caps. Not even one blanket had been issued them. One of Chiang Kai-shek's lieutenants later remarked cynically to me:

"The Reds boasted that they captured all their guns and supplies from us in the past. Let them do the same with the Japanese!"

One month after the Eighth Route Army left for the front, I joined General Chu Teh's headquarters in the Wutai mountains in northeastern Shansi, which by then was in the Japanese rear. On September 25 and 26, the 115th Division under Lin Piao's command had fought and won the first Chinese victory over the Japanese at the Great Wall pass, Pinghsinkwan.

During all this time, communist representatives in Nanking were urging Chiang Kai-shek to permit them to assemble all the old Red Army guerrillas that had been left in Kiangsi and Fukien provinces when the main Red Army went on the Long March. However, it was not until Nanking fell to the Japanese and 200,000 civilians and captive soldiers were slaughtered that the Minister of War issued an order to these guerrillas to concentrate along the lower reaches of the Yangtze to be reorganized into the New Fourth Army.

As these emaciated, ragged, and battered peasants marched from the mountains of the old Soviet districts, landlords and their Min Tuan waylaid them, sniping and killing whenever possible. With gnawing bitterness, Hsiang Ying and Chen Yi, their commanders, ordered that not one shot be fired in return, and that the columns march at night through dangerous areas.

The New Fourth Army, numbering 11,000 men, assembled in south Anhwei in April 1938 and was placed under the command of General Yeh Ting, with Hsiang Ying as vice-commander. Chen Yi was commander of a division, which left at once to penetrate the Nanking area. The whole army was assigned a fighting zone about 50 miles wide and 150 miles long, directly along the banks of the Yangtze. The War Ministry had planned things beautifully. The New Fourth Army was ordered not to leave its zone even for maneuvering operations against the Japanese. In their rear, in the Nanking area, was stationed an army made up of the same terrorist bands of Shanghai and Nanking gangsters that had once been used to exterminate villages in Soviet territory. These gangsters, whose supreme commander was General Tai Li, chief of the Kuomintang secret police, were very well equipped and provisioned and were assigned the task of hemming in the New Fourth Army and driving it directly against Japanese columns.

There was no doubt in the minds of informed Chinese and foreigners that the Kuomintang expected the Japanese to achieve what they themselves had been unable to do: the extermination of the Eighth Route and New Fourth Armies.

When I arrived at General Chu Teh's headquarters in the Wutai mountains in late October 1937, the Japanese were already driving on Taiyuanfu, the provincial capital, from two directions: through the mountains from the north, and from the east along the branch railway that ran from Shihchiachuang up through deep gorges to the capital. Kuomintang and provincial armies were holding the Japanese on the northern front; Tungpei and other Kuomintang divisions, with the 129th Division of the Eighth Route Army, were holding them on the east. The other two divisions of the Eighth Route Army were using mobile and guerrilla tactics in the enemy rear.

Ho Lung's 120th Division was ranging far and wide in north Shansi, while regiments of Lin Piao's 115th Division were campaigning through northeastern Shansi and eastern Hopei provinces, where they had already driven the enemy from a number of occupied district cities and even attacked the Peking-Hankow railway.

Like all the Kuomintang forces, the old warlord governor of Shansi, Yen Hsi-shan, would not permit the people to be organized and armed unless they were already in enemy-occupied territory. The Eighth Route Army, which operated in enemy-occupied territory, was therefore organizing, training, and arming the people on the same pattern that had proved so powerful in south China during the civil war years. Organizations of peasants, workers, merchants, women, youth, and children had been founded. The older men in villages and towns were being organized into Local Self-Defense Corps. Able-bodied young men, formed into Anti-Japanese Guerrilla Detachments, were fighting as auxiliaries of the Eighth Route Army. Armed with captured rifles, these detachments were the reservoir from which the Eighth Route replenished its losses.

General Chu Teh's headquarters in the Wutai mountains were in a large white building, formerly a landlord's home, where two Chinese newspapermen and I found him sitting on a stool while a barber shaved his head clean. He waved and shouted a greeting and later led us into a room papered with great military maps that stretched from floor to rafters. After pointing out Japanese and Chinese positions, he explained Eighth Route strategy and tactics:

"Strategically, we aim at sustained warfare and at the attrition of the enemy's fighting power and supplies. Tactically we fight quick battles of annihilation. Because we are militarily weaker than the enemy, we always avoid positional battles but engage in combined mobile and guerrilla warfare to destroy the vital forces of the enemy, while at the same time we develop guerrilla warfare to confuse, distract, disperse, and exhaust the enemy. Our guerrilla warfare creates such difficulties for the enemy that our regulars can launch mobile attacks under favorable circumstances."

He explained future plans:

"Our plan is to establish many regional mountain strongholds in the enemy rear throughout north and northwest China—such as this one in the Wutai mountains, where the enemy's mechanized forces cannot operate. Our regulars can return to such bases for rest, replenishment, and retraining; guerrilla forces and the masses can be trained in them; and small arsenals, schools, hospitals, and cooperative and regional administrative organs can be centered there. From these strongholds we can emerge to attack Japanese garrisons, forts, strategic points, ammunition dumps, communication lines, railways. After destroying such objectives, our troops can disappear and strike elsewhere. We will consolidate and use these strongholds to enlarge our fields of operation until our defensive strategy can be turned into a strategic offensive. Chiang Kai-shek has agreed to this plan and the Wutai Regional Base is being organized with his permission."

As we talked, General Peng Teh-huai entered. Generally a grim, dour man, he was now very gay as he told us of hourly reports of small victories over a vast territory in the enemy rear. General Chu listened with narrowed eyes, his shabby cap with its faded red star shoved back on his newly shaved head.

"You must investigate our methods of mass mobilization and training," General Peng exclaimed, with a happy wave of his hand. "The people are like the sea, and we are like the fish swimming through it. This is a national revolutionary war. Victory will depend on the courage, self-confidence, and fighting power of our troops and on brotherly relations between commanders and fighters; and on our close cooperation with other Chinese armies. We are carrying on intensive political work among our troops and the people. The people have rallied to us to the last man, woman, and child."

General Peng braced his hands on the table and continued:

"You'll find a lot of inspiring slogans and posters, of course, but of greater importance is the gradual process of educating our troops, the guerrillas, and the people. Our aim is to develop deep national consciousness and to educate and inform our troops and the people about the condition and designs of the enemy. Everyone must realize that victory cannot be had for nothing. The war has only begun!"

General Chu's eyes remained narrow, tense points as he replied:

"True! But the Kuomintang armies must also make many changes! Kuomintang officers still curse and beat their soldiers—they enforce unreasonable obedience. These are feudal practices! They must be replaced by friendship, mutual respect, confidence, and help. Sorrows and happiness must be shared by all. Living conditions of officers and soldiers should be approximately equal so everyone can take part in the war wholeheartedly!"

"Will all that be done?" I inquired skeptically, and the ever optimistic Chu Teh answered:

"It will take time. Our army must be the model. As the war continues, the Kuomintang armies will have to reform or be defeated. Why are so many Chinese puppets fighting in the Japanese army? Why do the Japanese boast that they will conquer China with Chinese? Why! Because the Kuomintang has done nothing to wipe out feudal conditions in the country and feudal practices in the armies. We must convince the Kuomintang, and we must win over the puppet troops."

Chu and Peng told us of the destruction by Lin Piao's division of one Japanese brigade at Pinghsinkwan, and of other battles in which the Japanese never surrendered unless wounded. Even the wounded pretended to be dead, they said, and when Eighth Route stretcher-bearers bent over them, they sprang up and killed on the spot. When Ho Lung's troops destroyed enemy transport columns, the Japanese clung to the trucks until cut off. Searching the pockets of the Japanese dead, Ho Lung's troops had found a number of antiwar handbills signed by the Japanese Communist Party and the Japanese Anti-Fascist League. . . .

The years 1941 and 1942 tempered the spirit of the people and troops in the Liberated Areas in blood and suffering.

The lines were drawn so clearly that even the most obtuse could see them: while the Kuomintang cut the communists off from all supplies and hemmed them in with a blockade of steel, the Japanese tried to exterminate them on the field of battle.

In the first six months of 1941 the communists prepared for the attacks from the rear and battles at the front. Immediately after the establishment of the Kuomintang blockade, Mao Tse-tung officially announced the "Production Movement of Self-Sufficiency." This, with time, transformed the face of north China and made sustained military resistance possible. Of this movement Mao said:

> Our policy is of resurgence through our own efforts. The reduction of rent and interest has raised the enthusiasm for mutual aid and raised the productive power of the peasants. Our experience shows that through mutual aid the productive capacity of one individual becomes four-fold. . . . Once mutual aid has become a habit, the productive output will not only be greatly increased, but all

kinds of new creations will appear. Political standards will be raised, and people will also improve culturally. Loafers will be reformed, customs changed, and our rural society led to new productive power. It will then be possible not only to carry on the war and cope with the famine years, but also to accumulate huge amounts of food and daily necessities for use in a counteroffensive. Not only peasants, but the army, party, and government institutions must also organize to engage in production together.

The Production Movement began with planning conferences of every group of the population, including the armed forces, across the thousands of miles of the Liberated Areas. Tens of millions of people began working in Mutual Aid Teams, Labor Exchange Groups, in industrial, consumer, and transportation cooperatives, or in new small factories or other institutions. No one was exempt.

The Japanese offensive began in July 1941. In the eighteen months of fighting to the last day of 1942, the Eighth Route and New Fourth Armies suffered 82,456 casualties; 30,789 were killed outright. The number of civilian and local partisan dead and wounded could not be reckoned but was much greater.

The Yenan press, for the next two years in particular, pictured General Chu Teh moving here, there, everywhere—writing, speaking, advising, laboring in his headquarters under candlelight until the small hours, and, early every morning, working in the fields like the peasants from whom he sprang.

Newspapers, pamphlets, and books put out by Yenan in those years are peppered with his writings, and reports of his speeches and interviews alone would fill volumes. His tenacious figure can be seen speaking before conferences of cooperatives, women, labor unions, and youth; at soldier-commander congresses; at peasant gatherings on rural reconstruction, Labor Hero conferences, memorial meetings for the dead; in classrooms filled with Japanese prisoners of war; and at exhibitions on industrial and military achievements.

From Communist Party congresses where the strategy and tactics of the national revolutionary struggle were determined, he would go to such gatherings as the Production Conferences of the Women's Alliance of the Border Region, where, in the autumn of 1941, he sounded like Mayor LaGuardia talking to New York housewives on how to cook spaghetti and care for children:

We produce salt in this region, so we can put down large quantities of vegetables for the winter months. In Szechwan we always salted down vegetables. We did it in this manner: . . .

Now, let us talk about the soya bean, which should become a major crop in this region. Soya beans can be used in many forms—as green vegetables, as bean curd, as sauce, or dried for winter use. They can also be pickled for winter use. Each Manchurian household puts down at least one large *kan* (vat) of salted soya beans for winter use, as well as another of sauce. They do it in this manner. . . .

After discussing crops with the women, he turned to the breeding and care of pigs, sheep, goats, cattle, rabbits, and bees. "Every bit of every animal—bones, meat, hoofs, and hides—should be used, and the care of bees and the increase in honey production should become one of the major industries of the Border Region," he told them, and went on to the care of children:

I sometimes find a woman sitting on her doorstep and weeping because her baby has just died. Why do we suffer such losses? One reason is because the people of north Shensi pay too little attention to sanitation. For ages our people have made very little progress in this respect. Poor sanitation can result in the extermination of a whole herd of swine, but when babies die as they do the loss is infinitely greater. Our production propaganda must therefore go hand in hand with improved sanitation both on the farm and in the home. Cleanliness must be constantly stressed. We now have cooperatives that produce good, cheap soap. . . . Babies must be washed each day and children taught daily habits of cleanliness. Even under the most difficult conditions our soldiers try to keep themselves clean and always wash their feet each night. If they can do this, people in the rear can do much more.

From the care of children he went on to the industrial cooperatives, which, he said, should be developed on a large scale "to serve as a bridge between agriculture and industry and to activize commerce." Cooperatives should never become mere money-making organs, nor should their products be hoarded to raise prices and "propagate an economy of scarcity." The Yenan Border government, he reminded them, laid great emphasis on cooperatives and home industries, exempting some from taxation and imposing only a nominal tax on the others, and also honoring men and women who achieved high standards of production as Labor Heroes.

> Some of our women production leaders tell me that they have a fund of [two hundred dollars] but don't know what to do with it. I should think you would use that money to make two twenty-spindle spinning machines. After two weeks' practice, a woman can produce fourteen pounds of wool yarn a day on such a machine. From this yarn you can select five pounds of the best and spin it into good yarn for which our weaving factories will pay you [thirty dollars]. The inferior wool can be woven into blankets and carpets. . . . Hemp, which we produce in large quantities, can be mixed with wool and woven into strong, durable, warm cloth.

After such a meeting he would sometimes mount his big horse, captured from the Japanese, and ride down into the Nanniwan area. A brigade of the Eighth Route Army under Wang Chen garrisoned this zone to protect Yenan from the Japanese across the river and from Kuomintang troops blockading from the south.

The army production movement, which he called "the Nanni-wan movement," was General Chu's pride and joy. When this powerful brigade was brought into the Nanniwan area, it found a wasteland. There were no buildings or caves and only the ruins of an occasional village or abandoned temple.

The Kuomintang blockade of the Border Region, General Chu told the troops, was intended to starve soldiers and civilians while the Japanese destroyed them in battle. Neither the army nor the people had any intention of allowing themselves to be starved or destroyed, nor could the army live off the people.

General Wang Chen's Nanniwan brigade looked about and found a two-thousand-pound bell in an ancient abandoned temple. From this they fashioned their first plow and hoes, the first picks and shovels to excavate living quarters in the hillsides, the first tools to make furniture and dig wells. The troops began transforming the wasteland into fields of grain and vegetables. From distant villages they bought a few draft animals, goats, sheep, and pigs, which produced and multiplied. They held frequent production conferences, founded their own spinning and weaving cooperatives, and continued their education as well as even creating a dramatic group. When thousands of refugees from battle zones streamed into the Border Region, they helped settle them on the land, dug wells and made spinning wheels for them, and helped them found cooperatives, primary schools, night schools for adult illiterates, and Labor Exchange Groups.

The Production Movement was under way when, in early July 1941, General Yosuji Okamura, Japanese commander in north China, turned 300,000 Japanese troops loose on the Liberated Areas in what he called his "three-all" strategy—kill all, burn all, loot all.

The Okamura "three-all" offensive of 1941 was fought with one main aim: "Clean up north China to prepare for the great Pacific War." Japanese columns moved in, surrounded whole districts, and closed in for the kill. In one small southeastern Shansi district, typical of others, the Japanese slaughtered 13,000 civilians who had remained in their homes, sparing neither babies nor the aged. In one town that the Eighth Route Army recaptured, the troops found and photographed the naked corpses of hundreds of women and girls of all ages, lying in the public square.

Before and during this "three-all" offensive, the Japanese built 2400 miles of deep trenches and 400 miles of protecting walls along the motor highways in central Hopei Province alone. High walls and protecting ditches also ran parallel with Japanese-controlled railways throughout the north and northwest. The Japanese constructed chains of blockhouses with underground chambers for food and ammunition.

The people on the northern plains also utilized the bosom of the earth. They dug underground air-raid shelters, which they extended into long tunnels that often connected different villages. Inhabitants of a village under enemy attack could take shelter in another, while enemy troops entering a deserted village would find themselves suddenly surrounded by Eighth Route Army troops who arose out of the earth beneath them.

The people, who had been taught to make land mines of every kind, sought to protect their homes by sowing mines along all paths leading to them. Some of the "People's Heroes" produced by this struggle were little boys who wandered out to meet advancing enemy troops and reply innocently to requests:

"No, I cannot guide you to my village because that is forbidden, but it is along that path over there—" pointing to a mountain path sown with land mines where troops and partisans lay in ambush.

In his annual report on July 1, 1941, General Chu stated that

Eighth Route and New Fourth Armies often went into battle with only five or ten rounds of ammunition and that the heavy losses suffered by the people and the troops of the north were the bitter fruit of the Kuomintang blockade.

By the first week of December 1941, Chu later reported, just when the Japanese thought they had crippled the people's forces in the north and could begin the Pacific War with a safe rear, "we launched a counteroffensive which prevented them from transferring troops to the south Pacific against the Allied armies."

This counteroffensive was accompanied by an upsurge of the Production Movement. As the people's forces recovered district after district and the civilian population returned to rebuild their destroyed homes, Yenan transferred grain and livestock into these just-recovered areas.

In his 1943 report, General Chu Teh was unable to estimate the amount of ammunition, food, and medicine captured during the counteroffensive, because, he said, all such supplies had been put to immediate use. The captured rifles, however, numbered 95,000; light and heavy machine guns, over 2000; pistols, 4027; antitank guns, 29; field guns, 73; "quick-firing guns," 225; and 2 antiaircraft guns. Other trophies included 272 radio transmission sets with generators; 939 field telephone sets; 112 cameras with film; 7201 gas masks; also bicycles, gramophones, parachutes, Japanese flags, and thousands of head of horses. One item on the New Fourth Army list of trophies read: "592 drums of American gasoline."

One of the most significant sections of General Chu's report dealt with the change that had come over Japanese troops during the preceding five years. By mid-1942, he said, the surrender and desertion of Japanese had become frequent.

These prisoners of war were never put in chains or herded into concentration camps. They were given Chinese uniforms and placed in classrooms to study much the same subjects that the anti-Japanese armies studied, with special emphasis on the feudal structure of their own country, the history of the Japanese working class, and the principles of scientific socialism. Many graduates of the "Japanese Workers and Peasants Training School" at Yenan, in particular, later worked as special political propagandists with the Eighth Route Army at the front. By the end of 1944, thirty of them had been killed in action. . . .

III.   The Yugoslav Partisans

VLADIMIR DEDIJER

*Vladimir Dedijer, Tito's companion during
the Second World War, writes about the
period 1941-1944. The Yugoslavs
organized the most powerful resistance to
the Germans. Yugoslavia and Albania
were the only countries in Europe where
communists were able to seize power
without heavy Soviet interference.*

. . . On June 22, 1941, Hitler's orders to the German army to
move against the Soviet Union were being read over the loudspeakers in almost all the cities of occupied Europe. That afternoon, the Politburo of the Yugoslav Central Committee met in a
house in the outskirts of Belgrade. It was unanimously decided
that the time for the uprising had come. While the meeting was
still in progress, Tito began to write a proclamation to the
peoples of Yugoslavia to rise in revolt against the German, Italian, Hungarian, and Bulgarian invaders. That very night, that
proclamation was printed in secret presses in Belgrade and carried by courier to all parts of Yugoslavia. . . .

Only a few days after the proclamation of June 22, 1941, was
issued, action against the invaders began. In the night between
June 23 and 24, the first act of sabotage was committed on the
Belgrade-Zagreb railway line. The Central Committee met again
on June 27 in Belgrade. General Headquarters for the armed
struggle against the invaders was established under the name of
the G.H.Q. of the National Liberation Partisan Detachments.
Popularly, the new people's army was known as the Partisans, a
name taken from the uprisings of the Spanish people against

Napoleon in 1808 and from the Russian revolts against Napoleon in 1812. This G.H.Q. included all the members of the Politburo of the Central Committee and was subsequently expanded to include certain military leaders. The Military Committee of the Party ceased to function, and its chairman assumed command of the new G.H.Q. Tito was appointed to this command by unanimous decision of the Politburo. It was also decided that the flag of the National Liberation Movement should be the Yugoslav flag, with a five-pointed star in the middle. Tito had already worked out instructions for the formation of detachments and for the scope and nature of their activities, for sabotage, for raids, for the organization of quartermaster and medical services. It was also decided that the G.H.Q. should immediately start issuing an official bulletin.

The atmosphere in Belgrade was particularly bleak in those days. German propaganda provided tremendous publicity for the communiqués in which the High Command registered its advances into Russia. Huge maps showing the breakthroughs of German tanks were posted on large boards; the whole city—all the trolley cars, all the walls—was covered with German posters. Loudspeakers were installed in the streets blaring communiqués from the eastern front. Quisling newspapers brought out special editions.

To counter this, young communists of Belgrade decided to burn publicly the Quisling newspapers. Groups of three approached more than a hundred newsstands; one seized the papers, the second poured gasoline over them, the third touched a match to the sodden mess. The effect of this act was tremendous throughout the city, for few well-frequented newsstands had been missed. Of the hundred groups that had taken part in this burning of Fascist papers, only one was caught. All three young men were shot the following morning by the German command.

Two days later, the young communists decided to repeat the action on a larger scale. The leaders of the organization themselves went to the most crowded spot in town in order to be the first to take part in the action. The Germans did not expect that the first action and their reprisals would be followed by a second wave. This mass burning of Quisling newspapers had a huge political effect on all Belgrade. The common people were proud of this action of the young people of Belgrade, who were prepared to face death in order to accomplish such things. And, suddenly, many of these people started to do similar things, in a spontaneous, unorganized manner. Someone had been brave enough to begin.

The wave of sabotage swept ahead with tremendous vigor. Telephone wires serving the Germans were cut; German soldiers were attacked in dark streets and their weapons wrenched from them; the burning of German military trucks and motorcars began on a mass scale. The most effective weapon was a small incendiary that set gasoline aflame after a brief delay. Young people crept near German trucks, surreptitiously opened the gasoline tank and tossed in an incendiary, then moved away. A few minutes later, while the truck was rumbling through the streets, it would burst into flame.

High explosives, too, were being put to good use. All these weapons were prepared by young people whose previous experience in that field had been very limited. Many died in their primitive laboratories and workshops.

Meanwhile, ruthless persecution of all communists and other suspicious persons began in Belgrade. The former Yugoslav political police rendered tremendous services to the Gestapo, drawing up lists and carrying out the arrests in association with German officials. The procedure was an extremely summary one. As the majority of communists had already left their homes, German military cars, manned by soldiers with light machine guns, circled the town. When the Yugoslav agents pointed to a communist whom they recognized in the streets, the German soldiers would open fire from their light machine guns without warning.

The German command also ordered a curfew. All citizens had to be in their homes before seven P.M., later changed to six P.M. Mass searches of sections of the town and of all the houses and apartments were carried out. In reprisal, the Partisans decided that all Yugoslav policemen should be punished by death. They were shot in the street, and a number were killed. One of them was lucky. A student approached him from behind and attempted to fire a bullet into his temple. The revolver missed fire, however, and the student was immediately caught and shot. . . .

In this situation, a meeting of the G.H.Q. was convened on July 4, in the home of a friend of the Party in Dedinje, a wealthy residential suburb of Belgrade. In order not to attract the attention of the police, Party members entered the house one by one at fifteen-minute intervals. A detailed plan for the further development of the uprising was worked out at this meeting, and Tito explained the main tasks of this phase of the struggle.

With a view to a successful development of the uprising, it was essential, in the first place, to destroy the governmental machinery of the old Yugoslavia, which had placed itself completely in the service of the invaders, and particularly the police, the municipal administrations, and so forth. In this way the occupier's mainstays in the villages and smaller localities, where the power of their army or military police could not as a practical matter reach, would be destroyed. In disarming the police and destroying their headquarters, the Partisans would also obtain the weapons of which they were so badly in need.

In the towns, the sabotage and diversionist activities were to be pursued with unabated vigor, and a hell was to be created for the enemy in which he could never feel safe. The Partisan detachments, however, were to be created in the countryside, where detection and arrest were less likely than in the towns. The activities of the detachments outside the towns would have considerable effect in the towns themselves.

At this meeting it was decided where the leaders were to go in order to assume the direction of the uprising in the different parts of the country. Edvard Kardelj was already in Slovenia. Milovan Djilas was designated for Montenegro, Svetozar Vukmanović for Bosnia and Herzegovina, and Tito himself and Aleksandar Ranković-Marko were to take over the leadership of the uprising in Serbia.

Only a few days after this meeting, the first results began to be felt. The wave of sabotage activities in Belgrade increased. A German military garage was blown up, and over a hundred German military motor vehicles were burned. The first six Partisan detachments were founded in Serbia. The manner in which the Partisan detachments obtained their weapons is highly characteristic. Some weapons that had been hidden at the time of the April catastrophe were recovered, but there were not enough to equip a large detachment. The main source of supplies was the enemy. Thus the Kragujevac detachment obtained its first six army rifles by disarming a police post, into which the insurgents suddenly broke armed with unloaded sport rifles. The police immediately surrendered, and the Kragujevac Partisan detachment, which later increased to six hundred fighting men, had six army rifles. In the town of Kraljevo, in central Serbia, a young peasant was standing behind a tree at the side of the road with an ax in his hands. When a German motorcyclist drove past him with a submachine gun flung across his back, the young Serbian peasant struck him on the head with his ax—and the detachment thus got its first submachine gun. The wave of attacks on police stations and municipalities swept over Serbia, and the Partisan detachments were very soon armed.

One summer day a Partisan detachment arrived armed at a people's carnival in the village of Bela Crkva near the town of Valjevo. When the police opened fire, a Belgrade journalist and veteran of the Spanish civil war drew his revolver and killed two policemen, while the rest fled. That was the first open clash between the Partisans and the German flunkies in Serbia. That day, July 7, is now celebrated as Serbia's national holiday.

The uprising developed in other parts of the country. Violently in some places, steadily in others, the whole of Yugoslavia was swept by the wave of resistance to the Germans, the Italians, the Bulgarians, and the Hungarians. In Montenegro, where most weapons had been hidden at the time of the short-lived war against the Germans in April of that year, the uprising soon broke out and spread to the whole of this mountainous area. Beginning July 13, 1941, when the Italians were organizing a parliament in the capital city of Montenegro to proclaim Montenegro's unification with Italy, Partisan detachments were flooded by peasants asking for arms to fight against Italians. The peasants said to the Partisans: "Why do you think you are our betters? Why do you not let us fight the invaders?" Within two days and two nights the whole of Montenegro, with the exception of three towns, was liberated from the Italians. Two Italian divisions were disarmed. Huge quantities of weapons fell into the hands of the Partisans. Captured Italian soldiers were very well treated, told about international brotherhood, and released; these same divisions were armed again by the occupation authorities and sent back to fight the Partisans. The rapid growth of the revolt in Montenegro was, to a very large extent, a result of the general conviction prevailing there that the war would soon end by a decisive victory of the Red Army over Hitler's hordes. Woe to those who in Montenegro at that time ventured to prophesy that the war would last as much as another six months.

Uprisings spread rapidly in Bosnia and Herzegovina, as well as in certain parts of Croatia, such as Lika, Kordun, Gorski Kotar, Banija, and Slavonija. In many parts of the country, the population rose to fight with hoes and wooden forks, closing in on the police in a wide circle and attacking them from all sides. The police usually surrendered before the weight of the onslaught. The uprising developed with particular rapidity in the parts of Croatia populated by Serbs, whose complete annihilation Pavelić had vowed. . . .

News arriving from all Yugoslavia showed the uprising was growing constantly. The German command resorted to the most ruthless measures in order to quell it. One morning four Partisans were hanged on Belgrade's main square, Terazije. Their bodies swung from the gallows all day, with German soldiers and Serbian Quislings on guard. At the same time, the Belgrade broadcasting station gave the names of the "Communists and Jews" who had been shot. . . .

Many villages and even a few smaller towns were liberated in Serbia. What was known as the liberated territory, cleared of the invaders, was established. In Slovenia the German authorities themselves put up a signboard a few kilometers before the liberated territory began, with the warning *"Achtung! Banditengebiet!"* (Beware! Bandit territory!). The time was approaching when it would become imperative to move the G.H.Q. from Belgrade, where conditions were becoming increasingly difficult, to the liberated territory. . . .

. . . Tito sought direct contact with the colonel of the former Yugoslav army, Draža Mihailović, who had gone to the woods with a group of his men after the April surrender. His supporters were called Chetniks, "One who is in the company." His units were organized in many parts of Serbia at the same time that the Partisan units were formed. But there was a marked difference between the two military organizations. I remember when I was in the field in Serbia in late summer of 1941, as a political commissar of the Kragujevac detachment, I used to pay visits to the Headquarters of the Chetnik units. There was a strong contrast between these units and Partisan ones. The Chetnik units were usually made up of older men, married men, peasants from rich families. They remained in their villages, they slept at home, and from time to time they were called to the Headquarters where they drilled. I had great difficulty persuading the Chetnik commanders around Kragujevac to take part in the fighting against the Germans. They said they had no orders. But they criticized our command because we "wasted mercilessly the blood of the Serbian people fighting against the Germans in an uneven struggle." They advised us that we should wait until the Germans were weaker to fight against them. The Partisan units were usually made up of younger people who wanted to fight against Germans. However, there were some Chetnik units who did fight Germans in some other parts of Serbia, like Vlado Zečević, Colonel Misita, and some others. But Colonel Misita was killed fighting Germans and Vlado Zečević joined Partisan units because he did not want to accept orders of Mihailović to stop operations against Germans.

A meeting was arranged, and Tito set out to visit Draža Mihailović, accompanied by a few Partisans. Their first meeting took place in a peasant house in the village of Strugarik, where they plunged directly into the question of action against the invaders. Draža Mihailović's point of view was that the time for the struggle had not yet come, and that it was better to wait for the Germans to be weakened and to save one's forces until that moment arrived and a fatal stroke could be delivered. Actually, Draža Mihailović's purpose was to maintain in Yugoslavia the pattern that had prevailed prior to 1941, and then, after the Germans had been defeated, to hand the country back to King Peter and to the Government in Exile. Tito proposed to Draža Mihailović that they launch joint operations against the occupation forces. But no agreement could be reached.

A few days later, the first meeting of the Partisan commanders took place in the village of Stolica. Commanders from practically all Yugoslavia except Macedonia attended this meeting. Most of them arrived on horseback or by foot through liberated territory; commanders from Slovenia and Croatia came illegally by train. They were all dressed as Partisans, in half-military, half-civilian clothes, furnished with chest straps and belts from which hung submachine guns and revolvers. The majority of them had yielded to a short-lived custom that dictated the wearing of fierce mustaches. The most fierce adorned the commander of a detachment from Serbia, Koča Popović. Tito had no mustache.

The meeting lasted several days. The political and military situation in every part of Yugoslavia was examined in detail. Several important decisions were taken:

First, it was decided to establish a G.H.Q. in each of the provinces of Yugoslavia to facilitate the coordination of the activities of the numerous detachments, and the existing G.H.Q. was to be transformed into Supreme Headquarters of the National Liberation Partisan Detachments of Yugoslavia.

Second, a detailed plan was worked out for the creation of new liberated territories in Yugoslavia, as had been done in Serbia. A plan was also worked out for extension of the liberated territory in Serbia, and decisions were taken with regard to the points that were to be attacked, the timing of the attacks, and the forces that were to be involved.

Third, it was decided that new National Liberation Committees were to be established in the place of the former authorities throughout the liberated territory.

Fourth, it was resolved to form larger Partisan units, in battalion strength, and to avoid frontal clashes with an enemy superior both numerically and in fire-power, but to rely instead on numerous mobile and closely connected Partisan detachments capable of simultaneous action. Such detachments could, when the need arose, be welded into powerful shock units for the purpose of waging a battle that they had been compelled to accept, or could disperse and strike suddenly at the enemy and at definite objectives, only to disappear again from the area of the attack. The essential point was to keep the manpower as intact as possible, while dealing the greatest possible blows to the enemy. The enemy should be compelled to strike into a vacuum.

The fifth decision of the Stolica meeting was approval of Tito's report on his interview with Draža Mihailović. It was decided to pursue the talks with Draža Mihailović in order further to investigate the possibility of a common struggle against the invaders.

The decisions taken at the meeting in Stolica speedily showed their effect. The twenty-four Partisan detachments in Serbia began to coordinate their activities, and a German garrison was soon captured by the Partisans, who took more than three hundred German soldiers prisoner and appropriated their weapons. Tribute must be paid to the enemy, and it must be recognized that the Germans in Serbia in 1941 fought with extraordinary determination. When they attacked the positions of the Partisans they advanced calmly as if they were on parade ground; when one fell, another soldier immediately took his place and continued to advance with the same calm, deliberate step. In order to avoid the further loss of isolated garrisons, the German command was compelled to evacuate the whole of western Serbia, including the principal town, Užice. The Supreme H.Q. immediately moved to Užice and remained there for almost two months. The town of Užice thus became a kind of symbol of the first liberated territory in Yugoslavia, which the people called the "Užice Republic." While evacuating Užice, the German garrison was compelled to leave behind an armament factory, whose capacity amounted to four hundred rifles and a large quantity of ammunition daily. The workers of this factory soon reassembled, the machines were transported to an underground shelter near Užice, and the rapid production of rifles bearing a special Partisan sign began. These rifles meant a lot to the Partisan detachments.

The liberated territory in Serbia was linked with the liberated territory in Bosnia, and the latter was in its turn connected with the liberated territory in Montenegro. A very considerable part of Yugoslavia was thus liberated; with ordinary care to avoid the larger enemy-held towns, it was now possible to travel from the Adriatic Sea to the outskirts of Belgrade without leaving liberated territory. A Partisan railway ran 100 miles through this territory, and a mail service was established throughout.

People's committees replaced the local governments that had placed themselves in the service of the invaders. These committees were formed by people who were in favor of the struggle against the occupation forces and against the Quislings. They were elected by the people themselves at meetings. In Serbia, a National Liberation Committee for the whole of Serbia was established and became the embryo of the future government. . . .

The situation in Serbia was causing concern to the German command. It had at its disposal in the whole of the territory of Serbia only three divisions of occupation and some police units. It therefore began bringing in reinforcements in the middle of September, in order to wipe out the liberated territory in Serbia.

The German command launched its attack from the north, but its front column, which had been provided with tanks, encountered the determined resistance of the Partisan detachments, which put fifteen tanks out of commission with the aid of land mines and hand grenades. The attempts of the German infantry to penetrate liberated territory also met with failure. . . .

The German command had embarked on the second phase against the liberated territory. They had for this purpose brought reinforcements from other areas: the 342nd Division from France, the 125th Regiment from Greece, and the 113th Division from the eastern front, where the offensive against Moscow was in full swing. The liberated territory was thus attacked on a 125-mile front by the complete 342nd and 113th Divisions, considerable elements of the 714th and 717th Divisions, the 268th Artillery Regiment, and the 125th Regiment. These forces were strengthened with tank units and more than fifty light bombers. The German forces were joined in the attack by large Quisling formations consisting mainly of Milan Nedić and White Guard units.

This time the Germans changed their tactics. They advanced cautiously along the main lines of approach, clearing the way with artillery and aircraft, while endeavoring to outflank the Partisan positions by means of powerful infantry elements.

Partisan reinforcements were dispatched to the north from Užice. Suddenly on the night of November 1-2, the alarm was sounded in Užice. Enemy units had made their appearance only two and a half miles from the town! They had already been engaged by our forces. Partisans hurried from the town to the scene of the fighting, and workers from the arms factories seized rifles and rushed to the battlefield. Toward dawn, the enemy attacks had been repelled and the Partisans were beginning to encircle the enemy, who was by now in full flight.

They had not been Germans but Draža Mihailović's Chetniks! With the rifles and ammunition we had given them to fight the Germans, they had now struck at the heart of the liberated territory at the very moment when a violent German offensive was threatening us from all sides. After they had been defeated near Užice, the Chetniks began withdrawing rapidly and were soon in desperate flight. They rallied momentarily at the town of Užička Požega but were again defeated. It was there that Streten Žujević-Crni, a member of the Supreme H.Q., was wounded in the stomach by a Chetnik dumdum bullet. The Partisan units pursued the Chetniks, surrounded them on the mountain Ravna Gora, where Draža Mihailović's headquarters were located, and awaited Tito's instructions.

That evening I was with Tito in his Užice headquarters, a large building that had been a bank in prewar days. Tito was in touch by telephone with the commanders of the units that had surrounded Draža Mihailović's H.Q. They were awaiting a reply. Tito was walking up and down the large room while I was sitting near a wireless set listening to a Moscow broadcast in Serbian. Suddenly I jumped up and told Tito:

"Listen, Moscow is speaking of the fighting in Serbia against the Germans. Listen, listen! They say Draža is leading all the forces of resistance."

Tito stood still, aghast. I had never seen him so surprised, either before or after that day. He merely said: "But that's impossible."

I repeated what I had heard. Tito was shaking his head, pacing the room, when the telephone rang again. It was commanding officer Jovanović-Bradonja calling. Tito ordered: "Cease further troop movements. Send representatives to Draža and start negotiating." Lola Ribar entered the room at this moment. Tito told him of Radio Moscow's broadcast and then added: "We must not destroy Draža Mihailović, although we have surrounded him. We must be careful not to cause difficulties in the foreign relations of the Soviet Union."

I frowned from my chair near the radio. Negotiations started the next day. I was in one of the commissions, but I had little to say, for I was thinking of my comrades who had been killed by the Chetniks and of the increasingly violent German onslaughts against our liberated territory.

The German offensive developed steadily. First our positions near Valjevo, north of Užice, fell. The German infantry carried out broad enveloping movements against our positions. The German air force was a particularly heavy menace, for there was nothing we could do against it, lacking as we did antiaircraft guns or even effective small arms. The Germans dived to a hundred yards above our positions, and the best we could do to retaliate was to open rifle fire against them.

An ever-growing number of wounded was arriving in Užice.

The Germans were advancing methodically, and it was obvious that Užice could not be held. . . .

Only twenty minutes before the German tanks entered Užice, Tito left—one of the last of the fighting men to go. He was at a front-line position overlooking the town when the German tanks broke into Užice. Without pausing, they continued along the road to Zlatibor. The bridges had not been well mined, and the tanks soon crossed them, followed by trucks carrying infantry. In a few moments, Tito and a handful of men were cut off by German infantrymen who leaped from the trucks and deployed in battle formation while the tanks continued on their way along the road up the mountain. Tito was only about one hundred and fifty yards from the German infantry and came under their direct fire. He began withdrawing up the mountain with the German infantry in hot pursuit. . . .

. . . The Supreme H.Q. and the decimated units around it were retreating. It was in the last days of November and already freezing in the mountains. The first snow was about to fall. But the German command had not achieved its purpose. At that very moment, ninety-two Partisan detachments numbering eighty thousand men were fighting in the mountains and in the plains of Yugoslavia.

Thus ended the first year of the uprising in Yugoslavia. It had started in one of the most difficult moments in the struggle against the Axis powers, when the prospects of victory over Hitler seemed more remote than ever. It would undoubtedly have been one of the moral contributions to the war effort of all the united nations had it become generally known in Allied countries to what extent this uprising had developed, what were its successes, how much territory had been liberated, and how severe had been the losses of Hitler's troops.

But at that time Yugoslavia, at least as regards the National Liberation Movement and Partisan Tito, had been blacklisted by the leading powers of the united nations. Not a single word about it was publicly mentioned in Allied countries, in their press, their broadcasts, or their public observances. One had to be in Yugoslavia, fighting the Germans, to understand the painful impression it made upon us. Even silence might have been borne, but, instead of silence, attacks were made on Partisans, and the greatest tribute was paid to the very man who had the least merit in the struggle against the Germans in Serbia in 1941: to Draža Mihailović. . . .

These were difficult days for the Partisans in Yugoslavia. They were fighting to the death, they were giving their lives not only for the freedom of their own country but for the general war effort of all the united nations, and all was hidden and distorted. When Moscow was boosting Draža Mihailović, there arose a conflict between the Communist Parties of Yugoslavia and Bulgaria concerning the character of the struggle against the invaders. The Bulgarians ordered the Secretary of the Communist Party of Macedonia, Šarlo, to take no directives from the Yugoslavs regarding the necessity of an armed struggle against the invaders. . . .

The experience gained in the first German offensive, in a frontal struggle with a technically very superior enemy, was extremely valuable to the Partisans. The Supreme H.Q. and nine Serbian detachments withdrew to the frontier between Serbia and Sandžak and liberated several towns held by the Italians. The detachments, which were somewhat exhausted by considerable losses in their struggles against Germans and by the immense efforts they had made, rested briefly on the mountain Zlatar. Tito visited almost every company of his forces and talked to the soldiers. In some of these companies, the majority of fighting men were workers from Belgrade or miners from Serbian mines. These inspections led Tito to form proletarian brigades: special Partisan units characterized above all by their firm discipline and by their methods of warfare. These proletarian units differed from the detachments in that they would not be bound to the regions where they had originated but would fight in all parts of Yugoslavia. In a way, the proletarian units became the symbol of the struggle of all the peoples of Yugoslavia. To distinguish them from other units, the proletarians carried a sickle and hammer over the red star. In the first encounter with the enemy, in a battle against Italians and Chetniks, the First Proletarian Brigade achieved a considerable victory, in which more than 120 Italians and many arms were captured. This encouraged the Partisan units considerably, after their losses in the fights against the Germans. . . .

Since the First Proletarian Brigade had been formed in the

meanwhile, Tito left for Bosnia with this brigade. Their arrival meant a lot for the uprising of this part of the country. Winter had already come. There was deep snow in the mountains, and the temperatures sank to 20 degrees below zero.

The German command, however, did not heed these adverse weather conditions but ordered the launching of a new offensive against those portions of territory where the Supreme H.Q. and the First Proletarian Brigade were to be found. This time, the Germans threw ski battalions into the battle. In an unexpected attack on the Romanija Mountain, in snow so deep that even wild beasts could hardly be expected to move through it, a German ski battalion took by surprise a battalion of the First Proletarian Brigade and inflicted heavy losses. The Partisans could not make use of their rifles and machine guns because these weapons had been frozen. But this German offensive failed, and the proletarian brigade broke through the German ring. During the retreat to Igman Mountain, 150 of the fighting men were put out of action by the cold. Toes—even the entire feet—had subsequently to be amputated. Most such operations had to be carried out in the absence of any form of anesthetics, because the Partisan medical units lacked both medicaments and surgical instruments. On one occasion, when in a village a Partisan was to have his leg amputated, the doctor for lack of proper instruments borrowed a saw, which he boiled and then put to use on his operating table.

No sooner had it emerged from this offensive than the First Proletarian Brigade entered the town of Foča, which had been occupied by Italians and Chetniks and which housed the Supreme H.Q. for more than three months. . . .

Finally, on April 23, Tito asked Moscow for the last time what was happening to the aid. He was brief:

"Can we hope for ammunition soon?"

To this he received the following final reply:

"As we informed you earlier, for reasons which you understand, you unfortunately cannot expect to get either ammunition or automatic weapons from here at an early date. The principal reason is the impossibility of getting them to you.

"It is therefore necessary for you to make the best and most economic use possible of all possibilities that do exist, including the slenderest and most difficult possibility of obtaining supplies there on the spot. You will have to carry on like that, regardless of the devilish hard conditions, developing a war of liberation, holding out and beating off the enemy until it becomes impossible. It is certainly necessary to unmask the Chetniks to the people completely, with convincing documentary proof, but for the present it would be politically opportune for you to do so through a general approach to the Yugoslav government, emphasizing that the Yugoslav patriots who are fighting have a right to expect support for any Serb, Croat, Montenegrin, and Slovene fighters who are waging a struggle, either in Yugoslavia or abroad, on the basis of a National Liberation Partisan Army.

"Please consider our advice and communicate your observations, also what concrete steps you may take in that direction."

So the Partisans fought throughout that winter and spring in all parts of Yugoslavia without Soviet help. The proletarian brigades on liberated territory around the town of Foča ran out of ammunition. The enemy jeered, calling us "five-bullet men" because there were five bullets to each soldier. . . .

These were the relations between Moscow and Yugoslavia during 1941 and 1942. Stalin thus, in one of the most difficult periods of the Yugoslav uprising, instead of sending all possible aid to the Partisans made every effort to seize key positions in Draža Mihailović's H.Q. in order to make use of him in the interest of Soviet foreign policy. The Yugoslav people, the interests of the progressive movement in Yugoslavia, were of secondary importance to him.

Because of the constant strengthening of Partisan detachments and the growing of liberated territory in the face of repeated offensives, Hitler and Mussolini decided to take even more drastic action. Toward the end of December 1941, Mussolini wrote to Hitler:

"Balkans. It is necessary to eliminate all the hotbeds of insurrection before spring. They might cause the broadening of the war in the Balkans. We should pacify Bosnia first, then Serbia and Montenegro. It is necessary for our armed forces to collaborate according to a common plan, in order to avoid a loss of energy and to reach the desired results with the least amount of men and material."[1]

[1]Benito Mussolini, *Diary* (Cavallero), p. 177.

The preparations for the offensive against liberated territory around Foča ended at the end of March, and passed over to the beginning of the so-called Third Offensive. Italian, German, Ustashi, and Chetnik forces took part in this offensive. For the first time in the course of this war, the Draža Mihailović Chetniks openly collaborated with Italian troops against Partisans. The offensive developed sluggishly, and the Italians advanced slowly. We first had to withdraw from Montenegro, and then the enemy encircled us around Foča. The Germans advanced only up to a certain point and then stopped, whereas the Italians had to withdraw from several spots. But it was clear that we could not maintain Foča. Our tactics consisted of attacking the enemy at night, offering the strongest possible resistance but refusing to accept a frontal battle, and destroying all communications. . . .

The number of proletarian brigades had increased. Three more brigades had been constituted from detachments from Montenegro and Sandžak, so that the Supreme H.Q. had direct command over five proletarian brigades. The enemy tried to encircle these units in the high mountains on the border between Bosnia and Montenegro, but failed. It is true that our units suffered immensely from lack of food. Neither bread nor fats could be found in the mountains. The Partisans used to drive herds of sheep before them, and for weeks our only food consisted in lean, boiled mutton. The worst was that there was no salt. We also suffered from scurvy, for there were no fruits or greens in the mountains. We could only eat young beech leaves, or press the juice out of the beech bark and drink it. When we broke through the enemy ring, our brigades found themselves in the valley of the Sutjeska River. This is one of the most beautiful spots in Yugoslavia. . . .

That night the Supreme H.Q. held a meeting in which it was decided to start a long march to the north, toward the liberated territory of western Bosnia, at a distance of about 200 miles. It was planned on this occasion to make a powerful attack on an important enemy line of communication, the railroad between the Adriatic Sea and Sarajevo, as well as on a series of enemy garrisons.

Thus began the "long march" of Yugoslav Partisans. The attack on the railroad over a stretch of 30 miles achieved complete surprise. Many trains were captured together with the material they were carrying, a great number of enemy places were destroyed, and there was little resistance. At the railroad stations we also got hold of many enemy newspapers with large communiqués of the Italian Second Army, describing the total defeat of the Partisan forces! I looked forward to only one prize for myself from these attacks, a bottle of ink. My fountain pen was almost empty. I thus had to limit the writing of my diary before the attack as much as possible, because of the lack of ink. Imagine my joy when I discovered a bottle of ink on the table of an office in the Bradina railroad station.

A few days later, the Partisan brigades liberated Konjic, an important junction of the Adriatic-Sarajevo railroad. Arms with adequate ammunition were also captured. There two Partisan soldiers of the First Battalion of the First Brigade entered a house and by force took food from a woman. She then came to the battalion H.Q. to complain. The entire battalion was gathered, and the two soldiers admitted what they had done. They were summoned before the battalion and condemned to death. Both requested to be permitted to speak before the entire battalion on the eve of their being shot, and one of them said:

"Comrades, I consider the punishment to be just. I have committed a grave crime. You see, our brigade has gone from one end of Yugoslavia to the other, liberating one city after the other from the invader. It carries freedom, and I have soiled its name, I have soiled this star with the sickle and hammer. . . . Shoot at me without compunction, comrades, do not allow your hand to tremble, because the punishment must be imposed. . . . "

And both stood quietly before the guns. A shot was heard. The soldiers who did the shooting had their eyes full of tears. But there was no other way. The only assistance the Partisan brigades had came from the population. A conflict with the people would mean the end of the brigade, the end of the struggle against the invaders.

The enemy did not expect our offensive. Tito selected his line of advance in a masterly fashion, the demarcation line of the occupation zone of the Italian and German army. While the enemy generals were making up their minds who should attack and where, and who would stop the advance of the brigades, town after town fell, garrisons surrendered, and hundreds of new fighting men joined the proletarian brigades. Thus the five brigades of

Tito's advanced rapidly to the north, toward western Bosnia, where extensive liberated territory was located. The Partisans freed several large cities there in the spring of 1942. The first Partisan aviation was founded there too. Three light German bombers had been captured on an Ustashi airfield. There were some pilots among the Partisans, and a few days later the Partisan aircraft made their first flights. The enemy did not expect it, and only when they were bombed did they realize these were not their own planes. However, the Partisan aviation could not remain active long, since there was not enough gasoline or bombs. But its moral effect was immense. The population believed that Stalin himself had sent those aircraft to the Partisans.

German fighters soon discovered the Partisan aircraft on the ground and destroyed them. At the same time the enemy began an offensive from all sides against the liberated territory. Partisan units as well as over fifty thousand women, children, and old people took refuge on Kozara Mountain, which the enemy promptly encircled in strength. After several weeks of heavy fighting, the Partisans broke through the ring and freed themselves. A considerable part of the population was saved with them, but many women and children fell into enemy hands. Some were immediately shot and the rest taken to concentration camps.

At this moment five proletarian brigades broke through in the south. Thus the liberated territory was saved and considerably extended, as the proletarian brigades overpowered several strong enemy garrisons. The Supreme H.Q. was located first in the town of Glamoč, and later in Bosanski Petrovac. A courier connection was resumed with all parts of Yugoslavia. *Borba* was again published as the organ of the Communist Party of Yugoslavia, appearing three times a week. People's committees functioned in all the liberated territory. The first elections for these committees were held in October 1942, and for the first time women were granted the right to vote. Many women became members of committees, a matter of real consequence in these mountainous regions, where relations toward women were of a conservative kind. But war brought on many changes, including this one. Women worked very efficiently in the committees.

In many parts of western Bosnia, particularly in those inhabited by Serbs, all churches had either been destroyed by the Ustashi or closed since the first days of war. When the Partisan brigades arrived, the army chaplains who accompanied every brigade were kept busy. They first cleaned the churches where the Ustashi had not allowed service, then found the bells and hung them in the belfries. On the following Sunday, the bells rang, and the peasants in their white dresses crowded from everywhere. . . .

In the fall of that same year, the Supreme H.Q. decided to form larger units, and corps were organized, composed of several divisions each. This rendered possible more complex military operations, where the coordination of larger units was needed. . . .

Thus, in the fall, the National Liberation Army increased to over 150,000 fighting men, divided into two corps with 9 divisions, 36 brigades, and 70 separate battalions in 70 detachments. It was decided at the same time to convene the A.V.N.O.I. The most outstanding representatives of the National Liberation Movement from all parts of Yugoslavia attended this assembly in the city of Bihać. It was originally intended for the A.V.N.O.I. to elect a provisional government, but Moscow requested that this be done under no condition. The idea was thus given up, and the council had only the character of a manifestation.

The convention of the A.V.N.O.I. had a great effect in all Yugoslavia. The enemy again made preparations for the final liquidation of the Partisan movement. In October 1942, Hitler invited Lieutenant-General Alexander von Leer to his Supreme H.Q. on the eastern front at Winitza. Von Leer was then the commander of the German Twelfth Army, and later commander of the entire German southeastern front. His troops were chosen to lead the offensive against the Partisans. Ante Pavelić, the head of Quisling Croatia, attended this meeting, according to the testimony of General von Leer at his trial. A final plan of operations was set up, and it was decided to invite the Italians to participate in the operations. On January 5, 1943, a special meeting was held in Rome. General von Leer represented Germany, and Italy was represented by General Hugo Cavellero and the commander of the Second Army, General Roata. An Ustashi general was also present. General Roata declared that in the winter of 1941-1942 when his garrisons had been surrounded he had to be supplied by air. At this consultation, the Italian generals suggested that Chetnik units be used, but General von Leer declared that he was not authorized to do so by his command.

All the preparations were finally made, and the offensive started in the second half of January 1943. The following German divisions advanced from the north: 7 SS Prinz Eugene, the 369 Legionary Teufel Division, and the 714 German Division. The 717 German Division attacked from the east. The Italian Fifth Corps was to attack from the west with the divisions Lombardia, Re, and Sasari, and Chetniks. The main blow was to fall on the liberated territory in western Bosnia and Lika. This is a mountainous wooded region.

The enemy had powerful aviation at its disposal. The Supreme H.Q. immediately worked out its operation plans. It was decided to offer the toughest possible resistance to the enemy but to accept no frontal battles under any conditions. At the same time, the order was given to all units in the other regions of Yugoslavia to start day and night attacks on enemy communications and garrisons. The Supreme H.Q. also ordered the First Proletarian, the Second Proletarian, and the Third Division to assemble in order to break through the enemy ring and to liberate Herzegovina and Montenegro, which were at the time completely occupied by the enemy. This meant changing from an enemy offensive to a Yugoslav offensive.

Several thousand wounded Partisans lying in various hospitals in the liberated territory represented a great difficulty for the maneuvering of Partisan units, since it was impossible to let them fall into enemy hands. The enemy usually killed all our wounded soldiers. All the wounded were divided into separate battalions, those with light wounds who could move without help in one kind of battalion, those more severely wounded but who could ride a horse in so-called cavalry battalions, and those who were very severely wounded in stretcher battalions. All wounded soldiers were armed against enemy attack. . . .

The German offensive developed powerfully. However, the measures undertaken by the Supreme H.Q. proved efficient. The proletarian divisions attacked toward the south, liberated the city of Livno, then Imotski, captured a large amount of armament, and then attacked in the Neretva valley, where the units of the Italian Sixth Corps were located in several fortified towns. It became necessary to stop the German advance in the north, and also to break through the Italian ring along the Neretva.

We made a strong attack on the town of Prozor, where a

regiment of the Italian Division Murge was located, but the town did not fall on the first night. There was a pause during the day, and on the next night we again attacked the Italian pillbox. Victory was achieved at dawn. The Italian regiment surrendered, and our units broke into the valley of the Neretva River, where Italian garrisons fell one after the other. In three days the entire Italian Division Murge was defeated and fifteen tanks were captured, along with a great many cannons and huge quantities of ammunition, food, and medical supplies. Almost two thousand Italian soldiers were taken prisoner in that sector.

Our proletarian divisions could easily ford the Neretva and disappear in Montenegrin mountains. But it was necessary to rescue the wounded, whose number had now increased to forty-five hundred. The evacuation went on slowly. We also had to rescue hundreds of thousands of old peasants and mothers with children who were fleeing before the enemy. This was pitiless war. . . .

Tito then told me about the plans of our further operations. We were to await the arrival of all the wounded and destroy all the bridges on the Neretva River, so that the enemy might think that we had given up the idea of a crossing. We should then send our basic forces to the north to push back the Germans as far as possible, and then unexpectedly break through the Neretva River.

Tito's order was quickly carried out. The German divisions in the north were amazed by our counterattack. In this battle we used the fifteen Italian tanks we had captured, as well as the entire artillery that had been captured in the Neretva battle. The Germans had to retreat ten miles, and we took many prisoners. . . .

When the Germans had been pushed away, the Second Dalmatian Brigade received the order to break through the Neretva River first, and to establish a bridgehead. There were fifteen thousand Chetniks of Draža Mihailović on the other side of the river and on the neighboring hills. They had been sent here by the Italians to close the front after the defeat of the Division Murge. The Chetniks had not expected our attack, believing that we were forcing our way to the north. A group of Dalmatian Partisans carrying unfused bombs in their teeth crept over a destroyed railroad bridge, which was standing practically erect.

When they reached the other end of the bridge, where a Chetnik pillbox was located, they threw two bombs into it and then jumped in. Thus a bridgehead was established after a struggle that had lasted only three minutes. Our engineers immediately erected a wooden bridge over the ruins of the old iron one, and then unit after unit crossed the river on the run and landed on the other bank, broadening the bridgehead. At dawn our first units had already reached the mountain summits on the other side, pursuing the defeated Chetniks.

Columns of wounded followed. The crossing of the river lasted for seven days. German and Italian aircraft bombed the bridge violently, but the crossing went on. And thus our last wounded soldier and our last unit reached the other side of the river. . . .

After the break across the Neretva, the Partisan divisions advanced rapidly through Herzegovina and Montenegro, liberating town after town. The problem of the wounded Partisans was a very difficult one. There was a severe epidemic of typhus. We all lived in villages in which the majority of the houses had been burned down. There were no medicaments whatsoever. The food was insufficient. Those who recovered from typhus were suffering especially from hunger. I remember many scenes from these days: a peasant plowing a field and sowing oats, and, as soon as he went away, a wounded Partisan throwing himself on the furrow and digging out the oats with his fingers. We had more victims from typhus in March and April 1943 than we had from encounters with the enemy.

In other parts of Yugoslavia that had not been included in the offensive, Partisan units made violent attacks against the enemy, especially in Slavonia, where the main Balkan east-west railroad line runs.

The fighting was extremely severe in western Bosnia, where German divisions succeeded in surrounding two Partisan brigades in the mountain of Grmeč. This happened in the middle of the winter, and the whole mountain was covered with six feet of snow. Partisan brigades and German columns lost their way in the snow-bound mountain. The Fifth Partisan Brigade marched once for more than seventy-two hours without food or rest. From exhaustion, hunger, and sleeplessness, people developed mass hallucinations. . . .

The victory achieved in this offensive, as well as the size of the

Partisan movement in other regions, forced Hitler to start immediately a new offensive against the Partisans. However, it became clear in Allied circles that the Partisans were the most powerful force in Yugoslavia, that Draža Mihailović was not as strong as it had been believed, especially after the defeat in the Neretva valley. The British government therefore decided to send an observer to the liberated territory. And so, one night, as a "Liberator" was flying over the liberated territory in Lika, an officer in a British uniform parachuted from the aircraft, accompanied by three noncommissioned officers. He landed in a forest in the dark and at dawn reached the fringe of a village where he found a sentinel who directed him to the Supreme Partisan H.Q. for Croatia. The officer in the British uniform sat in a motorcar and drove some forty miles over liberated territory before he reached the H.Q. He introduced himself there. He said his name was William Jones, that he was a Canadian, a volunteer in this war, since he had remained an invalid after the First World War, where he lost an eye, and that he had been sent here as an observer. Major Jones made an excellent impression from the very beginning, because of his sincerity and his courage. The Partisans liked him because he was very brave and never wanted to bend down or to take cover in a battle. He always stood erect, wearing his beret defiantly. Major Jones was remembered among the Partisans to the end of the war as the most popular Allied officer in Yugoslavia.

Supreme H.Q. were informed through Major Jones that a special British military mission would be sent them. Meanwhile, in mid-May, the Germans started a new great offensive against three proletarian divisions and several other units that were located with the Supreme H.Q. on the border between Montenegro and Bosnia. The enemy effected a very deep pincer movement. Twelve German and Italian divisions and one Bulgarian regiment took part in this offensive, which was marked by the bloodiest of battles. The Germans no longer limited themselves to lines of communication but, entering the territory itself, climbed upon mountain summits the way we did. They sent supplies to their units by plane. They fortified themselves powerfully in some sections.

When the offensive began, we had to delay our breakthrough because we were expecting the arrival of the British military mis-

sion. When it parachuted at last, the Supreme H.Q. was located
on Durmitor Mountain. William Dicken, a don at Oxford who
was then a captain of the British Army, was the head of this
mission. He gave the impression of being a quiet and courageous
man. Dicken arrived with his mission in the middle of one of the
most terrible battles fought by the Partisans in World War Two.

This offensive was a short one, but it was more violent than
any previous campaign. The basic Partisan forces broke through
after a bitter struggle and suffered tremendous losses. Tito himself was wounded in the arm, a member of the British mission,
Captain William Stuart, was killed, and the head of the Dicken
mission was also wounded. The Germans also suffered heavy
losses. This is what General von Leer wrote about the result of
the battle:

> The fights were extraordinarily heavy. All the commanders
> agreed that their troops were going through the most bitter struggle
> of the war. A ferocious Partisan attack which struck the Second Bat-
> talion of the 369th Division in particular effected a breakthrough on
> this front near Jelašca and Miljevina. All the enemy forces managed
> to retreat through this front and to disappear in the mountains to-
> ward the north. The German troops were too tired and exhausted to
> be able to do anything about it, and there were no reserves.

Thus the First and Second Divisions with the Supreme H.Q.
and some other smaller units broke through the ring, but the
main enemy blow fell on the Third Division, which was protecting the wounded and acting as the rear guard. Milovan Djilas
was at the head of these columns. When the tired fighting men
of this division crossed the River Sutjeska, everything seemed to
be quiet and the enemy had apparently retreated. When the
Partisans found themselves in the valley on the other side of the
Sutjeska River and were approaching the first hills, Germans
behind hidden pillboxes opened fire with all their weapons. To
return would have meant sure death. Therefore Milovan Djilas
and Sava Kovačević, the commander of the division, ordered an
assault. They were both the first to advance toward enemy pillboxes. More than half the Partisans fell before reaching the first
pillbox and throwing bombs into it. It was necessary then to
capture an entire system of pillboxes in order to widen the
breakthrough. . . .

It was not until the following night that Djilas finally managed to break through, and a week later he reached the Supreme H.Q. Thus ended the Fifth Offensive. The crack units had been decimated. Tremendous losses had been suffered. But moral victory was achieved. New fighters soon flowed into the ranks of the units. . . .

Then came the surrender of Italy. Although our Supreme H.Q. had not been informed in advance of this event, eleven Italian divisions were disarmed, which was of tremendous significance for the arming of Partisan units. . . .

IV. The Huk Guerrilla Struggle in the Philippines

WILLIAM J. POMEROY

*William J. Pomeroy, an American radical
married to a Filipino, was a unique witness
to the guerrilla war of the Huks in the
Philippines. He participated in it for two
years (1950-1952); then he was captured
and spent ten years in jail. After his
liberation he wrote a personal record of the
struggle, which unwittingly shows why the
movement failed.*

August 1950

Something is astir in the Sierra Madre.

G.Y. packs up and departs, staying away for several days,
attending a conference, he says vaguely. When he comes back he
is very tired and muddy and sits down at the riverside for a long
time with his feet in the water before plunging in. He comes up
to the house dripping, rubbing himself pink, very cheerful, but he
has nothing to say about his trip.

Couriers come in more frequently from the Secretariat in
Manila, bearing reports. G.Y. is up late into the night, poring
over papers and a map, scribbling. We do not ask him what is
up; in this movement few matters are spoken of freely, for
security reasons. We are given the task of preparing a leaflet for

From William J. Pomeroy, *The Forest: A Personal Record of the Huk Guerrilla Struggle in the Philippines* (New York: International Publishers, 1963). Copyright 1963 by International Publishers. Reprinted with permission of International
Publishers.

August 26, the day of the Cry of Balintawak, when the Katipu-
neros began the revolt against Spain in 1896. It is to be a stir-
ring call to the people to support the Huks in destroying the
imperialist-puppet regime. Great piles of the leaflet are run off
on the mimeograph machine and carried away from the camp in
sacks.

Large groups of armed Huks, heading south on the trails beyond the camp, pass by from the Field Commands to the north.
Their commanders and a few others come in to confer with G.Y.;
their packs are light, but they themselves are weighted down with
ammunition. They have the taut and confident look of men upon
a mission.

Other groups come through the camp, too, from the production bases. They carry empty sacks tied across their shoulders,
like the squad *balutan* on an errand of supply. It is unusual to see
the production base people on the move this way. The whole
population of the forest seems to be in motion.

On the evening of August 25, as we are about to retire, G.Y.
comes and sits beside our *banig*. Even when he is excited, it is a
calm excitement. There is no longer need for security, he says. I
can tell you now. Tonight we capture Santa Cruz.

The story of Santa Cruz comes up to us in driblets.

First there is the radio, with a garbled, almost incoherent report by a rapidly talking newscaster about thousands of Huks
pouring out of nowhere into towns and military installations, not
only in Santa Cruz but elsewhere in southern and central Luzon.
The big constabulary headquarters at Camp Makabulos, in Tar-
lac, has been captured, its garrison killed, and its installations
razed to the ground. As for Santa Cruz, it is, in that voice of
despair, "in the hands of the Huks."

In mid-afternoon a running courier is up from Longos. He had
left the town at ten o'clock in the morning, and at that time the
sound of firing was still audible from the direction of Santa Cruz
and a great pillar of black smoke hung in the sky. The alarm had
come in to the P.C. detachment at Longos shortly after midnight,
and the captain there with a jeepload of men had sped off toward
Santa Cruz. Near Lumbang, however, they had run into a barricade of coconut trees felled across the road and had been fired

upon by Huks in ambush. The captain fled back to Longos, but he had no sooner arrived there when somebody—Huks or town partisan units—fired a volley out of the darkness into the P.C. barracks, and the whole detachment ran away.

At dawn the courier had clung to a truck crowded with curious civilians and had traveled down the road toward the heavy firing going on at Santa Cruz. However, the barricade was still maintained near Lumbang, with a group of Huks strolling up and down behind it, telling the people politely, "Don't go there. Let us take care of the enemy." All along the road people had swarmed out of houses and were milling in the highway, laughing and telling each other in high spirits, "The Huks are killing the P.C.'s." They clustered at the barricade, asking the Huks, "Is it true that you are now the government?" It was like a fiesta.

It is not until after two days, however, that we get a full report. A special courier arrives with an armed escort. He carries a heavy black bag, which is emptied out upon the table. It lies there, a heap of banded sheaves of pesos, tens of thousands of pesos, confiscated funds for the struggle.

From the courier and his escorts we get our picture of the raid on Santa Cruz. All talking at once, they give to us some of the splintered turmoil of the event:

Four hundred Huks in two main bodies had gathered east and west of the town, waiting in concealment for the prearranged hour. Then they climbed into prepared trucks and drove into Santa Cruz simultaneously from both directions. Ambush parties on all the roads leading to the town at that moment felled trees across the highways and cut telephone wires.

These images loom out of the night: The packed anxious men in the trucks as they approach checkpoints at the town's entrance and at the gateway to the P.C. camp. The P.C.'s caught in the headlights coming out at a routine gait for inspection, shot down at once in the road, and the trucks roaring into the town and into the camp. The trucks driving round in the night quiet of the plaza and spilling out armed men in the heterogeneous garb of the forest. The wild scene of men with guns scattering in the headlight glare, shouting to each other for contact as they rush to assigned missions.

In the camp there is something awry. Some of the officers are caught in their quarters and killed, and everywhere P.C.'s are trying to flee. Some of them run out into the mudflat swamp along Laguna de Bay and bury themselves in the mud. Others try to hide in houses in the town. But a sizeable number with a lieutenant get into a concrete barracks and turn it into a fort. The Huks surround it, and a frantic siege begins. A clean sweep of the garrison is wanted. Here the night becomes a chaos of gunfire.

All the other targets in the town are taken: The jail, where several imprisoned Huks are released and where one who has turned informer is shot in his cell. The bank, where cashiers are brought from homes previously pinpointed and made to open safes. The homes of informers, who are dragged into the streets and shot. The hospital, where a production base man, skilled in the paths of the forests, gets lost in the corridors while trying to collect medicines and shouts desperately for someone to let him out.

Government buildings and military installations are burned, and the glare of flames lights up the town. Civilians pour into streets despite Huk urgings to remain inside. They hug the Huks and bring out food to them. They guide Huks to the hiding P.C.'s, who are shot. They swarm in the marketplace where the attacking party, going by a list drawn up in advance by intelligence units in the town, breaks open the stores of elements hostile to the movement and confiscates their goods, piling them in trucks—canned goods, clothing, shoes, anything useful in the mountains. The civilians help, and all that cannot be carried is turned over to them; people hurry in streets under great burdens of goods. Looting of other stores is halted by armed guards. Up on the back of a truck, in the glare of flames, a Huk with a rifle strapped over his back is delivering a speech, denouncing the criminal acts of the Constabulary who abuse the people, denouncing the traitorous government that sells out the country to imperialists, urging the people to support the Huks. Squads go about distributing our leaflets to the people in the marketplace and plaza, and throwing them into the frontyards of homes. Everyone is hoarse from shouting.

In the camp the seige of the barracks goes on, in the dark hours and into the morning. Molotov cocktails are thrown against the building that is scarred with the black smoke of their burning and with hundreds of bullet marks, but it holds out. Gasoline drums are set afire and exploded against the doors, but the P.C.'s fight on in desperation. The camp commander is discovered behind a barracks hiding in an empty oil drum, but the Huks are impatient now and when the man pleads for his life, promising to order his men to surrender, they shoot him. Time is running out.

Erning, Huk vice-commander of the attack, one of the best of the military cadres from Pampanga, stands up in a truck to direct firing on the barracks and is killed. He is one of the three casualties suffered in the raid.

It is crude and clumsy, this taking of a town by guerrillas, but it is the way the people fight in a civil war, until they have learned how to do better.

By now it is late in the morning, and Samonte, the overall commander of the attack, is concerned about planes. Planes may come and catch trucks on the road. He gives the order to withdraw. Units assemble and climb into the laden trucks, speed out of town.

A strange silence comes over Santa Cruz. The smoke of burning still drifts, and there is the heavy smell of gunpowder. Mashed, trampled goods lie littered in the streets, and the scattered bodies of P.C.'s and informers lie where they were shot in the streets, lie, too, across the area of the camp. But the people have all disappeared, hurrying home before the reinforced enemy returns, after the Huks have gone.

It is several days before Samonte, commander of the attack, comes up the trail to the Big House. He comes slowly and wearily across the log spanning the river. Tall, raw-boned, he stands awkwardly on the ground below the house and removes his hat, wiping his arm over his reddened brow.

"We lost Erning," is all that he says.

This revolution is a battle of strategy and tactics. It is not an armed mob rushing through streets bent on death and destruction. It is not destruction and death that is its end, but creation and birth, and the blood that is shed is like the placenta that accompanies the arrival of life.

For all its appearance of disorder, this revolution is not disorderly or blindly spontaneous but is led, led with a scientific knowledge of society and with the precise guidance of main forces, allies, and reserves, based on the most nearly correct estimate of given situations.

In the Philippines it has been decided by a leadership, after much debate, that a revolutionary situation exists. A revolutionary situation, says the socially scientific definition, occurs when the ruling forces can no longer rule in the old way and the forces of the people can no longer accept the old rule. Here in the Philippines the ruling forces are discredited and can no longer maintain themselves with a semblance of democratic processes; they resort to frauds, to terror, and to the suspension of rights. Here the people can no longer stand for the old rule and look about for changes; with no other means for change permitted, they are prepared to resort to the ultimate means of arms.

The situation is estimated by the leadership in this way:

The main enemy is the imperialists, and their allies are the puppet comprador groups that profit from a close relation with the imperialists. They defend themselves with the armed and suppressive agencies of the state that is within their grasp. Their reserves are the unenlightened, uncommitted masses of the people.

The main force of the revolution is an alliance of peasants, workers, and intellectuals. Their allies are all the elements that suffer from, are exploited by, and are denied development by the imperialists and proimperialists. Their revolutionary fighting arm is all those who are prepared for advanced struggle. Their reserves are the unenlightened, uncommitted masses of the people.

At present the fighting forces of both sides are already joined in battle. The revolutionary situation is flowing toward a revolutionary crisis, which is the eve of the transfer of power. We are in the period of preparation for the strategic aim of seizing power. Our tactical aims are all those steps that can effectively mobilize the allies and the reserves of the revolution into an increasing assault on the main enemy and its allies.

At this time the most crucial concern is the battle for the reserves, for the unenlightened, uncommitted masses. To win them to the side of the revolution, it is necessary to heat up the struggle, to demonstrate the power of the revolutionary forces, and to expose the weaknesses of the ruling forces. We do this in two ways: through the propaganda of word and through the

propaganda of action—by explaining to the people, and by showing them and involving them in advanced struggles. Hence expansion of the H.M.B. Hence armed attacks on the suppressive
agencies of the state, and the temporary seizure of towns to
exhibit the strength of the H.M.B. to the people.

Main forces and reserves. Exhortation and implementation.
Strategy and tactics. . . .

September 1950

We have become overconfident, and now we pay for that carelessness.

The attack on Santa Cruz, it is felt, has demoralized the enemy
in this region. Without waiting to investigate conditions in the
lowlands, therefore, it is decided to send couriers to Manila, to
the central command, with reports on the details of the attack
and with part of the money confiscated in Santa Cruz. G.Y.'s two
young girl couriers and the boy, Ruming, prepare to leave. They
are excited about going to the city, where they always have the
bonus of a movie. Messages and the money are stuffed into *bayongs* that are doubly woven, with a space between the two layers
of *pandan*. They are off with an armed escort, their gay voices
carrying back to us.

In the early morning the escort returns, hurriedly. They are
very grave and squat outside the house with G.Y., in a head-
bent circle, scratching at the ground with twigs. It is a serious
report. They brought the couriers to the edge of town, as usual,
at nightfall, and the couriers entered between the usual houses.
In a few moments there was a great commotion, with shouting,
and shots were fired. When the men went back to investigate,
the town was swarming with P.C.'s and they barely escaped
having an encounter. They waited at the outside post in the
coconut groves but no one came, so it looks as if our couriers
were all caught.

It is an anxious time. No one in the camp can work. We
wonder if the lesson of Vergie[1] has had its effect, but even then
there are the captured messages. In the afternoon there is partial
relief. Ruming arrives! We are overjoyed, until he tells his story.
He and the girls had entered the town and were almost at the

---

[1] A messenger executed by the Huks for having spoken under torture.

house used for a post when they ran right into a pair of P.C.'s who nearly encircled them all with their arms. The three couriers ran and tried to get into some of the houses, but the people were afraid and shut their doors or let the *nipa* window panels fall because the P.C.'s were shouting and firing in the air. Ruming saw both girls caught only a few feet from him—yes, and they were carrying the *bayongs*—but he is small, and he ran under houses and got away, in the dark.

What to do? There is nothing to do but wait, and worry. Only a cursory reading of the messages will enable the enemy to know that top organs of the movement are nearby. We will need to send out patrols, in all directions, to feel out enemy movements. Ruming wants to volunteer; he is only ten years old, but he thinks he has failed as a courier and he wants to redeem himself. G.Y. grins and gives his consent. Ruming's carbine is almost as long as he is. He and Sisu, the youthful security companion of Samonte, go out together.

Late in the afternoon there is the sound of firing in the distance, in the direction of the coconut groves, single shots at first, then a long burst of rapid fire that lasts for three or four minutes. After that there is silence that is drawn out like a rubber band into the twilight and into the night. We lie with everything packed, waiting for it to break, but it does not and the night passes. In the morning the patrols are back.

There is much news, and all of it is bad. Longos is full of heavily armed P.C.'s, and more are arriving in trucks. The civilians have all been ordered out of the fields and forbidden to go into the forest or into the coconut groves. Civilians are being hired as carriers, to bear the equipment of troops. All signs point to an operation of some size, and it will be into the forest, there can be no doubt.

As for the firing, there is a story to tell, and Ruming to tell it. He and Sisu, scouting in the coconut groves, ran into a full company of P.C.'s. The enemy had a guide at the point, whom Ruming recognized, an ex-Huk informer named Caballes. The two boy Huks, without hesitation, promptly knelt down and opened fire on the company of the enemy. Caballes was hit and fell, and a P.C. fell also. Then the two ran, bending low, in a storm of bullets from the whole enemy force, and got away untouched. So Ruming is redeemed and is a hero, the ten-year-old Huk.

It is a small victory, but it doesn't reverse events. Now it is our turn to run. . . .

Supper is over, and we are sitting crosslegged around our tiny lamp, reading, when there is the sound of hurrying footsteps in the mud outside. We look up, and Reg is in the doorway, the canvas raincape thrown over his shoulders dotted with the dark spots of rain. The lamp throws shadows over his face, highlighting the solemn mouth and the strain at the jaw.

"Comrades," he says, "I have bad news, very bad news. It came on the radio a few minutes ago."

We continue to sit there, waiting.

"All of our leading comrades in the city have been arrested."

We continue to look at him, blankly. "All?" we say.

"All," he repeats. There were mass raids. They were caught in different houses in a simultaneous operation. The names were all given, and there can be no doubt. The Secretariat of the movement is in the hands of the enemy, and so are most of our city cadres. They claim to have hundreds of documents, and some of them were quoted. They have our whole tactical plan and our details of organization.

It is the worst possible news, for the whole direction of the struggle was in the hands of those arrested.

We are all upon our feet, talking, trying to place the blame, to estimate the errors and the damage. It was a traitor. It must have been a traitor. It was carelessness. How could they be so careless with so much at stake? Security! Who was in charge of security? It's a disaster. Let's wait until we get the details before we leap to conclusions. . . .

November 1950

Reports come in from all along the Sierra Madre. The enemy is becoming more aggressive.

Spies are everywhere in the towns, and patrols are often in the forest now, where once they never came. Our F.C.'s ambush them, shoot up their vehicles on the roads, make death traps of mountain paths, but the patrols do not stop. They know our plans now; they know roughly our dispositions. And they have power.

The docks of Manila are crammed with great crates of military equipment, American military aid rushed to the Philippines, and trucks shuttle endlessly from army bases, bringing it to the new army that the Joint U.S. Military Advisory Group (the J.U.S.M.A.G.) is creating to fight the Huks. The Constabulary, discredited and hated and incapable, is no longer the instrument used against the people. The Philippine army, put on a war footing, has been thrown into the field, and American military specialists from Greece and from Korea, where imperialism has had the experience of suppressing people's movements, are organizing and training it.

The Philippine army has been reorganized by these professional interventionists into Battalion Combat Teams, each assigned to a sector where the Huks are known to be, groups of them clustered in areas of Huk strength. The B.C.T.'s are 1,200-man units, independent fighting teams, each with its infantry and artillery and service companies, with its intelligence and psychological warfare teams, heavy with fire power based on an abundance of automatic weapons. They are equipped from helmet to shoes, from howitzers to pistols, from tanks to jeeps, by American military aid.

Twenty-eight B.C.T.'s are being organized. These are in addition to the normal headquarters, service, and supply units of a standing army and a vast intelligence apparatus that bring total Philippine army forces up to 54,000 men. To these are added the Philippine air force and the Philippine navy of coastal patrol boats, both fully committed to the anti-Huk campaign. A Constabulary force of 8,000 continues to guard roads and towns. This does not include the 20,000–30,000 civilian guards hired and paid by the landlords, the town police forces, and the innumerable agents hired and armed by senators, congressmen, and the various government departments, all employed against the Huks and to terrorize the people.

All told, there are at least 100,000 government-armed forces or suppressive elements being flung against the Huks, with a ratio of perhaps ten of them to one Huk. That is the measure of our challenge to imperialism and its allies.

As for us, with the arrest of leaders in Manila and with the seizure of documents in their possession, we are in the position of troops caught by a flank attack while in movement. Our major operation for November 7 is completely known and must be discarded. A broad conference of the movement's leadership, scheduled for the near future to map the tactics of the decisive period of the struggle, must be reset and prepared for by an entirely new set of leaders, who are now scattered from one end of the country to the other. All we can do in the meantime is tighten our security, prepare for mobility, and shadowbox with the enemy's offensive. . . .

Somewhere in this general area, in the Luisiana, Cavinti, Sampaloc triangle, the enlarged conference of the movement's leadership will be held. Communications have gone out by courier to every corner of the mountains and to the southern islands, and, gradually, after sneaking through cordons and taking long, circuitous routes, leading cadres are filling the camps and the production bases around us, waiting for the time to assemble at a meeting site and waiting for the accumulation of supplies to maintain a large body of people for a period of several weeks. Not only must the leaders be provided for, but also a large number of picked security forces. It is not easy to prepare and to hold a conference of this type, which must be well guarded and kept absolutely from the knowledge of an alert and active enemy.

On a wet morning, figures come one by one out of the veil of rain. We recognize the man in advance, and we jump out of the hut to greet him. It is Luis Taruc, walking in the mud like a long-legged bird, under a great pack, with an automatic carbine cradled in his arms. We embrace in the rain. We have not seen him for two years. Beneath the familiar peaked cap his face is thin but laughing as ever. He and his group have come from Pampanga, a month's journey over muddy and dangerous mountain trails.

Another figure, like a slim boy in slacks and jacket, comes up beside him. It is his wife, Patty, recently wed, a pharmacy graduate of the University of the Philippines. I take her slender fingers. She is thin and extremely weary from the march, but there is warmth and strength in her grip and I like her at once.

Security men, unshaven, muddy, resembling camels with their ponchos draped over baggage, file in—tough, picked men, carrying B.A.R.'s and Garands slung downward with the rain dripping off the barrels. Paul Aquino and his brother Felix are there, sons of old Bio Aquino, the Pampanga peasant leader. Another stands quietly and at ease to one side, so casually that I do not recognize for a moment Linda Bie, the most famous of all the Huk military commanders. He grins at the greeting, surprisingly shy for a man with his fighting record, which is easily unique in Philippine history.

Luis and his party jam into the household of Reg Taruc, who is his brother. It is a boisterous, crowded hut, but they do not mind; they are all Pampangos, and in the regionalistically minded Philippines people of the same province gravitate together. It is something that is fought against in the Huk movement but never entirely overcome. Only G.Y., among the leading elements, is largely free of the tendency. . . .

Other leading cadres have arrived from scattered points in the mountains, and the following day we have a long political discussion—Jesse, G.Y., Reg, Luis, Mateo del Castillo, Jorge Frianeza, and myself. The central problem is the tactical line to pursue in the context of the arrest of the movement's leadership and of the counteroffensive by the enemy. There are some sharp exchanges of opinion, especially over the ideas of Jorge Frianeza. He was removed from leadership in 1948 for advocating what was termed an appeasement policy, which involved the projection of legal struggle tactics and support by the trade unions of elements in the ruling Liberal Party. He is now pessimistic about the course of the armed struggle in the face of a strong imperialist enemy. In general, however, the main trend of the discussion is in favor of a continuation of the tactics devised by the arrested leadership—expansion, building of the armed forces, and general preparation for the gaining of power. The basic contentions are that the material conditions in the country have not altered and that the subjective revolutionary force, the Huks, has not been defeated or weakened. . . .

January 1951

Clean wind and broken fragments of the sun are in the forest, drying up the littered avenues. We wipe and dry our things, ready for work again. Then, suddenly, not far away, there is the sound of gunfire.

All households are on alert. In two hours the report is in. A group of our security men on patrol were seen by a large body of government troops across a stream uncomfortably nearby and were fired upon. Our men fired back, and the enemy retired the way they had come. However, we do not feel secure now and we decide to move our camp. The enemy is smelling out the trails we use. Reg, however, has a bad case of malaria and cannot walk, so we put off moving for a day. In the meantime, half of our security force is sent out to form an ambush at the top of a gorge where the trail is precarious.

At noon I return to the hut after a conference with Luis and Reg. We have been studying a map, choosing a site to which to move. I drop my muddy shoes at the door, and we sit about on the floor, eating a lunch of rice and a soup made out of *togue*, the sprouted *mongo*. Belen, our courier, gets up and walks over to the little waist-high cubicle of *anahaw* adjacent to the *batalan*, used for a urinal.

Suddenly she is back across the floor in violent haste, skirts flying, shrieking, P.C.! P.C.!

For a moment we do not comprehend what she is saying, but in that moment a deafening outburst of gunfire comes from but a few yards beyond our hut. The enemy is in our camp, firing upon us!

In one single motion, without thought, we are up and out of the hut, running for the river. The pop-pop-pop, bang-bang-bang of automatic weapons fills the air behind us. . . .

. . . There is no way of telling how many in the camp have fled, have died, or live. We could look for others, but we might run into enemy patrols. Knowing that we are around, the attackers are likely to base themselves at the camp and comb the forest for us. Our total arms are the carbine of Carlos, for which he has two clips, and the .45 pistol of Paul, which has one clip. We decide to get as far away from the camp as possible, and we strike out at once toward the northeast where we know there are no trails that the enemy could use.

I have not noticed before that my feet are bare, but now feeling begins to return to them. In all my life I have never gone barefooted, unless on the soft sand of beaches. But there is little softness on the forest floor, only rocks, roots, and carpets of thorns. My feet are cut and pierced before we have gone a hundred yards. I know that Celia, too, is having difficulty. Nevertheless we hurry.

As we go, little scraps of memory return through the shock of the raid. Reg, who was too sick to walk. Jesse Magusig, who is paralyzed and unable to do more than crawl. Jorge, who was hit and fell. Our belongings. We have lost everything that we own, left behind with our packs in the hut, all of our money, our clothes, my typewriter, our personal papers, my passport. . . .

July 1951

For months we have been pouring out our literature, our directives, our appeals, sending them from this far point in the Sierra Madre to Recos, to the lowlands, to people in barrio and in city. We are like those who lean over a deep well and drop pebbles into its interior, waiting to hear the far hollow echo of them striking water. Now when the sound comes back to us it is a strange echo, like the lost cry of someone drowning in that depth.

The echo that comes is that only a part of the leaflets and the pamphlets that we send out are being distributed. Fear is beginning to replace daring in many places. Enemy agents swarm everywhere and have arrested some distributors in Manila and in towns. In areas where our leaflets appear there are retaliations, with serious abuse of the general population. Our members in nucleus and in section begin to lie low, afraid. Literature piles up in huts and in homes, rots unused in hidden places.

In the Recos there are continuous operations by army troops, and our people have to be mobile, to change camps often. Camps have been raided, and the mimeographing equipment seized. You are sending us too much, comes the complaint. We do not have the means or the time to reproduce it. Or there is the report that the school we planned has been postponed because of the operations. Or there is no report at all.

Stranger still is the echo of something of which we have not heard before: the surrenderee.

In Nueva Ecija, a leader of Reco 1, Taguiam, surrenders. In Rizal and in Laguna, H.M.B. soldiers surrender to the authorities, taking their arms with them; they reveal the location of camps, and raids follow. In the districts and in the sections too there are surrenderees, and, eager to avoid punishment or maltreatment, they turn over the names of comrades and sympathizers to the enemy; arrests follow. An uneasiness is in our camps; every time a man surrenders a camp has to be abandoned and relocated.

Why do they surrender? Because many have joined in the hope of quick victory, and now that the struggle is prolonged they have lost their taste for it. Because the enemy has the advantage in firepower and in modern weapons and more Huks are dying now than ever before. Because the raids and the bombings are often and the food runs out and they lie often hungry on the wet ground in flight. Because they worry about a family back in a barrio without a breadwinner. Because their families are contacted by government agents and word is sent up that they will be treated well, that their offenses will be forgotten, if they come down. Because they violate discipline in the H.M.B. and surrender to avoid revolutionary punishment. Because in the long history of the Filipino people there has always been oppression and hardship, and is it not better to endure it than to starve in the forest? There are many reasons. When the tide of the struggle is running our way, individual weaknesses are submerged in the flood of high spirits; when the enemy is strong and the tide is not our way, those weaknesses emerge and turn men into the slimy things that scuttle for safety on the exposed shoreline.

The dead leaves are falling from the tree, says G.Y.

The dead leaves.

A storm is shaking the forest, and the leaves are falling. In the forest there are always falling leaves, and new ones that grow to replace them. But in the H.M.B. there are fewer recruits now, too, and no arms for the new ones. It is a bad season.

We had thought that the people moved at our pace, to the rapid click of the mimeograph machine. We had thought that the morale and the discipline in this camp was the morale and discipline everywhere. We had thought that by the leaders setting a high tempo we could set high the tempo of the revolution.

We have been living in a fool's paradise.

Lawin, one of the security soldiers assigned as security to our household, is sitting in the hut, cleaning his Garand rifle. He is leaning on a corner pole, his feet upon a railing that was once a sapling, those feet that never know shoes, with soles like brittle horn. While he works he murmurs a little song to himself, *Ang ibon pipit.* . . . It is the rifle that makes him happy. Rubbed to gleaming, it lies across his ragged lap.

Something is curious about the gun. The sights have been

removed. *Ka* Lawing, I say, why are there no sights on your gun?
Sights? I have to point out the place. Oh, that. It got in the way.
It was always catching on something.

It seems that he doesn't know the use of the gunsight. In the
camp I begin to notice the guns of the others. Many have the
sights removed.

The men in our camps are supposed to be picked men, security
men for the leading organs of the movement, but many do not
know the full use of the weapons they hold to defend us. They do
not know how to take aim or how to hit a target. In an encounter
they merely point the gun and fire it. In an ambush they just
blaze away and knock over the enemy, when they do knock him
over, with a hosing effect rather than with accuracy.

There are, of course, many H.M.B.'s who know how to shoot.
They have learned before joining the movement or simply from
holding a gun for so long a time. The average recruit, however, a
peasant who has never had a gun in his hands before, receives no
formal training in the H.M.B. Ammunition is very limited; none
can be spared for target practice. There are few H.M.B.'s, indeed, who are in a position to give instruction. The recruits go
along with the veterans and do what they see them doing.

The gunsight question gives one an inkling of the very low
technological level of this people's army. It is on a par with the
half-primitive methods that the average peasant uses to work his
farm. It is a matter that could, of course, be overcome, if the
know-how were supplied. However, in the entire Philippine national liberation movement there is not one military leader of any
professional caliber. Neither G.Y. nor any of the staff of his
Military Department has had formal military training or has had
the means for studying it. On the Field Command level, one,
Victoria, has been a Philippine army non-com. Less than half a
dozen cadres have had some R.O.T.C. training—Cente, Ledda.
Others who are well known as guerrilla commanders—Linda Bie,
Viernes, Malabanan, Estrella, Dimasalang, Bundalian, Nelson,
Sumulong—have picked up competence in mobility, ambush,
and surprise attack from experience in doing it. Elementary am-
bush tactics are about the limit of understanding in the others.

Huk weapons themselves are almost entirely of the small arms
category, the Browning Automatic Rifle being the heaviest, and
that relatively scarce. In this important camp there are perhaps

ten. A few machine guns have been captured from the enemy, but they rust in the mountains, unused and lacking ammunition. No one has grenades or would know how to employ them. There are no mortars, and very few Huks have ever seen one; no one knows how they operate; when we are shelled by mortars by the army, no one knows what kind of weapon is shooting at us. The bazooka is known only by its name.

With regard to other techniques usually associated with guerrilla warfare there is incredible ignorance. The knowledge of dynamite or explosives of any kind is extremely meager, and they remain unemployed. An effort was made to develop explosives in Bulacan, but the man experimenting was blown to bits and the project was dropped. Land mines are wholly unknown, with no application. Even a technique such as that of the Vietminh of denying highway mobility to the enemy by digging ditches across roads is unconsidered here. Economic or military sabotage to cripple the enemy's potential has neither been tried nor conceived of. The fact is, the H.M.B. does not have technicians or any branch assigned to develop techniques.

Yet this is the movement that years of repression have failed to crush, against which the entire weight of the Philippine army has been flung, that is enduring in the face of massive military aid from the country that has had the most advanced technology and the greatest abundance of weapons in world history. Some of the best minds from American military academies are out here meeting their match from untrained peasants.

What do the Huks have? They have their courage and their hope. Put but an idea as a weapon in their hands, and they are ready to storm the future. . . .

There was a time when the forest was wholly ours and we lived in it as within a fortress, issuing forth at will to spread panic among our foes. The enemy does not dare to enter, we would say. We will carry the fight to him.

Now the forest is like a breached wall through which the government troops pour at their will. There is no place in the forest to which they cannot go, armed with their massive firepower, and we are the ones who move, step aside, take cover. There are Ranger units, American-trained, that enter the forest at a far point and travel through it quietly, seeking out our camps. Our forces, too, rove about, seeking them. It is like two blind men in a darkened room who, when they come into contact, lash out desperately, bloodily.

We do not seek encounters now, only rarely entering a town or attacking army garrisons. Ammunition is hard to get, and it is difficult to replace a gun that wears out or is taken to the enemy by a surrenderee. Ambushes, once a prime source of weapons, are hard to stage now, when army troops move on the highways in large convoys, heavily armed. Of course, there is always the black market and the smugglers, but the prices have gone up fantastically, and we lack also funds.

The trails, too, are no longer ours. When our units go down to the towns to pick up purchases, the army often lies in ambush, and our men are slaughtered. At times ten or twelve die upon emerging from the forest. Our squad's *balutan* return to camp with one man missing, two men missing, familiar faces gone from the huts and the social hall. We used to ask them, "Where is Pedring?" or "Where is Sorsogon?" and they would go on by with averted eyes, answering in the brief way of men who do not wish to talk about the matter, "He is dead." Now we merely count them, silently, as they come in tiredly, one or two at a time. The others are not discouraged, after losing a comrade. They tie on the empty sacks and go off on the trail whenever their turns arrive. We will be more careful this time, they say.

Enemy raids go on continually along the forest edge, striking at our district committees that have the direct contact with organizations in the barrios. Our organizers die in lonely huts in sudden bursts of fire that come out of underbrush. And yet, somewhere, a new hut goes up, smaller, more skillfully hidden, with someone new assigned to occupy it. But we are being bled of cadres.

In the barrios the army or the civilian guards have permanent barracks now and are always among the people. There are more informers because they feel protected and it is harder for Huks to reach and to liquidate them. Our contact men have to crawl past guards to get into a barrio.

Some of the Huks are bitter about the people. The people, they say, are opportunistic. When we are with them they are friendly to us; when the enemy is with them they are friendly to the enemy. But it is wrong to be idealistic about the people. They are flesh and blood and they suffer much. We are in the forest, where we can hide and fight, but they are naked to suppression. They are helpless before abuse, and who can stand up to abuse and robbery month after month after month? They make their compromises, but the other side does not win them. They are ours, and they will always be there, ready to follow us when we are able to lead them.

But when we try to take the offensive today, our comrades die, die by the dozens, and arms and equipment still pour ashore in Manila from American ships, and new B.C.T.'s still take to the field.

The truth is, we have lost the initiative that we sought to take. We are back where we started from, completely on the defensive.

There is the sensation, now, of being in a vise. From the beginning of this struggle, in 1946, the movement was on the defensive. The struggle began with the use of the mailed fist against us, and not with our bold launching. For years the Huks have fought to get out of the vise of repression. For a time, many months ago, we thought that all signs favored it, and we took the offensive ourselves, but now the iron sides of circumstance close in on us again.

In Manila, where a few months ago we had sent a whole new team of cadres, almost the entire City Committee is arrested in a single night of raids. It has sought to organize too boldly and too quickly, without proper safeguards against a greatly intensified enemy intelligence. Here, too, there is betrayal, by a woman whom we had trusted, who had been approached by Magsaysay with money and who had put agents on the trail of a courier who had visited her.

In the Visayas, on the island of Panay, Reco 6 is broken through the act of a leading cadre, Alfredo Gloria, who went over to the enemy and who led military intelligence agents disguised as Huks into the Reco camp and who himself helped to shoot down his former comrades. And a civilian informer from a barrio, on Panay, leads army troops to the camp of Guillermo Capadocia, and they shoot him down in the dawn when he emerges from his hut. (Cap is gone, the slim electric Cap.)

These are betrayals. There are uglier forms. The district committee member who kills the district secretary, decapitates him, and brings the bloody head in a sack to the army to claim the reward. The Huk in the outpost who rises in the middle of the night and tommy-guns his two companions, trading their heads, too, for his freedom and money.

Betrayals seldom occur when the tempo is high, when victory is a talked-of thing. They happen when the ground gives way and uncertainty yawns. Then the weak run to make their accommodations with those who appear strong.

The tempo is slack. The struggle is now prolonged.

It is the time when renewals are needed, but the well of determination is not equally deep in us all. We sit upon this island and see the guns pour in for those whom we fight. Whatever allies we might have, they can reach no hand to us; the sea is there between us. The sea, too, is a vise that squeezes in our isolated lives.

We do not have space here. We live and move in the same space that the enemy occupies. There is no place to retreat, no place that is not accessible by road, by plane, or by a couple of days on a trail; no question here of liberated areas. And the sea is always at our backs. In this confined space, with an aggressive enemy, there is only continual movement that can preserve us. But mobility, too, has its menace. Our armed forces fight, march, fight, march, fight until they are exhausted, with no time or place to rest and to recuperate.

We look at a map and wonder where to move next.

It is no longer victory that preoccupies us. It is survival.

V. The Journal of a Vietminh Combatant

NGO VAN CHIEU

*Ngo Van Chieu was a Vietminh cadre. The
following account covers the period
1946-1950 and is the only account of the
war presented by a sympathetic but
independent observer. It is also the only
testimony not published through the
regular Vietnamese propaganda service.*

July 1946

News from France indicates that the negotiations will probably
fail and that we may have to start fighting again. We have had
many conferences on the subject, but one thing is quite clear. If
the war with the French continues, we will not be able to fight
and win by using conventional modern tactics.

We are fully aware of this, which is why we have been attending a special training course for guerrilla cadres during the last
few days. If the war continues, we cannot hope to fight in any
other way for several years.

A higher cadre told us one evening that we are beginning to
plan for dark times; *Chien Khu* (little fortresses or centers of
resistance) will be organized to function as bases or rear outposts
for the troops who are called upon to fight in the plains. The two
main ones will be set up in the Tuyen Quang area, north of Bac
Kan, right in the middle of the mountains, and in the steep chalk
hills of Chi Ne-Hoa Binh, to the west of the Day.

From Ngo Van Chieu, *Journal d'un combattant Viet Minh,* translated from
Vietnamese into French and adapted by Jacques Despuech (Paris: Editions du
Seuil, 1955). Copyright 1955 by Editions du Seuil. Reprinted by permission of
Editions du Seuil.

Food depots, armament factories, troop regroupment centers, training schools for cadres, and so on will be situated in this *Chien Khu*. In fact, I am soon to go to one for military and political training.

August–October 1946

The camp is bare, made of apparently disordered rows of straw huts. We number some fifty cadres and future cadres, trickling in from every part of Vietnam to undergo the training that is supposed to turn us into real "officers." The commanding officer (C.O.) of the training center is a higher cadre, with a political commissar as his assistant. His technical adviser is a high-ranking Japanese officer, a one-time lieutenant colonel on the General Staff of the 38th Japanese Army. The course is to last three or four months.

We are housed six to a hut, and we sleep between bails of woven bamboo. No bedding is provided, and everybody has to fend for himself one way or another. The course is in two parts: one purely military, in which we are taught about the armaments of the French troops, how to use unfamiliar weapons, and the most appropriate tactics for the sort of unit we shall be operating with. We also learn about "jungle warfare," how to lead troops under pursuit, how to lead a column through untracked areas, and how to set up camp, with sentries and runners posted to keep a tight watch and ensure that the alarm will be sounded early enough: we must be able either to organize ourselves defensively or to disengage without loss. This is certainly the most important part of our training and will no doubt prove useful quite often.

Our political education concentrates on the misdeeds of colonialism and capitalism. We also have lessons in Marxism-Leninism. We have to read and report on pamphlets we are given, such as Lenin's *State and Revolution*, extracts from *The Dictatorship of the Proletariat*, and a piece by Giap on organization and discipline in the popular army.

The cadre who teaches the political education classes constantly repeats simple, easily assimilated maxims. He explains that we have a double mission: to liberate our people from the yoke of the French colonialists and to pave the way for constructive socialism by bringing peace to the country. The government's land policy is outlined again and again. Vietnam is a country of

fields and forests. Peasants account for 90 percent of our population. Under the colonialists and the feudal mandarins, the peasant masses were treated inhumanely; in the south, they still are.

. . . He gives us the example of his family and his village
(Xom), where some couples owned only one pair of trousers
between them; they often had to make do with a rag worn as a
loin cloth, and the children, boys and girls alike, usually walked
around naked until they were six or even ten years old, because
there was no money to buy clothes. This poverty existed alongside the incredibly luxurious life-style of the notables, mandarins,
and French administrators and settlers, who thought themselves
gods and spoke contemptuously of the Vietnamese peasants and
workers, whom they called *Nhaqués*. Those among us who have
spent time with French families remember that the servants'
quarters were in a mud hut with a few banana leaves for a roof;
the hut, which was often next to the pigsty, was called the "boy-
erie," and we often heard the French pronounce the word as
though they were talking about a stable or a manure heap.

Our teacher would say, "It was you and your brothers they
were talking about. Do not think I am a racist or that I am
expressing hatred for any country or any race. The people of
France did not know what was going on. I have lived in France,
and it was over there that I learned what freedom was. But those
you see here, facing you, are representatives of the reaction and
of sordid, self-seeking colonialism. Never forget it."

. . . In early October we are gathered together again. The
training period is over, and we are off to rejoin our units. We
have all learned quite a lot about many subjects, but we have
benefited especially from the advanced level of political and civic
education we have received. I now know why we must support
the government, and I am no longer a member of the popular
army simply out of blind, stubborn patriotism and a hunger for
glory. I now feel that my country's destiny and that of the
workers and peasants of Vietnam is closely linked to the success
of the Popular Republic Government.

I also know that we are weak, that our regular army numbers
only some 32,000 to 35,000 ill-equipped and poorly officered
men. We must strive constantly to build up our strength. Out of

our faith and struggle a great and powerful popular army will be born in the years to come. Our armaments are disparate; we are short of ammunition; we have no weapons factories, no cannons, no tanks, no air force, no navy. Too bad! We have the will, the love of freedom and independence. Whatever happens, I am confident that, in the end, we will win. . . .

October 1950

As we march down the river with our trousers turned up, our weapons and kit held over our heads, the splashing of the water is almost hypnotic. We are fording an arroyo; in the distance we can hear the mortar that has been firing all night. Toward morning, when we are about to make a halt, we suddenly change course and turn northward, hurrying toward the battle. What is going on? The C.O. tells me to tell my men that something has happened and that a message has been received indicating that French troops are heading south. We are going to cut them off and set an ambush.

We march all day, now in the water, now on the lower banks of the river, and suddenly, just before nightfall, we arrive at the battlefield. The batallion is ensconced between two hills; mortars and machine guns can be heard.

Suddenly we get the order: "Up that hill, double time." The men climb, and the whole batallion moves like a stream of ants, with one company dragging up the heavy machine guns and mortars. "Into the bushes." Everybody takes cover. A terse order is passed down. "All company commanders, come to the front."

I try to find my batallion leader. He is where he should be, and I relax: everything's alright, his problems were only on the surface. Now that he is seeing action, he is in his element. He is crouched beside a machine gun crate and has sketched a rough map on the ground. "Down there, there's a road." He points to the bottom of the hill. "And somewhere in that direction, there's a French column that has left Cao Bang and is trying to escape by breaking through to the south. They are being pursued by three of our regiments and chased straight into a trap." He turns and points again. "Over there, another column is heading toward us, a second French regiment that is coming to help the first one."

He wrinkles his nose and grins: "That one's for us. When it passes along the road, the Second Batallion will attack it. We're supposed to stay here as backup. The idea is to force them to take shelter on the plateau on the other side of the road, where one of our regiments and two batallions are waiting for them with mortars and three field cannon. When the French have been pushed onto the plateau, we come down and snap the trap shut. After that, it's just a matter of shooting it out. Our batallion will adopt a motto for this battle: 'Better to die fighting for Independence than to live like a slave.' "

. . . The French were attacked two hours ago, but they are still holding the road. They are hanging onto it as if their very lives depended on it. In fact, they're right: that road is their only way out. If they can hold the road, they can still hope that trucks and tanks will come to save them from the disaster they can feel looming over them. Two companies have already been annihilated. There are now only three thousand men left, stretched out over several kilometers.

My company moves forward down the passes while a mortar provides covering fire. We are about to attack. Our job is to take the road, force the French to pull back toward the plateau. In the twilight, I can see my soldiers lying flat in the bushes, their long, thin rice sacks slung over their shoulders, their helmets garnished with leaves. I tighten my grip on my rifle. The political commissar slips by, reminding us: "Remember the batallion's motto for this attack: 'Better to die fighting for Independence than to live like a slave.' " He holds an old revolver; the yellowing pages of a book stick out of his jacket pocket.

"For the homeland!" We rush forward like madmen. All hell breaks loose as we charge toward the road. As we run, my men are being cut down by bullets and grenades. Behind us, the mortars have opened fire and are pounding the road. Just ahead, behind a bush, I catch sight of khaki uniforms, running away, hauling a machine gun with them. Three of my soldiers have seen them.

"*Lin tay* . . . [the French . . . "]

"*Di, Di* . . . "

Get to the road, get to the road. Hell is nothing compared to an attack. I try to regroup my men for another advance. Suddenly, the road is only 20 meters away, strewn with enemy corpses. Twenty of my troops are right at hand. We spring forward. To the left, other foliage-covered helmets are bobbing behind bushes. We reach the road, and I stand up to cross it. There is a volley of shots, a shout, and a man leaps up on the other side, black, bearded, howling. He throws a grenade. Then, like a herd of demons, the French charge, rifles at the ready.

"Pull back, quick."

They're counterattacking. I fire a volley and flee, followed by some of the men. Behind me, I can hear one of our machine guns chattering wildly. I dive into the clump of bushes where we were hiding just before, and others follow. We find two of our volunteers lying there, dead. Perhaps they crawled there to die.

The men pick up the corpses. We are only 100 meters away, and from time to time we catch sight of the French, who have retaken the road. Night has already fallen, and the moon is about to rise.

"Regroup at the foot of the hill, behind you."

The batallion *must* regroup. We slip from bush to bush. Another batallion, the one that was covering our advance with mortar fire, is already in position behind us. Doubled over, we move between their positions. The odd volley shatters the silence of the night. Have we failed?

"Form a column behind those big trees over there."

When I get the order, I have already let myself collapse on a mound of earth. The survivors of my company begin to regroup. Sang was killed when we crossed the road, and the second position was practically annihilated by the French counterattack.

"Company Commander Chieu . . . "

The *Can Bo* (political commissar) is looking for me. He is bleeding from a head wound and from a gash along his arm. His helmet is crushed and only stays on because of the strap. "Regroup your company behind those mounds. Let your men rest and wait. The batallion commander will send for you."

Gradually my men join me. Apart from the second troop, which was wiped out (there are only three survivors), the troops have come through pretty much intact; each has lost about five or six men.

The battle has quieted down a bit. Shots still crack in the distance, but everything is much calmer. I cannot sleep. I try to eat some rice balls, but earth has gotten into them and they taste like death. I stare with half-closed eyes. I am so exhausted! I wonder whether I will be able to carry on tomorrow. Are we going to stay here all night? I am incapable of moving; my eyes fix on a white stone shining in the moonlight. I am so tired I cannot stop the saliva dribbling down my chin. Men pass by, bent over, carrying one of the wounded; others follow. Behind me, far away, I hear something that sounds like a cart. They are coming to pick up the dead and wounded. The French must have heard it too, because bursts of rifle fire and grenades come from the road toward us. Suddenly a rocket rises straight up. The little flame, dancing for the men who are about to die, gives off an unreal glow.

"Comrade Pham is asking for you, comrade Chieu."

A soldier, one of the batallion commander's guards, is tapping me on the shoulder. I get up and follow him behind a thin hedge of bamboo. The batallion commander is leaning on a tumulus. He is not alone. With him is a little group carrying a box with a long stem sticking out. A radio: that means we are going to attack again.

"Chieu, your company was one of those that suffered least just now. You will head the attack. Our mission is not complete yet. We intend to carry out the task we have been entrusted with."

I do not have the strength to protest that my men are worn out. What would be the point? Everybody is in the same state. And our batallion has adopted a motto for this attack.

The political commissar comes up to me and says, "I will go with you to tell your men."

The C.O. is talking on the radio. He is receiving orders and hardly seems concerned with making himself heard. He calls me over.

"You have just one order. Get to the road, cross it with all your company in a mass attack. Once you get to the other side, stay there and fire on the enemy wherever you see him. You alone will attack. You must get across the road; the whole operation depends on you. The radio operator comrades will be behind you. As soon as you get across, they will send a signal. Listen carefully: the French will counterattack, and that is when the rest of us will move in. Three platoons of reinforcements, specially picked troops, will join you. Don't forget, comrade, you must get across that road."

I return to my company. The C.O. is already giving other orders. The political commissar comes with me and says, "I will join your company for the attack, comrade."

"But you're wounded."

"After so many years in the revolutionary struggle, one stops feeling one's body, one's tiredness. The French burned my village. My mother was paralyzed, and she was burned in her hut, burned alive, comrade. I cannot forget that. And then, comrade, I am used to fatigue. I come from a poor family."

We call the men, who gather round in a tight group. The political commissar continues, speaking to everybody but very calmly, as if he were thinking out loud:

"I was myself one of the oppressed poor, like hundreds of thousands of others in our popular army. It is the peasants in our rice fields and mountains, the buffalo keepers and the plantation workers that are the real strength of our people. Do not forget, soldiers, your task is a sublime one: you are fighting for the freedom and independence of your people, for the greatness of your homeland. You fight and die that the colonialist oppressors and their mandarin hirelings will finally be kicked out of the land of your fathers. This company is going to attack again tonight. Somebody had to do it, and I insisted that the best and most combative unit be chosen. That's you. The cadre who will lead you, your company commander, was one of the first cadres to join the popular army. He has been with us since 1945, and even before that he was active in the underground. It is an honor for this company to be led by cadres of such high worth. A cadre was killed just now. You all knew him. It was Sang, old Sang. He was not so good at reading, but he knew how to handle men and he fought with tremendous courage. Sang was killed, but *on the other side of the road*. Will you let him down? The whole of Vietnam is looking at you. Soldiers of ——— company, face the enemy; death to the colonialist occupiers: *Forward, for the revolution and for Vietnam*."

That was it. He had shouted the last words. The men huddle around me.

"Line up in fours, leave your rice sacks, take only your weapons. Keep it quiet. Forward." We go back the way we came, gripping our rifles. "Keep together." From time to time, a shot is heard. Behind me, the political commissar says, "Move faster. They're still full of what I told them; we must attack quickly."

"For Vietnam and Independence . . . "

"Forward, *Doc Lap, Doc lap!* . . . . "

Howling and bent over, with rifle fire and explosives breaking out everywhere, we charge.

"*Di, Di* . . . "

Forward, forward. Rockets pierce the night, bodies hunch under the bullets. The road is barely 50 meters away when a machine gun suddenly starts firing just 10 meters from us. The French have set up on this side of the road, something we did not know. The attack swirls around the machine gun, and already some of the men are falling back. "Forward, forward," I yell. "We must get past that machine gun and cross the road."

Suddenly six men hurl themselves toward the machine gun nest, fall, and rise again. An explosion shatters the air. The special troops have blown up the machine gun, and themselves with it.

"*Tien lien!*"

The road is just ahead; we must get across it. Shadows are moving about on the other side, and we cannot tell who or what we are firing on. Behind me there is a flash, and my arm is jolted.

"*Ban, ban!* [Fire, fire!]"

I carry on shouting, but we have stopped advancing. We have reached the road but have not crossed it. The battle continues, with grenades and the occasional shadowy figure firing a burst of machine gun fire.

We must get across. I have a vision of calm and peace; calm and peace lying just across the road.

"Company . . . forward, cross the road! *Doc Lap!* "

I get up. Firing breaks out everywhere, and I leap forward alone. The others follow, yelling at the top of their voices. The French stand up. It seems there are so many of them. . . . We engage in hand-to-hand combat. I fire at random until my magazine is empty. Then I leap into a hole and strike madly at a helmeted shape in pale khaki. I twist my rifle butt into it; I pull out my knife and plunge it into the back of the shape, again and again. I am wild, wild with fear, which is why I am fighting with a corpse. The Frenchman has been dead for hours, his head is attached to his body only by a thin strand of skin.

"The French are pulling back!"

There were only about ten of them on this bit of road.

"Regroup and hold on, they're going to counterattack."

But they do not. After two days' fighting, we now know we have won. We have taken many prisoners and the battle conti- nues to the bitter end, but tomorrow it will be over. It was very hard. Why do the French fight so well for such a bad cause?

November 1950

We are marching toward Hanoi. I am going to see my house again. Like an irresistible tide, the general counteroffensive has been launched. The colonialists are fleeing like smoke before the wind.

We advance straight through jungle, forest, and rice fields, without even bothering to deal with those French outposts that are still holding out (special units have been assigned to eliminate them). We are marching victoriously toward the town.

This morning we arrived in a big village where we are going to stay for a few days. The population welcomed us enthusiastically. Every house was decorated with banners and little flags. We lined up on either side of the main street, and all the women, young and old, filed past to give us presents. Our batallion was given highest honor because we suffered the heaviest casualties and were involved in the toughest fighting on the R.C.4 a few days ago.

A group of soldiers, women, and children have gotten together to sing patriotic ballads. Accordions, guitars, and harmonicas have been brought out from who knows where.

I wander through the calm and peaceful town, amid scenes of a joy that I have never known. I think of Mai. Where is she now? Will I ever see her again? I should not be sad, since victory is at hand, but I keep coming back to the same thing; I cannot help it. Some girls go past and give me a bunch of flowers. "May Presi- dent Ho live a thousand years," they chant.

The propaganda section has already installed an information center, where a record player is pounding out military tunes. From a box draped with flags a propagandist is haranguing the crowd: "The popular army will reach Hanoi in time for Tet. It will be our new year's present to President Ho. Come on, join us now, while you are still needed. Soon it will be too late, we will already have thrown out all our enemies."

As I pass a group of cadres and political commissars, our regiment's political commissar calls me over: "Chieu, a family has invited you to stay with them. They are peasants, and the mother will be your War Mother." He points them out to me. There are two of them, one about sixty, the other about forty. They come toward me, making tiny steps. Their hands joined in front of their chests, they greet me with awkward little smiles.

"*Chao Ong* . . ."

They have not yet learned how to say hello.

"Call me comrade, little mother."

They live in a straw hut at the other end of the village. The streets are full of people, children in black rags, women in black and white *cai quan* and *cai hao,* the older wearing headscarves, the younger with their hair in a tight bun at the back of their heads. The soldiers are sitting on either side of the street, their weapons beside them on the ground and their helmets still decorated with the foliage of assault camouflage.

The people who are putting me up are wealthy peasants. They have prepared a feast and obviously consider it a great honor to have been deemed worthy of housing a military cadre. They have two sons, both of whom are also fighting in the popular army. One of them has been gone three years, and they have received no news of him.

War Mothers are an institution that has existed since the beginning of the war. They have been one of the decisive factors in the all out struggle waged by our regular, regional, and even guerrilla units. The War Mothers are usually elderly women who take it upon themselves, as a matter of honor, to adopt a soldier in the popular army for the duration of the war. The War Mother's whole family becomes the adoptive parents of a young soldier or cadre stationed in the sector. Should it happen that the "adopted son's" unit is dispersed by an enemy attack, he can seek out the family, who will provide him with shelter and civilian clothes, present him as a relative, vouch for him to the enemy authorities, and generally help him rejoin the popular army as quickly as possible. Such families are usually "safe" families, with a son, nephew, or other close relative fighting in some other sector for the popular army. They know that their own relatives will benefit from a similar welcome should the need arise. This institution maintains the links of affection and class solidarity between the army and the mass of the people; it also facilitates infiltration of enemy lines and brings the whole nation into the war.

Indeed, women fight on the same footing as men in our army. Under the mandarins and colonialists, women's conditions had remained as backward as in Chiang Kai-shek's China, but their situation has now completely changed. Women are no longer subordinated to their husbands; on the contrary, they participate in political life, vote, and run for office in elections for the village committee. They will probably soon gain access once and for all to key administrative posts. Women participate in the work of the revolution through the Women's Public Works Committee. This body centralizes and distributes all the work women can do, ensuring that they participate directly in the war effort; they are assigned appropriate military tasks, including sabotaging roads and trenches, carrying supplies and ammunition according to an established scale (15 kilos for those over 18, with women more than five months pregnant exempt), washing the clothes of the sick and the wounded, cooking, nursing, surveillance, keeping watch, and gathering information in areas occupied by the enemy.

VI.   Street Without Joy

BERNARD B. FALL

*Bernard B. Fall, a specialist on Vietnam,
worked first in France and then in the
United States. He stepped on a mine in
1969 during one of his many research trips
to Vietnam and was blown up. A lucid
historian, he understood the motivations of
the adversaries. This story covers the
period 1953–1954.*

For years, communications along the central Annam coast had
been plagued by communist attacks against Road 1, the main
north-south artery along the coast. The principle source of
trouble was a string of heavily fortified villages along a line of
sand dunes and salt marshes stretching from Hué to Quang-Tri.
By 1953, the French High Command had assembled sufficient
reserves in the area to attempt to clear up the threat once and for
all. In the meantime, losses had been heavy; one French convoy
after another passing on the road had been either shelled or
ambushed by the black-clad infantry of Vietminh Regiment 95, a
battle-hardened regular communist unit infiltrated behind French
lines. This inspired the French soldiers, with that kind of black
humor proper to all soldiers, to christen that stretch of Road 1
"la rue sans joie" (Street Without Joy).

In July 1953 the French High Command decided to clean up
the "Street Without Joy." Called "Operation Camargue,"[1] the
action involved a simultaneous landing of troops along the sandy
coast of central Annam, coupled with two coordinated thrusts by
armored units, with airborne forces remaining in reserve to seal

---

Reprinted from *Street Without Joy: Indochina at War, 1946–54* by Bernard B.
Fall, 1961, by permission of Stackpole Books, Harrisburg, Pa. 17105.

[1] The Camargue is the name of the swampy coastal plain west of Marseilles.

off attempts at escape by the communist forces in the trap. With the elements of ten infantry regiments, two airborne battalions, the bulk of three armored regiments, one squadron of armored launches, one armored train, four artillery battalions, thirty-four transport aircraft, six reconnaissance aircraft, twenty-two fighter-bombers, and about twelve Navy ships, including three L.S.T.'s, this force was not very inferior in size to some of those used in landing operations in World War Two in the Pacific. Communist Regiment 95 and the few guerrilla forces around it, obviously, had very little chance of escaping the encirclement. . . .

At first view the forces assigned to this operation appeared impressive. Using a total of more than thirty battalions, including the equivalent of two armored regiments and two artillery regiments, the operation against the "Street Without Joy" was certainly one of the most formidable ever carried out in the Indochinese theater of operations. Yet the enemy amounted to a maximum of one weak infantry regiment. What made the operation so difficult for the French was, as usual in Indochina, the terrain. . . .

H-Hour was at dawn on July 28, 1953. The lumbering L.S.T.'s had left their assembly areas the evening before and had steamed throughout the night toward their landing zone in the center of the coast facing the "Street Without Joy." Disembarkment of the amphibious landing craft began at 0400 in a clanking of metal and a howling of engines, as the Crabs and Alligators of the 3d Amphibious Group took to the water. . . .

Both types of vehicle were considered fragile and required a great deal of maintenance, which was often hard to come by in the swamps of Indochina. The Crab—initially built for carrying cargo in Alaska!—lacked floatability in water and towered too high on land, thus offering an easy target to enemy gunners who soon found out that it was not armored. However, it was small enough to be transported on an Army truck when not in use and could be embarked in light landing craft or barges. The Alligator, much heavier and armored, took well to the water but was too heavy on land for its fragile tracks and its relatively weak engine. Also, it could not travel great distances on land but had to be transported on special tank carriers, since it was too big and too heavy to be transported on trucks.

Yet it was an impressive sight as the 160 vehicles of the 3d

Amphibious approached the central Annam coast, each leaving a wide wake in the leaden-colored water, with the bright recognition streamers of the various squadrons flapping in the morning breeze on the tips of the radio aerials. At 0600, the first landing wave of the Amphibious Group hit the beaches, immediately fanning out through the coastal villages and occupying the first hill crest line overlooking the coastal dunes. The French assault against the "Street Without Joy" had begun.

The regular infantry elements of the Tonkinese Mobile Group had a tougher time of it. Of the three battalions, only one—the 3d Battalion of the 13th Foreign Legion Half-Brigade—had had any experience in seaborne operations; the two other battalions, the 1st Muong Mountaineer and the 26th Senegalese Rifle Battalion, had had no such experience. Unfamiliar with the landing ship's cargo nets and the rocking landing craft and plagued with seasickness, it took them close to four hours to get ashore instead of the two hours assigned to that part of the operation. In the meantime, the men of the 3d Amphibious Group were struggling with their vehicles atop the dune line. Many of the heavily loaded Alligators had bogged down in the sand as soon as they left the coastal strip and had to be unloaded on the spot. In many other cases the lighter Crabs had pushed on atop the dunes only to find themselves face-to-face with a deep precipice. However, they finally found a break between the fishing villages of Tan An and My Thuy and soon began pushing inland on their own. Communist resistance was almost nonexistent. A few men were seen fleeing the first line of fishing villages near My Thuy, and farther to the north two enemy platoons were seen pulling out.

In the meantime, Groupment "B" under the command of Colonel du Corail had not remained inactive. By 0630, two battalions of the Central Vietnamese Mobile Group reached and crossed the Van Trinh Canal, and, by 0745, the lead elements of Groupment "B" saw the squattish shapes of the 3d Amphibious Group's Crabs crawling over the hill line; the "Street Without Joy" was sealed off to the north.

To the right of the Central Vietnamese Mobile Group, the 6th Moroccan Spahis was not as lucky. It ran head-on into the bottomless swamps and sand holes east of Road No. 1, where most of its vehicles, with the exception of the M-24 light tanks, soon bogged down. It succeeded in reaching the canal—which was to be the line of departure for the mopping-up operation on the land side—at about 0830. In its sector also, there was no evidence of enemy opposition. In fact, the whole countryside seemed absolutely dead. No farmers were to be seen on the roads, and in the small villages the population stayed in their houses. Throughout the whole desolate landscape, the only moving objects were the French armored columns and truckborne infantry struggling through sand dunes and morasses to the Van Trinh Canal.

Only at the extreme right flank of Groupment "B" was there any shooting. There, an Algerian rifle company ran into unexpected fire from what appeared to be no more than 20 or 30 Vietminh. Private Mohammed Abd-el-Kader of 2d Company fell forward as a B.A.R. burst of fire caught him directly in the chest. Warily, his comrades fanned out in skirmish formation and shot back at the invisible enemy hidden behind clumps of bushes and in sand holes. Abd-el-Kader was the first French casualty in the assault.

To the right of Groupment "B," Groupment "C" under Lieutenant Colonel Gauthier had to execute the most complicated maneuver of the operation. The bulk of its troops crossed Road No. 1 in the direction of the canal to the north of My Chanh. A second column started along a path running parallel to Road No. 1, then veered sharply to the right to reach the canal between the village of Van Trinh and the lagoon. Lastly, the 9th Moroccan *Tabor* (Battalion) embarked on landing craft, went ashore at Lai-ha at 0630, secured a beachhead, and then swung southeast along the inland coast of the lagoon in order to complete the sealing-off of the "Street Without Joy" on the land side. By 0830, it had reached Tay-Hoang and completed its part of the operation's first phase.

Groupment "D," under Lieutenant Colonel Le Hagre, was to seal off the long peninsula reaching down along the lagoon almost to the city of Hué. Composed of experienced troops, it encountered few of the difficulties that had faced Groupment "A." The landing began at 0430, with the 7th Amphibious Group in the lead, followed in rapid succession by Marine commandos and the 3d Battalion of the 3d Algerian Rifle Regiment. The commandos and the Amphibious Group hit the beach almost without stopping; the Amphibious Group immediately headed north in the direction of the head of the lagoon, while the commandos secured the little city of Thé Chi Dong and, cutting straight across the peninsula, reached the north side of the lagoon at 0530. For all practical purposes, Vietminh Regiment No. 95 was trapped.

Now began the hardest phase of the whole operation—the mop-up. General Leblanc ordered the Navy ships standing offshore to move 6 kilometers to the north to the villages of Ba-Lang and An-Hoi in order to seal off any attempt of the rebels to flee by sea. On the northern end of the "Street Without Joy," Groupment "B" began a methodical sweep of every village, a painstaking operation that had to be carried out with the greatest care, regardless of results. Each village was first surrounded and sealed off by troops. Then heavily armed infantry moved in and searched the houses while mine detector and bloodhound teams probed in bamboo bushes and palm-tree stands for hidden entrances to underground caches in the midst of the sullen and silent population.[2] As a matter of routine most of the young men from the villages were arrested and detained pending a screening by intelligence officers, but even this had become a sort of rite in which everyone concerned participated without any great conviction.

By 1100 in the morning, Groupment "B" had worked its way about 7 kilometers south through the labyrinth of tiny villages without having encountered any resistance; then it reached the village of Dong-Qué, located almost in the center of the "Street Without Joy" at the intersection of several paths leading across the dunes toward the Van Trinh Canal. In the old days it had contained a customs post, whose brick structure was still standing, and this also gave it a certain importance.

Dong-Qué lay in the hot midday sun, snugly nestled in its swaying bamboo hedge, the very image of rural peacefulness in the monsoon season, when there is little else left for the farmer to do but to pray for rain and watch the rice grow from a tender green to a rich brownish yellow. But now, Dong-Qué was the target of the M-24 light tanks of the 6th Moroccan Spahis. In fact, the whole northern thrust seemed to be a Moroccan show, what with the Spahis being screened by the 1st Battalion, Moroc-

---

[2] The French Army had "K-9" teams in every major unit. Their successes were extremely variable, considering the effectiveness of Vietminh concealment.

can Rifles, and the whole force being covered by the howitzers of Colonel Piroth's 69th African Artillery Regiment, which, in normal times, hailed from Fez, in northern Morocco. These were battle-hardened troops; they had fought Rommel in Tunisia, waded through the Rapido, and clambered up the Petrella in Italy; they had knocked out the German 19th Army in the Black Forest and raced the Americans to Berchtesgaden. They were the elite of France's North African troops, and more Moroccans had risen to senior ranks—even to general—in the French Army than any other nationality. Here again, they were doing a workmanlike job clearing their sector.

Keeping their intervals carefully, the M-24 tanks had worked their way towards Dong-Qué at a pace which permitted the infantry to keep up with them. With the innate sixth sense which the Moroccans seem to have for detecting mines and booby traps, they had come to within 1,500 yards of the village without losing a man or a tank, but that same sixth sense told them that something was wrong with Dong-Qué. In silence, the infantrymen began to peel off the dike on either side of the tanks.

Atop the vehicles, the tank commanders had so far remained sitting on their open hatches, as much to see more of the countryside around them as to catch a breath of the breeze. . . .

Major Derrieu, commander of the leading squadron, looked straight ahead into the small town; the road appeared clear of any obstacles or the suspicious mounds of hastily dug mine emplacements. Nevertheless, the tank churned to a halt to let the mine-detector detail make one last sweep before rolling forward. Methodically, the tanned men with the long-handled frying pans and the earphones worked their way towards Dong-Qué, still quiescent under the tropical sun. Later, it was impossible to decide who had fired first—the Moroccan sergeant at the head of the demining detail who saw a rifle barrel flash in the sun, or a nervous Vietminh who felt that the Moroccans were getting too close for comfort. In any case, the fire fight developed with incredible violence at very short range. It was only due to the hair-trigger reactions of the Moroccans atop the road, who simply dropped to the ground and rolled off into the saving mud of the adjoining rice paddies, that none of them was seriously wounded.

The tanks were equally lucky that the Viets had probably

tipped their hand ahead of time, for the two bazookas of the defenders opened fire only as the lead tanks were already leaving the dikes in a clatter of tracks and a howl of engines for the comparative safety of the deeper lying fields. Now "buttoned up" (i.e., with their hatches shut), the turrets swung out in the direction of the suspected targets, still holding their fire. No point in wasting high-penetration shells on thatch huts when the machine guns could do a much more effective job. The infantrymen, in turn, had spread in an arc around Dong-Qué, but without moving closer. Behind one of the many grave mounds that always dot the Far Eastern countryside, the battalion commander had squatted down on his haunches in the mud, a map case on his knees and the combination earphone-microphone of his radio set in his hand. The set itself was affixed to the back of a Vietnamese P.I.M.,[3] who had also squatted down and who looked stolidly ahead under his battered hand-me-down campaign hat at the heat haze shimmering over the rice fields.

The howitzers of the 69th got the range of their target within a few rounds, and, minutes after the first radio call for support, Dong-Qué began literally to disintegrate under the impact of their high-angle fire. One by one the rice thatch of the roofs began to catch fire with a deep crackling sound that could occasionally be heard even above the din of the shells. Still, nobody ran; save for the agitation in the bamboo bushes around the village and the occasional flashes (hardly visible at high noon) of gunfire, the village might as well have been deserted. Then, all of a sudden, a tremendous explosion shook the village and a pillar of dense, black smoke rose in its center.

"The shells must've hit an underground depot," said Derrieu to his crew as he watched the shelling over the tank's scope. "Let's saddle up." With a howl, the idling tank engine shifted into high gear, and the lumbering vehicle, followed by the other tanks of the squadron, began to roll forward in the direction of the inferno that had been Dong-Qué. "Follow in line," said Derrieu over the intercom; he added, no doubt as an afterthought

---

[3] P.I.M. stood for "*Prisonnier-Interné-Militaire* " or "Prisoner of civilian interest arrested by the French Army," in contrast to detainees of the French or Vietnamese civilian police authorities. The P.I.M.'s often served as noncombatants in French units and became very devoted to their leaders. Others, of course, redeserted to the Vietminh.

due to his farmer ancestry, "and watch where you're going. No sense in ruining their whole rice crop."

Now, small black figures began to appear seemingly out of nowhere: from the windows of the houses, from the roof frames, and from dugouts on the side of the road, a veritable flood of human beings, completely blocking the advance of the tanks as they rolled into the village. This was phase 2 of the usual Vietminh defense pattern: once the position had become untenable or breached, use the civilians as a shield for the withdrawal of the combatants. But this time the ruse failed. The tanks were not alone, and the black-clad figures that now began to leave the village ran straight into the machine gun fire of the Moroccans. By 1300, it was all over for the 3d Company, Battalion 310 of the 95th Independent Regiment, "Vietnam People's Army," but its sacrifice had bought exactly what the commander of the regiment had needed—two hours of time to have the bulk of the unit withdraw toward the southern end of the pocket, where the Van Trinh Canal ended in a sort of marshy plant-covered delta that no one could effectively hope to seal off.

On the French side, General Leblanc also realized that the enemy, far from fighting to the death, was trying desperately to buy time to last until the evening in order to withdraw into the nearby hills west of Road 1, and he ordered the dropping-in of the first of the two paratroop battalions still held in reserve. At 1045, the 2d Battalion, 1st Colonial Parachute Regiment, having flown in all the way from Hanoi, dropped into its assigned assembly area near the village of Dai-Loc at the border of the dune zone close to Groupment "D," and immediately began its drive toward the mouth of the Van Trinh Canal. The race for the closing of the net around Regiment 95 had begun in earnest.

By mid-morning of D-Day, there were still wide gaps to the south of Van Trinh Canal near Phu-An and Lai-Ha as the 9th *Tabor* struggled through the sand pits and marshes to reach its line of departure. Apparently the communists had correctly surmised that this was indeed the weakest point in the French perimeter and had reacted accordingly. At 0845, just as the Moroccans were about to enter Phu-An, heavy machine gun and small arms fire began to smash into their ranks from the surrounding dikes. Silhouetted against the blue sky as they advanced over the dikes, and against the watery surface of the rice paddies as they plodded through them towards Phu-An, they offered perfect targets and immediately suffered heavy losses. Pinned down in the open, the 9th now began to call for help. It is here that its subordination to the faraway Groupment "C" rather than to the nearby amphibious Groupment "D" began to backfire; radio liaison to the Group's field C.P. at My-Chanh failed to function properly. and it was not until 0910 that Colonel Gauthier found out that things had gone sour on his extreme right wing.

But the Vietminh were not placing all their tactical eggs in a single basket. At 1100, smaller units of the communist 227th Battalion also attacked the assault guns of the 1st Foreign Legion Cavalry with heavy mortar fire and followed up this attack with an equally heavy mortar shelling of the 2d Battalion, 4th Moroccan Infantry. By 0940, Gauthier decided to commit his last reserves, two companies formed from trainees of a nearby Vietnamese N.C.O. school and three Vietnamese infantry companies hastily brought up from Hué. Finally two additional infantry companies were ordered into the Lai-Ha beachhead via L.C.M. but landed only at 1500. They then floundered in the marshes for almost three hours until they finally reached the Moroccans. When they got their wind back and had been beefed up by the reinforcements, the Moroccans counterattacked vigorously and finally occupied Phu-An at 1730. . . .

By nightfall, with Phu-An and Van Trinh occupied, the enemy had been constricted into a pocket about 14 kilometers long and 4 kilometers wide. To all appearances, Operation "Camargue" was a success.

However, this success was more one of appearance than of reality. To be sure, one-half of the "Street Without Joy" already had fallen into French hands—but without the expected booty of enemy prisoners and equipment. This meant that the enemy forces and equipment were still in the pocket. The latter, in order for the operation to be successful, had to become an airtight trap.

The trap, however, had *not* become airtight. Along the southern sector of Groupment "C," the last-Ditch defense of Phu-An and the counterattacks of Battalion 227 had kept the French from reaching the natural boundary of the Van Trinh Canal. The result was that four French battalions had to guard a front close to 12 kilometers long in order to prevent the escape of about 2600 men. It was obvious that this pocket had several important gaps, particularly the whole network of tiny rivulets and canals cutting across the Van Trinh Canal toward Road 1.

To be sure, the amphibious Crabs and Alligators were stationed near or even in many of the canals, and hundreds of infantrymen spent an uncomfortable night standing in the knee-deep mud of the rice paddies watching the black expanse ahead of them, where the slightest noise could be that of a frog jumping or of a communist infiltrator stumbling over a branch. There is nothing that sounds more like a patrol seeking its way forward in the mud than a stray buffalo plodding to its stable. . . .

When dawn broke, the men resumed their march forward, this time on all fronts at once. The countryside appeared completely empty in the morning sun. The farmers again did not come out of the villages to till their fields, the little Vietnamese boys who are always riding the lumbering buffalo out to pasture were nowhere to be seen with their charges. Again, the only things that seemed to be moving in the countryside were the French tanks, the amphibious vehicles with their long aerials dipping in the breeze, and long lines of grimy, weary, mud-caked infantrymen now plodding through the fields in an almost unbroken line from horizon to horizon.

By 1300, with the sun beating unmercifully on steel helmets and berets or campaign hats, Groupments "A" and "D," along with parts of Groupment "B," reached Van Trinh Canal throughout its whole length on the side opposite to Colonel Gauthier's Groupment "C." The trap had been sprung on the "Street Without Joy." The steel jaws of a modern armed force, supported by naval ships, amphibious tanks, and aircraft, had slammed shut on a force of hurriedly trained farmers led by men who in only a few cases had received the training of corporals and sergeants. A trap ten times the size of the force to be trapped had shut—and had caught nothing.

To be sure, "suspects" were found; that is, men of military age who could not prove that they belonged to the village where they were arrested and who could, therefore, be assumed to have been members of communist fighting units. A few weapons were also found, and at the northern end of the pocket, where the Vietminh had made its stand at Dong-Qué, some prisoners were taken arms in hand. But on the whole, as of D-Day plus-36 hours, Operation "Camargue" already was a failure. However, it was not entirely over.

Some of the low-flying "Morane" observation planes had detected suspect movements in the direction of An-Hoi—proof that some elements of Regiment 95 had escaped toward the north. At 1300, therefore, General Leblanc ordered a marine commando and some infantry from Groupment "A" to carry out a seaborne raid on An-Hoi. The raid was carried out swiftly enough; the troops landed at 1500, mopped up rapidly whatever suspects could be found, and returned to their ships by 1800, their mission accomplished.

There remained one more task to be accomplished in the now occupied villages, the methodical house-to-house search for hidden entrances, camouflaged storage dumps, and the one-in-a-thousand chance of finding a really important communist "cadre," one of the unassuming black-clad *can-bǒ* who, often barely 20 years old, really ran the war for the enemy. Hundreds of infantrymen swarmed out with mine detectors or simply long metal rods, thumping their rifle butts on the ground to detect suspicious hollow areas; others would strip and, holding hands, form a chain and slowly walk through marshes and ponds in the hope of finding weapons and equipment dumped into the water at the last moment—a sort of giant-size human rake slowly moving up and down the countryside. . . .

By the end of D-Day plus-2, all organized resistance had ceased, and on the following day began the withdrawal of the first-line units, the paratroopers, amphibious groups, and marine commandos. Now came the real job of permanently controlling the newly occupied area. Bridges that had been dynamited over the past years had to be rebuilt; roads cut into ribbons by Vietminh saboteurs had to be filled in; the whole artificial desert which the communists had created around the "Street Without Joy" had to be eliminated. Vietnamese government administrators made their timid appearance in the face of a hostile or frightened population that, after a week's fighting and years of life in a state of siege, needed everything from rice to antimalaria tablets.

"Funny," said Major Derrieu from the 6th Spahis, watching some of the new administrators in the village of Dong-Qué, "they just never seem to succeed in striking the right note with the population. Either they come in and try to apologize for the mess we've just made with our planes and tanks or they swagger and threaten the farmers as if they were enemy nationals, which—let's face it—they are in many cases."

"That may be so," said young Lieutenant Dujardin, standing on the shady side of his M-24, "but I wouldn't care to be in his shoes tonight, when we pull out. He's going to stay right here in the house which the commie commander still occupied yesterday, all by himself with the other four guys of his administrative team, with the nearest post three hundred yards away. Hell, I'll bet he won't even sleep here but sleep in the post anyway."

"He probably will, and he'll immediately lose face with the population and become useless."

"And if he doesn't, he'll probably by dead by tomorrow, and just as useless. In any case, there goes the whole psychological effect of the operation and we can start the whole thing all over again three months from now. What a hopeless mess."

"Well, if the Vietnamese can't lick that, we certainly cannot. After all, it's *their* country. Let's saddle up." With a shrug, both men walked back to their tanks, climbing into the turrets with the litheness of long practice.

Below them, on the tiny square of ruined Dong-Qué, the young, earnest, Vietnamese administrator in his khaki shirt and slacks was still talking to the villagers. They stood there, impassively, like so many wooden statues.

On August 4, 1953, the High Command called off Operation "Camargue." According to the newspapers, it had been a "total success, demonstrating once more the new aggressiveness and mobility" of the French and the value of great amounts of motorized equipment in swamp warfare. In their own reports, the French treated the operation with mixed feelings.

To be sure, Regiment 95 had for the time being disappeared as a constant menace along the central Annam coast. Two dozen villages or more had been placed under at least partial influence of the national authorities. But this had been no operation "on the cheap." Important numbers of troops and matériel had to be withdrawn from other vital sectors where they were sorely lacking and where their absence began to create emergencies of their own.

And the results in *actual loss of enemy combat potential* had been frustrating. For French losses of 17 dead and 100 wounded, the enemy had lost 182 dead and 387 prisoners, along with 51 rifles, 8 submachine guns, 2 mortars, and 5 B.A.R's—and how many of the dead and prisoners were regulars of the 95th Regiment and not merely local farmers or members of the always-expendable *Du-Kich* (communist village militia) remained open to question.

As regards swamp warfare tactics, "Camargue" had once more proved that it was impossible to seal off a pocket in an airtight fashion as long as a battalion had to hold more than 1,500 yards of ground—and most of the battalions along the southern flank of the pocket had held more than 3,000 yards. Thus, the fact that the bulk of the communist forces could slip through the *"bouclage"*—the ring of French infantry and armor—was a foregone conclusion as soon as the slow progress of the infantry on the first day eliminated all hopes of constricting the pocket to manageable size by nightfall.

For the progress of the infantry had been slow. In fact, it had been a crawl of about 1,500 yards an hour, on the average. But here again the tactical commander was caught in a dilemma. The purpose of the operation was *not* the surface occupation of the villages but the *flushing-out* of the enemy from his well-camouflaged hiding places and underground installations; hence any speed-up of the advance would be at the expense of the thoroughness of the search for weapons, men, and secret administrative organizations. This dilemma was one that posed itself time and again in the course of mop-up operations and was never satisfactorily resolved.

But, basically, the major defect of Operation "Camargue" was one which was shared by practically all similar operations in the Indochina war: no sealing-off of an enemy force could be successful unless the proportion of attackers to defenders was 15 to 1 or even 20 to 1, for the enemy had in its favor an intimate knowledge of the terrain, the advantage of defensive organization, and the sympathy of the population. . . .

VII.

Story of a Guerrilla in Algeria

SI AZZEDINE

*During the Algerian war, Si Azzedine
commanded Wilaya 4 and eventually
became one of the main officers in the
autonomous zone of Algiers. Here he tells
of an attempt by the French military to
"turn" a senior Algerian official. Many
similar attempts succeeded. This account
was recorded in Tunis by Jean Daniel.*

I was born in Bougie on August 8, 1934. My father was a butcher
by trade, but I hardly knew him. He died when I was three years
old. I have three brothers and one sister; I was brought up by one
of my sisters-in-law. I attended the Sadi-Carnot school in Bône
until receiving my diploma. I have fond memories of my French
classmates, but we lost touch and I have no idea what became of
them.

Upon graduation, my brother and I went to work for a milk-
man; then I became a stoker and later got a job on the assembly
line at the electrical goods factory in Bône. I was earning as much
as 18,000 francs a month. I was not at all involved in politics. My
brothers were, but I did not really understand what it was all
about. In 1948 one of my brothers was arrested, and, when my
second brother went to find out what had happened, they put
him in prison too. My third brother went to get news of the other
two, and they arrested him as well. When I went to see if they
were alright, I was sent back because I was only 14 at the time,
but the authorities made it clear that if I did not want to join my

This interview was first published in *L'Express*, in a printing that was seized
by the French government. It was reprinted in *Témoignages et Documents* in
March 1959 by the *Centre d'information et de coordination pour la défense des
libertés et de la paix*.

brothers in the cells I had better keep my nose out of the whole business.

Later, I went to Algiers and got a job on the line at the big Caterpillar factory, making American tractors. I was leading a very normal sort of life; with bonuses and overtime, I would sometimes manage to make 25,000 francs a month. I liked football and even joined the Algiers Muslim team, where I met others who were soon to become my best friends. I would discuss most things with them.

I remember November 2, 1954. We had all read *L'Echo d'Alger,* which announced the beginning of the revolution. At the time, the only references were to a few bandits and murderers operating in the Aurès mountains. They were also said to be communists. At first, like many others I believed everything I read, but I immediately tried to find out more.

From that time on, I wanted to educate myself. I would absorb all the newspapers, and I tried to find out why my brothers had been put in prison. A few months later, I met someone I admired greatly, a composer of Arab music named Abderhamane Lala. God rest his soul: he died on May 10, 1957, as a captain in the Palestro region. Abderhamane Lala had often spoken to me, but he hesitated a long time before using me. I was always asking him how to get in touch with the underground, but he would pretend not to know.

Then one day, on March 6, 1955, a date I will remember all my life, he told me I had been admitted to the Secret Organization. He himself had long been a member, of course, but he had kept quiet about it. I was very proud and happy. The organization had set my subscription at 2,000 francs a month. I paid 5,000. I made contacts, gathered information, and collected funds till July 31, 1955, when I was finally admitted as a *moussebiline* (auxiliary) and sent out on my first attack mission.

In the Maison-Carrée factory where I worked, the manager had summoned us one day and called us cowards. He had said, "The F.L.N. tells you not to smoke, so you're afraid of smoking. They tell you not to go into cafés and cinemas, and you obey like sheep. You're not men at all. From tomorrow onward, I want everybody to smoke."

The factory had become my political responsibility. I had learned that the night watchman, although a Muslim, was denouncing us. I discussed the matter with my brothers, and I was assigned to eliminate the watchman. It was the first time I had contemplated killing a man.

I was quite sporty and known to be tough, so I was told to do it "the hard way"—by strangulation. We did not want to attract the attention of the police by using firearms. It was my first test, and I almost failed it. I did strangle the watchman, but somebody raised the alarm, a patrol fired at me, and I was wounded in the calf. I hid and eventually managed to escape.

I was immediately sent to the Palestro maquis, where I stayed until July 14, 1956. Meanwhile, I picked up a second wound, during the attack on Laperrinne. From July 8 to 14, 1956, the army conducted a house-to-house search in the Blida area on what was for those days a massive scale; 28,000 men were involved. Today such a number may not seem outlandish, but in 1956 it was practically unheard of. In the outpost I was commanding, everybody was killed. I was hit by three Thompson submachine gun bullets. I can still hear the voice saying, "We'll nurse this one, then squeeze him like a lemon."

I was nursed and then interrogated.[1] I had long feared such an interrogation, the more so as my responsibilities increased and I became more knowledgeable. I had been promoted to adjutant and had traveled from village to village. In many cases I knew where the hiding places and arms caches were.

During this period I had an idea that proved very useful subsequently—to tell a big lie made up of little verifiable truths. I told them I had just arrived from Algiers because I knew how to make bombs (I never did know how to and still do not). It was a type of confession they were not used to, because it was enough to have me condemned to death. I even gave them the names of those who had supposedly sent me: Lala and "Blue Eyes." I knew they were on the wanted list. I said they were still in Algiers, since I knew they had gone into the maquis some time before. My interrogators believed me, and I was taken to Tablat prison. I was frustrated to find that the other inmates were

---

[1] Si Azzedine had previously signed a text declaring that "General de Gaulle's accession to the leadership in France authorized him to declare that the continuation of the struggle was senseless and could only perpetuate considerable unnecessary suffering in Algeria." "I regret," he added, "that the relevant authorities in the Exterior failed or refused to understand General de Gaulle's words."

mainly old political prisoners who lacked character and energy. Despite all my efforts, I could not get them to join in an escape plan. At last, four young people who shared my attitude arrived.

On October 13, 1956, we killed the guard with a blow from a stick, knocked out five auxiliaries, and burned the archives. When we got out onto the street, we found it was a market day. We merged with the crowd milling about Tablat's main square. Within a few minutes everybody knew our story. Almost instinctively, they split us up, absorbed us into different groups, gave us money, clothes, and weapons. Shortly afterward, I rejoined the underground.

I was immediately summoned by Colonel Ouamrane and Colonel Slimane, who heard my story and gave me a provisional commission. From that moment on, I was constantly busy. In two months, I mounted five ambushes and captured 110 weapons; in the course of these attacks only one of my men was wounded, lightly, although the Algiers papers reported my unit had suffered heavy casualties.

I was promoted to sublieutenant on February 4, 1957. On the seventh, I managed to disengage a *katiba* (platoon) from the pincer movement organized by Lieutenant Servan-Schreiber's Black Commandos.[2] Not that we deserve much credit for avoiding the trap: the Black Commando policy of living among the population ensured them a certain popularity, but it also meant we were told about everything they were up to.

Soon after, I was promoted again, this time to the highly prized zonal command. The man for whom my command was named, Ali Khodja, died on March 4, 1958. I was standing next to him when he was hit by an explosive bullet. Then in May 1958 I was promoted again. From captain, I became a commander in my own right.

I was arrested on November 17, 1958. Three generals—Massu, Fauré, and de Maisonrouge—had decided to deal with us once and for all. Their quarry was Colonel Amirouche, Colonel Si M'hamed, the Wilaya 4 Council, and myself. They mounted a gigantic operation, involving 30,000 men, planes, helicopters, ar-

---

[2] Si Azzedine is mistaken here. On February 7, 1957, Lieutenant J.J. Servan-Schreiber, the reservist who organized the Black Commandos, had already been demobilized for a month and had left Algeria.

tillery, and paratroops, to comb the area between Palestro, Aïn Bessef, and Bou Zegza.

When one of our liaison agents was captured, I moved camp from where he knew we had been staying. It was standard practice: prisoners could then tell the truth without betraying anybody. Our liaison agent was brave enough not to tell the truth and to give false information instead. By an extraordinary coincidence, his intended lies turned out to be accurate; we were found in a place where the liaison agent could not possibly have known we were going.

I was once again severely wounded, in the arm and leg; this time, I thought, I would have been better off dead. They fired tear gas into the grotto where we were hiding; they wanted me alive. I recall little else of what happened then.[3] When I woke up, I was in a French military outpost, and a procession of captains, colonels, and generals began to file past. My arm was in plaster. I remember a French commander who came to see me, saying, "You're the one who was at Bou Zegza on August 3, 1957, aren't you. Congratulations, old boy, that was nice work." Others were less elegant.

Then I met General Massu, who also mentioned the battle of Bou Zegza. One of the first things he said to me was, "Well, Azzedine, you can count yourself responsible for the only defeat that has gone down on my record."

The battle had been commanded by Si Lakhdar, who died a great hero of the revolution. On August 3, 1957, we had indeed outmaneuvered General Massu in all respects.

A short while later, I was taken to Algiers, where everybody wanted to see me, to ask if Captain so-and-so or Commander X was well known in the maquis. When I replied that they were

---

[3] French and F.L.N. accounts differ on this point. According to the French General Staff, Colonel Trinquier and his troops were making for a waterhole where the rebels often met. At noon on November 17, the paratroopers came upon two *katibas* armed with submachine guns. Further south, the F.L.N. Zonal Command was also under attack. Si Azzedine was completely cut off and had no option but to fight alongside his men. The paratroopers apparently found an F.L.N. man dressed in khaki, lying behind a bush, half submerged in a pond and holding a wounded arm. He then called out, "Don't shoot, I am Commander Azzedine and I am unarmed." The General Staff account adds that Si Azzedine's first reply was "I am a regular soldier. You may have taken me, but in a way I have won. You will never again be able to look upon us as mere dogs."

not, they were surprised and I think a little vexed. Then I had my first long conversation with General Massu. I had been well cared for, well treated; I was provided with everything I needed. General Massu lectured me at length about peace, arguing that there was nothing to fight about anymore, that the leaders abroad were deceiving us, and that it was time for a reconciliation. I listened and said nothing. I told my story, as I have just told it to you, but without mentioning my most recent responsibilities, which they knew nothing about.

And then one day a captain arrived, Captain Marion, who asked to be left alone with me. He told me that everybody I had seen up to now had been on military business; their job was to get information out of me, whereas he was not concerned with what I could tell and was only asking that I listen to him. And indeed every time I tried to speak, he interrupted me, telling me to think about what he was saying and to keep my answer until the next day.

He said he wanted to trust me; he knew I was well liked in my own area, both by the underground and by the local population. They were going to release me, he said. I did not believe him at first. I could not understand why they would make such an offer. Surely, with my record, they could not think that I would accept working for them. But Captain Marion explained his proposition more fully: as soon as I accepted, I would be freed and would rejoin the maquis, contact my leaders, and convince them to declare a cease-fire; I would transmit the French generals' promises that they would be given big villas, chauffeur-driven cars, a good salary, and administrative responsibilities.

As for the troops, they would simply hand in their weapons and return to their families and regular jobs. The Constantine plan, Captain Marion suggested, was enough to make our military aims irrelevant. It would be no treason to convince my fellows of this truth.

They let me think it over for a night, during which I weighed the pros and cons. I came to the conclusion that my place was with my men, fighting, and that any price was worth paying to get back to them. When I was in prison in Tablat, I had escaped. Here I did not need to escape, since my captors wanted to release me. In any case, my duty was plain: to rejoin my men and my superior officers. I decided to accept the proposition.

One of General de Gaulle's phrases had been particularly striking. He had said "I have understood you." So the next morning I said to Captain Marion, "I have understood you."

"That means you accept?"

"Yes, I accept."

Ten minutes later, General Massu came to see me. He called me "my son," drank champagne, and had some fruit juice brought for me. My bed linen was changed, and I was constantly asked if I needed anything. General Massu said that, thanks to me, peace might return to Algeria: even if my chiefs refused to listen, my men would follow me, and if the Wilaya 4 willingly stopped fighting, the other wilayas would follow suit. I was given a laissez-passer signed by General Massu himself.

Eventually it was agreed that Captain Marion would accompany me to my parents' house. We went to see my sister-in-law, who, as I have mentioned, brought me up and whom I love as though she were my mother. She lives in Belcourt, in the suburbs of Algiers. She welcomed me, as did all the children and cousins. It was a feast day. At one point, I felt tears in my eyes—for the first time in my life, I think. I saw Captain Marion watching me at that moment.

My sister-in-law took me aside. Seeing the captain with me, she had concluded I had gone over to the other side. She explained that although she was glad to see me again she did not want a traitor in her house. I tried to reassure her, and I think she understood immediately. We went out, and Captain Marion said to me, "You love them and they love you, so don't do anything stupid; don't double-cross us."[4]

I rejoined the underground and told the whole story to my brothers, who were gathered together. I wanted to leave it there, but they decided it would be useful for me to do a bit of intelligence work, to play the French along for a while. But as I had had a lot of press coverage and it was important to show my men where I really stood, we called in all the companies in the Wilaya to reassure them.

[4] According to the French General Staff, Si Azzedine stayed in Algiers for some time, making many contacts with Muslims of every persuasion. "He attended the legislative elections and grasped the importance of the changes in the general mood in response to the newly instituted social reforms." Supposedly, he had become convinced that General de Gaulle's accession to power meant that the prevailing situation had nothing in common with that of 1954.

I went back to Algiers and met up again with Captain Marion, who told me the last week had been one of the most tragic in his whole life. I also saw General Massu, who bombarded me with questions. I said that I had not yet seen my colonel, who was away on a mission, but that one of the commanders of the Wilaya was in agreement with my plan. The general was delighted: "That's already something, it's a big step forward in the right direction. This could be the most successful part of all my action over here."

I returned to Belcourt to see my family. Eventually I completed the intelligence mission I had been entrusted with; the point had been to find out what sort of information the French were getting about us and who was giving it to them. When I finally went back underground, I had done everything that had been asked of me, as well as facilitating the passage of a convoy of supplies, equipment, and pharmaceuticals.

During my stay in Algiers, General Massu had asked me if I wanted all operations in my sector to be suspended. I had said no, but he had insisted: "You can do as you like; in any case we are going to suspend ours." And the French did indeed suspend their operations in my area for two weeks.

Contrary to what has been written, I carried out only one mission in Algiers, after which I returned to get new orders from my chiefs. Since I was not yet completely recovered from my wounds, I participated in the Wilaya Council but not in its operations. Later the High Command called me to Tunis, and so here I am. . . .

VIII.   Mau Mau from Within

DONALD L. BARNETT
AND KARARI NJAMA

*An American anthropologist, Donald L.
Barnett, has interviewed at length Karari
Njama, a Kikuyu schoolteacher who
participated in the Mau Mau insurrection
in Kenya (1952–1956). He brings out the
magical and religious dimensions of this
armed movement, its organization,
motivations, and weaknesses.*

Karari Njama

. . . The following day was a Sunday in the first week of
September. After Sunday service I met Mr Samuel Ndiritu Njagi,
a clerk in the Ministry of Works, a true friend and a schoolmate
at Kagumo who had recently married my relative. He kindly
invited me to his home. When we arrived, I learned that he had
brewed beer in his mother's hut. We spent the whole of the
afternoon drinking and talking on one's job and the country's
politics. A few persons came and shared the drink with us. In the
evening we left toward home. On the way, Ndiritu told me that
he had been invited to a feast by my neighbor, Charles Ngatia
Gathitu, a pitsawyer and license holder on timber trades, situated
about 400 yards east of my home. We passed many people on the
way and arrived at the house at twilight. There were some people
standing outside, including Charles, the owner of the feast. He

From Donald L. Barnett and Karari Njama, *Mau Mau from Within: Autobi-
ography and Analysis of Kenya's Peasant Revolt* (New York and London:
Monthly Review Press, 1966). Copyright 1966 by Donald L. Barnett. Reprinted
by permission of Monthly Review Press.

led us into one of his big huts. Inside, were many people sitting and a hurricane lamp was burning. We were told to wait there while some preparations went on in the other hut. Groups of men and women continued to come until there was very little room for anyone to sit. A few persons would be called by names and moved in the next hut. When I was called to go to the next hut, I was very pleased, but arriving outside in a clear moonshine, I could see hundreds of people standing, some armed with *pangas, simis* (swords), and clubs. They formed a path on both sides leading to the door of the next hut. I became certain that the day had arrived for me to take the oath, and I had to face it manly, I thought.

As I led my group marching in the cordoned path, they waved their *pangas* and swords over our heads and I heard one of them asking whether there was an informer to be "eaten." With a reply that we were all good people from another person, we entered the next hut.

By the light of a hurricane lamp, I could see the furious guards who stood armed with *pangas* and *simis*. Right in front of us stood an arch of banana and maize stalks and sugar cane stems tied by a forest creeping and climbing plant. We were harassed to take out our coats, money, watches, shoes, and any other European metal we had in our possession. Then the oath administrator, Githinji Mwarari—who had painted his fat face with white chalk—put a band of raw goat's skin on the right hand wrist of each one of the seven persons who were to be initiated. We were then surrounded [bound together] by goats' small intestines on our shoulders and feet. Another person then sprayed us with some beer from his mouth as a blessing, at the same time throwing a mixture of the finger millet with other cereals on us. Then Githinji pricked our right hand middle finger with a needle until it bled. He then brought the chest of a billy goat and its heart still attached to the lungs and smeared them with our blood. He then took a Kikuyu gourd containing blood and with it made a cross on our foreheads and on all important joints, saying, "May this blood mark the faithful and brave members of the Gikuyu and Mumbi Unity; may this same blood warn you that if you betray our secrets or violate the oath, our members will come and cut you into pieces at the joints marked by this blood."

We were then asked to lick each other's blood from our middle fingers and vowed after the administrator: "If I reveal this secret of Gikuyu and Mumbi to a person not a member, may this blood kill me. If I violate any of the rules of the oath may this blood kill me. If I lie, may this blood kill me."

We were then ordered to hold each other's right hand and in that position, making a line, passed through the arch seven times. Each time the oath administrator cut off a piece of the goat's small intestine, breaking it into pieces, while all the rest in the hut repeated a curse on us: "*Tathu! Ugotuika uguo ungiaria ma-heni! Muma uroria muria ma!*" (Slash! May you be cut like this! Let the oath kill he who lies!).

We were then made to stand facing Mt. Kenya, encircled by intestines, and given two dampened soil balls and ordered to hold the left-hand soil ball against our navels. We then swore:

I (Karari Njama), swear before God and before all the people present here that . . .

1. I shall never reveal this secret of the K.C.A. oath—which is of Gikuyu and Mumbi and which demands land and freedom—to any person who is not a member of our society. If I ever reveal it, may this oath kill me! ([Repeated after each vow while] biting the chest meat of a billy goat held together with the heart and lungs.)
2. I shall always help any member of our society who is in difficulty or need of help.
3. If I am ever called, during the day or night, to do any work for this society, I shall obey.
4. I shall on no account ever disobey the leaders of this society.
5. If I am ever given firearms or ammunition to hide, I shall do so.
6. I shall always give money or goods to this society whenever called upon to do so.
7. I shall never sell land to a European or an Asian.
8. I shall not permit intermarriage between Africans and the white community.
9. I will never go with a prostitute.
10. I shall never cause a girl to become pregnant and leave her unmarried.

11. I will never marry and then seek a divorce.
12. I shall never allow any daughter to remain uncircumcised.
13. I shall never drink European manufactured beer or ciga-
    rettes.
14. I shall never spy on or otherwise sell my people to Gov-
    ernment.
15. I shall never help the missionaries in their Christian faith
    to ruin our traditional and cultural customs.
16. I will never accept the Beecher Report.
17. I shall never steal any property belonging to a member of
    our society.
18. I shall obey any strike call, whenever notified.
19. I will never retreat or abandon any of our mentioned de-
    mands but will daily increase more and stronger demands
    until we achieve our goals.
20. I shall pay £62 50s and a ram as assessed by this society as
    soon as I am able.
21. I shall always follow the leadership of Jomo Kenyatta and
    Mbiyu Koinange.

We repeated the oath while pricking the eye of a goat with a
kei-apple thorn seven times and then ended the vows by pricking
seven times some seven sodom apples. To end the ceremony,
blood mixed with some good smelling oil was used to make a
cross on our foreheads indicating our reception as members of
Gikuyu and Mumbi [while] warning us: "Forward ever and backward never!"

We were then allowed to take our belongings, put on our coats
and shoes and were welcomed to stay. We paid £2 50s each for
registration. During the course of our initiation, one person refused to take the oath and was mercilessly beaten. Two guards
were crying [out] seeking permission from their chief leader to
kill the man. The man learned that death had approached him
and he quickly changed his mind and took the oath.

After we had all been sworn, the house was very crowded that
contained about 80 people; nearly all of whom were initiated on
that night. About the same number of old members were working outside as guards. A speech was made by the oath administrator, Githinji Mwarari, and his assistant Kariuki King'ori, who
told us that they had been sent from the Head Office in Nairobi

to give people an oath that could create a real unity among all the Africans which would make it easier for the African to gain his land and freedom. He told us that the society was called Gikuyu and Mumbi or K.C.A. He remarked that the struggle for the alienated land started as long ago as 1920 by Harry Thuku and the Kikuyu who attempted to fight for the land which caused many deaths in Nairobi and the deportation of Harry Thuku to Kismayu. He said that the K.C.A. was the society that had been struggling for the return of our alienated land. He told us that we had been initiated so as to strengthen the African struggle for the alienated land—the chief African demand. He went on: "We have learned that the Kenya settlers are the chief obstacles to our claims. They do not want to leave the bread and butter which they obtain from these lands at the exploitation of our blood on the so-called white paradise. Some of you here might have been fined or imprisoned under the trespass ordinance on stepping on a settler's farm while you visited your relatives under his employment or else you had gone there seeking employment only. We cannot tolerate this any longer. We are going to shout to the Kenya Government, which we know that it is controlled by the settlers, until we are heard or else their eardrums would burst. We are going to pursue our demands through reasons and if this fails we would not hesitate to revolt. We have already sent Mr. Mbiyu Koinange to England to represent our case to the British Government.

"You have heard that some of our members have been prosecuted for taking Mau Mau oath. This is the same oath you have taken today. You are now members of that 'Mau Mau.'" . . .

Up to this stage, the plans and actions of "Mau Mau," the name of the society made popular by the Government pressmen, were only known by persons who had taken the second oath. In fact, one was ignorant of the movement until he took the second oath. At about 10 A.M. David Wahome, my assistant teacher, and I were knowingly led by Johnson Ndungu, one of my teachers, to an oath administrator, Daniel Muthua, about three quarters of a mile from the school. On the way I noticed a few scattered guards.

Inside the house was Daniel Muthua alone; his assistant was doing something else in the next hut. We were the only two persons to be initiated. He dipped some herb leaves in a Kikuyu gourd containing a mixture of goat's blood, its abdominal dung [i.e., the undigested stomach contents of the goat], and water, then sprayed us with it uttering words of cleansing and blessing. Each at his own time, we were initiated.

Naked, I stood facing Mt. Kenya, holding high a dampened ball of soil (damped by milk, animal fat, and blood—the most important dairy products) in my right hand and the other ball against my navel by my left hand. There were five two-foot pieces of the goat's small intestines lying on the ground about a foot and a half apart and I was instructed to step over these one at a time when completing the set of vows I was about to take. Then, repeating the words of Daniel, I said:

I swear before God and before the people who are here that . . .
1. I have today become a soldier of Gikuyu and Mumbi and I will from now onward fight the real fight for the land and freedom of our country till we get it or till my last drop of blood. Today I have set my first step [stepping over the first line of the goat's small intestine] as a warrior and I will never retreat.
    And if I ever retreat:
    May this soil and all its products be a curse upon me!
2. If ever I am called to accompany a raid or bring in the head of an enemy, I shall obey and never give lame excuses.
    And if I ever refuse:
    May this soil and all its products curse upon me!
3. I will never spy or inform on my people, and if ever sent to spy on our enemies I will always report the truth.
    And if I fail in this:
    May this soil and all its products curse upon me!
4. I will never reveal a raid or crime committed to any person who has not taken the *Ngero* Oath (*Muma wa Ngero*, Oath of Violence or Crime) and will steal firearms wherever possible.
    And if I ever reveal our secrets or fail to use or turn over to our warriors any firearms I acquire:
    May this soil and all its products curse upon me!
5. I will never leave a member in difficulty without trying to help him. And if I ever abandon a member in trouble:
    May this soil and all its products be a curse upon me!

6. I will obey the orders of my leaders at all times without any argument or complaint and will never fail to give them any money or goods taken in a raid and will never hide any pillages or take them for myself.

And if I fail in these things: May this soil and all its products curse upon me!

7. I will never sell land to any white man.

And if I sell:

May this soil and all its products be a curse upon me!"

I dropped the two balls of soil in a Kikuyu gourd which contained a Kikuyu knife and a Kikuyu needle. I then sat down on a stool. He gave me the well-stripped chest of a billy goat, from the neck to the testicles. It had a hole in the bottom and he told me to put my penis in that hole and hold the goat's chest upright with both my arms. I then repeated the vows for a second time, each time biting the goat's chest and ending, " . . . May this *thenge* kill me," and finishing by crossing the second small intestine line.

He then took away the chest and brought a Kikuyu pot and kept it upside down in front of me. He then put the *ngata* [the bone, containing seven holes, which joins the head and neck] of the billy goat on the pot and gave me seven small *mugere* sticks. I repeated the oath for the third time, putting a *mugere* stick in each *ngata* hole and each time ending, "And if I . . . May this *thenge* kill me! " I crossed the third line of small intestines.

He removed the *ngata* and brought an eye of the goat on the pot. He then gave me seven kei-apple thorns. I repeated the oath for the fourth time, each time pricking the eye with a thorn and ending, " . . . May this *thenge* kill me!" As I stepped across the fourth line of intestines, he removed the eye and brought seven sodom apples strung together on a thin hard reed and put them on the pot. He then gave me the same kei-apple thorns, and I repeated the vows for the fifth time, pricking a thorn at every sodom apple and each time ending, " . . . May I be pricked thus if . . . !" and also crossing the fifth line of the small intestines.

He removed the pot and the sodom apples and picked up the Kikuyu sword, knife, and needle. Swinging these over me seven times, each time banging them down on my head, he uttered the blacksmith's curse, condemning me to death if I violated the vows I had sworn. He then brought a very small Kikuyu gourd that contained a mixture of lion and leopard fat. He dipped a reed in it and with the fat made a cross on my forehead wishing me to be as brave as a lion or a leopard and to have their personality which would frighten my enemies. He then asked me to lick the remainder of the fat off of the reed. The ceremony was over. I dressed and started back to the school with David Wahome, who took the oath before me.

On the way to the school we discussed the oath we had taken. We resolved that it was a horrible oath, though typically Kikuyu. All the vows had been militant. We had definitely been employed in the Gikuyu and Mumbi military force.

"But what would happen if one disobeyed these vows?" Wahome asked.

"Well," I replied, "In my opinion, though the oath itself may have no reaction, I consider that I have repeatedly vowed under God's name and that if I disobeyed the oath, my lies would anger God whose wrath might result in all the curses I have made . . . and most likely I would meet a death penalty from the society."

"You are quite right," replied Wahome. "Remember that hundreds of people have been killed, even the well-armed European families—the Ruck family on North Kinangop and Commander Mikeljohn of Thomson's Falls. To violate any of the vows would mean to taste death. At present the Government is completely unable to control Mau Mau."

"Oh! I care very little for Europeans having been killed. For many years they have killed many Africans but none of the Europeans has ever been sentenced to death by their courts of justice for killing an African in the whole 60 years' history of their rule. They regard us as sykes or baboons. I wish Mau Mau courts had power to sentence many of them to death until they feel the result of their injustice and their hypocritical teaching, 'Love thy neighbor as thyself,' which they never practiced. It is useless for them to teach us of the great Chinese philosopher Confucius who taught his people, 'Do to others as you would have them do unto you.'"

"What do you think," I enquired, "of *Utuku wa Hiu Ndaihu*" (The Night of Long Swords)? As the rumor goes, if all the Kenya tribes are taking the oath as we are doing—which I hope they are doing—and a well-organized plot is carried out, it may be possible to kill all the Europeans at a given time since every one of them has at least three Africans serving him, while many of them have hundreds of African servants.

"Did you note that the vows we made are of fighting plans?" I asked.

"Yes," answered Wahome, "that we were told frankly. But you see, the plan might have been in existence for many years, and since the society is very secretive, even within its own members, it would be difficult for the ordinary person to know about it unless he was involved in the activity."

"Now, since all the top leaders are detained, who do you think would carry on the plans?" I asked.

"Well, their lieutenants of course," replied Wahome. "Mathenge and Kimathi are likely to lead the war and they will soon become heroes."

We arrived at school, took lunch, and prepared for the afternoon lessons. . . .

At 10 A.M. we visited Wanjau's camp about 300 yards south uphill. We were escorted by two armed warriors. We didn't carry the pass letters, for the leader was known and respected and the distance was very short. One of our escorts gave signals to the guards and we passed. Like the others, the guard's houses were built some 60 yards away from the camp and beside the path that led to the camp. All the houses were of the same plan. This camp had a place with sunshine where we found all the people warming themselves. We met Generals Wanjau and Nyama discussing a cattle raid for food. They resolved that they would raid Ihithe Village the following night. I expressed my wish to get to Kariaini Headquarters, and they promised me some escorts the following day.

The cook was sent to prepare lunch for the leaders—some well-fried meat. I came to understand that they would not eat maize or beans, which could be stored for a long time without going bad, while they had meat which could not be stored for as long a time before it went bad. This must be the reason why I have eaten only meat in these camps.

I wanted to know whether the leopards and hyenas ate their meat which they hung on trees. Wanjau told me that all the animals had become friends and that they would neither attack anyone nor eat that meat. He went on, "We pray for these animals who have kindly welcomed us in their homes and who have been put in our category by the security forces—in other words they regard us as animals. The rhino is our only enemy here inside the forest. We call him "Home Guard," as he resembles those who did not take the oath. But there are no rhinos in the Kigumo Forest. We take it for granted that all the rest of the animals have taken an oath of allegiance. They have stopped running away from us; in fact the monkey and ndete bird are our guards. They tell us the approach of an enemy by their alarms."

Because these animal alarms were often true, it made it easier for many to believe that God had given them such powers so as to help us to defeat the enemy's approach. This led to the passing of a rule prohibiting the killing of an animal, as it was thought that if we made these animals angry, they would probably fight against us and chase us from their home. The birds, mice, rats would come right in the kitchen to eat any food that might have fallen as though they were tamed. *Gituyu,* a type of big rat, as big as a cat with a two-foot whip-like tail, were so daring that they would eat maize from a person's hand and were not at all afraid. They broke their allegiance, [however], by going into our stores. They would eat as much maize as they could and carry as much as they could, [make] as many trips as were possible for them, to fill their stores in which they buried our maize. They were therefore killed.

The sun went behind the western mountains and we were back in the camp saying our evening prayers, after which fires were lit to warm ourselves. . . .

I returned to H.Q. in the evening, during the prayer time. I was surprised to see more than 2,000 people (to my guessing) in the camp. Many of them dressed in the ordinary clothing while about 800 of them wore different Government uniforms which must have been acquired mainly from the dead security forces. A few had long and shaggy hair and beards. Some had woven [or braided] their hair like women while others had wool braided in with the hair to imitate the Masai. In fact, they could approach any Government force without being suspected. Nearly half the people were armed with swords or *pangas* while the rest had various types of European guns and more than 600 homemade guns. I could guess their ages; most of them were between 25 and 30 years old. There were a few old ones, well over 60 years. The leaders could quickly be recognized. They all tied turbans around their heads, looked more clean and healthy than the rest, wore shoes or boots, possessed either a wrist or pocket watch, and carried a hidden pistol and a walking stick. . . .

. . . As we approached the meeting place, we could see leaders sitting down on the little grass which grew under the big trees some 150 yards in front of us. On our arrival, they stood for Mathenge and after exchanging greetings we all sat down in a circle.

All the twenty-seven leaders were from Nyeri. Many of them were new to me and curiously focused on me their long shaggy hair and beards on black and dark brown faces with their protruding dark brown eyes. These bloodshot-eyed leaders, or most of them, were armed with different types of pistols; three had Sten guns and three others big game-shooting guns. Figuring out that all the powers of law and order were vested in the hands of those people and that their decision was final, I felt uneasy.

The meeting started with prayers. We all stood facing Mt. Kenya with soil in our hands while Mathenge said the prayers. Then only Mathenge remained standing in the center of the circle. Taking a small stick about a foot long from a pile of them, he proceeded to curse the traitors: "Let any leader who would reveal confidential matters to the warriors or to anyone else not entitled to the matter, let the person who creates hatred between others, the witchdoctor who kills people by poison to enjoy his practice, etc., etc., be destroyed along with his entire family and vanish from the earth." We all had to repeat the curse after him and he threw away a stick into the bush after the completion of every vow.

One person enquired whether all the persons present had taken the Leaders Oath. I said that I had not taken it although I had been working as a leader. I was then asked to take the Leaders Oath.

With a little worry about the oath I was going to take and a little pleasure of my promotion, I stood in the middle of the leaders facing Mt. Kenya, raising my hands high over my head with soil in my left hand and a piece of goat's meat in my right, I repeated the vows after Mathenge:

I swear before Ngai and all these people here that . . .
1. I will never reveal the leaders' secrets to a warrior or any other person who is not a leader.
2. I will never run away or surrender leaving my warriors behind.
3. I will never abandon the leadership of my people but I will go wherever my people would send me and do whatever they ask me to do in my country's name.
4. I will never disdain [i.e., degrade or criticize] any leader in the presence of warriors.
5. I will never by any means cause or plan the [injury or] death of another leader."

I ended each vow by chewing some meat and a little soil and saying: "If I fail to do this, may this oath kill me. If I lie, may Ngai kill me."

At the completion of my oath, I was asked to take my books and sit down with the others and start recording the minutes. I wholeheartedly accepted the vows I had taken. Mathenge went on to introduce me to the leaders as his secretary. . . .

Donald L. Barnett

Karari's account of the June 25 raid and, more specifically, of the failure of Kariaini forces to carry out their part in this "all-out attack" focuses attention on the role and influence of the seers among Aberdare guerrilla forces. It also provides a striking illustration of the seeming incongruity, in the context of a modern-day revolution, of prophets, omens, and magico-religious beliefs. To understand this phenomenon, it is necessary to view the role of the *mundo mugo* in term of both continuities in Kikuyu culture and ideological reactions to contemporary events.

The traditionally important role of the *mundo mugo,* as a member of the Kikuyu War Council with numerous military duties and functions, has already been alluded to in an earlier section, and it is easy enough to view his role within revolutionary forest groups of the 1950s—for example, advising on raids and other military matters, using his war magic against the enemy, conducting cleansing ceremonies, transmitting messages from Ngai (usually received in dreams) to the guerrilla leaders, etc.—as merely an extension or continuation of traditional belief and practice. This, however, would be to overlook the importance of contemporary pressures, internal and external, and their effects on the complex and developing ideology of the forest insurgents.

To provide a context for this discussion and, as ideological matters will be of continuing concern, a framework within which future developments can meaningfully be considered, it might be useful here to address ourselves to the general question of Mau Mau ideology. It must be noted at the outset that many writers have attempted to characterize this ideology, and not infrequently the entire revolutionary movement, in terms of one or another general and comprehensive category or label. Mau Mau, it has variously been asserted, "was in fact a religion,"[1] or, rather than a religion, " a self-conscious return to tribalism . . . based on synthetic paganism,"[2] "a wholly tribal manifestation aimed at tribal domination, not a national liberation movement, "[3] "a form of millenarism,"[4] or "a pseudo-religious cult . . . of the golden age."[5]

I must confess that I find all such attempts to "fit" the ideology of Kenya's revolutionary movement into a single, neat category wanting in both historical accuracy and utility. Unfortunately, the Movement issued no manifesto and all who address themselves to its ideology are obliged to make inferences from a wide array of songs, prayers, oaths, etc., which, in their variety, can be used selectively to support any number of sweeping generalizations.

My own investigation of Mau Mau ideology, viewed as the unifying set of aims, interests, and beliefs of the Movement, has shown it to be a rather complex phenomenon containing at least four major aspects or components, namely, secular, moral-religious, African national, and Kikuyu tribal. The weight or importance attached to these several aspects, as we shall see, changed over time and varied from group to group. Nevertheless, it will be useful at this point to consider the general characteristics of each component as part of the total ideology.

[1] L.S.B.Leakey, *Defeating Mau Mau* (Methuen & Co. Ltd., 1954), p.41.
[2] F.B. Welbourn, *East African Rebels* (S.C.M. Press Ltd., 1961), p. 133.
[3] F. Majdalaney, *State of Emergency* (Longmans, 1962), p. 70.
[4] L.P. Mair, *British Journal of Sociology*, Vol. 9, No. 2 (1958), p. 175,
[5] F.D. Corfield, *Historical Survey of the Origins and Growth of Mau Mau* (Her Majesty's Stationery Office), p.9.

Developing largely out of the manifold politico-agrarian grievances directed against European rule and white settler occupancy
of alienated African land, the *secular* aspect of Mau Mau ideology was revealed most clearly in the oft-repeated demands of the
Movement for higher wages, increased educational opportunities,
removal of the color-bar in its variety of discriminatory forms,
return of the alienated lands, and independence under an all-
African government. As a reflection of the developing relationship of inequality between black and white in Kenya society,
these secular aims were, in their political dimension, an expression of African nationalist ideology—that is, a demand for African "Freedom" and self-determination. ("You cannot build on
the work of a foreigner. His word should be drowned in deep
waters by God. His rule should be brought to an end. In this
country of ours, Kenya, let the black people govern themselves
alone." "If you look around the whole of Kenya, it is only a river
of blood; for we have our one single purpose, to lay hold of
Kenya's freedom.")

Within the revolutionary forest context, this secular-African
national aspect was reflected and symbolized in the demand for
"Land and Freedom." As will be noted, "freedom" was seldom
if ever viewed as a specifically Kikuyu or tribal objective, but
rather as the end product of a successful African struggle vis-à-vis
the European adversary for independence from colonial and
white settler rule. ("Mother, whether you cry or not, I'll only
return when our lands are recovered; when we obtain land and
African freedom.")

With respect to "land," however, the objective was more often
than not seen in tribal or specifically Kikuyu terms. Thus, in song
and prayer, the common reference is to the land left to the Kikuyu by Ngai or the mythical ancestors of the tribe, Gikuyu and
Mumbi; and its recovery from European hands is viewed as a
Kikuyu objective. ("O God, the most powerful! We praise Thee
for guarding us throughout the day. We have raised our hands to
show You that the soil You gave our forefathers is now being
used by strangers, who robbed us of our lands, our gift, our
inheritance. These strangers are killing us for our land." "I'll
never leave Jomo, I'll never leave him; since I've been solemnly
promised the return of our land.")

The secular aspect of Mau Mau ideology, then, had both an

African national dimension, centering largely aroung the aim and concept of "freedom," and a tribal dimension framed in terms of specific Kikuyu claims to alienated land. The revolution's political frame of reference was thus African national; its agrarian frame of reference, Kikuyu tribal.

The nonsecular or sacred aspect of Mau Mau ideology was framed largely in terms of moral-religious precepts, according to which the secular aims of the revolution were seen as sanctioned and legitimized by a higher, supernatural power. Most important among these precepts were the following, repeated over and over again in song, prayer, and oath. (1) *"We have been wronged by the Europeans; our cause and struggle are just and right."* ("God created Gikuyu and Mumbi and placed them in Gikuyuland; they were deceived by the Europeans and their land was stolen." "Sorrow and trouble came with the white man; when we accepted them they stole our land." "We are tormented because we are black; we are not of the whites and do not share their blessings, but our God is before us!") (2) *"God is just and powerful; right will prevail over might."* ("Please, O God! Look mercifully upon the spilt blood of our brethren and hear our call and cry. We have not weapons to fight against these people, but we believe Thy sword will defeat our enemies; for we are your sons and daughters and do not believe you created us to become servants of other people in the land you blessed and gave to our ancestors, Gikuyu and Mumbi." "Have no fear in your hearts, God is in heaven. Be brave, God's power is here and the Europeans will be driven out.") (3) *"A just cause must nonetheless be fought for; God helps those who help themselves."* ("Warriors of Gikuyu, awake! Ye who cannot see that the old man grows older. If you sleep the foreigners will seize all our wealth and then what will the children of Mumbi feed on?" "You of the House of Mumbi, even if you are oppressed do not be afraid in your hearts; a Kikuyu proverb says 'God helps those who help themselves.'")

Combined with a reaffirmation of certain common traditional values and customs, precepts such as these provided the Movement and revolution with a "moral force," a conviction that the struggle was just and a belief that right would prevail over might. It is quite likely that similar convictions have formed an integral part of all revolutionary ideologies.

Together with their incorporated secular aims, these moral-religious precepts and beliefs also performed an important unifying or integrating function, linking in common cause and brotherhood a vast majority of the previously dispersed and frequently conflicting Kikuyu, Embu, and Meru groups. To the extent, however, that this was achieved through the use of specifically Kikuyu symbols, persons of non-Kikuyu tribal affiliation tended to be excluded, if not alienated, from the revolutionary movement.

Though the religious aspect of Mau Mau ideology contained a syncretic quality, with various aspects of Old Testament Christianity found interwoven with their Kikuyu counterparts, it was framed largely in terms of traditional beliefs and concepts. Christianity, particularly in its institutionalized form as represented by the missions, was avowedly rejected. In the black-white struggle, it was viewed essentially as just another aspect of European domination. ("Between a missionary and a settler, there is no difference"—a Kikuyu saying.)

We are now, I believe, in a better position to understand the role and ideological implications of the *mundo mugo* among Aberdare guerrilla groups. Largely isolated within the forest and without the direct participation of their more highly educated and cosmopolitan leaders, the peasant forces of this period tended to place considerable weight on the specifically Kikuyu aspects of their composite ideology. Kenya African nationalism, though by no means disappearing, was forced into the background by a strong sense of Kikuyu "nationalism" or tribalism. The felt need for tribal unity—no mean achievement in its own right and in large measure accomplished by mid-1953—led to emphasis being placed on the more specific grievances of the Kikuyu peasantry, particularly those centering around land and the dominant position of the European settler. And the increasing antiwhite, antimission feelings, together with an equally strong desire to recover the lost dignity, the surrendered "manhood," of the tribe, conditioned the reaffirmation of certain aspects of traditional Kikuyu law and custom.

It is in this light that we must view the role of the *mundo mugo*. With the rejection, for the most part, of Christianity went a reaffirmation of the merits and credibility of the old religion and its legitimate "professional" practitioners. Traditionally, however, magical and religious beliefs were interwoven within a single system of thought which, particularly among the illiterate peasantry, had been supplemented rather than displaced by Christianity over the preceding fifty years. The magico-religious beliefs prevalent within the ranks of the guerrilla fighters, therefore, and the widespread acceptance of the legitimate military role and prophetic powers of the *mundo mugo* are best understood as continuities in traditional Kikuyu culture which were both reinforced and, to a considerable degree, reshaped by the forces operating within the revolutionary context of 1953.

As we shall see, the actual powers of the seers in determining or influencing military policy and tactics varied considerably from group to group, depending in large part upon the importance attached to magico-religious beliefs by the individual leaders. There was, in addition, considerable variation over time in the role and importance of the *mundo mugo*. Though the "moral strength" derived by the forest fighters from their beliefs in the prophecies and magical powers of the seers is difficult to assess, it must be objectively noted that the seer's role was of dubious military value and a source of both stress and internal conflict within the revolutionary movement.

Karari Njama

The following day, after cleansing and dressing my patients' wounds, of whom many were almost healed, I climbed up the hill with Mathenge and other leaders to spend the day warming by the sun's heat. At about 10 A.M., four Harvards started bombing the H.Q. area with much stronger bombs than before. The bombing lasted fifteen minutes, followed by five minutes of firing from their machine guns. During the bombing I saw a few persons run into their holes, while many others, including myself, ran under big trees and lay down on our stomachs with our noses almost touching the ground and held soil in our hands amidst the horrible thunder of exploding bombs, which echoed as death hoots to me, and the frightening earth tremors. In the fainting breath, each said his own prayers, asking God to save his life and to avenge against the injustices of our strong enemies.

After the departure of the Harvards we were very much anxious to know whether they had caused casualties. They had dropped one bomb right inside the camp and another at the edge. Luckily there were no people in the camp at the moment, for they were all on the hillside where the airplanes could not bomb successfully. Though there was no person injured, the day was referred to as "the first heavy air raid." We suspected that a captive—for there were no surrenderees by then—had pointed out to the Government the site of H.Q.; but since these airplanes went on bombing other areas in which there were no camps, we concluded that it was a mere guessing of where the camp could be and our warriors continued to live in the H.Q.

On June 21, under the authority of Mathenge, I wrote a letter to each leader notifying him that the "all out attack" would be on June 25, 1953, commencing at 7:30 P.M. I also wrote a propaganda letter to the Government saying:

> The June 25 raid is an example of our planned series of attacks. The Europeans and Asians who are with us are very much engaged in the making of guns and plans. We are certain that our next all-out attack will make you flee our country or commit suicide. The more you punish the civilians in the reserves, the more they hate you and the more they join our forces. We are glad that you are spending thousands of pounds daily paying pilots' wages, oil and bombs which kill hundreds of buffalo, elephants, deer, etc., and only supply us with plenty of meat right here in the forest. Whatever worst you do against us, God changes it to be our best help.
>
> Yours Victoriously,
> General Stanley Mathenge

After reading to Mathenge the propaganda letter I had drafted, he was very pleased with me and said that the letter should be posted as it was near Munyange Police Post. All the other letters were dispatched the following morning, and all the messengers were to report at H.Q. on the evening of the 24th that they had delivered the messages.

When Kihara Kagumu visited the hospital on the morning of the 25th he reported to Mathenge that the H.Q. camp had selected 1,600 warriors who would participate in the all-out attack in 32 groups of 50 men each. He said that each group was to be led by a lieutenant or an appointed warrior and that they would all leave H.Q. at 4 P.M. so that they could see the security forces going to their guarding positions by 6 P.M. and then mark the ambush places; they would then separate, each group heading to the place it would attack.

The following morning an injured warrior was brought to the hospital at about 7:30 A.M., his calf being badly torn by a grenade. I quickly applied a pad on the pressure point to stop bleeding and cleansed and dressed his wound. Meanwhile, hot soup was being prepared. As he was drinking the soup, he reported the [previous] night's raid to me, saying that they arrived at the forest fringe before 6 P.M. and saw over 800 Devonshire personnel assisted by military and Home Guards taking their positions at all possible paths. They became frightened. They could pass their ambushers and carry on the plan, but they thought that the Devons would block their way back in such a way that they would either be killed on their return journey or would remain in the reserve and continue a day battle which had not been planned.

The other reason [i.e., for their failure to carry out the raid] was the superstitious beliefs which were being taught by the witch doctors that if a deer or a gazelle passed across the path of a group that was going to raid, it indicated bad luck and the warriors should abandon their plan. Twice a deer and a gazelle had crossed our way. This [belief, he said,] was supported by many warriors who said that they disobeyed the same rule when they were going to raid Othaya and the result was very bad, as the seers had forecast. This caused their decision to put off the raid.

Two of the groups of 50 undertook the risk and decided to fulfill the plan, while the rest waited at the forest border. The patient was in one of the two groups that attacked a guard post and took away very many head of sheep and goats, of which some were lost in the darkness and only 160 arrived at H.Q. The other group managed to bring 40 head of cattle. The patient continued that he was one of the guards who remained behind to fight the enemy who might follow the livestock. "When we passed the Devons' ambush we were all happy about our success. We started talking loudly as we approached the forest but we did not know that the Devons had heard the first group and had followed it to the forest edge, and that they were lying there waiting for us. We unknowingly entered their ambush, which we realized [only] when they opened fire on us. We were so near them that they used grenades, [one of] whose shells injured me. I think we must have lost some of our people there."

The raid report was very disappointing. The seers had ruined our plans. It seemed to me that most of our warriors, including many of their section leaders, were under the command [i.e., influence] of the prophets. This was one of our great dangers I thought. If Government used these seers to help them, they could either lead our warriors into Government ambushes or induce them to surrender claiming that they had been directed by God to convey this message to the people. I talked the matter over with Mathenge and found that he also believed in witchcraft. I kept on thinking of a way which could turn our people from the prophets, but this was impossible until their messages were realized as a danger. I quickly learned that my attempts to make our warriors turn against the prophets were interpreted as urging them to disobey God's messengers and thus disobey God's instructions.

By nightfall, the report from H.Q. was that two armed warriors were still missing. It was suspected that they were casualties of the Devons. A group of people was sent out to search for them in the ambushed area near the forest edge while another group was sent in the reserve to find out the current news about the raids.

The following day we received the news from the reserve messengers saying that they were told that, when the day broke, the Devons with some Home Guards (who reported the story to our messengers) went to check how many people they had killed. When they arrived at the place where they had opened fire, they did not see any corpses but there were blood trails. They followed the blood track thinking that it would lead them to some corpses. They unknowingly approached two injured warriors who opened fire killing two Devons. They were then both killed, and their guns fell into Government hands. The corpses were exhibited to the reserve people.

Though the H.Q. camp failed to raid on June 25, the report in the reserve and from Government information through radio and newspapers indicated that the forest fighters were well organized, many in number, scattered everywhere, and that the raids had incurred heavy losses on the Government side in a single day.

Up to this date, the H.Q. had an average of two raids a week on either military, police, or Home Guard centers, followed by ambushes in which Government attempted to enter the H.Q. It just serves here to say that the Government had four and a half months of trial and error in which it lost many of its forces [as well as] arms and ammunition which increased the strength of our warriors. The road from the reserve to Kariaini H.Q. was as wide as many of the vehicle roads today in the reserve and had been known by the Government forces as "the road to death." I think that an account of some of our early successes would make the reader [better able] to figure out a bit of the fight in the forest.

It was about 10 A.M. on May 5, before my arrival, when our watchmen reported that they had seen about two thousand men and women led and guarded by military, Home Guards, and some Europeans marching toward Kariaini Forest squatter gardens with the intention of uprooting *nduma* (arrowroots), potatoes, and all the remaining foodstuffs so that our warriors would not get any more food from those gardens. Our guards were strengthened and set off to meet them in the gardens, with a warning to take care not to shoot the civilians. As soon as our warriors were ready, they sounded bugles at different positions which indicated the opening of fire. When the civilians heard the bugles they ran away. Five military persons fell dead, while the others made off following the civilians. They were quickly followed [and our fighters succeeded in] killing three more and capturing one Home Guard, thirty old men, and fifty women. A few warriors were left guarding the captives while the others chased the military right inside the reserve. Two military persons dropped their guns at Ihuririo about a mile from the forest fringe. Our warriors collected the guns and returned to the forest, releasing all the captives who wanted to go back. A dozen old men and eight women, who wished to join us, were taken to H.Q. Our warriors gained two Sten guns and nine shotguns in that unprepared fight.

Our enemies' ignorance of things in the forest was their great disadvantage. When we saw them coming, knowing the path they would have to follow—for we used to stay at the forest fringes, observe and count the enemies before they approached the forest—we would then deploy ourselves along the path, out of sight, and when their last man passed our ambush we would open fire, killing some and forcing the rest into the depths of the forest. Once caught in the heart of the forest it was very unlikely that they would escape; often they would run into others of our fighters or be killed by the wild forest rhinos or buffalo.

When, as sometimes happened, one or two Government soldiers escaped from the forest and returned to camp, reporting about the ambush, reinforcements were often rushed to the spot where the fighting had occurred with the intentions of collecting guns and their injured comrades. Knowing these reinforcements were coming we would usually move a mile or two from the place of ambush toward the reserve and deploy again along the paths we suspected the Government forces would follow. Not suspecting that we would come closer to their base and the reserves, these forces often walked straight into another ambush similar to the first.

Another way in which our fighters trapped the security forces was to go out of the forest and then march single file singing back into the forest, leaving a very clear track for Government to follow. They would then circle back and lie in wait for their trackers and forces to come along the path which they had prepared for ambush.

Many encounters were those in which the Government forces followed livestock, thinking that the camp would be far away inside the dense forest and perhaps that they would find us slaughtering the animals and even making a lot of noise which would make them detect our presence. We always had our ambushers in such tracks for a distance of at least five miles from the camp.

In successful such encounters indicated above, we gained a great deal of arms and ammunition. The other sources were raiding camps and posts and ambushing individual personnel in the reserves and towns, raiding European homes, stealing guns, buying from police, military, Home Guards, and from Europeans and Indian traders and opportunists. Among the Government servicemen were our members and sympathizers who supplied us with ammunition free of payment. When our members were issued with arms and ammunition by the Government in order to join the Home Guards, some of them fled to the forest with all their supplies. Bullets had become token payment [from security force personnel] to prostitutes who later sent them to our warriors. . . .

IX. Counterinsurrection in Kenya

FRANK KITSON

*Frank Kitson is one of the best British
specialists on counterinsurrection and has
operated in Malaya, Cyprus, Kenya,
Aden, and other countries. In the following
pages he relates how he and his group
"turned" some Mau Mau, who then helped
commandos destroy part of the leadership
of the movement by taking advantage of its
organizational weaknesses.*

. . . One day, toward the end of March 1954, we were interrogating a prisoner called George, who had been captured by the Kikuyu Guard in an action with a gang near the forest edge. We were not having much success with the interrogation because George kept telling lies and we did not know when he was doing so. One of the secrets of effective interrogation is of course to know the answer to most of the questions asked so as to trip the prisoner up when he lies. After a time the prisoner becomes resigned to telling the truth because he does not want to be caught out in his lies too frequently, and it is then that the interrogator slips in the questions which he particularly wants answered truthfully. Unfortunately we did not know enough about George and his former friends to work this system effectively.

Then I remembered that some weeks earlier we had found a book on the body of a gang member killed in the same general area from which George had come and which contained details of men and weapons. Thinking that this book might refer to George's gang, I shouted in English to the clerk who was sitting at the far end of the room to throw it to me, and I caught it as

Reprinted by permission of Faber and Faber Ltd. from *Bunch of Five* by Frank Kitson (1977).

it came over George's head. George had not noticed the clerk, who had not been in the room when we had started the interrogation; nor had he understood what I had said. All that he knew was that I had said a few incomprehensible words and a book, which he imagined to be in the possession of his gang leader deep in the forest, had suddenly appeared out of thin air and was going to be used to prove him a liar. To his mind this represented strong magic, and from that moment on he was my man, whose sole aim was to do all possible to help me.

After completing the interrogation, we took George out on a patrol and he pointed out several huts near the forest edge where his gang used to go for supplies. He went into one, pretending to be still in the gang, and the owner gave him some interesting bits of news. Over the next few days we did the same thing in other areas where George's gang was known to work, making up a suitable story each time to account for George's presence. On one occasion a contact made in this way told George that a supply group from his gang was lying up nearby. George went and met them and led them back to where we lay in wait, so that we were able to engage them with our weapons. In the subsequent skirmish we killed or captured all the members of this group. We had in fact done something far more important than that: we had at last broken through the great divide and had developed background information—represented by George's knowledge of a supporter's identity—into contact information.

Eric Holyoak was the man chiefly responsible for exploiting this breakthrough when eventually it came. Because he had been considered too young to be a Field Intelligence Assistant, he had been designated as the interrogator for my area. In order to fulfil this function efficiently he had collected together eight loyal Kikuyu to act as guards for any prisoners that might be passed to him for interrogation. These were the men who had built the huts around my house and who had fortified the whole complex as a defended post. He had also been involved in taking George out on his early patrols and had been responsible for thinking up the stories George told to his contacts. Eric soon found that there were grave difficulties in making up convincing stories to account for the presence of one stray gang member wandering around on his own, so George taught our team of loyal Kikuyu to dress and act like Mau Mau. Eric would go with George and some or all of our team and hide near a known gang supporter. He would then send George and the team, all of whom were acting as Mau Mau, to talk to the supporter, who might in turn put them into contact with a group from a real gang. The team would then talk to the gang before returning to Eric, who could direct a military or police patrol onto them or just note down the information for future use if that seemed more satisfactory.

Soon after we had started doing this, our team fell in with a real gang before Eric had broken away and taken cover, but in the dark the real gang failed to notice his presence. Realizing that he would soon be discovered, he ordered his team to attack the real gang, which being taken by surprise was easily overcome. From this incident we reckoned that, if we disguised ourselves with face blacking and wigs and if we put some yellow dye in our eyes, we could pass as Africans in the dark and accompany our team. This would be advantageous from the point of view of getting good firsthand information. Thus was born the pseudo-gang system, which we enlarged over the coming months, recruiting additional exterrorists like George as we went along. Sometimes I accompanied Eric on these operations in order to get firsthand experience, but I was rather a liability because of my uncertain grasp of the language and he never exactly welcomed the help that I so anxiously proferred. . . .

Near the area in which the gang operated were a number of farms which had no Mau Mau committee on them because they had all been arrested some months earlier. Eric decided to introduce a pseudo-gang, which would tell the laborers that they had been forced out of their normal area in Kiambu. Our gang would ask for support and encourage the formation of the normal chain of committees to provide it. Once the system was operating freely, Eric would arrest all the supporters of the real gang from the other group of farms. He hoped that the real gang would be forced into getting supplies from the committees that he had set up to support our pseudo-gang. Our gang would then be well within its rights to demand a meeting with the terrorists in order to coordinate operations.

The early stages of the operation went well. Our pseudo-gang found the laborers in the selected area only too willing to provide support, and the supporters of the real gang were removed according to plan. We then suffered a setback because the real gang went to the Fort Hall Reserve instead of moving into the area we had prepared for them. Luckily they came back after a few days and made contact with the new committees. Ten days later one of our men met three of theirs in the hut of a leading supporter. On this occasion it was arranged that the leader of our group, with a bodyguard of three, should at last meet the real gang. The matter being discussed between Eric and myself was the composition of the team to go to the meeting, which was due to take place the following night. The leader would have to be George, and the Thika Field Intelligence Assistant, suitably dressed up, would be the second member. These two had been part of the pseudo-gang that had built up the committees and were known to the supporters. Eric had agreed to go along to keep the Field Intelligence Assistant company, and he had undertaken to provide a good man from our team to make up the number. We ran through the names of our men to see who would be the most suitable, but there seemed to be a snag to each one.

We had finished eating and were still undecided when an African came wandering round from behind the house. He was carrying a dustbin lid full of posho, which he was scattering on the ground for the chickens. He wore a khaki shirt hanging outside a ragged pair of shorts; he looked undernourished, and his legs, which were swollen, were covered with jungle sores. His hair hung to his shoulders in the plaits of the hard-core terrorist; his nose was flat and wide, and he had huge, gentle eyes that were completely out of keeping with his general appearance. His name was Kamau, and when he saw us at the table he gave us a nervous but friendly smile. Kamau had been captured about a week earlier during a battle in the forest, and we had kept him on after his interrogation was finished to see whether he would be suitable for use in pseudo-gangs. For the first few days he had been confined, but he was now being allowed to walk around the compound by himself so as to get the feeling that we trusted him. In a week or two he would go out with another member of our team, visiting low-grade informers, and then when his reliability was proved he would go on his first pseudo-operation. That would have been the normal program, at any rate.

Eric suddenly said that he would take Kamau as the fourth member of the party. . . .

Soon after 8 P.M. they went to Thika and met the Field Intelligence Assistant who was running the operation. A police patrol commanded by a mutual friend of theirs was going to help round up the terrorists because the soldiers who had originally been given the task had been called away to help chase a big gang in the north of Kiambu District. That at any rate was Eric's story, and I did not press him on the subject. The police inspector knew where and when the meeting was to take place and intended to surround the hut. With a bit of luck the terrorists would surrender if they saw that they were outnumbered and in a hopeless position. We always made simple plans because experience had shown that anything elaborate could be relied on to miscarry. Also by leaving lots to luck we did not expect events to follow any particular course so we were less alarmed by what actually happened.

Our party drove away from Thika and left the Landrover about three miles away from where the meeting was due to take place. From there the men moved off on foot, with George leading, followed by the Thika Field Intelligence Assistant, Kamau, and Eric, in that order. George had a pistol stuck in his belt, and he carried a kiboko. Kamau had a simi, and the two Europeans each carried Mau Mau homemade guns. It was a clear, still night with a strong moon, and although it had been dark for nearly three hours it was still quite warm. The men walked fast and silently between row after row of coffee bushes. The moon made long shadows of the men and the bushes, giving rise to the illusion that four giants were gliding noiselessly through a forest. Once they left the coffee bushes for about a quarter of a mile and walked through some grass by a bit of swampy land where thousands of crickets and frogs were disturbing the night with their clamor. Soon they were back in the coffee bushes, and the silence seemed all the more profound by contrast.

Almost before they realized it they had arrived on the edge of a grass clearing. Thirty yards away a dozen conical huts with thatched roofs were outlined in the moonlight against a background of banana trees. According to recent regulations, African labor lines should have been surrounded by a strong perimeter fence, but on this farm the "Bwana" had not yet got round to completing the task. Our men sank down on the grass while George slipped out of the shadows and walked to the hut on the end of the line. He scratched on the door and was admitted almost at once.

To the men waiting outside the next twenty minutes seemed like an hour. Something might have gone wrong and the gang failed to appear. Alternatively they might be in the hut and be unconvinced by George, in which case they would probably be taking him apart. All the time the moon shone down and the tension rose, but the men had to keep still and quiet while the sweat cooled on their backs. Eventually the door opened and a form slid out into the shadow of the hut. Thinking it was George, Eric was about to move but stopped himself just in time. The man passed less than five yards away and disappeared into the darkness. Nothing more happened.

Then before they realized it, George was with them again. It transpired that only one member of the gang had been in the hut when George arrived; the rest were waiting a few hundred yards away. The terrorist had been suspicious, but George thought that he had convinced him. He had now gone to fetch his friends. Meanwhile our team was to go into the hut where two members of the committee were waiting.

So far so good, although the situation was not altogether satisfactory. For one thing the gang might not be convinced, in which case our men would be hopelessly trapped once they went inside the hut. Another hazard was that the gang supporters might become suspicious before the gang arrived. They had seen George often enough, but they had not met Kamau or Eric before. Finally, the preliminaries had taken longer than had been expected and the police might arrive before the gang assembled, or they might all arrive at the same time, which would give rise to an appalling shambles. Despite these considerations there was only one thing to do, and the four men went into the hut.

Luckily it was very dark inside. George and the two committee men sat on stools round the glowing remains of the fire in the center of the floor. They did all the talking while the other members of our party squatted in silence up against the wall as befitted the bodyguard of a gang leader. For the first time since his capture Kamau seemed to be entirely at ease and enjoying himself.

Five minutes later the gang appeared. No one had heard a whisper or the snap of a twig. Although momentarily expected, their arrival produced the effect of an electric shock. These were the people we had been hunting for so long, but as they crowded in through the door and squatted down on the floor it was an open question as to who was hunting whom. Altogether eleven terrorists had turned up. Of the other four, there was a good chance that two or three were away, so that only one would have been left outside as a sentry. Of the men in the hut, two had pistols, three had rifles, and the rest had home-made guns or simis. The first few minutes were taken up with formal greetings between George and the leader of the real gang, but then they got down to business.

Inside the hut, as the talks went on, conditions were quite disgusting. Smoke from a dozen cigarettes and from the fire mingled with the smell of food and of the men themselves. Visibility was down to a few inches. Under these circumstances it was difficult to think clearly, and decisive action by anyone, pressed together as they were like sardines in a tin, would be very difficult.

Unlike most settlers Eric knew a bit of Kikuyu as well as Swahili, so he was able to follow the gist of the discussion. He knew that George and the gang leader would go round and round the main purpose of the meeting for a long time before actually grasping the nettle, because this is the Kikuyu way of approaching a problem. At the same time he soon became aware that the negotiations were not going well. They had got on to the explosive subject of whether the Mau Mau in Kiambu or Fort Hall were contributing most to the movement. Our pseudo-gang and therefore George represented terrorists from Kiambu, whereas the real gang was composed of men of Fort Hall.

At one moment it seemed as though the issue would give rise to a free fight, but then a strange thing happened. Kamau had edged his way forward so that he was sitting between George and the gang leader, but slightly behind them. He now took a hand in the conversation, and, although he talked quietly and slowly compared with the other two, it soon became clear that he spoke as one having authority. As the minutes ticked by, the tension relaxed and friendship was restored. It seemed as though everyone wanted to be on Kamau's side, so there was no longer any point in having an argument. Watching from the wings Eric got the feeling that Kamau had forgotten that he was working for us and was back with the terrorists in spirit as well as in body.

Suddenly this newfound harmony was shattered by two terrific bangs followed by prolonged and piercing screams. Then the door of the hut flew open and the police inspector stood in the opening, submachine gun at the ready.

Our own men who had been expecting the interruption were none the less frightened by what had happened. The real gang members were naturally terrified. Kamau was the first to collect his wits: he kept shouting out that all was lost and urged surrender. The terrorists would undoubtedly have done so without delay had it not been for their leader, who raised his pistol to fire. At the same instant George pitched him forward into the fire and Kamau jumped on his back, thrusting his face down into the red-hot embers. His command to fight changed abruptly into a yell of agony.

For the next few moments all hell was let loose. The police inspector was followed into the hut by his askaris, who laid about them with their rifle butts, roaring with excitement. All our men received bruises, and the unfortunate George was knocked unconscious. Eventually order was restored and the prisoners secured. Outside in the moonlight two policemen bent over an African who was lying on the ground. His shrieks had given way to a persistent low moaning as a pool of blood seeped slowly out of his body into the grass. It was the sentry, and he died within a few minutes.

That was the end of Eric's story. There was no doubt that the operation had been an immense success, and the credit was due to the Thika Military Intelligence Officer who had planned it and to the Field Intelligence Assistant who had carried it out. Credit was also due to Eric for the part he had played and in particular for his selection of Kamau as backup for George. . . .

I knew Kamau's history well enough. He had been born and had grown up on a European farm in the Rift Valley, but when the Emergency started he and his parents had been sent back to that part of the Reserve from which the family had emigrated years before Kamau was born. They went to live in a seven-acre farm belonging to Kamau's cousin, but the farm could barely support the cousin's family let alone any extra. From all the country round about the young men were flocking off to join the gangs in the forest, and when Kamau received a summons he went without regret. While still in the Rift Valley Kamau had taken the first Mau Mau oath, which was designed to gain the support of all members of the tribe (this was the oath we had been administering earlier in the evening). He had not been particularly keen to do so, but the only person who had refused flatly was murdered, and in any case Kamau did not disapprove of the Mau Mau aim of getting back land stolen from the tribe by Europeans. He had no means of knowing that the land issue was largely bogus and was being exploited by African politicians for their own purposes.

When he joined the gang he took the batuni oath, reserved for the fighters, and was subjected to further propaganda in the form of songs that the terrorists sang, extolling their political leaders and expressing their determination to liberate the sacred soil. The gang lived deep in the forest, received ample support from the Reserve, and did very little. Sometimes they debouched from their hideout, burned a few huts, and murdered any supporters of the Government they could find. It was a good life. Later on, as a result of operations by the Security Forces, the gang found it was getting less support from the Reserve and was frequently obliged to move camp.Some members were killed, and others became ill from lack of a suitable diet and from constant exposure to the weather. Long before he was captured Kamau had begun to wonder whether the Mau Mau were ever likely to achieve anything by their actions. When he reached our post and started talking to our team, his doubts were confirmed. Whatever else happened the Mau Mau were obviously not going to beat the Kikuyu Guard, backed up by the police and the British army. Kamau decided that the best thing for the Kikuyu was to stop fighting and try and achieve their aspirations in conjuction with the colonial Government. He had nowhere in particular to go, so he decided to stay with us. He also felt that by making himself useful he might avoid being hanged, which was the penalty for being a gang member. . . .

. . . I was gradually arriving at a conclusion that I have found to hold good in various different places. Briefly it is that three separate factors have to be brought into play in order to make a man shift his allegiance. First, he must be given an incentive that is strong enough to make him want to do so. This is the carrot. Then he must be made to realize that failure will result in something very unpleasant happening to him. This is the stick. Third, he must be given a reasonable opportunity of proving both to himself and to his friends that there is nothing fundamentally dishonorable about his action. Some people consider that the carrot and stick provide all that is necessary, but I am sure that many people will refuse the one and face the other if by doing otherwise they lose their self-respect. . . .

X.   Reminiscences of the Cuban Revolutionary War

ERNESTO CHE GUEVARA

*Ernesto Che Guevara, who died fighting in
Bolivia in 1967, was a doctor and a
revolutionary. He was not a military
theoretician. His work on guerrilla warfare
is primarily a how-to manual; his "foco"
theory and the prospects of armed struggle
in Latin America have proved to be wrong.
In his* Reminiscences, *from which this
account is taken, he relates events of the
war in Cuba from 1956 to 1958.*

The "Granma" Expedition

. . . It was already daylight when we landed in Cuba, at a
place known as Belic, on the Las Coloradas beach.

A coast guard cutter spotted us and telegraphed Batista's
army. No sooner had we disembarked and entered the swamp, in
great haste and carrying only the indispensable, than we were
attacked by enemy planes. Since we were walking through man-
grove-covered marshes, we were not visible, nor were we hit by
the planes, but the army of the dictatorship was now on our trail.

We took several hours to get through the swamp. We were
delayed in this by the irresponsibility and lack of experience of a
comrade who had claimed he knew the way. We were on solid
ground, disoriented and walking in circles, an army of shadows,

From Ernesto Che Guevara, *Reminiscences of the Cuban Revolutionary War,*
translated by Victoria Ortiz (New York and London: Monthly Review Press,
1968). Copyright 1968 by Monthly Review Press. Reprinted by permission of
Monthly Review Press.

of phantoms, walking as if moved by some obscure psychic mechanism. We had had seven days of continual hunger and sickness at sea, followed by three days on land that were even more terrible. Exactly ten days after leaving Mexico, at dawn on December 5, after a night's march interrupted by fainting, exhaustion, and rest stops, we reached a place known—what a paradox!—as Alegría [Happiness] de Pío. . . .

Alegría de Pío

Nothing remained of our equipment but a few rifles, cartridge belts, and some wet bullets. Our medical supplies had disappeared; our packs had for the most part been left in the swamps. The previous day we had walked by night along the border of the cane fields of Niquero sugar mill, which in those days belonged to Julio Lobo. We satisfied our hunger and thirst by eating cane as we walked, and, inexperienced as we were, we left the peelings behind. We found out years later that the enemy did not in fact need these careless clues to our presence, since our guide, one of the principal traitors in the Revolution, brought them to us. The guide had been given the night off, an error we were to repeat several times during the war, until we learned that civilians of unknown background were always to be closely watched when we were in danger zones. We should never have allowed our treacherous guide to leave.

At dawn on the fifth only a few of us could go a step further; our exhausted men could walk only short distances and then needed long rests. A halt at the edge of a cane field was ordered. Most of us slept through the morning in a thicket near the dense woods.

At noon we became aware of unusual activity. Piper Cub planes as well as other military and private aircraft began to circle in the vicinity. Some of our men were calmly cutting and eating cane as the planes passed overhead, without thinking how visible they were to the low-flying aircraft.

As the troop's doctor, it was my job to treat the men's blisters. I think I remember my last patient on that day. He was Humberto Lamotte, and, as it turned out, it was his last day on earth. I can still see his tired and anxious face as he moved from our primitive clinic toward his post, carrying the shoes he could not wear.

Comrade Montané and I were leaning against a tree, talking about our respective children; we were eating our meager rations—half a sausage and two crackers—when we heard a shot. In a matter of seconds, a hurricane of bullets—or at least this is what it seemed to my anxious mind during that trial by fire—rained on the troop of eighty-two men. My rifle was not of the best—I had deliberately asked for it because a long asthma attack during the crossing had left me in a deplorable state and I did not want to waste a good weapon. I do not know exactly when or how things happened; the memories are already hazy. I do remember that, during the cross fire, Almeida—Captain in those days—came to ask for orders, but there was no longer anyone there to give them. As I found out later, Fidel tried in vain to regroup his men in the nearby cane field, which could be reached simply by crossing a small clearing. The surprise attack had been too massive, the bullets too abundant. Almeida went back to take charge of his group. At that moment a comrade dropped a cartridge box at my feet. I pointed questioningly to it, and the man answered me with a face I remember perfectly, for the anguish it reflected seemed to say, "It's too late for bullets," and he immediately left along the path through the cane field (he was later murdered by Batista's thugs). This was perhaps the first time I was faced with the dilemma of choosing between my dedication to medicine and my duty as a revolutionary soldier. At my feet were a pack full of medicines and a cartridge box; together, they were too heavy to carry. I chose the cartridge box, leaving behind the medicine pack, and crossed the clearing that separated me from the cane field. I distinctly remember Faustino Pérez kneeling on the edge of the field, firing his machine pistol. Near me a comrade named Arbentosa was walking toward the plantation. A burst of gunfire, nothing special about it, hit us both. I felt a terrible blow on the chest and another in the neck and was sure I was dead. Arbentosa, spewing blood from his nose, mouth, and an enormous wound from a .45 bullet, shouted something like, "They've killed me," and began to fire wildly, although no one was visible at that moment. From the ground I said to Faustino, "They've got me" (but I used a stronger expres-

sion). Still firing, Faustino glanced at me and told me it was
nothing, but in his eyes I read a sentence of death from my
wound.

I stayed on the ground; following the same obscure impulse as
Faustino, I fired once toward the forest. I immediately began to
wonder what would be the best way to die, now that all seemed
lost. I remembered an old story of Jack London's in which the
hero, knowing that he is condemned to freeze to death in the icy
reaches of Alaska, leans against a tree and decides to end his life
with dignity. This is the only image I remember. Someone, crawling near me, shouted that we'd better surrender, and behind me I
heard a voice, which I later learned belonged to Camilo Cienfuegos, shouting back: "Here no one surrenders . . . ," followed by
an oath. Agitated and short of breath, Ponce approached me. He
had a wound, apparently through the lung. He told me he was
wounded, and, indifferently, I showed him that I was also. Ponce
continued dragging himself toward the cane field, together with
the unwounded men. For a moment I was alone, stretched out
waiting for my death.

Almeida came over to me and urged me to move. In spite of
my pain, I did so, and we entered the field. There I saw our
comrade Raúl Suárez near a tree, his thumb shattered by a bullet
and Faustino Pérez bandaging it for him. After this everything
became confused. The light planes flew low over us, firing a few
shots from their machine guns. This only added to the Dantesque
and grotesque scenes around us: a stout guerrillero trying to hide
behind a single stalk of sugar cane; and another, without really
knowing why, crying out for silence in the midst of the tremendous uproar.

A group was formed, led by Almeida and including Lieutenant
Ramiro Valdés (now a major), comrades Chao and Benítez, and
myself. With Almeida at the head, we crossed the last row in the
cane field in order to reach a small sheltering forest. At that
moment we heard the first shouts of "Fire!" from the cane field,
and columns of smoke and flames rose from it; I am not sure of
this, for I was thinking more of the bitterness of our defeat and
the imminence of my death than of the specific incidents of the
battle. We walked until night prevented us from going any further, and we decided to sleep huddled together. We were attacked by mosquitoes, tortured by thirst and by hunger. Such was

our baptism of fire on December 5, 1956, in the district of Niquero. Such was the beginning of what would become the Rebel Army. . . .

On the March

The first fifteen days of May were days of continual marching. At the beginning of the month, we were on a hill close to El Turquino; we crossed regions which later were the scenes of many revolutionary victories. We passed through Santa Ana and El Hombrito; later on, at Pico Verde, we found Escudero's house, and we continued until we reached the Loma del Burro. We were moving eastward, looking for the weapons which were supposed to be sent from Santiago and would be hidden in the region of Loma del Burro, close to Oro de Guisa. One night during this two-week journey, while going to carry out a private necessity, I confused the paths and was lost for three days until I found the troop again in a spot called El Hombrito. At that time I realized how lucky it was that we were each carrying on our backs everything necessary for individual survival: salt, oil, canned foods, canned milk, everything required for sleeping, making fire, and cooking, and also a compass, on which I had relied very heavily until then.

Finding myself lost, the next morning I took out the compass, and, guiding myself with it, I continued for a day and a half until I realized that I was even more lost. I approached a peasant hut, and the people directed me to the rebel encampment. Later we found that in such rugged territory a compass can only give a general orientation, never a definite course; one has either to be led by guides or to know the area oneself, as we later knew it when I was operating in that same region.

I was very moved by the warm reception that greeted me when I rejoined the column. When I arrived they had just held a people's trial in which three informers were judged, and one of them, Nápoles, was condemned to death. Camilo was the president of that tribunal.

At that period I had to perform my duties as a doctor, and in each little village I set up my consulting station. It was monotonous, for I had few medicines to offer and the clinical cases in the Sierra were all more or less the same: prematurely aged and toothless women, children with distended bellies, parasitism, rickets, general avitaminosis—these were the marks of the Sierra Maestra. . . .

The guerrilla group and the peasantry began to merge into one single mass, without our being able to say at which moment on the long revolutionary road this happened, nor at which moment the words became profoundly real and we became a part of the peasantry. As far as I'm concerned, those consultations with the *guajiros* of the Sierra converted my spontaneous and somewhat lyrical resolve into a force of greater value and more serenity. Those suffering and loyal inhabitants of the Sierra Maestra have never suspected the role they played as forgers of our revolutionary ideology. . . .

One Year of Armed Struggle

By the beginning of 1958 we had been fighting for more than a year. A brief recapitulation is necessary—of our military, organizational, and political situation, and of our progress.

Concerning the military aspect, let us recall that our troops had disembarked on December 2, 1956, at Las Coloradas Beach. Three days later we were taken by surprise and routed at Alegría de Pío. We regrouped ourselves at the end of the month and began small-scale actions, appropriate to our current strength, at La Plata, a small barracks on the banks of the La Plata river, on the southern coast of Oriente.

During this period between the disembarkation and prompt defeat at Alegría de Pío and the battle of El Uvero, our troop was composed primarily of a single guerrilla group, led by Fidel Castro, and it was characterized by constant mobility. (We could call this the nomadic phase.)

Between December 2 and May 28, the date of the battle of El Uvero, we slowly established links with the city. These relations during this period were characterized by lack of understanding on the part of the urban movement's leadership of our importance as the vanguard of the Revolution and of Fidel's stature as its leader.

Then two distinct opinions began to crystallize regarding the tactics to be followed. They corresponded to two distinct concepts of strategy, which were thereafter known as the *Sierra* and the *Llano*. Our discussions and our internal conflicts were quite sharp. Nevertheless, the fundamental concerns of this phase were survival and the establishment of a guerrilla base. The peasantry's reactions have already been analyzed many times. Immediately after the Alegría de Pío disaster there was a warm sentiment of comradeship and spontaneous support for our defeated troop. After our regrouping and the first clashes, simultaneously with repressive actions by the Batista army, there was terror among the peasants and coldness toward our forces. The fundamental problem was: If they saw us they had to denounce us. If the army learned of our presence through other sources, they were lost. Denouncing us did violence to their own conscience and in any case put them in danger, since revolutionary justice was speedy.

In spite of a terrorized or at least a neutralized and insecure peasantry that chose to avoid this serious dilemma by leaving the Sierra, our army was entrenching itself more and more, taking control of the terrain and achieving absolute control of a zone of the Maestra extending beyond Mount Turquino in the east and toward the Caracas Peak in the west. Little by little, as the peasants came to recognize the invincibility of the guerrillas and the long duration of the struggle, they began responding more logically, joining our army as fighters. From that moment on, not only did they join our ranks, but they provided supportive action. After that the guerrilla army was strongly entrenched in the countryside, especially since it is usual for peasants to have relatives throughout the zone. This is what we call "dressing the guerrillas in palm leaves." . . .

This was a period of consolidation for our army, lasting until the second battle of Pino del Agua on February 16, 1958. It was characterized by deadlock: we were unable to attack the enemy's fortified and relatively easily defended positions, and the enemy did not advance on us.

Our zone of operations was to be broadly extended when Pino del Agua was attacked for the second time by our entire troop, under the personal command of Fidel. Two new columns were formed, the "Frank País, "commanded by Raúl, and Almeida's column. Both had come out of Column One, commanded by

Fidel, which was a steady supplier of these offshoots, created for the purpose of establishing our forces in distant territories. . . .

In this brief sketch of the country's struggle during the course of a year we must mention the activities, generally fruitless and culminating in unfortunate results, of other groups of fighters.

March 13, 1957, the Student Directorate attacked the [Presidential] Palace in an attempt to bring Batista to justice. In that action a choice handful of fighters fell, headed by the president of the F.E.U.—a great fighter, a real symbol of our young people, "Manzanita" Echeverría.

A few months later, in May, a landing was attempted. It had probably already been betrayed before setting out from Miami, since it was financed by the traitor Prío. It resulted in a virtual massacre of all its participants. This was the "El Corintia" expedition, led by Calixto Sánchez, who was killed together with his comrades by Cowley, the assassin from northern Oriente, who was later brought to justice by members of our movement.

Fighting groups were established in El Escambray, some of them led by the 26th of July Movement and others by the Student Directorate. The latter groups were originally led by a member of the Directorate who betrayed first them and then the Revolution itself—Gutiérrez Menoyo, today in exile. The fighters loyal to the Directorate formed a separate column that was later commanded by Major Chomón; those who remained set up the Second National Front of Escambray.

Small nuclei were formed in the Cristal and Baracoa mountains, which were sometimes half guerrilla, half belly-soldiers; Raúl cleaned them up when he invaded with Column Six. Another incident in the armed struggle of that period was the uprising at the Cienfuegos Naval Base on September 5, 1957, led by Lieutenant San Román, who was assassinated when the coup failed. The Base was not supposed to rise alone, nor was this a spontaneous action. It was part of a large underground movement among the armed forces, led by a group of so-called pure military men, untainted by the crimes of the dictatorship, which was penetrated by—today it is obvious—*yanqui* imperialism. For some obscure reason the rising was postponed to a later date, but the Cienfuegos Naval Base did not receive the order in time and, unable to stop the rising, decided to go through with it. At first they were in control, but they committed the tragic mistake of not heading for the Escambray mountains, only a few minutes distant from Cienfuegos, at a time when they controlled the entire city and had the means to form a solid front in the mountains. National and local leaders of the 26th of July Movement participated. So did the people; at least they shared in the enthusiasm that led to the revolt, and some of them took up arms. This may have created moral obligations on the part of the uprising's leaders, tying them even closer to the conquered city; but the course of events followed a line characteristic of this type of coup, which history has seen before and will see again.

Obviously an important role was played by the underestimation of the guerrilla struggle by academy-oriented military men, by their lack of confidence in the guerrilla movement as an expression of the people's struggle. Thus it was that the conspirators, probably assuming that without the aid of their comrades-in-arms they were lost, decided to carry on a fight to the death within the narrow boundaries of a city, their backs to the sea, until they were virtually annihilated by the superior forces of the enemy, which had mobilized its troops at its convenience and converged on Cienfuegos. The 26th of July Movement, participating as an unarmed ally, could not have changed the picture, even if its leaders had seen the outcome clearly, which they did not. The lesson for the future is: He who has the strength dictates the strategy.

Large-scale killing of civilians, repeated failures, and murders committed by the dictatorship in various aspects of the struggle we have analyzed point to guerrilla action on favorable terrain as the best expression of the technique of popular struggle against a despotic and still strong government. Guerrilla action is the least grievous for the sons of the people. After the guerrilla force was set up, we could count our losses on our fingers—comrades of outstanding courage and tenacity in battle, to be sure. But in the cities it was not only the resolute ones who died, but many among their followers who were not total revolutionaries, many who were innocent of any involvement at all. This was due to greater vulnerability in the face of repressive action.

By the end of this first year of struggle, a generalized uprising throughout the country was looming on the horizon. There were acts of sabotage, ranging from those which were well planned and carried out on a high technical level to trivial terrorist acts arising from individual initiative, leaving a tragic toll of innocent deaths and sacrifices among the best fighters, without their signifying any real advantage to the people's cause.

Our military situation was being consolidated, and the territory we occupied was extensive. We were in a state of armed truce with Batista; his men did not go up into the Sierra and ours hardly ever went down. Their encirclement was as effective as they could make it, but our troops still managed to evade them.

In terms of organization, our guerrilla army had developed sufficiently to have, by the year's end, elementary organization of provisions, certain minimal industrial services, hospitals, and communications services.

The guerrillero's problems were very simple: to subsist as an individual he needed small amounts of food, certain indispensable items of clothing, and medicaments; to subsist as a guerrilla force, that is, as an armed force in struggle, he needed arms and ammunition; for his political development he needed channels of propaganda. In order to assure these minimal necessities, a communications and information apparatus was required.

In the beginning the small guerrilla units, some twenty men, would eat a meager ration of Sierra vegetables, with chicken soup on holidays; sometimes the peasants provided a pig, for which they were scrupulously paid. As the guerrilla force grew and groups of preguerrilleros were trained, more provisions were needed. The Sierra peasants did not have cattle, and generally theirs was a subsistence diet. They depended on the sale of their coffee to buy indispensable processed items, such as salt. As an initial step we arranged with certain peasants that they should plant specified crops—beans, corn, rice, etc.—which we guaranteed to purchase. At the same time we came to terms with certain merchants in nearby towns for the supplying of foodstuffs and equipment. Mule teams were organized, belonging to the guerrilla forces. . . .

The problem of supplying ourselves with arms was another story. It was difficult to bring arms from the *llano;* to the natural difficulties of geographical isolation were added the arms requirements of the city forces themselves, and their reluctance to deliver them to the guerrillas. Fidel was constantly involved in sharp discussions in an effort to get equipment to us. The only substantial shipment made to us during that first year of struggle, except for what the combatants brought with them, was the remainder of the arms used in the attack on the Palace. These were transported with the cooperation of Babún, a large landowner and timber merchant of the zone. . . .

Our ammunition was limited in quantity and lacking in the necessary variety, but it was impossible for us to manufacture it or even to recharge cartridges in this first period, except for bullets for the .38 revolver, which our gunsmith would recharge with a little gunpowder, and some of the .30–06's, which were used in the single-shot guns (they caused the semi-automatics to jam and interfered with their proper functioning).

Certain sanitary regulations were established at this time, and the first hospitals were organized, one of them set up in the zone under my command, in a remote, inaccessible place, offering relative security to the wounded, since it was invisible from the air. But since it was in the heart of a dense forest, its dampness made it unhealthy for the wounded and the sick. This hospital was organized by Comrade Sergio del Valle. Drs. Martínez Páez, Vallejo, and Piti Fajardo organized similar hospitals for Fidel's column, which were improved during the second year of the struggle.

The troop's equipment needs, such as cartridge boxes and belts, knapsacks, and shoes were met by a small leather-goods workshop set up in our zone. When we turned out the first army cap I took it to Fidel, bursting with pride. It caused quite an uproar; everyone claimed that it was a *guagüero*'s cap, a word unknown to me until then.[1] The only one who showed me any mercy was a municipal councillor from Manzanillo, who was visiting the camp in order to make arrangements for joining us and who took it with him as a souvenir.

Our most important industrial installation was a forge and armory, where defective arms were repaired and bombs, mines, and the famous M-26 [Molotov cocktail] were made. At first the mines were made of tin cans and we filled them with material

[1]Guagüero is Cuban (and Caribbean) slang for "bus driver."

from bombs frequently dropped by enemy planes which had not exploded. These mines were very faulty. Furthermore they had a firing pin, which struck the detonator, that frequently missed. Later a comrade had the idea of using the whole bomb for major attacks, removing the detonator and replacing it with a loaded shotgun; we would pull the trigger from a distance by means of a cord, and this would cause an explosion. Afterward, we perfected the system, making special fuses of metal alloy and electric detonators. These gave better results. Even though we were the first to develop this, it was given real impetus by Fidel; later, Raúl in his new operations center created stronger industries than those we had during the first year of war.

To please the smokers among us we set up a cigar factory; the cigars we made were terrible, but, lacking better, we found them heavenly.

Our army's butcher shop was supplied with cattle that we confiscated from informers and *latifundistas*. We shared equitably, one part for the peasant population and one part for our troop.

As for the dissemination of our ideas, first we started a small newspaper, *El Cubano Libre,* in memory of those heroes of the jungle.[2] Three or four issues came out under our supervision; it was later edited by Luis Orlando Rodríguez. After him, Carlos Franqui gave it new impetus. We had a mimeograph machine brought up to us from the *llano,* on which the paper was printed.

By the end of the first year and the beginning of the second, we had a small radio transmitter. The first regular broadcasts were made in February 1958; our only listeners were Palencho, a peasant who lived on the hill facing the station, and Fidel, who was visiting our camp in preparation for the attack on Pino del Agua. He listened to it on our own receiver. Little by little the technical quality of the broadcasts improved. . . .

Help came in those days not only from the people in the neighboring villages; even the city bourgeoisie contributed equipment. Our lines of communication reached as far as the towns of Contramaestre, Palma, Bueycito, Las Minas de Bueycito, Estrada Palma, Yara, Bayamo, Manzanillo, and Guisa. These places served as relay stations. Goods were then carried on mule-

---

[2] A newspaper by this name was published by the *Mambís,* independence fighters against Spain in 1868–1878, and 1895.

back along hidden trails in the Sierra up to our positions. At times, those among our men who were in training but were not yet armed went down to the nearest towns, such as Yao or Las Minas, with some of our armed men, or they would go to well-stocked stores in the district. They carried supplies up to our retreat on their backs. The only item we never—or almost never—lacked in the Sierra Maestra was coffee. At times we lacked salt, one of the most important foods for survival, whose virtues we became aware of only when it was scarce.

When we began to broadcast from our own transmitter, the existence of our troops and their fighting determination became known throughout the Republic; our links began to become more extensive and complicated, even reaching Havana and Camagüey in the west, where we had important supply centers, and Santiago in the east.

Our information service developed in such a way that the peasants in the zone immediately notified us of the presence, not only of the army, but of any stranger; we were easily able to detain any such person while investigating his activities. Thus were eliminated many army agents and spies who infiltrated the zone with the purpose of prying into our lives and actions.

XI.

With the Guerrillas in "Portuguese" Guinea

GÉRARD CHALIAND

*The guerrilla struggle of Guinea-Bissau
(1963-1974) has been—with that of
Eritrea—the most important in Black
Africa. This text, which relates the overall
organization of the armed struggle, dates
from a visit the author made in May-June
1966. He accompanied Amilcar Cabral in
the liberated areas of northern
Guinea-Bissau.*

. . . We went to see the camp proper, three hundred yards
away behind a clump of trees. On the way, we passed the
kitchen, which had been set up under the protection of a giant
baobab tree. The fighters' daily meals were cooked over two
fireplaces. (The flames were extinguished at the first sign of an
air raid.) The food was mainly rice and was served in large pots
or enamel pans; the water was drawn from relatively clear
springs and kept in big gourds. We came into a clearing and saw
about fifty teenage girls, student nurses who had also been to
regular school. With them were some forty F.A.R.P. men in
khaki uniforms and plastic sandals, all armed with submachine
guns. They were lined up in four rows. Four bazookas, two
heavy machine guns, and a mortar were lying in front of them.
A hundred guerrillas, equipped with rifles, were standing at
attention beside the regular army men. The fighting men were
mostly very young, roughly between seventeen and twenty-five.

From Gérard Chaliand, *Armed Struggle in Africa: With the Guerrillas in "Portuguese" Guinea,* translated by David Rattray and Robert Leonhardt (New York
and London: Monthly Review Press, 1969). Copyright 1969 by Monthly Review
Press. Reprinted by permission of Monthly Review Press.

The camp was a spacious, well-sheltered cabin where the F.A.R.P. men slept on straw mattresses. The guerrillas had come from their own villages, which were all nearby. Further back was a cabin for the student nurses. Everyone observed complete silence as Amilcar Cabral walked up to talk to the troops. Throughout his speech, we could hear heavy guns in the distance.

"Comrades.

"I have already been to Maké; I have already seen quite a few of you. I am happy to be with you again and to find new faces. To be with a brother again is always a great pleasure, but here we are more than brothers. Two brothers may take different roads. We, members of the Party and fighters for our people, do not have two roads to follow, but one only: the road that leads to freedom and progress for our people.

"In our Party we have sworn to give our lives for the liberation of our people and the building of our country. For this reason we must have a clear picture of the struggle and its difficulties. Girls, women, *homem grande*—you are all sons and daughters of the people, and each of you must understand why we are fighting. It is time to put an end to the suffering caused by colonialism—but we must also put an end to the backwardness of our people. There is no point to our struggle if our only goal is to drive out the Portuguese. We want to drive them out, but we are also struggling to end the exploitation of our people, both by whites and by blacks.

"As far as we are concerned, no one has the right to exploit labor. We don't want women and children to continue living in fear. We want all the men and women in our country to be respected. We want to drive out the Portuguese and build. This work cannot be done by one person alone: it must be done by everybody, and, most especially, by those who understand the meaning of their actions. The people must work. A country in which everybody has a chance to work is a prosperous country, for work is what enables us to make progress. Every man and woman must learn that work is their first duty and that all the workers in the country are useful to the cause. I don't mean just the work of intellectuals or engineers; the jobs done by nurses, carpenters, and mechanics are also very important, but, as we see it, tilling the soil is the most important job of all.

"The country that we want to build is a country where people will work. Perhaps you're thinking to yourself: we've been working a long time and we have nothing to show for it. But you were working for the chiefs and the Portuguese. We're going to recover our whole country and work hard in it, but the beneficiaries of this work will be the workers themselves. We are fighting for justice; the product of labor must not be stolen. The only one more valuable than a worker is the one who works even harder. We are already in command in our country. But it means nothing to be in command if we lack schools and hospitals and if we don't manage to change living conditions in the rural areas—for in Guinea the rural areas are crucial. You must not think that we are already free. We are still at war. Of course, we have schools, nurses, and medical stations. We can already hold our heads high because of what the Party has helped us to do and because of what we have done by ourselves. We want our own labor to provide for all of the country's needs: that is what I was anxious to tell you. You already knew it, but it's good for you to hear it again. No one, including the leaders and myself, must forget this. A man must have a clear understanding of the struggle at all times.

"The armed struggle is spreading out all over our country. But in the liberated regions some zones are peaceful, whereas in others fighting takes place every day. This is not right. If ten of us go to the rice paddies and spend a whole day doing the work of eight men, we have no reason to be pleased with ourselves. The same thing applies to the struggle. There are ten of us, and we fight like eight. I've talked about this to Oswaldo and Chico. They told me our weapons were inadequate. I say that what is done with them is inadequate. We can always do more. Some people get used to war, and when that happens they're through. They load their rifles and go for a walk. They hear a motor on the river and don't use their bazooka—and the Portuguese boats get through. Once again, I say that we can do more. The Portuguese must be thrown out. I want to make one thing clear: we simply cannot allow the Portuguese boats to get through any more. I am going to talk about this a little later with your Party leaders, and all of us here will talk some more about it, too.

"You must understand that the leader doesn't have to be there in order for you to do your work. I have just come back from Boe—like some of the other Party leaders I have to move around a lot to see how our struggle is developing. Men and women worthy of the name don't need to be urged to perform their duty. They do it by themselves. Otherwise, what's the difference between them and a donkey who won't go forward unless he's driven? I can't be everywhere at once, and you shouldn't always be waiting for orders. Oswaldo and Chico don't have to tell you what needs to be done. We must be aware of the job and then do it. Every struggle plods on step by step, but there comes a time to carry it through to the end. Things are uneasy in our Africa: many peoples had hoped to manage their own affairs, but the colonialists who were leaving are now coming back. Having an African government doesn't mean that one is master of one's destiny. First our work and our wealth have to belong to us—to the people who work to create this wealth. There are others besides the Portuguese who don't want us to be masters in our own land. Once we are independent, they don't want us to be in charge. *They* want to be the leaders. But we're not going to let that happen to us. This is why we must defeat the Portuguese, for the others are their allies. Our Party leadership is strong and resolute, we have weapons, and the people are with us. We have everything we need to get rid of the Portuguese.

"The armed struggle is very important, but the most important thing of all is an understanding of our people's situation. Our people support the armed struggle. We must assure them that those who bear arms are sons of the people and that arms are no better than the tools of labor. Between one man carrying a gun and another carrying a tool, the more important of the two is the man with the tool. We've taken up arms to defeat the Portuguese, but the whole point of driving out the Portuguese is to defend the man with the tool. Teachers are important too. We can wage the struggle and win the war. But if, once we have our country back again, our people are unable to read and write, we will still have achieved nothing. I don't mean that those with an education are more important than the others; the entire people must learn how to read. They must learn how to read so they won't be deceived any longer. I do not speak of being deceived by the Portuguese. We no longer have anything to say to the colonialists. Our dialogue with the Portuguese is the armed struggle. We can already bear arms and speak freely in our country. Our victory is certain, but our struggle isn't really worthwhile unless we respect the people and unless we make it possible for girls like our nurses to be properly brought up and respected.

Our struggle is meaningless unless the people are not afraid of those who carry the guns. Our weapons are for use against the Portuguese and not against the people. We will win if everyone performs his duty fearlessly and with understanding. Our struggle will be triumphant if each of us understands that being a Party militant involves certain duties. Our struggle is hard. Our people say, 'Even eating is hard.' We must go on because nothing can stop our people's struggle. But one thing is even more important: we want every son of our land to acquire genuine political awareness. It's up to the Party militants and most especially their leaders to set an example.

"This year the Party will be ten years old. It's still a child, but we have already done a good deal. We've organized the people, we've armed ourselves, and we're going to defeat the colonialists, who used to be stronger than we were. Our Party isn't made up of one man or of its leaders. Many people think that I am the Party: there are others who think that Chico or Oswaldo are the Party. The Party is all those who understand the objectives of our struggle. And many do understand. This is why the Portuguese, the friends of the Portuguese, and even certain Africans want to destroy our Party. All these enemies won't be able to destroy our Party: they simply can't do it. Who can destroy our Party? Only we ourselves can, by our own acts. Every day we must ask ourselves whether what we are doing could endanger the Party. Those who help the Portuguese, of course, they are our enemies—we arrest them and kill them. But the destructive people in our own midst are even more dangerous.

"I am happy to see that your girls' organization is here today. Women belong in school, in the militia, and in village government. I hope you will have the courage and good health to carry the fight against the Portuguese through to the end. We may receive medicine, weapons, and all sorts of things, but nobody can send us crates full of courage. Supplying that is our own job. It was thanks to our courage that we were able to start the struggle, but we're going to need even more courage to win it. Tomorrow, our children will be proud not only of their freedom but also of the new foundations we have laid. Work well, comrades." . . .

Chico, age twenty-seven, political commissar for the northern interregion, speaks:

"We've held elections for a Party committee in each village of the liberated regions. We call it a *tabanca* [Creole for village] committee. In general, it is composed of three men and three women and is elected by the village assembly, in other words, by the entire adult population of the village. We explain beforehand the way in which they must get organized, the tasks they have to carry out, and, of course, the basic principles of the Party. Young people are often elected. The old people haven't always been happy to see their places in the village leadership taken over by the young. Almost all our fighters are young, too, of course. But then again, since everybody, old and young, had had enough of the Portuguese, even the old ones who at first dragged their feet finally came around. So anyhow, committee officers are elected by the villagers. We in the Party are consulted, and we decide to support a candidate on the basis of the work he has already accomplished for the Party and of the esteem in which the other peasants hold him. In principle, the peasants' choice is respected. If, in our opinion, they have chosen badly, we leave the candidate in office. We wait for the peasants to realize their mistake by themselves. Naturally, the Party reserves the right to remove those who use their prerogatives in their own interests. We don't want a new chieftainship system. A new committee is elected at the peasants' request, and elections are also held periodically just to avoid what you might call hardening of the arteries.

"The village committee has several tasks. At the present stage, one of the most important is to increase agricultural production, so that there will be plenty of rice for both families and fighters. The fighters also produce rice, millet, etc., but their food is supplied mainly by the village. We've created new collective fields so that the villagers can produce for the fighters. The village committee takes care of supervising and administering the work, and it also takes care of the militia. The militia consists of young people who are not F.A.R.P. fighters but guerrilla partisans with rifles and no uniforms. They are part of the village's self-defense group. In certain zones, they play an offensive role. They live in the village. The F.A.R.P. fighters, however, leave the village and are transferred from place to place according to the requirements of the struggle. Obviously, they are volunteers. They join us because of our political work in the villages. This work is done in the local languages. Around here, the village people speak Balante and Mandingo, and a certain number of peasants understand Creole. My own native language is Pepel, but I can't speak it because I always lived in Bissau. I've learned Balante and Mandingo in the course of the struggle.

"Political work means getting people to learn about the Party and explaining why we exist and what we want. We explain what colonialism means. At first, we explain that Guinea isn't Portugal and that we can govern ourselves without the Portuguese taking our livestock, without heavy taxes, and blows, and fear of the Portuguese. We explain that what's happening here isn't an act of God, and that it's already happened in a lot of other countries. We have to show our people that the world doesn't end at their villages. Our problem is to make them understand the present level of the struggle, the fact that the struggle doesn't concern just their village but all of Guinea, and that it's not simply a national but also an international struggle. We have to make them aware that in order to advance, *they* must guarantee the struggle's continuity, *they* must take charge of their own destiny by solving their problems on the village level, developing production, sending their children to school, and holding frequent meetings.

"In actual practice, meetings are regular as long as the Party is present. If the Party is not on the scene, meetings become fewer and farther between and finally stop altogether. Our people are just beginning to be free, and everything can't go on from one day to the next as the Party wishes. But bit by bit, there are signs of progress. In general, village committees meet two or three times a month. Even when it functions imperfectly, the village committee is respected because it's almost always made up of the best elements in the village. Of course, sometimes one of the committee members commits an error. In that case, he is removed. Recently, for instance, one of the neighboring villages had a problem about the rice that had been harvested and set aside for the fighters. One of the committee members appropriated it for his own profit. He was expelled from the committee, and someone else was elected to replace him. Depending on production, the villages give the fighters rice, palm-cabbage, corn, millet, and sometimes livestock when there is any available. The population feels protected by those who are doing the fighting. Some villages haven't seen any Portuguese in almost three years. The most difficult problem of all is getting the committee in motion—getting it to do what has to be done, and especially getting it to act much more often on its own initiative.

"We also have to give the fighters political training. The essential principle is that no difference must be created between the fighters and the people for whom they're fighting. We explain to them that our struggle is directed neither against the Portuguese people 'nor against white skin, that our enemies are all those opposed to our country's freedom, that there are Portuguese who are for us and Africans who serve the Portuguese, and that our weapons don't come from Africa but from countries where the people don't have black skin. Military training takes place at the same time as political training. We teach weaponry and the general principles of guerrilla warfare. But above all, there is actual field combat. There's no precise training period for a fighter: it's always coordinated with his concrete participation in combat. Political training, however, never finishes: that's why each unit has a political commissar. We also place great stress on discipline during and between combat engagements. We're very strict about alcohol and sexual relations.

"We explain to everybody, fighters and villagers alike, that our struggle is being waged not only to drive out the Portuguese but also to build and develop the country; that in order to be free, the people themselves must take charge of the country and that they must be the ones who profit from their labor. We explain that we need bridges, hospitals, and schools, and that tomorrow's construction will be the hardest phase of all. The people will have a new life, but only if they work for it. We have no intention of struggling now and relaxing later, because the things we hope to get won't come to us all by themselves. The outlook for the future is work, before everthing else: actually, work should assume top priority starting right now.[1]

"As far as the ethnic problems are concerned, the Party has devoted a lot of effort to them, and it alone could attempt to solve them correctly. These conflicts have just about disappeared in the course of the struggle against the Portuguese. Of course,

---

[1] The day before, when an old man complained about his hardships, Chico had said: "Since the day you were born, how much have you put together to leave your children? You're not going to leave anything, because the Portuguese have taken it all. The only inheritance you can leave your sons is freedom, and that's a great deal, because they can obtain everything else by working."

the Portuguese played the Fulah chiefs against the Party. The P.A.I.G.C. tried to explain the new situation to the Fulah population by demonstrating that it was in the Portuguese interest to support the chiefs in order to rule over all the rest of us. But there were many who didn't want to understand what we were saying, because they didn't want to lose what they already had. They have been considerably influenced and corrupted by the Portuguese. The Fulah chiefs fled to the cities for protection, and, although some Fulah elements joined the Party, others followed the customary chiefs.

"In 1963–64, there came a point at which the armed struggle reached a temporary stage of equilibrium and the Portuguese were using repressive methods to implant fear in the population. We explained that Portuguese colonialism was heaving its last gasps, and we increased our efforts to create a permanent state of insecurity. Since the end of 1964, the struggle on the battlefield has gone in our favor. At that time, certain Fulahs came to ask for the Party's protection. Of course, there are regions that we don't control, like the Balante coastal regions around Bissau, the Fulah highland regions, the Mandjak regions in the center, and the Felupe regions. But it's just a question of time—I mean, of getting enough cadres.

"In the present phase of the struggle, the essential task is to make the village committees function properly and to form section committees that will connect five or six villages. We've begun to set these up. According to the size of the villages, each section committee has ten to fifteen members. In addition, there is the necessary work of production. Of course, the major problem is still the armed struggle. We must continue to widen our encirclement of the Portuguese and begin the struggle in regions that have not yet been liberated. In order to begin the struggle in new areas successfully, we have to create a new relationship of forces. The first difficulty is the peasants' fear of Portuguese repression. In the Mandjak regions, where the struggle began about six months ago, the population has stopped frequenting the urban centers and now places itself under the protection of the fighters.

"We must first explain our struggle politically and make a precise study of the regional situation, which may or may not be favorable, depending on circumstances. We send in the F.A.R.P. only after completing this first task and only if it shows positive results. We prefer to send fighters who were born in the region and who speak its language. The people in charge are Guinean—and that's all that counts.

"After creating a new relationship of forces by virtue of our military action, we have to replace the colonial infrastructure with our own administrative and economic infrastructure, in order to affirm our presence and to take care of the population's elementary needs. That's why the people's stores are important. In the south, they function pretty well. Here, we need more.

"Our struggle has been successful because, two years before launching the armed struggle, Amilcar trained hundreds of cadres in Conakry and sent dozens of them to do the work of explanation and mobilization in the villages. When we began the struggle, we didn't have to hide from the Portuguese and the villagers, because the peasants informed us about every move made by the Portuguese troops. Since then, we have always taken precautions to avoid a split between the fighters and the population." . . .

Very early the next morning Cabral, Chico, Oswaldo, and a number of cadres set out for a Mandingo village three hours away.

We left to join them. For a few kilometers our route lay along the Bissora-Olosato road, which since 1963 had been cut in numerous places by the guerrillas. Big trees had been felled across it. During that period the guerrillas had had nothing but pistols, and they made ambush after ambush in order to get Portuguese weapons. The Portuguese have never since regained control of the road. Roughly ten kilometers from Morès we passed an immense clearing pockmarked with bomb craters and riddled with heavy automatic fire: the former site of the central base camp of the northern region, finally spotted by the Portuguese air force but evacuated before its destruction. A few kilometers further on we passed sentinels posted by the F.A.R.P. At a turn in the path, we suddenly came out into a clearing where a large crowd of peasants had gathered. At the sight of a white man there was a brief flurry of alarm among the women that was quickly brought under control by the soldiers. In the midst of the crowd, surrounded by Chico, Oswaldo, and Titina, stood Amilcar Cabral. He called for silence, showed his rifle, and said, "We are the ones who have the guns nowadays—nobody needs to be afraid. Not all whites are enemies. Whites who are on our side are our friends. The people who are afraid these days are the Portuguese, and they are afraid because we have the guns. And the guns we have are to serve our people."

The meeting, which had been going on for several hours, was about a village (actually a group of three Mandingo hamlets) where there had been "problems." Some 250 to 300 local people were there, the men on one side, the women and children on the other. The women, dressed in indigo robes, were seated; the men, standing, wore *boubous,* or loincloths, and short-sleeved shirts of the kind sold in Gambia. It was very hot and every face was streaming with sweat.

Amilcar resumed:

"As I was saying to you, we have got to open still more schools. But the schools are worth nothing if they change nothing. Why should a little girl go to school if afterward she must be married by force? I'm telling you that the Party is not going to tolerate any more of these transactions and business deals involving daughters. Soon we intend to remove the children from the base camp and place them back in their home villages. But they are not to be married off against their will. Some of the girls came to us at the base, as you well know, in order to avoid being married against their will. A woman should marry the man she has chosen and not one her parents have chosen for her.

"The women here have been doing what they could in production, and they deserve our respect for that. Meanwhile, a good many of the men have been content to go on trafficking. There are some who prefer trading in Gambia; others take their business to Casamance.[2] They buy and they sell, they sell and they buy, and finally they buy themselves a woman in order to put her to work. Now all that has got to stop. The land is good, there is no lack of rain. You have just got to get down to work. Every single man has got to work: the building of our country is not going to come from heaven. Everybody has got to work. The war is no excuse. The Balantes and Mandjaks are working, too. Our enemies are those who do not work. Here in your part of the country production has not been high enough. The Balantes are

[2] A market town in Senegal near the "Portuguese" Guinea border.

producing more and thus helping our struggle more. Here you must do as they are doing in the south of the country, where rice production has been so high that there is more than enough to go around. We can praise a person who works, but the work somebody did yesterday is not about to give him special privileges today. You have got to work every day. You have to work and keep on working. When I come back here, there has got to be rice and a lot of it. The only people who work around here are the women, and that has got to stop. They will help you and that's all. The only person who's got the right to complain that he doesn't have something is somebody who has worked and tried to get it. The Party provides guns; it provides nurses, doctors, and teachers; but it expects you to provide work. Now that we have liberated regions, we don't have to ask the Portuguese for a work permit, we don't have to pay them taxes anymore, there is no forced labor.

"Some people have come to see me and when they got home have been going around with a swelled head saying they'd been to see me. However, I am no better than anybody else. The only superiority around here is the superiority of work. But there are a lot of people who like to have chiefs and the customs that go with them. In a village when two or three people are elected to be responsible, the others get mad because they all want to be chiefs. But the Party is not a system of chieftainship; the Party is here to serve the people. A person with Party responsibility is not superior to anybody, and if he does a bad job he gets replaced. What is the Party in the last analysis? The Party is the people. If a person with Party responsibility does something wrong, it is up to you to say so and get him replaced. For us the people's opinion in these matters is extremely important, because the Party is fighting for the people.

"If certain people raise their hands against you and strike you in my name or in the Party's name, don't believe them. Tell your political commissar Chico and get them replaced. You have also got to get rid of this mania of everybody wanting to be a chief. The responsible Party person gives directions and that's all. He's not there to force anybody to do anything. Also, in every village you must have a people's militia. Don't be afraid of guns. Guns are there for our people to use against the Portuguese. And if some people work for the Portuguese, it is up to you to prevent them from doing any harm. If anybody is in favor of the Portuguese, he'd better go over to their side. Those who are on our side will have the country tomorrow and have no reason to be afraid of anybody.

"What I am asking is that you should work within the framework of what the Party needs. I am asking for higher production so that our fighters can be fed, and I am asking you to accomplish things on your own initiative because everybody must participate in the struggle. From now on we will have only soldiers in the base camps. The schools and the schoolchildren will be integrated with the villages. As for the soldiers, their job will be to attack the Portuguese every day. But the soldiers must never abuse the people. We must go on being united. Soldiers who turn their guns against the people are worse than the Portuguese. I have just returned from the region of Boe. We have had victories there. We have also had victories in Sao Domingos. Nothing can prevent us from winning now, but the people have got to help us as much as possible and keep us informed if we are going to finish this war really fast.

"There was a time when we said, 'We are about to start the armed struggle,' and some people did not believe us because we had no guns. Now we have liberated the whole of the Oïo region as well as half the country. We told the Portuguese government a long time ago that we were going to arm ourselves, and the Portuguese just laughed. They don't feel so much like laughing anymore. That's the difference between yesterday and today. We are going to win, but, if you produce more, you will hasten our victory. You must work, work, work, and never collaborate with the Portuguese, neither by having business dealings with them nor in any other way. As for the people on the Portuguese side, the Portuguese are going to drop them in the end. There are already some Portuguese who know they're finished here in Guinea, but they stay on only because of Angola and Mozambique. If every person has courage we are bound to win soon.

"And what about after our victory? What will happen afterward? We are not going to have people who steal others' labor then. Because it is not only whites who steal others' labor; blacks do it, too. But we won't have any more of that here. Everybody is going to work and enjoy the product of his labor. Now you've got to tell me if you really mean to get to work."

A great many hands were raised in agreement. Cabral then had three men and one woman elected for the purpose of discussing with him the concrete problems of the zone. A few peasants raised their hands and asked for seed. Two old men spoke and started to expatiate on their personal problems and on a quarrel that had arisen between them. Cabral interrupted them and asked them to come and see him afterward.

An *homem grande* got up and said, "People here need rice. Rice and clothing."

Without giving Cabral time to answer, another old man got up and said, "Our needs mean nothing. Petty questions mean nothing. Petty sacrifices mean nothing. We must unite all the sons of Guinea. When we were still unarmed, the whites came to steal our labor and we had nothing. And now we are doing nothing. Before, we produced more and fought harder. Now they leave us alone. They try to come in their cars, but they get blown up on the mines. But they still have their airplanes. And what are we doing? For several months the struggle has made no progress here. We have got to have as much heart as we did before if we are going to get rid of them for good and really win this war."

"I don't know any professors that can say it better than you do," said Cabral.

A woman got up and spoke: "I have been here since the beginning of the struggle. I have worked with the understanding that this was to liberate the people, so there would be no more slaps in the face, no more humiliations. There are a lot of people who went to Senegal as refugees after the Portuguese started bombing us. I lost one of my fingers" (she held up her mutilated hand), "but I don't feel like running. I worked in a base camp, and now I am working here. I want to stick with the struggle until we are free."

"It warms my heart to hear you," said Cabral. "I wish you all courage; take heart; my message is 'Work, and confidence in the Party!'" . . .

Very early one morning we left with Antonio Bana and half a dozen soldiers to visit two or three Balante villages. Sometime after seven o'clock two bombers passed overhead and dropped their bombs a few kilometers away as we continued our march. About fifteen kilometers from Morès, the Portuguese were trying to rebuild a bridge in order to make the Olosato-Bissora road usable again before the start of the rainy season, because supplies had had to be flown in by helicopter for the past few months. The heavy rains were due to start in about ten days. A couple of days earlier, F.A.R.P. bazookas had destroyed the part of the bridge the Portuguese had succeeded in rebuilding. The bombers were making frequent attacks in reprisal. In the course of our hike we heard numerous mortar explosions. After three hours on the road we passed through a Balante village that had been hit by bombs. The mud huts were gutted, and the trees surrounding them torn up. On the mud wall of one of these huts there was a drawing traced in black lines. It depicted a squad of eight men in formation, a truck with its driver, and beneath them three or four armed guerrillas. Two airplanes were shown diving on this scene, and three corpses were represented at the bottom of the picture.

"This," said Bana, "is one of the Portuguese' favorite spots. Whether the planes are going north or south, they always save one little bomb to drop here—just in passing."

We got a distinct view of the planes when we arrived in the first village. It was empty. There was no one but a little boy keeping watch over the village pigs. We went on toward the other village. There, too, almost all the inhabitants had left. The fear of being bombed and the distant sound of the bombs already dropped by the planes had made them leave.

We entered the village and found three women and an old man. Our arrival did not cause any surprise. Our guide, Antonio Bana, who had spent five years in the maquis, was well known and appreciated, especially for his sense of humor. It was a small village, its huts huddled together. The women were preparing palm-cabbage, crushing it with blows of the pestle. An old man was bringing firewood and laying it down. A few moments later, we heard the dull explosion of a bomb. The old man came up and greeted Bana, who spoke to him. The old man shook his head and started to speak:

"You see how things are now. The Portuguese are bombing us with their airplanes. They have killed people. But many of our young people have joined the guerrillas. Independence is something we are going to have; even if we don't get it, our children are going to get it and the Portuguese are going to leave our country.

"In the old days, we had forced labor. You had to work on road maintenance on the Mansaba-Bissora highway, and if you didn't work fast enough they flogged you. And when they did, they really laid it on. If you had two cows and they needed both, they would take both. You paid them taxes. A tax on everything. A tax on your wife—200 escudos. A man with several wives had to pay 50 escudos more for each extra wife. Sometimes they raised the taxes. The worse things got, the heavier they made that tax."

Now there were three planes and they were bombing much closer to where we were. We all left the village to take refuge in more heavily wooded terrain. Antonio brought along a big jug full of wine and pocketfuls of palm-cabbage. We took shelter to the sound of mortar fire that was to go on for several hours. There was nothing else to do but wait for night and calm.

So Antonio Bana, Party cadre, twenty-eight years old, told me the story of his life:

"At the beginning of my life, when I was thirteen, I worked as a houseboy for a white family in Bissau. I waited on the white man's son, served at table, ran errands, etc. I was making 150 escudos a month. One day I got to thinking, thinking about my life in the future. When I get married, I thought, how am I going to live with my wife on 150 escudos a month? After thinking it over, I decided to go out and learn to drive. An African truck-driver taught me how. But to become a driver you had to pass a test; you had to know how to read and write. And the Portuguese required an I.D. card, but since my parents were not *assimilados* I had no card. So I dropped my plans to become a truckdriver and went to work as a garage mechanic for a Portuguese boss.

"The boss had an Austin truck. When he saw I was a hard worker, he said, 'I'm going to let you drive my truck.' But he did not pay me like a regular driver with a proper license. One day he called me over and said, 'The truck is yours to drive.' I took it out, but first I asked him if I could get driving papers. He said no, but he could guarantee everything would be all right because the district commandant was a friend of his.

"I made trips inland to pick up consignments of peanuts. In order to get back to Bissau, I had a real licensed driver sitting next to me who would show his card and I would pass as his assistant. But other licensed drivers found out about it, and, since they were out of work themselves, they filed a complaint against me. Then the district commandant issued an order that persons without a card were not permitted to drive. And so my boss told me, 'You can't drive anymore.' So then I stayed at my job in the repair shop. I was a hard worker. The whites were free to do as they pleased. I had no right to talk back. At that time, they had the upper hand. And so it was that I worked with many white men but not one of them ever laid a hand on me because I knew how to live alongside white people: work hard and don't talk back. And when one white man had no more work for me, I would change my job and go work for another white man.

"One day—I had a friend and we roomed together—another friend came to our room and started talking. He said there was a Party. I didn't know what a 'Party' was. This friend explained that it was for independence, and the Party was created to fight against the Portuguese for the liberty of the people and to have a new life. Now I had always known the Portuguese were mistreating our people. When I was very small, I believed some people grew up white and others black, and it was the white skin that made them evil.

"When this friend finished telling us about it, we asked him questions. In a confused way, we had thought the same things ourselves. But when he explained them, everything became simple. We saw each other again several times. And that's how I became a volunteer fighting against the Portuguese.

"Since that time, I have given everything to the Party. The Party can do anything it wants with me. I worked for the Party and heard people talk about Cabral and Barbosa—that was around 1959—but I didn't know them. My job was to mobilize people. I arranged little meetings in places I knew, at first with people I could really trust, and I explained that the time had come to fight for our freedom and that the P.A.I.G.C. was engaged in this struggle for our people. One day Rafael Barbosa, the president, came, and I got acquainted with him. He explained the meaning of the struggle to me, and through him I came to understand many things. It was around that time that we were sent, me and some others, to the countryside to mobilize the peasants.

"We would try to get in touch with the village elders, the *homem grandes*. We did that because the old people have a lot of prestige. After that, the old men would explain things to the others. The oppression of the Portuguese was so heavy that they took us seriously, even though we were so young, and they would listen to us when we talked about independence. We explained what the Party is. The Balantes were the worst oppressed. They were always on the road gangs. They understood what we were talking about faster than any of the other tribes.

"Later on, when it came time to actually mobilize the people, Cabral made us play a game. One by one, we had to pretend, in front of him, that we were going into a village to talk to the *homem grande.* Everybody else would watch. If it wasn't right, if there was something wrong about it, Cabral would make us start all over until we found exactly the right openings and the right arguments. We would start over and over again until it came out right.

"Before going into a village to meet the *homem grande* we would try to find out all about him. You had to be very careful. So we would find out all about the old man's daily habits, his relations with the villagers, his relations with the Portuguese, etc. At first we never went into a village unless the *homem grande* was all right or, as the Mandingos say, a 'man of confidence.' If he was a man of confidence, then we went.

"You have to remember that the *homem grande* is not the village chief. The village chief is always an agent of the Portuguese, appointed by the Portuguese. The *homem grande*, however, is the oldest, the wisest, the most respected man in the village. The chief has nothing but administrative authority. The *homem grande* represents moral authority. Among my people we have more confidence in the words of the *homem grande* than in anything young people say. The *homem grande* is the center of every village's social life. Sometimes he and the village chief are friendly, but it is rare that the *homem grande* tells all the secrets of the village to the chief, because the chief is an outsider. That's how the Balantes are. And then sometimes the Portuguese take advantage of the prestige of an *homem grande* and appoint him village chief, on condition that he will work for them. The district chief is an outsider, too.

"The Portuguese impose a Muslim because the Muslims have more experience of chieftainship. Generally they impose a Mandingo on the Balantes. The district chief is not popular because he enforces the laws of the Portuguese administration. But these chiefs don't care because they have no tribal bonds with the population under them. And that is why mobilization turned out to be easiest among the Balantes.

"And so, after having found out what we could about the *homem grande,* we would arrive in a village dressed in the local style. The first thing I would do was to ask for the *homem grande.* Then, after going through the ceremony of salutation, I would ask to be granted his hospitality. The Balantes are an extremely hospitable people. The *homem grande* would answer my greeting and call for a meal to be prepared because he would expect me to stay to eat with him. It was very rare that both chicken and rice would be served. If there was only rice with some palmetto sauce, I would say, 'Papa, why aren't you giving me anything but rice? The Balantes are a hospitable people.'

"'I am poor. I don't have any chicken.'

"'How can that be, Papa? Do you mean that you have been working ever since you were born and you never had even a single rooster?'

"'Why are you asking me these questions, my son? Yes, I used to have cattle and sheep, but the white man took everything away with that tax.'

"'And are you happy, Papa, with what the white man has been doing?'

"'I'm not happy about it. But what can I do? They are powerful.'

"By this point I had had a chance to size up the old man. He had already said he didn't like what the colonialists were doing. I wasn't doing anything but asking questions; I hadn't yet said anything. But then I would push it further:

"'Papa, tell me, if something happened to come along that would make it possible for you to have a better life tomorrow, would you go along with it?'

"'I'd go along with it.'

"'Well then, you've got to get yourself ready. Right now there is a Party that is fighting against the Portuguese so that we can be free and so that if you work you can keep the fruit of your labor. If you have a son or a daughter, the Party will send them to school to get an education. But this is a secret you have to keep because if the Portuguese find out you know about it, they will kill you. That doesn't mean you can't talk about it to other people, but you have to tell it only to people you really have confidence in. Take me, for example; I have confidence in you, Papa, and that's why I came here, because I knew you were against what the Portuguese are doing to us.'

"After that, I would leave the village. I'd tell him that I would like to meet with him and a few trustworthy people from the village—outside the village in some quiet spot where I could talk to them.

"At that time, the Party was putting out leaflets. Every Party group was supposed to distribute leaflets in the city. The people living in the city come from the villages, and they often go back home for a visit. If one of them knew how to read, he was given the responsibility of explaining the leaflet to the people in the village. And since I would have already contacted the *homem grande* by the time the leaflet arrived with some other comrade, trust in the Party would grow. Also, it wasn't long after that that the Party started making radio broadcasts from Conakry in all the local languages. That gave people confidence and was very important. We had to make the peasants feel that the Party is strong, too, not just the Portuguese.

"The second time I came, the *homem grande* would summon the trustworthy people so they could meet me. He would say, 'Here are the people I explained everything you said to.' And he would introduce them to me, and I would say, 'Is there anything unclear in what the *homem grande* told you about our coming struggle? Ask me any questions you need to.'

"Often they would say, 'We are nothing but black men and don't even know how to make a match. The white man has guns and airplanes. How are we ever going to make him leave our country?' And I would answer, 'Our leaders created the Party, and they made it in spite of all kinds of difficulties, right in Bissau. You have to trust our leaders because soon they will have guns for us and with these guns we are going to fight the Portuguese.'

"Then after that I would ask them to explain what I had said to the other peasants of the village, so that the name of the Party and its existence would be known. In that way, people started waiting and expecting something to happen. Then I would go back to town. I was in contact with Barbosa, who was sending reports to Cabral.

"A little later, I would ask that a village meeting be held. I would explain to the peasants what the Party was and why we were fighting. I said that we wanted to get rid of the forced labor, the floggings, the excessive taxes, the theft of livestock. Then there would be a discussion period. I had to find out through discussion which people would be capable of becoming Party militants, and if the village agreed I would ask them to assume Party responsibility in the village. At the very beginning there was generally only one person who could take on such a role, and that was almost always an *homem grande*. The *homem grandes* were accustomed to assuming responsibilities, they knew how to speak in public, and, as the moral leaders of their communities, they knew what Portuguese colonialism was because they had collided with it often enough. Then we would summon the responsible people out into the bush and explain to them what they were supposed to say to the people in their villages.

"Later on, I went to Conakry to the school for Party cadres where I took a course from Amilcar Cabral. At that time there were seven of us. That was in 1961. There were Chico, Oswaldo, Nino, who is now in charge of the southern region of the country, then Domingo Ramos, Constantino, and Texeira. They had just got back from a year of military training. Cabral first gave us a short course in political matters and then explained the tasks we had to accomplish and how we were to get them done. Then he assigned the zones in which we were to undertake political agitation and activity.

"When I came back here, I felt stronger, more confident. But the action had developed to the point where we were becoming conspicuous, and it wasn't long before the enemy started cracking down. Some of the country people got scared. Others just hardened, saying things like the Portuguese had killed their fathers, or their brothers, or their sons, and that 'They're out to get me, too, and I am going to fight.' For us the crackdown was an added opportunity to explain the role played by the Portuguese in our country. The harder they cracked down and showed their true ugly face, the more they confirmed the truth of what we had been saying about them. But we also had our troubles. Some of the country people started saying it was all our fault and if we would only quiet down they'd be able to pay their taxes and live in peace. Of course, Cabral had warned us not to imagine that the entire peasantry would rise up in rapture at the mention of independence. Distrust was there all the time. You had to dress like a Mandingo to go among Mandingos, like a Balante to go among Balantes. And you had to watch out for the agents of the Portuguese who were bound to run straight to them with any information they could get on you.

"Our procedure was to speak in a village and then go out into the bush to spend the night. It was the only way we had of making ourselves and the Party known. Little by little, Party sympathizers among the village people would come out into the bush bringing us meals. Later on, we were able to call out the villagers—or at least some of them—and talk with them, explain the meaning of our struggle, and ask their help. As time went on, there were some in every village who were with the Party and others who were not actually with it but still sympathized. Then there were those who were neutral if not downright suspicious. So as to prevent this kind from doing any harm, we had to manage to isolate them bit by bit, which we did—thanks to the more determined people in each village. Believe me, mobilization is a much, much harder thing than armed struggle itself.

"I used to go back to Conakry two or three times a year. We would make our reports to Cabral and he would talk them over with us, trying to find a way of moving on to a higher phase of the struggle. He would then set new objectives and we would return.

"At the beginning of 1962, we returned as a group under Oswaldo's command. Our mission was to establish ourselves solidly enough among the people to be able to launch the armed struggle. There were eight of us. Three were assigned to the Balante zone, three to the Mandingo zone, and one to the Fulah and Sarakollé zone. Each person went to the part of the country whose local languages he was most fluent in. Oswaldo was in charge of the overall operation and was authorized to reassign us to this or that tribe, according to the work we each accomplished. At that time the Portuguese were very strong, and, when they felt the population getting ready to boil over, they started descending on the villages with their troops. Our first move was to settle down in the region of Cambedge, in order to study the enemy's activities. I was sent into the Balante region to observe conditions of work and organization. When I got there, I saw that the Portuguese had tortured and killed people in many villages. The peasants advised me to clear out. Oswaldo and some others who had entered the Morès region also withdrew to the Senegal frontier. At the border we tried to attract Guineans to Casamance (Senegal) in order to propagandize among them. At that time, however, Senegal had very little use for the P.A.I.G.C.

"In Senegal they had François Mendy's M.L.G. Party,[3] which has made many attempts to harm the P.A.I.G.C. The M.L.G. had serious support in Senegal, but it had no contact with the population inside Guinea. Certain members of the M.L.G. held important posts in the Senegalese administration. So at that period, Senegal had nothing to do with our Party and did not wish to have anything to do with it. The M.L.G. did its best to induce us to quit the P.A.I.G.C. They offered us money. They said the P.A.I.G.C. was a party of Cape Verdeans. When they saw that bribery wouldn't get them anywhere, they made accusations against us to the Senegalese authorities in Casamance, claiming we were engaged in subversive activities against the Senegalese government. And then they told us: 'If you want to stay here, you had better quit the P.A.I.G.C., or you'll be sent back across the border.' When they saw that that wouldn't work either, they had us jailed, claiming that we had stopped other Guineans from joining the M.L.G. And they mounted a big propaganda campaign against us by offering rice to the Guineans in Casamance if they would quit the P.A.I.G.C. Then Cabral arrived and convinced the Senegalese authorities to let us out of jail. When we got out, Cabral told us to go back across the frontier into the interior. But before Cabral even had time to get back to Dakar, the Senegalese authorities locked us up again. Cabral had us freed once more and accompanied us back to Conakry; from there we made an undercover march all the way across so-called 'Portuguese' Guinea till we were back where we'd started, in the northern region of our country, close to the Senegal frontier.

"By this time the worst of the crackdown in the interior of the country was over. We immediately got back in touch and redoubled our agitation effort. What with the activities of the Portu-

[3] The M.L.G. initially drew its support primarily from Mandjaks living in Senegal. It is now merged with F.L.I.N.G., a puppet party having its headquarters in Dakar.

guese, who were also busily propagandizing, the entire peasant population was made aware of our existence, which of course only increased our importance. The Portuguese in fact helped us indirectly by constantly talking about the *bandoleiros*. They went to villages with which we had never had any contact and ordered them to turn in the bandits. The Portuguese even went so far as to offer the country people liquor and tobacco, telling them: 'Pay no attention to these bandits, Sékou Touré is trying to take over the country.' In a Balante village, they would say: 'They are going to force you to accept Islam.' In a Fulah village, they would say: 'They will force you to drink alcohol.' Meanwhile we kept busy on the counterpropaganda front, making full use of the psychological errors committed by the Portuguese. After a period of preparation, we sent for all the cadres trained in agitation work. There were several dozen, and we were able to intensify our efforts correspondingly. The Portuguese had placed agents in every village, occasionally drawn from among the local population. We embarked on a series of acts of sabotage: blowing up bridges, cutting telegraph lines, etc.

"After that (toward the end of 1962) the Portuguese launched a big offensive and forced our cadres to pull back over the border. However, those who had really managed to get their village properly together and to merge with its population remained. Within a fairly short time, the Portuguese subsided. We immediately popped up again on this side of the border. And since that time we have never left. We camped in the bush and started setting up base camps at the same time. The population knew what we were doing and helped, mainly by providing food. There were some traitors, but our people in the villages put them out of the way. In any case, there weren't very many at the time. But then the Portuguese started giving big rewards for informing. So we started liquidating the informers.

"Twice I was in a village when the Portuguese surrounded it. The first time it was a Mandingo village. The Portuguese were making a house-to-house check. I was given a big Mandingo *bou-bou* to put on, and I strolled out of the village wearing it. The second time was in a Balante village. They were checking people's identification. I hid in an old man's house.

"'You seen anybody come this way?' they asked him. 'Nobody been through here,' said the old man. I got into a Balante loincloth and put a load of kapok branches on my shoulder, greeted the soldiers in Balante, and got out of there. Nobody in the village had talked. Mobilization had become a reality. Agitation was at its height. Now all that remained was to start bringing in the hardware so we could get down to direct action.

"The guns started arriving through secret channels. Back then, a gun running operation involved a nine-day march, avoiding villages and straddling the border of the two Guineas or the Senegal line. We had a rough time in those days—you had to steer clear of both the Portuguese and the Senegalese. Nowadays it's simple: we finally got transit privileges and the guns have been getting through in regular shipments.

"Oswaldo distributed the matériel, and we divided it up among our groups. Armed action started in the south around the end of 1962 and the beginning of 1963. In the north it started in June of 1963. At the very outset we had seven base camps. And three guns per base. It didn't amount to much, but we were getting there: one *pachanga*, which is our word for a submachine gun, plus two revolvers. There were far more men than guns. Only the real specialists in guerrilla warfare were given the firearms, and we promptly got busy ambushing Portuguese convoys (there were a lot of them in circulation at that time) in order to seize more guns.

"At this point, a certain number of the village people we had mobilized started getting scared and many of them fled. Others avoided contact with us because of the enemy's repression in the countryside. But then others helped us with food and information on Portuguese troop movements. When the score of our successful ambushes began to mount up, people who had been avoiding us recovered their confidence and helped us. The Portuguese imagined they were going to make short work of us. But we started getting regular arms shipments and every month were able to arm a larger number of militants. Lately, as you can see, the Portuguese are pretty scarce in these parts—except over our heads, of course. Oswaldo can fill you in on the overall picture of our military operations—that's his job."

When we returned to camp at nightfall, the doctors were working on two guerrilla fighters who had been wounded by mortar fire. No one had been killed or hurt in the bombing. We said goodbye all around, for this was to be our last evening in Morès.

Maké was a six-hour march away. As usual, small squads were posted along the road at two-kilometer intervals. In the course of that night, we crossed the Olosato-Bissau highway in bright moonlight. We could make out the fresh imprint of truck tires.

Next day Cabral ordered the demotion of the two squad leaders responsible for the surveillance of the road at that point.

Djagali

About nine o'clock the next morning, as we were having coffee at the Maké base, a bomber turned in the sky high overhead. An hour later, we heard its bombs as they began to fall somewhere in the distance. "That would be in the Farim region," said Oswaldo. That morning, for the first time since my arrival in the country, Oswaldo (who had the double responsibility of organizing the various night raids intended to harass the Portuguese and of making security arrangements for the secretary-general's protection) was at last free. All of us had had a long and exhausting march the day before.

Oswaldo, who at twenty-seven is military commander of the entire northern region, spoke as follows:

"At the very beginning, well before we had launched the armed struggle, we traveled all around the country mobilizing the people. The Portuguese responded quickly with repressive measures. They made motorized sweeps—columns of trucks loaded with soldiers would drive through the countryside spreading terror among the population in the hope of rooting out Party cadres. At that point our people were forced to regroup on the other side of the frontier. Later on they returned.

"When they returned they were armed, but not well armed: there were only three weapons per group. They got back in contact with the reliable people in villages where they had already worked. There were several acts of sabotage. Then the armed struggle proper got underway in the north in June 1963. Our objective was to kill Portuguese. The Portuguese were incautious enough to venture out on the roads, not realizing that we were armed. We took them by surprise. In those months we captured a great many weapons from the Portuguese.

"Soon we had five machine pistols and twenty-five hand grenades for each group of thirty men. The Portuguese continued to come and go, still imagining that they were going to have a quick and easy job of it. As more guns and ammunition came in both from the outside and from the Portuguese, our groups expanded. I organized new units.

"Around October 1963, four months after the start of the armed struggle, the heavy bombing raids began. It was a long time before the people were willing to leave their destroyed villages. They rebuilt on the very same sites. They refused to take refuge in the forest. You have to reckon with the fact that people in this country are afraid of the forest. A considerable change has taken place since, however, and entire villages have agreed to move into the forest and place themselves under our protection. The Portuguese used to bomb the villages by day and the peasants would go back and sleep in them every night, but since the Portuguese were using fragmentation bombs and napalm the situation became untenable. Little by little, following our advice and explanations, the peasants of the entire northern zone started leaving their destroyed villages and coming to live in the immense Oïo forest. This occurred toward the end of 1963 and the beginning of 1964.

"Arms shipments from the outside really started coming in in 1964. We set up new base camps, to decentralize as much as possible. This gave us greater mobility and let us harass the enemy a bit everywhere at once. Moreover, we were obviously less vulnerable ourselves. Following the Party Congress of February 1964, we did a great deal of reorganizing on this basis and little by little the north was secured.

"The basic structural unit of our armed forces was the group of eleven men. For certain problems there were squads of five. For important ambushes we often used groups of twenty-two. In the classic eleven-man group there was invariably a political commissar.

"At the outset of the struggle, we aimed at blowing up bridges, obstructing the highways—in short, preventing the Portuguese from moving freely from place to place. Our objective was to eliminate the small, isolated Portuguese units. Subsequently, we made night raids against Portuguese garrisons in order to hurt their fighting spirit and morale. Beginning with the

1964 rainy season, the Portuguese started making fewer and fewer sorties.

"During that entire period we had a twofold objective: to eliminate physically the maximum number of Portuguese soldiers and at the same time to organize the people more and more thoroughly. Although we were still suffering from a serious shortage of arms and ammunition at that time, by the end of 1964 and the beginning of 1965 our matériel had become somewhat more abundant. At any rate, even today we have more volunteers than guns, but at least those who are armed are well armed. And it was in 1964 that we organized our national army, the F.A.R.P. We took full advantage of the rainy season, giving the Portuguese no respite from harassment and for the most part seizing the initiative on all fronts. The beginning of 1965 saw a similar amount of action. There was a slump toward the end of 1965 and the beginning of 1966, due to our own successes and the security that was achieved as a result.

"We then proceeded to modify our political structures, setting up the interregions, the regions, and the zones. There were likewise modifications on the Portuguese side. They brought in reinforcements, both Portuguese and mercenary troops. In the beginning there were 10,000 of them; now there are 25,000. We made and have abided by the decision not to commit any 'barbarous acts' in answer to Portuguese repression. It should in fact be noted that the Portuguese do respect us—mainly of course for our strength, but also for our discipline, the reality of which is brought home to them by our very refusal to indulge in 'atrocities.' For example, it is our policy to let captured Portuguese civilians go.

"Their air force is now their main weapon. Naturally from time to time they do attempt a sweep through the liberated zones. They even try search-and-destroy operations. For example, they tried four times this year to make a sweep in the zone of Iracunda. They make these sorties several hundred strong. (In the southern region they tried to pull off a big operation on December 31, 1965. It was not much of a success. There were 3,000 men involved on their side. Our comrades in the south treated them to a riotous New Year's Eve.) They make these sorties armed with automatic weapons, mortars, and bazookas and have air support as well. Their infantrymen are equipped with Mausers and hand grenades. Since they come out in such large force, we quickly know that they are on their way, having been informed either by the peasants or by our own reconnaissance patrols. We pull back. We let them push ahead into unfamiliar country. Most of their infantry consists of raw recruits who are absolutely lost out here where we have been in control since 1964. At this point, we carry out a loose encirclement, using night attacks to break up the column. Thanks to our perfect knowledge of the ground, we ambush them again and again. At times a secondary ambush is laid at one end of their line so that once serious contact has been made we can take advantage of the general confusion to launch our main attack elsewhere along the line. Not one of these Portuguese operations has achieved its principal objective: namely, to force us to withdraw from a liberated zone.

"Since 1966 the basic unit of the F.A.R.P. has been a mobile group of twenty-three men: one group commander, one political commissar, and twenty-one men armed with submachine guns, plus one bazooka and one heavy machine gun. Some groups also have a mortar. These autonomous groups have extreme mobility and offensive capacity.

"As of now the Portuguese occupy only towns and fortified camps in the northern interregion. That's still a lot, and we are going to nibble some of that away from them this coming year. We are still short on matériel to arm more people. We could have a great many more combat people. Recruiting is done by the village committees. Obviously, we have only volunteers, and they are almost always very young: on the average, between sixteen and twenty-five. We are very young in general, as people's armies go: none of our cadres is over thirty. Recruits get a minimum of two months' training on our bases. First they cover basic political doctrine, then the handling and proper care of arms, and finally elementary guerrilla techniques. The rest is learned in the field and elsewhere in daily life under the supervision of the Party.

"As for the Portuguese, their morale is very low. We have had a dozen deserters since 1964 who have confirmed this. The war is not popular among the troops. Apart from a few young ones who have acquired a taste for it and apart from the Salazar regime's caste of fascist officers, the infantry has no morale at all. The fliers are another matter—these gentlemen are aristocrats. And they are not liked by the troops. The troops are disgusted with taking all the losses while the fliers are dropping their bombs at no great risk and from a very safe altitude. In fact, soldiers and sailors attacked the squadron barracks at Bissau once in 1964, after their planes had bombed Portuguese troops without having taken the trouble to verify the target.

"But now the rainy season's starting. It's our big season, the phase we like to call *Pincha Tugas* because this is the time of year we wear them down and worry them to death, you know. . . . "

A combat group arrived at the base camp that afternoon with one man slightly wounded. That morning the Portuguese had tried to open the Mansaba-Morès highway. They were turned back.

We had a conversation with Amilcar about his tour of inspection and the conclusions he had drawn from it about the coming rainy season. He said, in substance, that the bases as we now know them will be immediately abolished. The schoolchildren will be parceled out in small groups to the villages and will form the core of the future village militia. Women from the bases will likewise be reintegrated into the villages, where they will play a role in the activities of the village committees. Combat personnel will be made more mobile, to sharpen their effect. Portuguese camps must be attacked two or three times a night, as they were during our visit. Rivers must be staked out by special units whose only task will be the destruction of Portuguese boats by bazooka attack. Small units will likewise be restricted to antiaircraft defence. The atmosphere of insecurity might affect not only the Portuguese but also the fighting men of the F.A.R.P. but for nearly a year now this has not been the case. Neither the fighting men nor the villagers have ever been so much at liberty and ease, with liberated regions firmly in hand and no Portuguese presence other than that of the airplanes, aside from a few attempted sweeps that failed; with friendly relations between the troops and a population that feels that it is protected; with secure and comfortable bases, which are all the safer because the Portuguese no longer have sufficient morale to attempt any serious offensives. All this provides the impetus to enter a new phase that will evolve during the rainy season. . . .

XII.   Journal of a Colombian Guerrillero

ANONYMOUS

*This text was written by a member of the
F.A.R.C. It tells of events that followed the
success of a major counterinsurgency
operation, the "Lazo" plan of 1965. The
"independent republics" of Marquetalia,
Sumapaz, and other areas controlled and
administered by the F.A.R.C. were
destroyed. The story that follows takes
place in the province of Tolima.*

. . . We had left Riochiquito following the military offensive
against us in that zone. The first clash with the *chulos* occurred in
a place called Palomar[1]; one of us was wounded, and several
soldiers were killed. Later, we marched on toward the summit. It
rained a lot that day; it was as if the sky had been ripped open.
We arrived completely soaked. Marulanda, our leader, set up an
ambush. At eleven in the morning, we realized that the *chulos*
had cut across the bush in an attempt to head us off. We made
for the Bilbao canyon. On the way we were able to buy enough
veal, maize bread, and beans to replenish our strength. We went
on toward another canyon. Three days later, we returned to the
same spot; the trail was very confused.
We marched all the following day. We were crossing a ravine
when they fell on us. They tried to encircle us, but we managed
to lose them by taking another ravine, full of shrubs and
brambles, leading toward Montalvo. The commander organized
another ambush, but the enemy was right behind us. There were

From *Journal d'un guérillero Colombien* (Paris: Editions du Seuil, 1968).
Copyright 1968 by Editions du Seuil. Reprinted by permission of Editions du
Seuil.

[1] *Chulos* is a derogatory term for regular soldiers.

so many *chulos* that we could not tell if we were looking at *chulos* in camouflage gear or just at bushes. That was the day the sentries pulled back too early and the *chulos* attacked us as we retreated. Lucio Mesa was wounded; they got his equipment and his rifle. It was a bad wound; he told us to leave him behind because he could not walk, but we carried him. He died that night. We arrived at another canyon. It was impossible to get a fire going because of the storm, so we had nothing to eat. The next day we came to another ravine, somewhere between Montalvo and Chiquila. Leonardo could not take any more; he was not able to keep up. He let us go on, and, while we were waiting for him further up, he was taken. The *chulos* cut him up into little pieces with their machetes.

Marulanda called a meeting. We were tired, and the lack of food had demoralized us all. He said, "You know the situation as well as I do. It's a siege; we're trapped in these mountains. If we stick together, we may get out of it; if we split up, it'll be much more difficult. But if anybody wants to go, they're free to do so." Nobody left. As we came to the top of the hill, there was a volley of shots and one of us fell, dead. They were sticking to our trail like dogs on the hunt. Every few hours, there would be a shootout, and some of us would die. While most of us formed a rear guard to hold them off, a few would go forward, cutting a path through the bush, trying to break through before they surrounded us completely. They had a helicopter that would fly low and drop troops here and there, apparently at random.

We crossed another canyon. Craz was stiff with hunger, yellow-faced, barely able to speak. He died.

When we got out of that canyon, we split up. We left the families that had fled with us in a safe place. There were only six of us left: Marulanda and five guerrilleros. We continued toward Palomar. We passed many *chulos* strongholds but in the end got through. Of *finado* Salinas, only the bones were found.[2] Under cover of night we carried on to San Miguel. When we entered the Huila, we almost ran right into the *chulos,* but we froze and they passed. Then we went back down along the Aguache canyon, where we bought some grub—*panela* and *bizcochos.*[3] We followed the Pata and eventually came to a place where, on the other bank, a guerrilla had set up camp.

---

[2] *Finado* is a title of respect accorded by peasants to a person who has died.
[3] *Panela* is a sugar cake made from sugar cane juice; *bizcochos* are biscuits.

There was no way of making contact; we were stuck. Marulanda said, "*Bueno, muchachos, a encaletarse* till they get tired of looking for us."[4] He warned us that even under cover there was some risk. We looked for a place big enough for all of us and settled in at the foot of the mountain to wait till it all blew over.

The surrounding peaks were full of *chulos,* and the noose was getting tighter. They must have had some idea of where we were. Small patrols began to scour the terrain, meter by meter, bush by bush, ravine after ravine, as though they were trying to pry some secret from the earth. Six-man patrols would pass us repeatedly, searching, waiting for something to move. They were never in a hurry, and they left a big space between each man when they walked, in order not to get in each other's line of fire. They knew they had one crucial ally: hunger.

There was a little hut not far away. On the second day we contacted the old couple that lived there and met all their neighbors. They were not "organized," and Marulanda spent until midnight explaining why we were fighting for the revolution. They sold us a little manioc, which we cooked on the spot and then took back to our hideout. The old couple did not see which way we went.

The next day, we started out at about six in the morning. We could see *chulos* nearby. They passed not 200 meters away but did not notice us. On the way down to the hut, we found the remains of the sugar cane they had been sucking. We swam across the river, but when we saw the old man he was terrified. The *chulos* had wrecked his place and stolen all his manioc. He told us he could not sell us anything. In the end, he sold us 15 pesos worth of sugar cane. We put the cane on our backs and returned to camp at eight that night.

The day after, we ate the cane, but only at mealtimes. Nobody slept; everybody was alert, bags at the ready. We kept a keen lookout, but the real point was to sit tight without moving. We held a meeting. The commander said, "If you want, we can chance it. I passed by here some time ago, and I remember the lay of the land. But it would be better to sit tight for a while, at least three days, until the new moon."

Some of us would crouch low while the others kept watch. The

[4] "Quick, boys, under the tent . . . "

patrols repeatedly passed right next to us. With nightfall we returned to the hut to buy some sugar cane, which we cut in the dark. We could not suck it in the fields because the remains would have given us away. It was early morning when we got back, having swum across the river once again.

The next day, the *chulos* went back to the old man's hut and asked him why there were so many footsteps all around. He answered that they were animal tracks. Our commander told us, "The *chulos* will be here before long." He took out his machine gun and prepared his equipment. He told us to do the same. We looked at each other. He added that if we came out of it alive, we should not lose contact with the Party. Also, that if we had to scatter, we should not go too far lest we become isolated.

The *chulos* began to climb the ravine, and we started down it, very careful not to disturb even the roots we had to hang onto as we slid down the cliff. We walked along the streams, hopping from stone to stone, doing our best not to leave even one broken branch behind us. I was in the rear. It had been agreed that I would fire on the first *chulo* I saw.

"Watch out, the *chulos*!" I gave the alarm. It was a patrol sent out to draw our fire. The *chulos* were stretched out in a line with a wide interval between each man; they were wary and ready to shoot. They came to the crag but found no tracks. Everything was in its place. They left. We asked Marulanda the time. "Midday," he said. They would not come back today.

Three o'clock. All's well. He broke out laughing and we all joined in.

Five in the evening. Nothing to fear for the rest of the day. We felt the tension dissipate. We stared at the equipment, piled up and covered with branches so it could be burned if need be. We knew by heart just how many cartridges remained. We added the munitions in our heads. The movement's assets were safe, at least for the moment.

Nightfall. I do not really know why, but we all slept soundly.

In the early morning we went back to the hut. The river was swollen. I swam across and had to hide in the grass when some *chulos* went by. Evaristo and Pedro were still on the other side, and everyone else was at camp with the commander.

On the way back we each carried a big bag of sugar cane. The river was even more swollen; it had poured during the night, and now the current was violent and fast. Evaristo said, "You seem to manage in the water; as for me I think I prefer the *chulos*." Pedro and I crossed, just barely able to wade. Evaristo was still on the other side. I cut a branch and went back halfway across the river and called him, telling him to hang on to the branch. He grabbed it, hung on with all his might, and made it to the other side. We took our prize back to the cache. Three sacks of sugar cane: they would have to last at least three days. We had had a hard time convincing the old man. He was ill and did not want to sell. "If the *chulos* find out, they will kill me, *Dios Mio*."

We counted up the sticks of cane. We were each entitled to a little bit. We had found a way of eating it with bits of salt the old man had given us from his animals' salt licks. We were so pleased finally to have something salty to put between our teeth.

Marulanda was very punctual. "*Muchachos*, it is breakfast time." We would each bring out our bit of sugar cane. "*Bueno*, it is lunch time"—and we would start sucking again. "Don't forget it's time for dinner." Out would come the same old piece of sugar cane.

The nights were still very dark; no sign of the moon. We were calmer, breathing more easily but always on guard.

There was no more sugar cane. The old man had had enough; he gesticulated wildly and seemed very frightened. His wife backed him up. The *chulos* were coming by his place every day. Despite all our entreaties, the couple would sell us nothing. After all, they were not "organized" but yet had helped us and not given us away.

We returned to the hiding place. All we had left was bagasse, but, as Marulanda said, "We would have to content ourselves with it." When your stomach is crying out, you must give it something, even if only to deceive it.

The next day, the commander called us all together. "If we stay here, the *chulos* will get us or we'll die of hunger. We'll have to risk it and try to get through."

The *chulos* were everywhere. We traveled by night, under the light of the moon that had finally risen. It was not too dark to see, and we managed to figure out which way led up. Sometimes, in the bushes, we could barely make out who was in front. When the sun rose, we were at the top of the ravine.

We heard a noise. It was the *chulos,* busily setting an ambush. We kept quiet, glued to the face of the cliff and ready to fight. We could hear them breathing. We waited patiently for nightfall and at half past six headed off down a gorge. The army had left tracks. We walked until morning. It was the right path.

By sunrise, we were near *nuestras masas.*[5] We finally got hold of some *panela* and some shoes. We had been walking barefoot for so long. Restored, we set off towards Marquetalia. We had broken out of the circle.

. . . The *chulos* are attacking; they have prepared their move carefully; there is nothing to do but fight it out and try to save the gun. One of my comrades, startled, leaps up and runs off, leaving his sack and rifle next to his companion. Every path toward the mountain is blocked; we are caught in a circle of fire; the only way out is to cross a broad torrential river.

Some of us make it across. We see a woman run back through the chaos and gunfire, grab her sack and her companion's, sling both across her shoulders, and pick up the rifle. Then, with all that weight on her back, she launches herself into the water and starts swimming across. The current is fierce, but we are pinned down and can do nothing to help. Gunfire crisscrosses every-where. We can only stare and hope.

The girl in the river is named Oliva. I remember the first time I saw her. She was very young and always stayed right behind Manuel Castellanos's wife, who looked to be her mother. The older woman had told us their story: "They arrived at six o'clock in the evening of June 6. . . . The bastards! They said they had killed my husband and that they were going to kill my children one by one. Then they put a noose around my neck and began to tighten it, asking me if I was Manuel Castellanos's whore. They took me into the bedroom and made me undress, threatening me with their bayonets. They wanted to know where my brother was, and, as I had no idea, they kept hacking my hair off with a razor. They beat me with a leather whip and locked me up in the room with a padlock. They wanted to know where Israel Céspedes, Rafico Polania, and Benjamin Arias were. They said

[5] *Nuestras masas* means "our own people."

when they caught them they would make them regret the day they were born."

Then Oliva spoke for the first time: "They made me strip and threatened to cut my breasts off. They didn't manage to rape me, although they tried, at least six of them. . . . I fought all the time. But they raped Luz Céspedes's daughter. She was only twelve years old. They said they were doing all this so we would be ashamed to tell anyone about it and to show us just what they were capable of. They added that if we told anybody they would kill us and throw our bodies in a ditch. . . . "

"Why were you frightened when you saw us coming?"

"I thought I too was going to have to say to my husband, 'I can't sleep with you tonight, it's my turn.'"

"Your turn at what?"

"At . . . well, at sleeping with the chief of the bandits, of course—and perhaps with some of the others as well. That has been the custom around here. It's difficult to say who's worse, the *chulos* or the bandits. We were frightened when you turned up. I felt ill. All these weapons . . . "

So we explained to them that if they wanted to join us we would not prevent them—on the contrary, women are useful and there are not enough of them in our ranks. If a young girl wants to follow the guerrillas and join the organization or marry one of the fighters, everything is done correctly so they can live a decent life. The couple is told: you are free to organize your private life as you wish, as long as you have some consideration for your comrades. Of course, you'll have to put up with the way we live in the maquis; it is often hard, and there is little chance of settling down. The rules are quite straightforward: a guerrillero who attacks a woman, any woman, will be brought to trial. That sort of violence is simply not permitted. If the woman is willing, if it all happens naturally and she decides to follow the guerrillero, then she comes with us. This can cause problems, because sometimes we go for months without seeing a woman or at least without being able to have any sort of relationship. But although it is hard, we get used to it. The respect the guerrilleros have for a woman who lives among them is the same respect they have learned to have for peasant women.

That was all about two years ago, the day we first met her.

The hardest thing in the war is losing your comrades when the enemy wins. You have to dredge up reserves of strength just to keep fighting. All this passes through my mind as the *chulos* close in: we cannot bear to wait for them, but we must.

In our unit, there are four women. All are good comrades, that's for sure—they help a lot with the supplies and the cooking, and they help dispel morbid thoughts. But Oliva is something else. Her presence puts fire in your bones when hunger, fatigue, and lack of sleep have pushed you to the brink.

Time stands still. Centuries pass. At the slightest movement, there is a hail of bullets. When we see that Oliva has made it to the other side, we all burst out laughing. . . . With all that weight on her back, she managed to cross the torrent! Some of us give covering fire while the other slip into the bushes and disappear. One last volley and we pull back too.

When the danger has passed, we meet up with Oliva again. She hands her companion his equipment and his M-1. It is a pity there are not more women in our unit.

They must have picked them from the dregs of mankind. They chose perverts, drug pushers, thieves who would steal from the devil and sell their own mother in the bargain. Many were ex-guerrillas who had become *bandoleros*. They got all this rabble together and formed the *Barbados*.

These guys have no conscience. They can be turned loose upon their one-time companions, upon their own people, like hunting dogs. They know the terrain, the people, the old trails. They dress like guerrilleros, organize themselves and fight just like us; even their habits, their language, their jokes are the same.

The military authorities told them to let their beards and hair grow, in order to besmirch the symbol of the heroes of the Sierra: *los Barbudos*. But the peasants nicknamed them *los Barbados*. And now they roam the region, sowing confusion by passing themselves off as guerrilleros.

They come into the house and ask, "There are no soldiers about, are there?" They always ask that. Only two of them come, not a whole group, but they treat the place as though it were theirs. We watch them leave, pretending to flee, effacing their footprints as they go. The peasants help them mess up the trail; they have taken them for guerrilleros. Their whole behavior is an imitation of ours. Their beards and hair are very long, their clothes are a little torn, but they have automatic weapons, machine guns and M-3 carbines.

They enjoy many prerogatives—not only the best weapons, but preferential treatment in the barracks and at the guard posts. The soldiers know very well that whereas they earn 50 pesos a month, a *Barbado* gets 400 or even 900 pesos a month. And of course there is another special privilege granted them: they have a free hand. The army exercises almost no control over them. They do what they want and are accountable to no one. They dislike being treated as soldiers and prefer to be called counterguerrilleros. And the troops grudgingly respect them.

They have disappeared into the bush, in an effort to find a detachment of theirs that we detected lying in wait for us some time ago. There were 10 or 12 of them, we could not be sure exactly. They stayed there all day, waiting to ambush anyone heading along the trail to the peasant's house.

When they capture a guerrillero, they offer him a free pardon if he joins them. Then the training begins: the new recruit must give some proof of his loyalty. At first he acts as a guide for the army and the police. Then he becomes a spy and must denounce the inhabitants of the region. He gets a special safe-conduct, which enables him to go where he chooses. He knows the army's watchwords and can report to any military outpost. Having proved himself, he is admitted to a batallion. They give him a special uniform, weapons, equipment, and a ration.

The ones we saw received their papers at Natagaïna. When we heard they had pulled out, we sent a message to the peasant.

Many peasants still mistake them for us. In the south of Tolima, we had to abandon over a hundred farms after a detachment of *Barbados* had gone through. The courier returns with the friendly peasant. Fortunately, the troops have not yet arrived.

XIII.

On the Move

MICHAEL RAEBURN

*Michael Raeburn, who has lived in
Zimbabwe, collected the tales of members
of Z.A.N.U. and Z.A.P.U. about the
years 1964–1971. In the following account
he consolidates their tales and includes
some commentary on the context of the
struggle. Since 1971, and especially since
1977, the efficacy of the military schemes
of the two movements has greatly
increased.*

*Between 1967 and 1970 Z.A.P.U. organized several campaigns
in an attempt to launch a major military struggle against the
Rhodesian government.*

*The first campaign, in August 1967, heralded a much-publi-
cized but short-lived alliance between Z.A.P.U. and A.N.C. of
South Africa. A combined Z.A.P.U.-A.N.C. force of nearly
one hundred heavily armed men entered Rhodesia in the
Wankie area. The objective of the A.N.C. faction was to get to
South Africa. The Z.A.P.U. faction was to help the A.N.C.
men on their journey south, and then remain in the center of
Rhodesia setting up guerrilla bases.*

*The column came to grief in the Wankie Game Reserve.
Weighed down by their weapons in this depopulated and very
inhospitable region, the guerrillas were continually impeded by
inadequate maps and lack of food and water. Very little ground-
work or reconnaissance had been carried out, and no contacts*

From Michael Raeburn, *Black Fire! Account of the Guerrilla War of Rhodesia*,
J. Friedmann, ed. (London: Julian Friedmann Publishers, Ltd., 1978). Published
by permission of Julian Friedmann Publishers, Ltd.

had been established with local Africans in the neighboring Tribal Trust Lands. Communication with them was left to chance, with the result that the authorities soon heard about the guerrillas' presence. The heavy figure eight boot-patterns left by the soldiers in the uninhabited Game Reserve made tracking easy for the Rhodesian troops. The invading forces were devastated in a series of pitched battles—only a few escaped death or capture and found their way back to Zambia.

The participation of the A.N.C. in the Wankie Battles gave the South African Government an excellent excuse to send forces into Rhodesia to help the harassed regime defend its northern frontier.

In January 1968 another operation started in the Sipolilo area. This time a combined force of one hundred and fifty Z.A.P.U.-A.N.C. guerrillas were involved. Having learned something from the errors of Wankie, the leaders prepared the ground more carefully and built up arms dumps as well as good contacts with local people. The guerrillas also brought considerable supplies of food with them. But they were far too numerous to remain in hiding for long, although they did manage to do so up until March, when a game warden discovered the unmistakable boot-prints. There were several pitched battles between the two sides, and the Rhodesians spread havoc with their air power. Z.A.P.U. sent in reinforcements, and the South African government did the same. The fighting went on until July, and the guerrillas fought bravely, winning several battles. But they were overwhelmingly outnumbered, and they found it increasingly difficult to get food, since their local supporters did not come from a wide enough area. They were once again hindered by poor maps. As they went on the run they were forced to break up into smaller and smaller groups; some, consisting of two or three guerrillas, were never captured and managed to remain in the Sipolilo area.

But the Z.A.P.U. leaders were still determined on large-scale confrontation. In July 1968 in a third offensive, ninety Z.A.P.U.-A.N.C. soldiers were sent into the country from Zambia. Their defeat was so crushing—thirty guerrillas were killed and forty captured within four weeks of entry—that it wrecked the Z.A.P.U.-A.N.C. alliance.

Z.A.P.U. had begun searching for new tactics for waging

guerrilla war when the events of "On the Move" took place in
1970. But the leaders still did not appear to have learned the
lesson that big units are highly vulnerable in Rhodesia. They
sent in three groups, amounting to fifty men, to launch what is
now known as the "Victoria Falls Campaign" of 1970.

"On the Move" involves one man who fought in this campaign. In the story he is called Joseph Mpofu, although this is
not his real name. Joseph spent several months in a Botswana
prison after his escape from Rhodesia, where he wrote some
notes on his experiences. The main events and comments in
this story are based on these notes as well as on conversations,
both with Joseph and with other guerrillas who have fought in
Rhodesia.

Although "On the Move" is about one man's experience of
certain events in a widespread offensive, the story still provides
an invaluable personal view of what went wrong not only with
the Victoria Falls Campaign as a whole, but with the entire
Z.A.P.U. military strategy between 1967 and 1970.

The Crossing

An event occurred on the night of January 2, 1970, that started
everything off on the wrong foot.

Joseph Mpofu, age twenty-five, was part of a Z.A.P.U. platoon in a temporary camp on the Zambian side of the Zambezi
River, about 50 miles below the Victoria Falls. The nearest point
on the map was a Rhodesian fishing holiday spot at Deka, 10
miles downstream. Joseph's platoon—Platoon A—consisted of
ten men. They had come from Lusaka a few days earlier with the
twelve members of Platoon B. A third platoon of twenty guerrillas—Platoon C—had crossed into Rhodesia before the others
arrived at the Zambezi camp, and its men were hiding in the
forests near Matetsi Mission in the Wankie Tribal Trust Lands.
Platoons A and B were now waiting for orders to cross the
dreaded rapids of the Zambezi.

But there had been a delay. A three-man reconnaissance team
had failed to return at the designated time. For three days, members from "operations" kept a continuous watch for the flashlight
signal from a specific point on the opposite bank of the Zambezi.
When it finally came, on the night of the second, the message

was that the team needed to cross immediately. But they could not do so because a Rhodesian army patrol boat was too close. The "operations" section understood from the signal that the men were in danger. They wasted no time seeking a solution. They waited until the patrol boat came within fifteen yards from where they lay concealed in the bush, then opened fire with small arms, hitting one Rhodesian soldier. The launch beat a hasty retreat, allowing the local Tonga canoeists to hurry across the river and bring back the guerrillas.

The news that the three men brought from Rhodesia was not good. They had been detected on their return journey and had been chased by spotter planes, helicopters, and soldiers for 50 miles. Although they had managed to shake the enemy off and get back to Zambian territory, the damage had been done. Being fully armed, they had probably been mistaken for stray members of a full guerrilla column. The enemy had been alerted, and a security operation had most certainly been launched to comb the area for other infiltrators. . . .

Victoria Falls

Before leaving for Rhodesia, the guerrillas were reminded of the objectives of the campaign. All contact with the enemy was to be avoided. The guerrillas should remain in hiding in the Victoria Falls area. Relations should be established with local contacts with a view to recruiting and training. Strategic targets should be found and sabotaged. These targets should be limited to installations such as railway lines, bridges, government buildings, and banks. The objective of sabotage was to cripple the economy.

It was immediately clear to Joseph, once the platoon had reached its destination, that these aims would be impossible to fulfill in the Victoria Falls area. On their 20-mile walk from Deka to their base, in the forests along the Matetsi River, they had seen and narrowly avoided two army patrols. Local contacts in villages near their base spoke of considerable troop movement in the area. Soldiers had visited villages asking questions about "foreigners" and "terrorists," offering, on the one hand, rewards for information, and, on the other, penalties for withholding it. The guerrillas' military radio was so jammed with interpatrol communication that it was far too dangerous to use for their own purposes.

For seven days Joseph sat in the bush with his comrades and waited. Every day the commander went off with one other soldier, both in civilian clothes with pistols concealed in their trousers, to make contact with local village supporters. They returned to base, disheartened. The commander was not satisfied with the men he had seen. "They are not up to standard," he complained. News of army activities in the area had made the contacts extremely nervous and reluctant to help. It was clear that they were not real militants. The commander felt they had been recruited prematurely by Z.A.P.U. reconnaissance. Once again, thought Joseph, a job badly done.

The people in the area had grievances against the country's rulers, but they were on the whole unusually ignorant of nationalist politics. It was not a politicized area like the Matopo or Chipinga or dozens of other regions. The fact that they had reacted favorably to the Wankie battles, which had taken place on their doorstep two years earlier, was not sufficient grounds to assume that they were politically aware and determined nationalists. On the contrary, the opposite was now being proved to be true. Of the six men seen by the commander only one offered to continue helping. But the information this man gave on troop movements was extremely vague. A good contact would have done some research on the subject, but this man couldn't be bothered. Another old man had been overenthusiastic when he heard that "the men with gun" had arrived. When the commander returned to see him the next day, the old man had told all his friends who were gathered together to look at him. The commander wisely hurried away, never to return.

It was clear that none of the contacts supplied by reconnaissance really understood the struggle. They had not been prepared for war. When they met it face to face they dropped their obligations like a burning stick. The guerrillas could not rely on them for information, food, or support of any kind. All projects for giving military training to local supporters were idle dreams.

One night this depressing situation was the subject of conversation among the guerrillas. They sat around a fire eating beans and tinned meat. The general opinion was that they should move south to Matopo where they stood a better chance of establishing themselves. Although the commander agreed with the idea in theory, he wanted to wait for instructions. He also felt that trying to cross the enemy lines to move south was asking for trouble: at the moment, it would be better to wait where they were, see how the situation developed in the area, and hear what Headquarters suggested. . . .

The change in the commander's attitude had been produced by the realities of guerrilla war. Out in the field, certain major issues had come to the surface. The men who made up the platoon had all received military training. But they had been taught in different countries: Joseph and a young man called Tami Ndhlovu had gone to Cuba, Fireworks and two others had been in Algeria, the commander and three others went to Moscow, the young boy of sixteen had trained in Lusaka, and Lovemore had been in Cairo. In all these countries the men had been taught how to shoot, but they all had varying concepts of how the war should be waged, and they all had different political attitudes. . . .

When the Z.A.P.U. guerrillas returned from all these different countries, they were confined to military camps in Zambia, waiting to be sent to fight in Rhodesia. All of them had learned to shoot, but not all of them had absorbed the political theory they had been taught. Many of those who had been sent were illiterate: they had learned the practicalities, but the theory was above their heads. Others with some education had picked up what they could. A few came back with a powerful vision of how the struggle should be waged—in the eyes of the leaders, these were "troublemakers."

Because the leaders were themselves searching for the right way to carry on the war, they were particularly vulnerable. Without clearly defined policies, they laid themselves open to criticism. So they watched anxiously to see if the "troublemakers" would cause unrest in the military camps. They selected commanders who would do what they were told. They spread the "troublemakers" out in numerous camps so that they could not form powerful cliques. When they made up a column to send to Rhodesia, they made sure that the "troublemakers" were in the minority. . . .

Eight days after Platoon A arrived at the Matetsi River, a courier from Platoon C came to see the men. He announced that a local contact had turned informer: troops were swarming all over their area. As a result of this situation it was no longer possible for his platoon to remain in hiding. They had no choice but to take action against the enemy and try to break through its lines and move south. His platoon commander had decided to start the operation on the night of January 16, in four days' time, with an attack on the Victoria Falls Airport. The commander wanted Platoon A to engage the enemy on the same night, near where the platoon was based, further to the east of Platoon C. A similar request was being made to Platoon B, which was even further to the east. In this way it was hoped to divert the enemy's attention and spread out its military resources, giving Platoon C a greater chance of successfully breaking out of the area.

The commander of Platoon A thanked the courier for his message and told him he would let him know within two days whether he would agree to this plan.

Joseph was not surprised to hear that the campaign had been destroyed only a week after it started. Most of the men had sensed it was doomed all along. But this didn't stop him feeling let down. He noticed the commander was also depressed. Nobody spoke for some time after the courier left, until the commander stood up and asked Lovemore to go with him to talk to some villagers.

While they were gone, Joseph sat thinking. He wondered why Platoon C had been so big. He was surprised that it had not broken up into smaller groups once it had got inside the country. He could find no reason why Platoon C should be twice the size of the other two. He thought even his own group was too big. But twenty men couldn't move anywhere without the risk of being seen, nor could they hide themselves easily. Squads of five men or so could have much greater freedom. Platoon C was a small army. It needed an extensive, well-organized backup operation to survive. This meant getting local support on a very large scale. Five men could feed themselves with only a little assistance, but a group of twenty needed dozens of villages to supply them with food. Why hadn't Platoon C divided up? Perhaps now the pressure was on they would give up sticking together? Poor chaps! Because they were so numerous they had been forced into the sort of pitched battle situation that had been the downfall of the Wankie and Sipolilo campaigns. How could the leaders tell their soldiers to avoid engagements with the enemy, and then send large platoons into dangerous areas? Joseph wondered whether he would ever get any answers to these questions.

He was also very worried about Platoon C's suggested plan of action for the sixteenth. He was convinced that the only thing to do at this stage was to get everybody out of the region as quickly and inconspicuously as possible. Going in for this parallel action stuff was asking for trouble: if Platoon C wanted to blow up the airport that was their problem. However, if the men split up and slipped away, it was very unlikely that all of them would be caught. But if all the platoons went chasing after the enemy, the losses would be much higher all round.

When the commander returned and discussed the situation with the men, Joseph was very relieved to see that he was against the plan. According to village contacts, troop movements were increasing throughout the Wankie Tribal Trust Lands. There seemed to be no area where troops were in small enough numbers to risk an engagement. Or if there were such areas, the contacts had been unable to pinpoint them. Every day brought greater risk of detection. By attacking the enemy they would draw even more security forces against them. An attack would produce the same situation for them as the informer had produced for Platoon C. Then they too would be forced to withdraw in conditions loaded against them. The commander would not allow this to happen. They must lie low over the next few days, see if Platoon C went ahead with its attack as planned, and then slip out of the area while the enemy concentrated on finding Platoon C. In view of the density of the security forces, it was decided that they would stay together as a group of ten, because then, if they were forced to fight, they stood a better chance of survival. They considered that to avoid detection, the difference between five and ten men was not as crucial as the difference between ten and twenty.

The commander sent a coded message to a prearranged contact in a nearby village, informing Platoon C of their decision. Then they settled down to wait.

Three events occurred during this time. One night a young man named Moyo disappeared. He had been the most unreliable member of the group. He had spent three weeks in a Z.A.P.U. jail for refusing to go and fight in Rhodesia. Only threats had made him come along. They had needed to keep an eye on him all the time, and he had never been allowed to do guard duty at night, go off on his own, or accompany the commander on his village rounds. Now with the strain building up day by day, he had decided to make a run for it. They knew that if he was caught it wouldn't take much to make him talk. The need for them to move off was more urgent than ever. Joseph cursed the stupidity of those who had been responsible for sending such a man.

On the fifteenth an airplane passed overhead, showering the whole area with leaflets calling for all guerrillas to "surrender or die." The leaflets offered an amnesty to those who walked toward the security forces without weapons, hands raised high and shouting the words: "We do not want to die—save us—we are here."

On the same day news came from a nearby settlement that soldiers from the regime's African regiment (R.A.R.) had been going into several villages dressed like guerrillas in order to try to catch sympathizers. They had met with a certain amount of success—at least sufficient to terrify most contacts into refusing to have anything more to do with the real guerrillas.

On the day of the sixteenth, news came that Platoon C had carried out its plan of attack during the night. Two sections had assaulted the airport situated in the Fuller Forest. It was a daring action, since security forces were garrisoned there. The guerrillas caused severe damage to buildings, and several light military aircraft were destroyed. Five members of the security forces were killed. At the same time a third section blew up the Victoria Falls–Wankie railway line.

The Journey South

At sunset on the sixteenth, Platoon A began a 250-mile journey to Matopo. The one-month journey first took them east, to the edges of Gokwe; then they traveled south to Lupane and through the Gwaai Forest in Tjolotjo. This brought them down southwest of Bulawayo, where they were able to move east into the Matopos Hills.

They did not go directly south from Matetsi because at all costs they wanted to avoid going through the Wankie Game Reserve. In the 1967 Wankie campaign the liberation forces had suffered terrible hardship because the area was not adequately mapped and was totally uninhabited. Water was a great problem, and soldiers wasted days wandering about and getting lost in search of water holes. Some of them were spotted and picked up by the security forces, who then surrounded the few good water holes, forcing the guerrillas to come out of hiding in their desperate search for drink and food.

So at first Platoon A traveled east away from Wankie. They moved fast in order to get clear of the heavily patrolled area around Matetsi. In spite of their anxiety to travel as quickly as possible they took the precaution of brushing away the tracks of their figure eight boots with leafy branches as they went. They also covered their clothes and skin with fresh dung. In this way if they passed closely downwind of a herd of wild animals, it wouldn't be able to smell them, take fright, run off, and perhaps in so doing alert an enemy patrol. But the dung caused them endless agony from pestering flies, especially horseflies that drove them mad with their painful stings. With the flies, the heat, and the forced marching, the youngest member of the group, who was only sixteen, collapsed exhausted on the second night.

The Platoon had been on the move for forty-eight hours, interrupted only by short breaks of one or two hours. The army had so many ways of picking up guerrilla trails that the commander considered speed to be the best plan, rather than the traditional method of moving at night and resting during the day in hiding. They merely progressed more cautiously during the day, with an advance guard picking out the way in short bursts and, if all was clear, signaling to the rest of the Platoon to join them. This was even more tiring than night marching, and a greater strain on the nerves. The young boy had fallen to the ground even though Fireworks had relieved him of his submachine gun several hours earlier. The commander was angry, not so much on account of the poor boy himself, but rather because he resented that such a young man had been allocated to his platoon. He considered leaving him behind to fend for himself but abandoned this plan because the boy would more than likely be picked up and give the rest of them away. So they pressed on, taking turns at holding the boy on his feet.

By some miracle they did not come into contact with enemy troops. But they came close twice. While resting on the third day they heard a patrol walking through the bush only a few yards from where they lay in hiding. That night they were compelled to take cover when a helicopter crossed their path, flying low with powerful searchlights scouring the forests beneath.

On the fourth day they were running short of food. They had left their Matetsi base with only a few supplies, so that they could travel as lightly and as fast as possible. There was no question at this stage of risking detection by stopping at a village. So they relied on their bush craft: they ate berries, roots, and the sour jelly of the malala fruit, and when they were short of water they sucked the wood of the White Tree, which was plentiful in the region. This diet was supplemented with glucose tablets and vitamin pills.

When they got to the Lutope River they had covered over a hundred miles and were more or less clear of the danger zone. After a much-needed eight-hour sleep they moved on at a slower pace, entering Lupane Tribal Trust Land. They began progressing south. . . .

After only a day's rest, the commander began going off regularly to make contact with some of the Z.A.P.U. men who lived in the district. It was easy for him to walk about unnoticed, since the area was quite heavily populated. After a few visits he felt confident that he could organize the supporters fairly well. He told the guerrillas of his progress and said that this time they were going to take it easy and build things up carefully. He suggested that they remain based in the valley, as water was at hand and the cover was good. He had not yet announced to the Z.A.P.U. contacts that there was a guerrilla platoon behind him in the bush. He merely told them that he had recently arrived and was staying with relatives on the other side of the Trust Land. But he had warned them that he wanted to make arrangements for the arrival of a guerrilla group sometime in the future. They had accepted his story and seemed keen to discuss what should be done.

In order to maintain this low-key approach with his contacts, the commander suggested that his men remain self-sufficient as far as food was concerned. There were a number of African stores in the area that did quite a large amount of business. It was decided that in order to maintain a steady supply of food, a team of two guerrillas would go off every other day to a different store and buy a small number of items. In this way suspicions would not be aroused by the purchase of large quantities, and the risk of discovery would be kept to the minimum by always sending different men to different stores. Money was a problem, but the commander had sent a message to Bulawayo to request further funds from Z.A.P.U.'s underground headquarters there. In the meantime they would have to make do with what they had. As it was nearly all South African currency, it would be necessary to try to change most of it into Rhodesian. South African money could be used now and then, but it would be dangerous to set up a pattern of strangers going into stores and always buying with rands. The banks might register a sudden increase in the number of rands coming in from Matopo and spark off an enquiry by the extrasensitive security forces. To avoid this the commander decided to get his contacts to change some money in Bulawayo. He also asked the men to try to change a little in a couple of stores, using stories about coming back from the mines.

Whenever a team went off from the base camp on one of these supply missions, they were given a maximum time limit. If the men were late, it would be assumed that something had gone wrong, and the platoon would have to move out of its hiding-place.

On March 2, John Sibali and Edison Maleme had departed early in the morning and were due to return by 2 P.M. When they had not arrived by 3:30 P.M. the commander ordered his men to start abandoning camp. As they were gathering their weapons together, the observation post reported that he could see several black soldiers descending into the valley. The guerrillas were now unable to move out without being seen. The commander ordered his men to take up established defensive positions. Moments later the observation post reported that it could see white soldiers coming down as well: all in all, there were about twenty men advancing. The guerrillas sank back into the rocky crevices and waited.

Many months later when Joseph was back in Zambia, he learned what happened to Sibali and Maleme. They had entered a store run by a white woman which was not far from the Matopo Police Camp. This store had been used once before by Joseph and Tami, who had bought supplies there with Rhodesian money and without incident. But on this occasion the guerrillas offered the woman rands. The woman accepted the money, but for some reason it started her off talking. She asked them in Sindebele whether they spoke Afrikaans. They replied that they didn't, and that the money had been sent to them by a brother. Then she asked them whether it was legal to do this. They replied that they thought it was okay. The woman was not questioning them in a suspicious manner: she was just being friendly.

But one of the customers who overheard their conversation became very suspicious. He stepped up to the two men and asked for their registration certificates. When they refused to show them to him, the man explained that he was a policeman. The guerrillas told him they had left their *stupas* behind. The policeman said that if that was the case he would have to arrest them, as he was under orders to arrest anyone without a *stupa*. The guerrillas asked him if he could just forget about it, since he was not in uniform and therefore not officially on duty. But the policeman refused. He asked the shopkeeper and the crowd of customers whether they had ever seen either of the men before. When they all replied in the negative, he requested that the shopkeeper telephone the police station to get assistance, and he ordered the two men to sit in a corner and wait.

But Sibali and Maleme started making for the door. The conscientious policeman rushed round to block the exit and commandeered some meek bystanders to help him. For some reason the guerrillas did not put up a fight at that stage. They probably still hoped they could talk their way out of their difficulties.

Their hopes were dashed when they saw the size of the police contingent that rushed to the store. It consisted of not only a police Land Rover full of white armed policemen and soldiers, but also a jeep of R.A.R. troops. When the first policeman entered and asked "Who are you?" the guerrillas pulled out their pistols and started shooting. But it was far too late. John Sibali was shot in the stomach and died soon afterwards. Edison was injured in the arm. Then the security men jumped on him and beat him heavily enough to extract a promise that he would lead them to his guerrilla platoon.

As the column of Rhodesian soldiers advanced cautiously and with difficulty down the steep slopes of the Matopos Hills where the guerrillas were hiding, a helicopter began patrolling the valley. But the platoon was too far into the depths of the valley to be seen from the air. The column intermittently came into the guerrillas' view as it drew to within a distance of two hundred yards. Because of his white civilian shirt, Edison stood out clearly in front, leading the way down directly toward the hideout. The guerrillas watched the advance until the soldiers were only about eighty yards off, at which point Edison stopped for a moment. Then, instead of continuing the descent, he led the soldiers along the face of the hill parallel to its base where Platoon A was hiding. As the column drew level with the guerrillas below, it became clear that Edison was marching the security forces straight past his own men in order to provide them with the opportunity for an ambush. The soldiers were passing by like sitting ducks at a distance of only fifty yards.

The commander shouted the order to fire. . . .

PART TWO

Analyses

XIV.

Revolutionary Warfare and Counterinsurgency

*Eqbal Ahmad, a Pakistani living in the
United States, is a member of the Institute
of Policy Studies in Washington, D.C.,
and has helped create its European branch,
the Transnational Institute of Amsterdam.*

. . . Occupied nations and oppressed peoples have resorted to guerrilla warfare throughout recorded history. But only in modern times has it become the acknowledged weapon of the weak, a symbol of our age, registering successes no less than setbacks from China to Cuba, Malaya to Mozambique. Some 28 guerrilla insurgencies were reported by the Pentagon in 1958 and 42 in 1965; in 1969, about 50 were underway.

The unprecedented popularity of guerrilla warfare symbolizes the progressive severance of traditional social and economic links, the erosion of authority, and a moral explosion among the disinherited, disenchanted masses in underdeveloped countries. It indicates the increasingly perceptible gap between the sorrows of the poor and the contentment of the rich, between the coercive military capabilities of the rulers and the determined resistance of the ruled. It also constitutes man's supreme challenge to the awesome power of modern machines. Vietnam and Algeria are cases in point: small, underdeveloped nations, they engaged two of the most advanced war machines of our time and defeated the presumption of technology. . . .

Interest in guerrilla warfare has developed rapidly in the

Extract from *National Liberation and Revolution*, N. Miller and E. Aya, eds. (New York: The Free Press, 1970). Extract copyright 1970 by Eqbal Ahmad. Reprinted by permission of the author.

United States. The subject is studied with a sense of urgency in universities no less than in military schools, by policy makers no less than by professors and journalists, for America's security and power are believed to be at stake. In an address to the National War College, Hubert Humphrey reiterated the national concern when he spoke of this "bold new form of aggression which could rank with the discovery of gunpowder" as constituting the "major challenge to our security."[1] Guerrilla warfare is viewed as the latest weapon in the communist arsenal, and Vietnam is its testing ground. "If guerrilla techniques succeed in Vietnam," wrote James Reston, "nobody in Washington dare assume that the same techniques will not be applied in all Communist rimlands from Korea to Iran."[2] Scholars like W. W. Rostow have portrayed Vietnam as the war to end wars. He told a University of Leeds audience: " . . . if we have the common will to hold together and get on with the job—the struggle in Vietnam might be the last great confrontation of the post-war era. . . . "[3]

These views are based on two assumptions and at least one serious misconception. It is assumed that the Vietnamese situation is typical, historically and politically, of other underdeveloped countries, and that American policy toward other nations would be comparable to the one pursued in Vietnam. The misconception concerns the nature of revolutionary warfare.

Until recently there had been two main models—the establishment and the revolutionary—of guerrilla warfare. However, in the years following World War Two, two subsidiary models have been developing and are now distinguishable from their ideological and theoretical parents. The four models are: (1) the conventional establishment; (2) the classical revolutionary; (3) the liberal-reformist; and (4) the radical-heroic. The last two draw heavily on the classical revolutionary theory, but there is a fundamental difference between them. The radical-heroic theory, most popularly represented by Régis Debray and Che Guevara in his

[1] See *The New York Times,* serialized editorials on "Wars of Liberation," III-IV, June 30, July 2, July 3, 1965.

[2] "Washington: The Larger Implications of Vietnam," *The New York Times,* April 25, 1965.

[3] W. W. Rostow, "The Great Transition: Tasks of the First and Second Post War Generations," February 23, 1967. Similar views have been expressed by Mr. Nixon on several occasions, including his May 14, 1969, speech for "peace."

last years, is antiestablishment and revolutionary. The liberal-reformist doctrine, whose most prominent exponents come from France and the United States, has counterrevolutionary goals and represents learning from previous failures in suppressing internally generated revolutions, an improvement upon—not a departure from—the establishment model.[4]

The Conventional Establishment Model

Although the United States historically pursued an antirevolutionary policy with regard to the Latin and Caribbean countries, American interventions occurred along conventional lines. America's interest in counterinsurgency developed after World War Two. But under President Kennedy it became a dominant theme in the strategy of "limited war." The doctrine of limited war, which ran counter to the Eisenhower administration's preoccupation with "massive retaliation," had already found an important military advocate in General Maxwell Taylor.[5] Taylor's prescriptions for limited war favored larger buildup of conventional military capabilities. Under Kennedy they came to be supplemented by the notion of counterinsurgency. . . .

America's interest in revolutionary warfare began from a counterrevolutionary and defensive posture as a result of reverses in China, Korea, Cuba, and Laos—and of its protracted involvement in Vietnam. It was natural, therefore, for American officials and establishment academicians to be attracted more to the myths and methods of those who have had to defend themselves against guerrillas than to an understanding of the causes and characteristics of such wars. Americans are therefore unable to avoid the psychological and political pitfalls of colonial powers and regimes like France and Nationalist China. A symptom of this negative posture is that, while recognizing in it a "bold new

[4]Discussion of the radical-heroic model is not included here. For a partial discussion see my essay, "Radical But Wrong," in Leo Huberman and Paul M. Sweezy (eds.), *Régis Debray and the Latin American Revolution* (New York, 1968), pp. 70–83.

[5]See *The Uncertain Trumpet* (New York, 1960). Taylor, a close friend of the Kennedys, later became Chairman of the Joint Chiefs of Staff and Ambassador to Saigon.

form" of warfare, government publications (including the course books used at Fort Bragg) reject the term "revolutionary war" in favor of old terms which do not express the vital distinction between revolutionary and other types of guerrilla conflict. . . . The widely used term "guerrilla war" denotes some common features of such conflict but does not emphasize the peculiarities of its modern, revolutionary variety.

For example, like revolutionary wars, partisan movements (known to us from the Napoleonic wars and World War Two) were armed struggles by guerrillas against vastly superior armies, in which the overtly neutral but covertly engaged civilians provided the demographic "sea" to the guerrilla "fish." Yet the differences between these two types of warfare are significant: the partisans operated in support of conventional forces in open conflicts and expected liberation by the allies; they operated mostly as local bands that lacked nationwide structure and centralized direction; their aims were politically and socially limited to "liberation." A revolutionary guerrilla movement, however, seeks not simply to inflict military losses on the enemy but to destroy the legitimacy of its government and to establish a rival regime through the creation of "parallel hierarchies." The Chinese, Cuban, Algerian, and Indochinese conflicts are cases in point. Tito's partisan movement acquired many characteristics of revolutionary war, but perhaps its earliest western example is the Irish rebellion of 1916–1922.

Other features of the conventional establishment interpretation of revolutionary war can be summarized as follows: (1) There is a conspiratorial theory which views revolutionary war as being essentially a technical problem, that is, a problem of plotting and subversion on the one hand and of intelligence and suppression on the other. As the "chief conspiratorial group," the communists are believed to be the most likely initiators and beneficiaries of revolution. U.S. officials have used this argument to justify their military interventions, including the one in the Dominican Republic (1965). (2) A logical extension of the conspiratorial theory is the belief that any revolutionary movement is inspired, directed, and controlled from abroad. The active sanctuary—from which guerrillas can smuggle supplies and train their troops—is considered the primary factor in their success. . . . Indeed, so strong was the belief in the external origins of guerrillas that Washington promoted plans for "offensive use of guerrillas" against its communist enemies.[6](3) Conduct of the war is viewed as being mainly an exercise in military strategy and tactics. The military advantages of guerrillas—mobility, freedom from logistic anchors, good intelligence, surprise—are studied; countermeasures and devices are developed. Irregular and covered terrain is considered a primary condition for guerrilla warfare; therefore troops are trained in jungle warfare. (4) The guerrilla movement is believed to enjoy considerable advantage because, in the words of W. W. Rostow, "its task is merely to destroy while the government must build and protect what it is building."[7](5) The civilian population is considered important for providing information and protection to the guerrillas; it is believed that civilian-guerrilla cooperation is enforced by terror and does not manifest free choice. . . . Serious inquiry into other bases of guerrilla support and mass mobilization is therefore deemed of no great importance.

The Classical Revolutionary Model

The above assumptions are, at best, half truths—credible and misleading. . . . Studies in the field of revolutionary wars and my personal observation of the Algerian struggle lead to different conclusions which may be summarized as follows: (1) Revolutionaries consider mass support the primary condition for their success; winning and maintaining popular support remain their central objectives throughout the struggle. (2) The requirements of guerrilla war, as well as the history of its failures and successes, confirm the primacy of political factors in such a conflict. (3) Popular support for the guerrillas is predicated upon the moral alienation of the masses from the existing government. The revolutionaries' chief aim is to activate and perpetuate the moral isolation of the enemy regime until such isolation has become total and irreversible. (4) The conditions leading to revolutionary wars are not created by conspiracy. They are partly inherent in a

---

[6] Put into practice, these plans have ended disastrously. Such was the case with U.S. attempts to infiltrate guerrilla teams into North Vietnam, a practice that is believed to have begun in 1956 and continued at least until 1965.

[7] Cf. Lt. Col. T.N. Greene (ed.), "The Guerrilla and How to Fight Him," *Selections from the Marine Corps Gazette* (New York, 1962), p. 60.

situation of rapid social change, but the outbreak normally results from the failure of a ruling elite to respond to the challenge of modernization. (5) A revolutionary guerrilla movement concentrates on outadministering, *not* on outfighting, the enemy. This is a constructive and not simply a destructive undertaking. (6) The use of terror by guerrillas is highly selective; it does not constitute the reason for the favorable reaction of the masses to their cause. (7) The external sanctuary is of greater psychological and diplomatic than military or political value to the guerrillas. A discussion of these points follows.

The organizers of guerrilla warfare give prime attention, in practice no less than in theory, to the human factor. . . .

The guerrilla concern with mass support is understandable even on purely military grounds. Mobility, for example, depends on the availability of food, shelter, road gangs, labor for laying mines and booby traps, messengers, and stretcher-bearers—services which require active and clandestine civilian cooperation right under the enemy's nose. The guerrillas depend on mobility to surprise the enemy as well as to dodge him. Good information on enemy movements and plans enables guerrillas to choose their time and place for ambush and to escape antiguerrilla mop-up operations. Intelligence depends on intimate contacts with the population to the extent that it develops into a widely based rebel infrastructure which includes women, old men, and children. . . . Lastly, popular support is essential because the disparity of military strength rules out a clear-cut victory by the insurgents, and the struggle tends to be a war of attrition in which the guerrillas' morale is their ultimate trump card; morale cannot be sustained in isolation from one's people. . . .

The underdeveloped countries are experiencing a triple dislocation—political, social, and economic—in telescoped time. Politically, this dislocation is marked by the erosion of traditional authority, an increasing search for freedom from domination by foreigners as well as native oligarchies; by the gradual rise to political consciousness of a hitherto complacent and atomized peasantry, their hook-up with modern, ideological counterelites, and their growing collective expectation of justice, opportunity, and participation in national life. Socially, it is characterized by the emergence of new classes (urban workers, the extremely crucial but underanalyzed lumpenproletariat, and a new middle class) and by cleavages of world views between generations and classes whereby the young and the disinherited reject the old values and agencies of socialization in favor of new ones. Among its economic manifestations is the demand not only for rapid, rounded economic development, but also for the equal distribution of wealth—rather, for the distribution of austerity where there is not enough wealth to distribute.

In ideological terms the triangular character of this revolution is indicated by the simultaneous appeal of nationalism, populism, and socialism—movements which were historically apart and, at first, even mutually exclusive in Europe. The overall result of this development has been a moral explosion among the masses. Men no longer accept misery, exploitation, and inequality as ordained by God. The myth of divine rulers and superior races has exploded, alternative ways of ordering life and labor are increasingly understood to be available, and people believe that change in the old order of things is not only possible but just and therefore necessary. . . .

The pressures for change in the political, economic, and social relationships of the past inevitably lead to a confrontation with those whose interests lie in the maintenance of the status quo. In countries and colonies whose rulers are willing to abdicate their monopoly of power and privileges, where genuine reforms are introduced, and where new institutions begin to provide for sharing of power and responsibility, the change is effected in an orderly (if not entirely peaceful) and democratic manner. Periodic and limited violence occurs, mainly in the cities, and is often exploited by aspiring politicians. But organized violence of the type used in revolutionary warfare is discouraged, rarely breaks out, and so far has not succeeded in a single country where the government made a genuine and timely effort to satisfy the grievances of the people. Nor has it succeeded in countries where the rulers have maintained some contact with the masses or where there were institutions and mechanisms through which one could hope to influence and change the existing system. It was the relative willingness of its rulers to accept change, rather than the lessons in liberalism they allegedly taught their subjects, that explains the comparatively orderly liquidation of the British Empire. (In independent India the communist uprising of Telingana failed not because the Indian masses have few needs but because

India's leaders, the Congress Party, and the nascent parliaments had legitimacy and held some promise for change. Similarly India's troubles in Kashmir, in Nagaland, and with the Mitzo tribes point not to the potency of communist subversion but to what happens when a government finds little moral support among a people.)

When a ruling class resists fundamental reforms (which mean reduction, if not liquidation, of its power and privileges), its confrontation with the new political forces becomes increasingly violent. A regime unwilling to satisfy popular aspirations begins to lose legitimacy. Coercion increasingly becomes its primary instrument of assuring obedience; "law and order" becomes the favorite phrase of its governing groups. The revolutionary forces deliberately activate this process. By forcing the issues which augment the contradictions within the system and the divisions within the ruling class, they weaken the latter's efficacy and cohesion. By promoting activities which bring into sharp relief the parochial interests of the regime, they widen the perceptible gap between those in authority and the expectations of the collective. By setting examples of defying and challenging established authority, they break the inhibitions of habitual or reflexive obedience and help transform private doubts into public actions; examples of overt resistance establish new standards of defiance and produce new alternatives and skills.

A revolutionary movement must also give ideological thrust, organizational form, and programmatic content to the amorphous revolutionary conflagration. It must demonstrate, in practice, that there are alternative structures and arrangements which approximate the popular yearning for a just, communal, and participatory system. This last is a noteworthy point, for a guerrilla movement whose organization, leaders, and policies do not reflect the promises of the revolution (particularly in the base areas) is not likely to receive the sustained mass support necessary for protracted struggle. Achieving moral isolation of the enemy and legitimacy for the revolution require not only the severance of the old but also the forging of new political and social links.

Once a revolutionary movement enters the guerrilla phase, its central objective is not simply to achieve the moral isolation of the enemy but also to confirm, perpetuate, and institutionalize it by providing an alternative to the discredited regime through the creation of "parallel hierarchies." The major task of the movement is not to outfight but to outadminister the government. The main target in this bid is the village, where the majority of the population lives and where the government's presence is often chimeric or exploitative (conscription, collection of taxes, etc.). Here the chief and his council are often the main link between the people and the government. Breaking this link demands careful planning, organization, and hard work. The government is systematically eliminated from the countryside by the conversion or killing of village officials, who are then controlled or replaced by the political arm of the movement. The government is thus cut off from the population and begins, as the French graphically put it, to *légiférer dans le vide* (legislate in the void). The rebels must build an administrative structure to collect taxes, to provide some education and social welfare, and to maintain a modicum of economic activity. A revolutionary guerrilla movement which does not have these administrative concerns and structures to fulfill its obligations to the populace would degenerate into banditry. Even in clandestineness, the parallel government must prove its efficacy.

The official American view—that the guerrillas' tasks are easier because they only destroy while the government builds—contradicts the findings of those who have studied and observed these movements. It would be a rare revolutionary war indeed in which the government's destruction of civilian population and property did not surpass by a wide margin the losses caused by the guerrillas' selective terror and sabotage. During this phase of the movement, military confrontation is normally avoided. The embarrassed government also, at first, treats the assassinations as a police problem, and nonpayment of taxes is ascribed to administrative lags or a bad harvest. . . .

Most compelling, but also most self-defeating, is the myth that terror is the basis of civilian support for guerrillas. . . . Guerrilla warfare requires a highly committed but covert civilian support, which cannot be obtained at gunpoint. . . . Guerrilla resort to indiscriminate terrorism indicates lack of broad support, without which the movement soon collapses. Only degenerate or defeated guerrillas are known to have risked the loss of mass support by terrorizing civilians at large. . . .

An outstanding feature of guerrilla training is the stress on scrupulously "correct and just" behavior toward civilians. The rebel army code carries severe punishments for rape, robbery, and damage to property and crops. . . . Guerrillas' use of terror, therefore, is sociologically and psychologically selective. It is employed partly as an instrument of subversion and partly out of a need for survival. It strikes those who are popularly identified as the "enemy of the people"—officials, landlords, and informers. Its subversive purpose is twofold—to break the links between the government and the people and to free the poor peasants and landless laborers . . . of the oppressive power of landlords and the state bureaucracy allied to them. In order to be effective, terror must be regarded by the people as an extragovernmental effort to dispense justice long overdue, and it must have the effect of freeing the local communities from the felt constraints of coercive authority.

Killing a village chief, therefore, is often a very complicated affair and should generally prove to be unnecessary. Since most chiefs are local farmers who command legitimacy and loyalty through tradition and kinship, the revolutionaries ideally want to persuade them to join the movement. When that fails, it takes painstaking political work to convince the villagers that their chief is an "enemy of the people" and to bring about his elimination. . . .

Second-degree terror, which normally does not result in killing, is used to sabotage the government's belated effort to gain popular support, and thus to perpetuate its isolation from the people. Government school teachers and health workers are favorite targets of kidnapping and indoctrination. . . . Guerrilla sabotage normally guards against causing too much hardship on the population and long-range damages to the economy. Industry and even foreign-owned plantations are spared if they pay their "taxes" to the liberation front. And they normally do so when the government is unable to protect them. . . . Thus guerrilla sabotage too is selective, aiming at maximum psychological effects.

The success of a movement in acquiring legitimacy, support for its programs, and participation in its parallel hierarchies depends on a number of factors. A coherent, consistent, and functioning ideology appropriate to its cultural, political, and economic environment appears to be important for success in protracted conflict between antagonists of unequal strength; it is particularly crucial in assuring both the movement's continued legitimacy and the unity of its leadership after the armed phase of the struggle is over and the task of consolidation begins. . . .

The structures, values, and leadership style of a revolution must not only promise a new vision of society but also, at the same time, be congruent with the old culture. . . . Successful parallel hierarchies, therefore, are generally based on extant local patterns and experiences—a phenomenon notable in the Mexican, Russian, Chinese, Vietnamese, and Algerian revolutions.[8] Even more importantly, the symbols of revolution and styles of leadership derive heavily from the local culture and constitute the creative links between the old and the new, between the mystical and the rational bases of legitimacy.

But unlike the formal constitutions and administrative structures of most underdeveloped countries, such patterns are not the outcome of contrived, professional designing. They result from a profound and intense interaction between leaders and followers which often constitutes a greater learning experience for the urban-trained leaders than their rural comrades. Only a relationship of mutuality, identification, and coperformance between leaders and masses can release the creative energies necessary for the constant improvisations and the steady flow of new leaders (their attrition rate being very high) so crucial in revolutionary warfare. Personal background and class origins of leaders seem to be important factors in facilitating this development; the narrower the original social and cultural gaps between them and the populace, the more likely they are to create meaningful bases for authoritative leadership within a revolutionary setting. The majority of Algerian, Chinese, and Vietnamese revolutionary leaders are known to have rural family backgrounds, and few were trained in western universities. Frequently a relationship of mutuality and identification between city-trained revolutionaries and the rural masses develops when the repressive measures of the government drive the former to seek safety in the rural areas, forcing them to communicate and live with peasants not as prose-

[8] See for example Sir John Maynard, *The Russian Peasant and Other Studies* (New York, 1962); Stuart R. Schram, *The Political Thought of Mao Tse-tung* (New York, 1963); and Paul Mus, *Vietnam: Sociologie d'une guerre* (Paris, 1952).

lytizing outsiders but as suffering fellowmen. In the process, the leaders learn the realities of peasant economy, social life, and the meaning and power of rural myths, symbols, and rituals; peasants similarly begin to understand that their private and communal problems have wider public and political connections.

Congruence, however, does not imply absence of institutional or ideological innovation, nor even conformity to traditional structures and values. A revolution must necessarily destroy and replace the anachronistic traditional structures and values. As an organized, sustained, and largely clandestine struggle aimed at the destruction of the existing power relationships, revolutionary warfare itself represents a break from the rebellions of the past. It creates an environment in which the rural people themselves accept and introduce innovations which transform their communities; these often include innovations whose imposition by illegitimate rulers they had previously resisted. . . .

Finally, there are the well-known "rational" factors (involving the promise and performance of programs, elites, and institutions) which go into the making of legitimacy: (1) the success of a movement's program in creating common interests and collective goals (as against serving parochial interests); (2) the actual functioning of revolutionary institutions—the extent to which they remain accountable to the population and permit rapid recruitment and elevation of the young seeking new identities and roles in society; and (3) the integrity of leaders, their ability to practice and promote the principles proclaimed by the revolution and cherished by the people, their success in realizing (at least partially in the present) the popular dream of integrated, participatory, self-managing communities. Since the superior resources of the incumbents make coercion a poor basis of power for revolution, revolutionary movements often represent maximization of the positive basis for legitimacy. The most successful guerrilla movements, therefore, evince deep respect for local autonomy, self-management, rapid social mobility, egalitarianism, and accountability of leaders and cadres to the populace. (Although it is not relevant to our concern here, it should be noted that, during the period following successful termination of such conflicts, the new government's efforts at centralization of power often lead to clashes between the government and the self-governing communities and units of production and to the sabotage of self-management by the centralizing bureaucracy. Such was most clearly the experience in the U.S.S.R. and Algeria.) . . .

The desertion of the intellectuals and moderates often signals, not so much the irreversibility of a revolutionary war, but its take-off. Intellectuals, especially the Asian variety thereof, are a democratic, liberal group who view organized violence with distaste. Somewhat alienated from their culture, westernized, and city-centered, they distrust the peasants but desire an improvement of their condition. When an armed revolution breaks out, they are likely to play in the middle, hoping to get some reforms under way by using the armed threat as a counter for bargaining. These *attentistes* begin to go into exile or to defect to the rebels after the failure of the regime and the success of the revolution become imminent.

The incumbent army's pressure for conventional attack on an external sanctuary is yet another sign that a revolutionary war has been lost on home grounds. In revolutionary warfare, professional armies trained for conventional combat follow a vicious logic of escalation, which derives from acute frustration over an elusive war that puts in question not only their effectiveness but the very validity of their training and organization. Moreover, the morale of professional soldiers cannot be maintained if they know they are fighting a popular rebellion. Hence the compulsion to believe that behind the popular behavior lies the terror of an army trained, equipped, and directed by a foreign power, and the wish to draw the enemy into open battles. . . . Since reprisals against the population fail to produce the desired result, carrying the war to a sovereign nation becomes the most compelling and the only road to a conventional showdown with the enemy. . . .

The importance of an active sanctuary should not be underestimated, although it is not essential to guerrilla success. In Cuba, Yugoslavia, and China, the revolutionaries did not have active sanctuaries. In Burma and to a lesser extent in Greece, sanctuaries proved of limited value. Neither the Morice Line in Algeria, nor the Lattre Line around the Red River Delta, nor the armored Ping-Han Japanese railroad in North China had much effect on the outcome of the war. Politically and militarily, revolutionary guerrillas are by and large a self-sustaining group that can go on fighting indefinitely even if infiltration from across the border stops. . . .

External help, however, has great psychological and diplomatic value. In a war of attrition, there can be no decisive victory over a strong foreign enemy. At best, one hopes to inflict heavy losses, tire it out, and through international pressure force it to negotiate—not the status quo, but withdrawal. External help is important in internationalizing guerrilla demands; it keeps alive the hope of liberation. When a revolutionary army loses an ally, it loses not so much military support as hope. When the world is watching, when the fear of diplomatic sanctions and the threat of widened war are present, a foreign power caught in counterguerrilla operations is less likely to make the final and the only move that is likely to "win" the war—start committing genocide.

Finally, the assumption that a guerrilla outfit, like a conventional army, can be controlled and commanded by a foreign or externally based government ignores the organizational, psychological, and political facts of revolutionary warfare. As the case of Algeria clearly demonstrates, the distrust of the "home-based" guerrillas for even their own government-in-exile cannot be overstated. The resourceful and tough "interior" leaders and cadres who face the enemy daily, collect taxes, administer, make promises, and give hopes to the population are not easily controlled from abroad and make suspicious, exacting, and hard-to-please allies. Clandestineness does not permit the use of conventional channels of communication and authority. Therefore, zone commanders and political commissars are, for the most part, masters of what they survey. Tested in war, seasoned in politics, accustomed to command and to quick decisions, these soldier-politicians have their own constituents, dreams of power and community, and commitment to expressed goals. As a group, they are joined together by shared experiences, by a common mood which is defiant and insular, by a shared suspicion of "politicians and diplomats over there" selling them out, and by a collective will to defy a settlement that is not of their making.

The Liberal-Reformist Model

At the start of this section an explanation of terminology is necessary. The use of the "liberal-reformist" label may be regarded by some as inaccurate. An argument can be made that counterinsurgency violates the fundamental tenets of liberalism and therefore should not be associated with liberal ideology or institutions. In this view French and American roles in Algeria and Vietnam were unique instances in which the countries concerned deviated from their liberal norms. It is pointed out by exponents of this view that in fact the metropolitan peoples' recognition that the practice of counterinsurgency violated liberal values and democratic institutions eventually contributed to their opposition to the wars in Algeria and Vietnam.

My preference for this term is based on the evaluation that western liberalism has been concerned essentially with procedural freedoms while neglecting substantive ones. As a result, it could support—even produce—colonialism and racism. Hence the paradox that western democratic institutions not only developed alongside but even drew sustenance from the parallel growth of colonialism and racism. Second, I prefer this description because the term "counterinsurgency" fails to denote the differences between the conventional, punitive-militarist, and liberal-reformist approaches to it. Third, the term liberal-reformist describes more accurately than any other term the expressed goals as well as the background of individuals involved in articulating and practicing this form of counterinsurgency. The rhetoric which defines its goals is reformist and liberal: "freedom," "progress," "reforms," "democracy," "participation," and "self-determination" are its most favorite working words and concepts. Generally speaking, its practitioners are men of impeccable liberal credentials in the United States. Prominent among them are many of Kennedy's New Frontiersmen and well-known university professors of liberal reputation at prestigious campuses. . . .

In theory, the liberal-reformists draw heavily on the revolutionary model, although they often deny its originality. They postulate that, although guerrilla wars result from conspiracy and are waged by remote control, the cooperation or at least the neutrality of a population is essential to their survival and effectiveness. They recognize that politics plays the dominant role in such conflicts, and that for revolutionaries civilians are the first and remain the primary object of attention. They admit the central importance of ideology and the existence of a "cause" around which the masses could be mobilized, and they allow that the presence of acute economic and social grievances is causally linked with popular support for revolutionaries. Their main difference with the conventional-establishment approach lies in their comprehension of the interdependence of political, military, and psychological factors in revolutionary warfare.

The theory and practice of counterinsurgency suffer from severe psychological handicaps that result from its antecedents, antirevolutionary ideology, and the managerial attitudes of its exponents and practitioners. Its antecedents are colonial and bureaucratic; in the theory and practice of psychological warfare, it draws heavily on fascist doctrines and practices. It derives inspiration from colonial history and learns from its example. The French theorists, much like their American colleagues, emphasize that "pacification" is part of the western tradition, that conventional warfare gained ascendancy only during the two world wars, and that it is again being superseded by "limited," unconventional conflicts. In their search for western models and cultural continuity, the French theorists of *la guerre révolutionnaire* invoked the memories of pacification in the heyday of colonialism. They frequently cited examples and works of General Bugeaud, Marshal Lyautey, and Galliéni. The latter's doctrine on the identity of civilian and military authority (the role of *officier-administrateur* and *officier-éducateur*) was extolled; their methods were emulated.[9]

In the United States. the experience with the Indians and other colonial exploits provide the source of learning. For the uninitiated, American counterinsurgency literature holds many surprises. Here is Roger Hilsman, a well-known scholar of liberal persuasion, advisor and aide to President Kennedy, and, at the time of this writing, the Director of Intelligence and Research in the State Department:

> . . . We Americans have also forgotten that it was we who fought one of the most successful counter-guerrilla campaigns in history—in the Philippines back at the turn of the century. We learned some fundamental military lessons then, and it is time we remembered them.[10]

[9] See Peter Paret, *French Revolutionary Warfare: From Indochina to Algeria* (New York, 1964), ch. 7.

[10] "Internal War: The New Communist Tactic," in Greene (ed.), *op. cit.*, p. 26. [The "successful" Philippine campaign was " . . . the bloodiest colonial war (in proportion to population) ever fought by a white power in Asia; it cost the lives of 300,000 Filipinos" (Bernard B. Fall, *The Two Viet-Nams* [New York, 1967 (second revised edition)], p. 464, note 1).]

Mr. Hilsman goes on to give some gory details and to draw some "fundamental lessons" from defeating the "extremists" and "bands of religious fanatics" who were vile enough to resist American occupation. The lessons include: (1) maximum use of native mercenaries as demonstrated by the "fabulous exploits" of the "famed Philippine constabulary"; (2) leadership role for Americans—"over each group [of native recruits] we put a trained American officer—a bold and determined leader" (the official euphemism is "advisory role"); and (3) adoption of "Indian fighting" tactics of surprise and nighttime attacks—"the solution is to adopt the same weapons to fight him."

Despite their rhetoric, which stresses the primacy of politics and calls peaceful revolution their goal, the liberal-reformists treat counterinsurgency essentially as an administrative problem subject to managerial and technical solutions. . . .

The liberal-reformist theorists are ultimately concerned with order more than participation, obedience more than the consent of the governed, stability more than change. The people are to them objects of policy, a means rather than an end, a manipulable, malleable mass whose behavior toward the government is more important than are their feelings and attitudes. Since they are interested only in operational payoffs, the counterinsurgents' investigation into revolutionary theory and practice tends to be selective, superficial, and systems-oriented.

For example, the military writings of Mao Tse-tung are reproduced and cited out of their political context, their specific local character is ignored, and Mao is presented as a system builder rather than the leader of a historical revolution. The "systems" orientation as well as the conspiratorial view produces a bias in favor of seeking similarities among revolutions. Hence the fact is often ignored that, despite many similarities, the Chinese, Vietnamese, Algerians, and Cubans fought very different wars and owed little to Mao's "doctrine." Yet the same theorists rarely acknowledge that the similarities among those revolutions resulted more from common conditions (e.g., Japanese, French, and American occupation) than a common doctrine or source of conspiracy.

The liberal-reformist theorists dissipate their limited insight into revolutionary warfare as they focus on the links between the people and the revolutionary cadres. They conclude that the effectiveness and strength of revolutionaries rest in their ability to manipulate ("techniques of mass deception") and coerce the masses ("terror"), and in their ruthless organizational skills ("infrastructure"). As a result, their prescriptions reveal considerable technical expertise, an obsession with administering and manipulating the masses (e.g., strategic hamlets, psy-warfare, etc.), and an oblique if not altogether distorted view of the needs and demands of the people. Their indebtedness to what they construe to be the insurgent model is unmistakable, but their understanding of it remains crooked. I. F. Stone wrote in 1961:

> In reading the military literature on guerrilla warfare now so fashionable at the Pentagon, one feels that these writers are like men watching a dance from outside through heavy plate glass windows. They see the motions but they can't hear the music. They put the mechanical gestures down on paper with pedantic fidelity. But what rarely comes through to them are the injured racial feelings, the misery, the rankling slights, the hatred, the devotion, the inspiration and the desperation. So they do not really understand what leads men to abandon wife, children, home, career, friends; to take to the bush and live gun in hand like a hunted animal; to challenge overwhelming military odds rather than acquiesce any longer in humiliation, injustice or poverty. . . . [11]

The conspiratorial theory—the argument that contemporary revolutions can be understood in the light of a worldwide communist conspiracy—continues to provide the needed rationale and justification for counterinsurgency and foreign interventions. The French theorists are notorious for their ascription of communism to all insurgencies. In their view Algeria's F.L.N. was a puppet variously of Moscow, Peking, and Cairo, just as their American colleagues view the N.L.F. as a puppet of North Vietnam and/or China. . . .

Their counterrevolutionary commitment leads these theorists to at first qualify, then distort, and finally abandon their central (albeit only) positive theme—that revolutionary warfare has its basis in the existence of acute grievances, and that the achievement of social, economic, and political progress will reduce the chances of its outbreak and success. The qualification is introduced by the argument that, although "modernization" is essen-

[11] I. F. Stone, *In a Time of Torment* (New York, 1968), pp. 173–174.

tial in the "long run," social and economic inequities and injustices pose no real threat to stability until they are exploited by conspirators. The essential requirements of stability are, therefore, efficient administration . . . and policing of the population. . . . Hence reforms are seen only as useful auxiliaries to "pacification." . . .

The distortion develops from continued focus on "terror" as the basis of mass support for guerrillas. At their best, counterinsurgency experts display obvious contradictions between their rhetoric and their perception of reality. . . . For example in his book, *Viet Cong,* Douglas Pike presents an impressive amount of evidence illustrating that except in rare instances the N.L.F.'s use of sabotage and assassination is sociologically selective, politically judicious, and psychologically liberating. Yet his conclusions stand out in glaring opposition to his facts. One is struck by the schizophrenic quality of this otherwise impressive study.

It is probably impossible for counterinsurgency experts to perceive the truth, for doing so entails admitting a revolution's legitimacy and their own side's lack of it. . . . These attitudes provide the justification for government's "counterterror," which begins with "selective" reprisals only to escalate into massive and indiscriminate violence. In reality, "terror" is effective mainly when it has the effect of freeing people from the felt constraints of coercive, illegitimate authority. As a result, incumbents belatedly discover that terror produces results quite opposite of those expected or desired. This realization increases their frustration and feeling of moral isolation. Instead of providing a basis of correction, this belated and hazy perception of reality only augments their desperation and leads to incredible acts of inversion. Two widely known examples should suffice: (1) In an effort to undermine the popular support of the N.L.F., the United States and its Vietnamese collaborators send out armed squads imposturing the Vietcong to terrorize the peasants. (2) The bombing and burning of villages is justified on the ground that the affected villagers blame the Vietcong for "exposing" them to government reprisals; it is believed that the enemy thus loses popular support.

In practice, the liberal-reformists seek to wage counterrevolutionary campaigns by adopting the organizing principles, "attitudes," and behavior of the revolutionaries. The pacification teams in Vietnam ("revolutionary development cadres") and Algeria were modeled after the F.L.N. and N.L.F.; the "hunting commandos" and special forces sought to imitate the Algerian and Vietnamese liberation armies. . . .

The tactics of counterinsurgency are appropriated by inverting what is construed to be the insurgent model: a counterideology is sought to compete with the revolutionary one; "strategic hamlets" are the intended opposites of "popular base areas"; "psychological warfare" counters revolutionary propaganda; "pacification" teams are designed to duplicate the revolutionary cadres; "reeducation camps" seek to reverse the guerrillas' political commitments. Yet incumbents are incapable, by definition, of effectively seeking the removal of the causes upon which a revolution may be based. France, the United States, and their local collaborators could not credibly claim national liberation to be their goals in Algeria and Vietnam; Algerian *colons* and Vietnamese landlords who formed the backbone of incumbency could not be serious about instituting meaningful land reforms. Lacking genuine revolutionary commitments, unable or unwilling to acknowledge the real aspirations of the people, the liberal-reformists' effort at counterinsurgency misses the heart of the matter.

Contemporary revolutions have been occurring in the non-western world. Yet all the counterinsurgency theorists are westerners. More than their native clients they need ideological and moral arguments to justify their intervention to the natives no less than to the western soldiers who are sent to wage a confusing war on alien soil. Hence the counterinsurgent ideology seldom develops in response to local needs; it is mechanically manufactured or imported and characteristically lacks not only native roots but even the necessary adaptations to the local culture and values. . . .

It should, however, be noted that foreign efforts at fostering political development are doomed to fail; they often result in western military interventions and enlargement of local conflicts. Improved techniques and professionalism are not the primary factors in political and social development. Rather it involves a vision of society, the choice of values and goals. These are not exportable goods or skills that can form part of foreign aid programs. Furthermore, no foreign power has the ability to equip a native government with legitimacy, nor with the will and capacity to open channels for peaceful change. In fact, the reverse is true; identification with a foreign power erodes the legitimacy of a regime. And the correlation between growing legitimacy and willingness to open new channels for participation is known to be positive.

Vietnam is a case in point. It is fashionable now to blame Diem, once billed as a democratic alternative to Ho Chi Minh, for his many failings. Yet few liberals have acknowledged that it was morbid optimism on their part to expect an absentee aristocrat, propped up by American dollars and guns, to substitute for the heroic leaders and cadres who had devoted a lifetime to the independence of their country, and to defeat a movement whose organic ties with the peasants were cemented by a bitter struggle for social justice no less than national liberation. Given the historical situation, Diem had little choice; his only possible weapons were a power apparatus to regiment the population, all-out support of the Catholic minority and the privileged, and widespread terror. These were not the aberrations of a program, but the program itself. The fundamental responsibility for the totalitarian and corrupt character of successive Saigon regimes does not lie with Diem or the degenerate generals who once collaborated with colonial France and are now sanctioning the systematic destruction of a people they claim to govern. It rests with those who created Diem and who still sustain in authority men who can only be regarded by their countrymen as traitors to Vietnam. . . .

Counterinsurgency experts believe in what one may call the "doctrine of permanent counterinsurgency." No price—not the distortion of their professed values by the advancement and acceptance of totalitarian practices and institutions, not the destruction of a culture, not the dispossession and displacement of a people—is ultimately too high for these men who play with the lives and future of the masses in the manner of obsessed gamblers intent on a final win. There is much emphasis in their rhetoric on "realism," "rationality," and "objectivity"; but they are rarely influenced by these characteristics in rejecting the realities that threaten the presumption of success. Their rationalizations lie more in the realm of political pathology than of "objective" analysis. They tend to explain away their failures by pointing at flaws which underscore the need for "greater effort"—lack of execution, paucity of trained personnel, sabotage by politicians or conventional generals, and finally the failure of public will in the metropolitan country to sustain a protracted struggle.

The doctrine of permanent counterinsurgency presupposes the refusal to recognize the absence or loss of governmental legitimacy.

XV. The Communist Insurrection in Greece

CAPTAIN LABIGNETTE

This text provides a pertinent analysis of the military and political causes of the Greek defeat. It lacks a proper political dimension, however, for it does not cover Stalin's turn-around and the Yugoslav crisis, which had such drastic consequences for the Greek Communist Party, leading to an abrupt change of leadership and a serious internal crisis.

The Greek insurrection of 1946–1949 is the most famous example of a revolutionary war that failed in spite of long preparation and an excellent start. Since the war developed in the context of post-Second World War international tensions, the public has tended to concentrate on the annexationist character of this new manifestation of Stalinist policy and on the Anglo-American riposte, which took the form of support for the Greek government.

The history of the uprising and its suppression is particularly interesting to students of the techniques of revolutionary war; firm conclusions can be drawn from the mistakes and experiments of the two sides, which is rarely the case with this notoriously elusive subject.

. . . Greece seemed an easy target for a war of subversion: it had suffered terribly from the war, and its economic situation was dreadful. The communists had thoroughly penetrated the E.L.A.S. resistance organization, and, although far from constituting the majority of its members, they effectively controlled it. However, at the Liberation a regular army, composed of a brigade of 2,000 men and the "sacred squadron" of 700 officers,

From *Revue militaire d'information,* no. 281, special issue "La guerre révolutionnaire," February-March 1957.

returned, and the communists dissolved E.L.A.S. and gave up their arms at the Varkisa convention. But whereas most of the resistance fighters were happy to go home, four or five thousand communist members of E.L.A.S. left the country and set up frontier bases in adjoining Russian satellite states. Under the leadership of Marcos, who was assisted by Soviet advisers, they began to organize an insurrectional movement. At the time, Tito had not yet broken with Stalin, whose orders were still accepted in Yugoslavia. Greece therefore bordered on three satellite states; Albania, Yugoslavia, and Bulgaria. This was of course a major asset for the insurgents, who were always sure of a safe place to which they could retreat when necessary.

The outbreak of the insurrection was accompanied, as usual, by a series of assassinations of politicians and representatives of the regular authorities. The government had a police force only 15,000 strong to send against the rebels; the army, with help from the British Army, was right in the middle of self-reorganization. The police were called in to protect the citizenry, but their patrols, like their small, local headquarters, came under constant attack. Anybody found giving the police information was likely to be killed; this severely restricted the scope of police operations. Before long the various regular and mobile police squadrons were being attacked so heavily that they were forced to withdraw to the major villages, leaving much of the countryside under rebel control. The communists were thus free to elicit contributions in nature and in kind from the peasantry and to recruit volunteers for the partisan groups. They managed to secure effective control over important "bases" wherever the ruggedness of the terrain and the lack of proper roads enabled them to cut an area off altogether.

At first, the terrorist campaign spread throughout the country, but it soon concentrated on three locales: Mt. Grammos on the Albanian frontier, Mt. Vitsi on the Yugoslav frontier, and the Pindus mountains in the center of the country. The government's position was critical: it was already struggling with a disastrous economic crisis whose effects were worsened by the need to resist the partisan insurrection.

Yet the communists did not owe their success to a large partisan army: they had started with fewer than 3,000 guerrilleros, by late 1946 their numbers had doubled, and in April 1947, when they overcame the police, they numbered about 15,000. These figures refer only to armed partisans. There were also, of course, a great many sympathizers (about 200,000) who helped them move from place to place, kept them supplied with food, and gave them information.

Faced with this revolutionary upsurge in a hungry and disorganized country, the Greek government could only call on an ill-equipped, demoralized, and poorly trained army of 120,000 men, later enlarged to about 150,000.

The officers that led this army into battle against the partisans were accustomed to the classical forms of warfare and proved quite incapable of adapting to the requirements of their mission. The partisans used the same tactics they had brought to bear against the police: they ambushed patrols and attacked outposts, operating mainly at night. Informers were eliminated and the population intimidated. The soldiers reacted much as the police had done: they sought shelter in the bigger villages, left the population at the mercy of the raiders, and emerged only to mount large-scale search parties that never found a thing. Furthermore, as the revolt spread, the army scattered itself throughout Greece, in small units that proved defenseless against partisan attack. It was at this stage that the government set up the National Defense Corps.

The sole purpose of this new body was to relieve the Greek Army of its static duties by protecting small outposts and sensitive areas. The army would thus be free to concentrate on the more dynamic role of attacking the partisan units in their strongholds. As a first step toward correcting the original mistake of scattering the regular forces, the measure worked. The National Defense Corps was later reorganized into 100 batallions of 500 men; these light infantry units eventually carried out many local missions, whereas the defense of specific locales was entrusted in part to armed civilians organized in the M.E.A.

Just as the government, inspired by the hard lessons of trial and error, was beginning to institute these necessary reforms, the rebels began to make serious mistakes. After a brilliant start, in which they had seized control over large parts of the country, the "Democratic Army," probably numbering over 20,000 combatants by 1948, made two decisions that were to prove fatal.

First, they sought to compensate for their extremely high

casualty rate (about 1,500 combatants per month) by compelling people to join their ranks, without being adequately selective. As a result, many of their men lacked conviction in and dedication to the cause, as became obvious during the latter stages of the campaign.

Second, they changed the articulation between units and went over much too quickly to a classical form. This mistake was particularly pernicious since their infrastructure was not very solid and they did not always find the transition to even a parallel hierarchy smooth. Now that the population was under the umbrella of the National Defense Corps, those who came forth to denounce this or that rebel leader had less to fear. In short, the partisan army was reorganized at a time when it lacked the full support of the population and when its infrastructure was too weak and too new.

Guerrilla bands, each numbering about 100 and used to operating as a light infantry company, a role they had admirably filled, were now regrouped into brigades, which in turn formed divisions. The administration of these excessively large divisions required full-scale logistics bases and therefore restricted the men to a definite area, denying them the mobility and fluidity that are guerrilla units' main assets.

[Within the "Democratic Army"] . . . some cells were assigned the task not of disrupting operations but of simply spreading the Party ideology and promoting a climate of opinion favorable to the partisans. The government's actions were openly criticized, and there was no one to answer back on the regime's behalf. A definite lack of morale within the army resulted, which manifested itself as lack of will to fight. On top of this psychological handicap, the Greek Army's organization was totally unsuited to the task at hand.

It is therefore not surprising that the army suffered several defeats in its first offensives against rebel strongholds: the terrain favored the enemy, and heavy infantry soon became both physically and mentally exhausted. The High Command had planned an assault on the Pindus mountains, which were lined with rebel bases, hoping that once the army had pacified this area it could head toward the frontiers and push the communists back into the adjoining satellite states (Albania, Yugoslavia, and Bulgaria). The pacification campaign, launched in April 1947, failed dismally. Thanks to the Greek Army's heavy-footed lack of dynamism, the partisans had ample time to withdraw and seek refuge in their other bases.

The following year, on June 29, 1948, an offensive was launched against Mount Grammos, on the Albanian frontier. For two and a half months, 15,000 partisans held off the 50,000 soldiers of the regular army and eventually operated an orderly withdrawal into Albania, passed into Yugoslavia, and reappeared soon after around Mt. Vitsi. The government troops attempted in vain to dislodge them again. These defensive victories were a great boost to rebel morale in all parts of Greece. Terrorist and guerrilla activities became widespread throughout the entire country, especially in the Peloponnese. The situation was becoming critical for the government. The authorities were profoundly demoralized, fearing that the uncertainty of the struggle, along with the prevailing misery and despair, would further the progress of communist propaganda. In fact, their anxieties were unjustified. The partisans had just committed their most serious mistake: they had prematurely weighted themselves down by adopting classical military regimentation. Instead of being everywhere, they were concentrated in clearly defined regions within which they could be surrounded and starved out. Since Mt. Grammos and Mt. Vitsi are devoid of arable land, food supplies had to be brought in from abroad by mule train along mountain paths that were susceptible to army commando raids and air force bombardment. It was at this stage that Sophondis, the Prime Minister, entrusted the command of the army to General Papagos.

. . . The first stage of Papagos's reforms involved a change of personnel. The officer corps was purged of "politicos" and incompetents. The infantry units' equipment was made lighter and adapted to the requirements of guerrilla warfare in mountain terrain. An elite corps of "commando groups" was formed, attracting the strongest and bravest recruits. Their exploits soon generated the sort of publicity that encouraged other units to emulate them. Much more stress was placed on training, and the soldiers' food was improved. Useless trucks were replaced by mule trains. Alongside this military reorganization, the authorities launched several initiatives to stimulate the economy and reduce the poverty level.

The battle was reengaged in the Peloponnese, where 3,500 partisans were killed. In the center of the country, a series of massive operations pacified almost all the rest of Greece. On August 10, 1949, the Mt. Vitsi area, in which the partisans had been holding out for two years, was taken in a three-day offensive. Of the 7,000 communist partisans who had sought refuge there, 2,000 were either killed or taken prisoner; the rest escaped to Albania. On August 24, the 5,000 partisans ensconced on Mt. Grammos succumbed. The last bastion of the insurrection had fallen; the war was over.

The events that marked the stages of this failed revolution would seem to confirm various theories concerning revolutionary war. Three main causes for the rebellion's collapse have been noted:

- The spirit of the masses did not crystallize around a common ideal.
- The underground movement did not develop a solid infrastructure or an alternative hierarchy acceptable to the population.
- The guerrilla bands were prematurely militarized and tied down to particular bases.

In 1946, Greece had roughly 7,500,000 inhabitants. Of the adult male population, only about 200,000—less than one twelfth—were communists or communist sympathizers. For all the talk about active minorities, it seems clear that, without a certain amount of support, a party cannot wage a war of insurrection. By terror and intimidation the insurgents may force the people to provide them with information, food, shelter, and even recruits. But such collaborators will also collaborate with the government, and much more willingly. In Greece, entire populations evacuated the areas occupied by the partisans. Toward the end of the campaign, despite the general chaos, a countercurrent to communist propaganda developed, based on Greek patriotism and the fear that Greece would be dismembered by the three neighboring states, Albania, Yugoslavia, and Bulgaria. The regular soldier may not have been particularly committed to the cause of his generals, but he was usually not a communist, and the eventual outcome of the conflict shows that, given decent officers, soldiers could match the dynamism of the partisans.

Without complete popular support, it is always difficult to establish a solid infrastructure in a particular region. The logistics of the tightly organized Greek underground suffered badly as a result of overconfidence in the populace. Since the partisans were based in mountainous and sparsely populated regions, they could not live off the land. Those who inhabited frontier regions could be supplied from depots built up in other countries, but the men in the center of the country, in the Peloponnese, or in the Pindus mountains had no fixed bases and thus had to be supplied by mule train (bases would have hindered their mobility). It took between 50 and 100 mule loads per day to keep the partisans in the interior supplied. From 700 to 1,400 mules were constantly on the move along the mountain trails, easy prey for the air force. This problem of supply led commanders to set up depots in the regions they occupied. In order to centralize the supply to the various guerrilla bands, small groups of 80 to 100 men were set up under a specific administration, and this logistic and administrative reorganization was the first step toward the more formal militarization that rapidly went into effect.

A guerrilla war can only be fought by light infantry units that can live off the land and conduct brief, quick-moving raids, laying ambushes and making every use of the element of surprise. When a guerrilla army is organized into large units backed by artillery and dependent on a quartermaster's store for supplies, it becomes a regular army, capable of confronting another regular army of equivalent size, but it has lost its original mobility and fluidity. The Greek communist partisans were outnumbered ten to one by the regular army. To face an enemy that can muster ten times your strength in a pitched battle is a sure recipe for disaster, yet it was the option adopted by the Greek communist leadership. The defensive advantages of their chosen terrain enabled the partisans to hold off their adversary in 1948 but were not enough in the face of the superior numbers and improved morale of the government troops in 1949. It was this move away from the very principles of guerrilla war and an overhasty transformation into a regular army that hastened or indeed caused the eventual defeat of the Greek partisans.

XVI. Emergency in Malaya

JULIAN PAGET

*Julian Paget is one of half a dozen
counterinsurgency specialists in Great
Britain. Like Frank Kitson, he has been
present at practically all the major colonial
campaigns since the Second World War,
particularly those in Malaya, Kenya,
Cyprus, and Aden. The following is an
excellent account of the Malayan state of
emergency.*

The Enemy

The Malayan Emergency is a classic example of a communist
takeover bid, based on insurgency and guerrilla warfare. We shall
doubtless see other attempts along similar lines, and it is therefore worth reviewing the enemy's aims and how they were
thwarted.

The insurgents were 90 percent Chinese, but they hoped to
win over the Malayan half of the population by posing as a "nationalist anti-British" movement. There was, however, no genuine anti-British feeling in Malaya, no strong nationalist feeling,
and no real local grievances to be exploited. The communists
failed to provide any cause that might arouse the sympathy of the
Malays, and they therefore never gained the willing support of
the majority of the population.

The communists lacked two other things that could have
helped them. They had no political support for their military
campaign and so never managed to arouse world opinion to rein-

force their military efforts, as Grivas was to do so successfully in Cyprus. They also lacked any friendly base outside Malaya that they could use safely for reorganization and reinforcement. They had no border with China, as had the Vietminh in Indochina. Thailand to the north was hostile to communism, and, although the insurgents could lurk astride the frontier, they could not establish a firm base there. At sea, the Royal Navy controlled the Malayan coast. They were forced, therefore, to set up their bases in the Malayan jungle, which was unsatisfactory, as they had to be limited in scope and were always liable to attack.

The communist plan of campaign was based on three phases. First, they would organize an insurgent movement by "the masses" against the British government and would adopt guerrilla tactics to tie down and demoralize the police and the army. Second, they would dominate or occupy certain specified districts, where they would create "liberated areas" under communist control. Finally, as the populace rallied to their cause, they would create a "liberation army" and sweep the British from the country.

The insurgency never in fact got beyond Stage One, primarily because the security forces successfully broke up in the large groups of guerrillas from the beginning and so prevented them from setting up bases or dominating the vital areas around the populated districts. The insurgents could not, therefore, win over the masses as they had hoped, and they were in no position to set up "liberated areas," except harmlessly in the jungle.

The government then followed this up with a policy of isolating the guerrillas from the populace, and this finally defeated the revolt.

The Battle for Hearts and Minds

The communists failed to win the minds of the people of Malaya as a whole because of several errors of judgment. First, they believed that the Malays were so discontented with British rule that they would willingly join the revolt against it. This never was and was unlikely to become the case, as Britain had made the promise in 1952 that the country would be granted independence in the near future. Second, they alienated the populace by their policy of sabotage, which caused unemployment and loss of income to the workers but did not win them the war. When the communist leaders realized this and issued the 1951 Directive ordering a policy of conciliation, it was too late. Finally, the only political solution they could offer to the Malays was a communist State and this had little or no appeal.

The British government in Malaya, however, early appreciated the need to win the support of the populace, both in the short-term and as a long-term objective, and they achieved their aim. The Briggs Plan was a first step, when action was taken first to protect and then to isolate the populace from the insurgents. This was followed in 1952 by the promise of independence, which was a trump card. It won over the Malays very effectively, though the Chinese needed more convincing, because they feared that they would be treated as "second-class citizens" in an independent Malaya. They were convinced gradually, and once they turned against the insurgents the revolt lost all hope of success.

The active participation of the populace in the campaign was encouraged by the establishment of a Home Guard, by recruiting for the police, and by constant exhortation. At first only the Malays responded, and the police force and the Home Guard were both almost entirely Malay. The Chinese sat on the fence until it was evident, first, that the insurgents were not likely to win, and, second, that support of the government would be in Chinese interests.

A further feature was the official policy of improving the conditions of the people, both Chinese and Malay. "Operation Service" was one example of it, and the social measures undertaken in the "new villages" was another. Throughout the country, every effort was made to show that the government had the interests of the people at heart, and this policy achieved results.

Alongside the battle to win over the waverers among the populace was the psychological warfare and propaganda campaign to win over the insurgents themselves, and this was also very successful. The insurgents lacked any propaganda or political support themselves, such as E.O.K.A. had in Cyprus, and this was a great weakness.

The Malayan Emergency illustrates well the importance of winning the hearts and minds of the people in the short and the long term, and how this can be achieved by the government.

Civil-Military Cooperation

The Malayan Emergency was the first large-scale counterinsurgency campaign, and much pioneer work was required before the most effective machinery was worked out and put into effect. A good example of this was the problem of civil-military cooperation, particularly between the army and the police.

At first, the army was "in support of the police," as though the situation were only a larger-than-usual "internal security" operation. This soon proved unsatisfactory, and a system based on the triumvirate of "civil, military, and police" at all levels came into being as part of the Briggs Plan. This was developed into an extremely efficient machine, which became the model for the Kenya and Cyprus emergencies.

This teamwork extended to Intelligence, where all sources and resources were coordinated under a single Chief of Intelligence, so that there was eventually very effective liaison, with the result that by 1954 the organization was good.

An important feature was that in the later stages the Malay and Chinese officials were included in much of the discussion on policies for the conduct of the campaign, and this helped to develop confidence between them and the security forces. Relations with the European population were close from the start, and the planters and miners played a decisive part by their stubborn resistance to terrorism and subversion.

The Malayan campaign eventually produced the highest standards of civil-military cooperation and demonstrated that it is a decisive factor not only in defeating the insurgents but also in establishing a political solution. The machinery did, however, have to be built up after the Emergency had been declared, and the twelve years' struggle might well have been shorter, or indeed never have got going at all, if the cooperation that was finally attained had existed in 1948.

XVII.   Steamroller in Kabylia

JEAN-PHILIPPE TALBO-BERNIGAUD

*Midshipman in the Navy artillery from
1958 until 1959, Jean-Philippe
Talbo-Bernigaud was also one of the
founders of the* Partisans review. *He was
present during the realization of the Challe
Plan and analyzes it in the following essay.
He maintains it was militarily successful
but does not lose sight of the political
dimension of the conflict.*

"Steamroller": This word, now a part of the Algerian military
jargon, first appeared when the Challe Plan was launched at the
beginning of 1958. Those in command had decided to employ the
general reserve troops more systematically, using them to scour
the country from west to east and "treat" the principal rebel
strongholds. These regions were mountainous, traditionally difficult to reconnoiter, and impossible to control completely, for
there were no means to increase the number of permanent lookout posts. After Opération Ouarsenis, the reserves conducted
Opération Jumelles in Greater Kabylia and Operation Pierres
Précieuses in Lesser Kabylia.[1]

There was a great deal of fuss made about what *Opération
Ouarsenis* accomplished: it became possible to create and/or rees-
tablish the trails, guardposts, and the S.A.S.,[2] and it was said that
the region was decidedly purged of rebels. Nevertheless, although with the approach of the Steamroller we received opto-

From *Les temps modernes,* number 180, 1961. Reprinted by permission of *Les
temps modernes.*

[1] Later evaluations of *Opération Jumelles* found that 11,000 "rebels" were
killed (out of an estimated 30,000 rebels in all the Algerian territory).

[2] S.A.S. were special administrative sections in charge of military conduct,
composed of former officers of the defunct department of "Native Affairs."

mistic communiqués describing with satisfaction the hundreds of "rebels" killed each week or each day, more direct reports that reached us from the embattled territory afforded less optimistic conclusions. We heard of a section surprised by a group of fella-ghas while the men were resting during the day—three-fourths were destroyed. Squadrons (*peletons*) of military jeeps that went out alone to patrol or on reconnaissance were brutally assault-ed—one time a platoon was riding in trucks; another time they were on a road near Cavallo. We lost men; vehicles were burned; rifles and machine guns were carried off so quickly that reinforce-ments had no time to intervene. What did it all mean?

In fact, the Ouarsenis experience corresponded to a change in rebel tactics, and the outcome was quite logical: the katibas (companies), occasionally composed of feileks, or light infantry, fought on an entirely different level than did the French, who were weighted down with artillery, aircraft, and tanks. Docu-ments that fell into the hands of the Deuxième Bureau and were incidentally made known to the press attested to the success of our arms. The new directives to the maquis recommended that we avoid pitched battle, disperse our effective force, be ex-tremely mobile, employ ambushes and hand-to-hand combat to exploit the element of surprise and thus make our actions more likely to succeed, and, finally, that we intensify our efforts to organize and politically indoctrinate the populace. Soon the re-bel bands were reduced to the size of the ferka (section), and the fellaghas—of the opposition—began to take the initiative. In northern Constantine, there were several ambushes on convoys at the end of 1958 and murderous attacks were made on the yard. Afterward we learned that the five or six participating ferkas had been brought together only for these actions, meet-ing after a forced march from three different regions of the country.

One of the command's objectives had been attained: the rebel units, having suffered heavy losses, were broken. It was now necessary to deal with the small, difficult-to-find bands that were more than ever inured to the hardships of war and that had learned to coordinate their actions. The period of spectacular success was over; whenever a band of 10 or 20 fellaghas was spotted during operations, it would usually split up into even smaller groups in an effort to slip out of the net. Furthermore, the Front's influence on the population was growing, far more rapidly than the authorities were prepared to admit.

The situation had been more or less static in our sector for over six months. In M'cid Aïcha, 75 rebels were eliminated, one third of whom were forced into caves and killed by sappers and by SSII ground-to-ground radio-controlled missiles. But most troop units never came into contact with groups of less than 10 fellaghas. Although our fatality rate was lower than theirs because we could evacuate our wounded by air, the total number of casualties was more or less the same on both sides.

We therefore had high expectations that the new "search and destroy" troop units would help improve a thoroughly rotten situation. We made appropriate preparations. In an investment of manpower that would normally have seemed excessive, new watchtowers were built to protect the main routes; sappers reestablished strategic trails or built new ones designed to bypass the expensive necessity of repairing the bridges and corniches blown up by the enemy. Every available ford was used. The officers that had already spent some time in the area did not hide their anxiety at the idea that the reinforcements might not arrive before winter set in.

However, the army was not alone in making preparations for the new arrivals. Trails were being sabotaged left, right, and center. In the middle of the djebel we met a little shepherd boy who could not have been more than twelve years old; he asked us if the paratroopers were arriving this week or next! Encounters with the fellaghas became rare; the whole region seemed miraculously to quiet down. We heard that some members of the underground had simply taken a bus and left Philippeville; clearly there was nothing wrong with their identity papers! The same thing was no doubt happening all over northern Constantine. Probably only small, essentially local, commando groups remained, along with the armed members of the O.P.A. who would know the terrain like the back of their hand. Where could the others have disappeared to? Perhaps "behind" the Steamroller, in Greater Kabylia for instance, or elsewhere. In any case, we would certainly not have the element of surprise working for us.

The "search and destroy" troops eventually arrived. . . . We soon realized that they were used to large-scale operations, indeed, to operations conducted in the grand style. They expected to function in regimental units, leaving at dawn in transport vehicles whenever possible; in fact, a detachment of engineers was available to precede them, paving the way for the troops as they penetrated deeper and deeper into the djebel. When it was raining too hard, excursions would be put off, and it took a great deal of persuasion to get the regiments to set out at night so that they could be on the spot at dawn. This comfortable way of going about things soon provoked a certain friction with the sector commander, whose orders the new troops were to follow. For the rest of us, accustomed to a very different rhythm, these operations offered something of a break, or at least a relaxation. Actually, even the reinforcements were not inexperienced.

But most important is that we did exactly the opposite of what one is always taught about pacification in guerrilla warfare: we treated the terrain well but abused the populace. The units maneuvered in formation over many square kilometers of countryside. I can still see one of those magnificent artillery firing plans that we would receive at the time: no less than 96 shots to be fired in a rectangle 10 by 15 kilometers; one third were to fall 200 or 300 meters apart. It was as though Rommel was expected to arrive fully armed any minute. . . . The difficulties we experienced finding the fellaghas naturally caused a heightening of our level of activity among the civilian population.

Registration of the population in the ex-authorized zones was pursued. Temporary classification camps were built in El Milia by current P.I.M.'s[3] for future P.I.M.'s. The peoples' names were entered on a roster; one by one they were interrogated in an isolated tent in order to drag from them information about those present and those absent: "Who is the *messoul* (tax collector) in your *mechta?* Who has political responsibilities?" The interrogation officers tried to penetrate that wall of silence; from among the gossip, the fantastical declarations, and the false denunciations, they had to determine who was truly concealing information about the Front. "Suspicious characters" were detained while new fragments of information were crosschecked against old. Even trustworthy S.A.S. workers were questioned, then released to the S.A.S. The person in charge of public works com-

---

[3] P.I.M. stands for interned military prisoners. Both the expression and the institution were inherited from the war in Indochina.

plained bitterly that the army had at one time or another imprisoned all his machine operators.

The situation in the countryside was no better. The Sector Headquarters, the Regional Command, the S.A.S., and the headquarters of operating regiments issued more or less conflicting orders, directives, and recommendations. This produced much discontent, in particular among the unit commanders who were charged with transporting the unhappy fellahs and who lost face when asked to follow contradictory commands.

This inconsistency was certainly still more troublesome for its victims, who were thus made game of. For example, orders would come down to release those who had been registered so they could return home that night. But the administrative control units were inadequately staffed and the transport was overflowing, so the companies would spend the night guarding the fellahs, who would return home only the next evening, having been fed nothing while in camp. In the morning we would apprehend every person in a certain area, and in the evening orders would come down to release the children—many kilometers away from their home in the djebel. It was the same for the herds, which one moment we decided to brand, and then decided not to. . . . At the other end of the line, the S.A.S. felt they had fulfilled their task quite well if they distributed a few mugs of powdered milk to nourish the infants whom their mothers had carried in a kerchief on their backs. These events, of which I heard only rumors, occurred in the course of the same operation. On another occasion, people who had already been registered and released were triumphantly apprehended yet again by the rear guard. . . .

The military operations that actually involved investigations of rebels were more murderous. From the very first, the intervention troops were not well informed on the particularities of the sector, which had a terrible reputation for lack of security. As a result, the ex-Forbidden Zone[4] experienced a new wave of irresponsible killing, a sort of death to all comers. Unless by mistake, the paratroopers did not generally kill women and children, but they acted otherwise toward men. The men, however, would

[4] In "Forbidden Zones" (*Zones Interdites*), normal residence is not allowed. This allows better control of those people who are enclosed in surveillance hamlets.

usually disappear in time, so only the aged who were unable or unwilling to leave their shelter would remain. Their risk of being searched increased with the density of vegetation, because often they would establish a refuge in the deepest part of the bush in order to avoid air surveillance.
. . . Some fellaghas nevertheless remained visible. Three were captured. . . . The supply path of a regiment camped in the djebel was cut off. . . . We placidly watched as an armed patrol passed some 500 meters away, not realizing they were indeed fellaghas until some fifteen minutes had passed. Stopped on a road during the night, waiting for orders, we watched an armed soldier approach another who slept on the embankment but four meters away; suddenly the sleeper arose and bounded into the underbrush, vanishing before the two or three men who had mistaken him for one of their kind had time to react. . . . Incidents like these were not the exception. It was obviously more difficult to keep one's eye on a warhardened fighter in the maquis than on a civilian, which enables us not to condone but to understand the presence of so extraordinary a number of slaughtered "suspects," reported or not in the Daily Information Bulletin. This state of affairs is now known to the public, including the French, who have always wanted to escape their collective responsibility by burying their heads in the sand.

I could present even more examples of atrocities committed as a matter of course in order to maintain order; they would clearly demonstrate how the actions involved in "pacification" have changed little in either method or result for the interminable years of this war. For the purpose of comparison, I cite the work of Colonel R. Barberot, who expresses perfectly the unchanged logic of the system:

It is precisely because such actions [the murder of Muslim civilians] are not only useless but contrary to our purpose that it is imperative they be condemned outright.

But condemning them is not enough; the incoherence of the system results in such a multiplicity of such mistakes that they can no longer be treated as exceptions.

In its present form, the military apparatus is incapable of adapting itself to the form of revolutionary war being waged in Algeria. When it is not simply doing nothing, it actually frustrates its own ends.

Without special information, the French troops are quite incapable of distinguishing the rebels from the law-abiding citizens. They are therefore forced to impose blind repression. Miscarriages of justice are more than frequent. But for each ordinary citizen shot down for a fellagha, ten real fellaghas will spring up, until the army finds that the whole population has turned against them and they are faced with a choice between exterminating everybody—which is patently absurd—and capitulation.[5]

The "torrential absurdity" Colonel Barberot refers to elsewhere still prevails, with devastating results, but whereas he managed to ensure that some of those responsible for the more outrageous "errors" were punished, I never saw or heard of any such prosecutions during my whole stay in Algeria. Colonel Barberot was not alone in believing that circumstances required reforms in the structure and methods of the military apparatus if the situation in Algeria were to improve. None of the reforms was seriously considered at any stage during the past three years. We continued to practice a policy of petty extermination without admitting it—or, worse, accepting it as inevitable. And the well-named Operation Steamroller, which was the core of the Challe Plan, was the most impressive illustration of that policy.

Does all this imply that the Steamroller was unsuccessful? Certainly not, for the temporary concentration of troops in one region put a number of fellaghas out of combat and allowed a superficial purge and better control of the area. However, after two months' occupation the improvement was small considering the tremendous number of enlisted men involved. Before the arrival of reinforcements, the guerrillas were everywhere and the fixed units were quite likely to encounter them frequently and at close proximity. But after the regiments arrived and established themselves in the south and west, the majority of the guerrillas fled to the north and east.

Even if the military situation did improve, in order to judge the success of Operation Steamroller one must consider what happened to the area after the troops had left and the "treatment" was over.[6] Ouarsenis again developed a bad reputation in

[5] R. Barberot, *Malaventure en Algérie* (July 1957), p. 116.

[6] In April-May 1960, it was necessary to remount *Opération Tentacule* in the Daïa mountains (Oranais); *Opération Couronnes*, of Ouarsenis (1959), was repeated as *Opération Cigale* (1960); the efforts of *Opération Rubis* in the Kerrata region would be a continuation of *Opération Jumelles*.

the communiqués, and security deteriorated daily even though new posts were established. Further, we knew that Si Saleh, the commander of the Algerian Wilaya 4, chose to install himself and his group in Ouarsenis in 1960, preferring that area to the Blidean Atlas or to the Cherchell area. Evidently the area's geography favored the Front militarily. But in addition to that the passage of the Steamroller probably promoted rebellion among the populations it quashed with so little judgment; troops more familiar with their zone of action would have been unlikely to exhibit as much insensitivity.

It is of critical importance that the A.L.N. had the hearty support of the populace and never lacked volunteers to take the place of its dead. As in any revolutionary war, the attitude of the Algerian people as a whole will determine the balance between the two forces in the final analysis. On the one side there is an occupying army that represents a country torn between imperialism and liberalism (France) and that is manipulated by the material power and political maneuvers of elements on the far right who rely for support on the Algerian Europeans' fear. On the other side there is the liberation army and the Front, both of which enjoy the support and approval of the Muslim masses of the entire Maghreb.

XVIII. The Failure of the Guerrillas in Peru

HÉCTOR BÉJAR

*In 1965, Héctor Béjar headed the E.L.N.
in the Ayacucho region of Peru. Like Luis
de la Puente's and Guillermo Lobaton's
M.I.R., his movement was crushed after a
few months. The E.L.M. tried to operate
in isolated areas inhabited by Indians
whose language the guerrilleros did not
speak. Béjar wrote this autocriticism while
in prison.*

La Mar Province is located in the central range of the Andes within the acute angle formed by the deep, narrow canyons of the Pampas and Apurímac rivers.

The communities of Chungui and Ancco are perched on the summits of the range, almost 16,000 feet above sea level. From these heights hundreds of little streams run rapidly down incredibly steep precipices toward the Pampas and the Apurímac. In the south the precipices are barren and baked by an implacable sun. In the northwest they are covered with thick, eternally humid forests.

There are no roads. The traveler who dares to cross the province has to use a mule or go by foot, painfully climbing and descending gigantic stone stairways and crossing interminable bogs and enormous accumulations of sand.

There is little arable land, and what exists is poor. The Indian communities grow potatoes and *ocas* on the heights. On the slopes and in the warm zones they grow corn and sugarcane and coffee and cacao in the "forest eyebrow." After transporting

From Héctor Béjar, *Peru 1965: Notes on a Guerrilla Experience* (New York and London: Monthly Review Press, 1970). Copyright 1969 by Librairie François Maspero. Translation copyright 1970 by Monthly Review Press. Reprinted by permission of Monthly Review Press.

their meager crops on muleback for several days, the peasants sell them at low prices in the roadside markets. These markets are their point of contact with capitalist civilization, whose spearhead penetrates farther and farther into the Andes as the road advances.

The vast majority of Indians speak only Quechua, although some of the young people do go to school in the provincial capital.

According to the 1940 census, the province had 38,590 inhabitants. Of these, 35,129 lived in the countryside and 3,461 in the towns. The 1961 census showed 40,961 inhabitants over five years of age, of whom 32,598 did not speak Spanish or know how to read and write.[1]

Land ownership is shared by the communities and the haciendas, and there are numerous points of conflict. The *yanaconas* —Indians who are forced to serve on the haciendas—almost always want to free themselves from the haciendas and join the communities.

April in Chinchibamba, a small village in the forest.

We are but a few individuals who move only at night to avoid encounters with the peasants. We don't want them to know of our presence yet, but they can't be deceived. They discover our tracks, see us through the foliage, and hear our steps. The rumor spreads, and fantastic explanations are invented: that we are cattle thieves, *pishtacos,*[2] communists. . . . But what do they know about communists except what they have heard from the village priest, the *Aprista* landowner, and the prejudiced schoolteacher?

We obstinately continue to travel at night. Our food supply gives out, and for several weeks we eat little or nothing. Finally there is no other solution. We have to speak to the peasants.

We begin to make friends. There are different reactions. Some of them distrust us, others perhaps fear us, but none of them refuses to help us. When we first sized each other up, the word *papay* ("papa") separated us. The *papay* is the boss, all whites and mestizos, all foreigners. We have to cease being "papas"— the success or failure of our mission depends on it.

---

[1] National Planning Institute, National Bureau of Statistics and Censuses, *VI Censo Nacional de Población, Tomo V* (Lima).

[2] According to local superstitions, the *pishtacos* are murderers who sell human fat.

The language is another barrier. Very few of us speak Quechua (I know only a few words, and those I pronounce very badly). One comrade knows the Quechua spoken in the Cuzco region, which is pronounced differently. Only one of us knows the local pronunciation.

In spite of these difficulties our friendships grow and there are frequent invitations. We explain who we are, why we have come, and, in the process, our language becomes more understandable to them. We have to be careful of the words we use, because the peasants are hearing many of them for the first time. Those who know Quechua act as interpreters or speak to the peasants themselves.

These peasants live in their own world, with its tragedies, its rivalries, and its happy moments. They are members of a community and are not basically dissatisfied with their lot. They don't feel that they are victims, since they are used to seeing poverty as their inevitable fate. They are defending themselves against an aspiring landowner who wants to use fraudulent titles to take over communal lands. They threw out the shyster, and the police protecting him prudently withdrew. The community's officials were later arrested.

This is the world we must become part of, and we are cordially, even enthusiastically, welcomed.

June 1965

We are no longer "papas." Now we are "brothers."[3] We help them in whatever ways we can. Everyone needs a doctor. There are no doctors or medicine, and people die from lack of care. An aspirin tablet has incalculable value. We treat the sick and distribute the few tablets we have, which is a double reason why we are welcome. Many are in agreement with our objectives. Others just listen and two or three distrust us, but at least almost everyone knows that we are not thieves or bandits. They no longer fear us, and we can go into any home, sure of finding food and aid.

[3] We used the words *compañero* and comrade very little. The term "brother" spread spontaneously throughout the zone. It is more expressive, and it is closer to the psychology of the peasants, who identify love and friendship with family links (one's best friend is always a "spiritual" relative). Thus, a guerrilla was referred to as brother so-and-so. And to find out of someone was worthy of trust, we asked if he was a brother or not.

We discover that the population of this village is sparse and seasonal. Most people live farther up and only come into the ravines and to the banks of the Apurímac River for a few months. We want to contact the entire population, but going up to the higher areas poses the tactical problems of how to travel and where to hide. It is not just a problem of terrain, but also of equipment. It's no laughing matter to spend a night under the stars at 15,000 feet. We would need overcoats, scarves, and thick clothing, but we don't have them, and even if we did they would be too heavy to carry on the 10,000-foot climb to the peak. Nevertheless, we take the risk, climbing painfully up one night with a pitiless rain soaking us to the bone.

We learn some interesting things 15,000 feet above sea level. It's possible to withstand the cold by walking at night and resting during the daytime in the hollows heated by the weak sun of the high plateau. If one marches constantly the cold doesn't matter; and it's good training, in that it accustoms one to move about in darkness. Visibility is a hundred times better at night. It is necessary only to pull oneself up to the top of a peak to see as far as one could march in a couple of days. A good pair of binoculars and the problem is solved. Caves are good protection from aviation, and guerrillas can hide in rocky areas, which are good natural camouflage. Will future rebels republish the descriptions of the legendary exploits of the *montoneros,* those guerrillas of the nineteenth and the first years of the twentieth century? They should, because it would be one of the most interesting contributions to guerrilla tactics in Latin America.

Peruvian guerrillas must become accustomed to traveling constantly from the mountains to the forests and back again. They have to descend almost vertical slopes with no paths, protected by the vegetation which grows on the eastern Andes, and then climb up again to the heights without any transition. They have to live perpetually between 4,000 and 16,500 feet above sea level. It does not require supermen, but one does have to be completely adapted to our diabolical geography.

Large landholdings prevail in the high regions, but the landowners, who are merciless exploiters, live under the same primitive conditions as the peasants. The only place in the whole zone where we found beds was at Chapi. Landowners in other areas sleep on rudimentary platforms or on sheepskins and eat *mote*[4] and potatoes boiled in salt and water, just as their serfs do.

Although these are large landholdings, their size indicates not wealth but avarice and criminal neglect. Greedy, ignorant, and miserly, the landowners are the main obstacle to progress. They not only stubbornly oppose schools and make life difficult for the teachers, but they also keep their laborers from cultivating more land than they think is appropriate, punish those who breed too much livestock, and carry out fierce reprisals against offenders. Their mental poverty means hopeless material poverty for hundreds of families. Afraid of having to work like their serfs, and knowing that they themselves are useless and parasitical, they fiercely defend the prerogatives which allow them to live off the peasants.

Although the workers on the haciendas are more exploited than are the members of the communities and although their social problems are more violent in nature, they see their condition more clearly. We don't need to convince them that the boss is their enemy. They know this and hate him wholeheartedly. Many of them have tried to form unions or build schools, and have been punished with a few lashes, imprisonment in the main house of the hacienda, or a denunciation to the authorities for engaging in "communist agitation." "Why do you want to go to school, to learn to steal?" growls the landowner.

There are discontented people everywhere, and they receive us enthusiastically. When we begin our operations against the landowners, which are indispensable for earning their complete trust, their enthusiasm grows. Our armed propaganda, which consists not in speeches but in concrete actions against the landowners, produces results.

It hasn't taken us long to expel the large landowners, many of whom fled before we reached them. The workers are beginning to realize how different it is to live without bosses. All our actions have their support. . . .

The guerrillas' supporters grow more numerous, and the first peasants join the band. Many others promise to do the same in Sojos, Muyoj, Palljas, and Chapi. We begin to see how, in a very moving way, a strong link is being forged between the peasantry

---

[4] *Mote* is boiled corn.

and our unit. With the landowners removed and the army unable to locate us, we become the only authority in the zone.

But we have made some serious mistakes. Our friends and their contact with us, whether open or supposedly secret, are well known. One day a peasant tells his wife that he guided us to such and such a place, she tells a neighbor, and the neighbor tells everyone else. Another day a young man who has gotten drunk at a town festival shouts proudly that he is a communist and a friend of the guerrillas. On another occasion we ourselves give someone away by visiting him in broad daylight. Not everyone can be trusted. There are stool pigeons, ex-major domos from the haciendas, people who betray others, or inform on them, or simply store up information for the future.

We finally realize the danger and encourage our supporters to join the guerrilla band. Some of them follow our advice immediately; others say that nothing will happen to them, that we shouldn't worry, and that, in any case, they know how to take care of themselves.

October 1965

The first army patrols appear. They are small mobile groups that pretend to be guerrilla units. "Do you know where our comrades are?" they ask the peasants. "We're bringing them messages from Lima." The device is too clumsy for them to succeed in learning our whereabouts, but some of the more naive peasants reveal themselves. We warn them of the danger, but it's too late.

When the invasion finally comes, all of our supporters are tortured and shot. The terrible vengeance extends to their nearest relatives, their crops, and even their homes, which are remorselessly burned. . . . It is planned barbarism to terrorize the population and inflict exemplary punishment for their friendship toward us.

But it also reveals cowardice and insecurity. On no occasion did the troops use persuasion or separate the guilty from the innocent. It was more practical to kill them all than to carry out an investigation. How could they convince the people that they were defending a just cause when their desperation impelled them to end the danger as quickly as possible without regard to the means they employed? In slaughtering their victims, they were really trying to stifle their own fear.

All of which contains extremely valuable lessons. The first is that the peasants are willing to help. The second is that it is necessary to protect the lives of one's supporters as carefully as one protects one's own. Our survival depends on our mobility, but the survival of our supporters depends on secrecy. We observed the first requirement up to a point, but we were sadly remiss in the second. . . .

These are the facts. Did we have peasant support? If by that is meant a general and well-elaborated theoretical conviction and massive and well-organized aid, then evidently we did not. To ask for that kind of support would be to deal with metaphysics, not realities. If, however, by peasant support we mean the collaboration of most of the people, originating in their certainty that we were there to defend them, then we did have it and, moreover, it surpassed anything we had expected. . . .

After numerous experiences had made us well liked by the local inhabitants, overconfidence proved to be our undoing. One success after another caused us to overestimate our own strength. There were also some desertions that lowered the number of guerrillas and thus affected our firepower.

We were actually a small group. In the most difficult moments there were barely thirteen of us. One reason for this was that our lack of communication with the urban centers made it impossible for us to depend on a steady flow of recruits. We were also surrounded. The encirclement did not threaten the existence of the guerrilla unit, which even under such conditions could operate comfortably, but it did keep us from setting up reliable lines of communication with the outside. By the end of 1965 our efforts to do this had failed.

One of our errors certainly lay in not considering that type of liaison sufficiently important, and in depending on recruiting men in the zone where we were operating. Our intention was to provide ourselves with supplies and guerrillas right on the spot. The provisions were easy, especially for a group as small as ours. The recruiting was feasible, but it was too lengthy a process due to the slowness with which a peasant makes a decision. The peasant may finally choose to join the guerrilla unit, but before doing so he will think it over carefully and take his time about weighing all the possibilities. However, a guerrilla unit needs to recruit rapidly and in quantity in order to strengthen the group and bring it up to the best combat level.

The small size of our unit kept us from undertaking any large-scale operations against the army. Nevertheless, we trusted in our knowledge of the terrain and in the numerous friends that we had everywhere. We began to move about by day along known roads, relying on the people's reports and neglecting the most elementary precautions. Our confidence was based on the fruitless efforts the army was making to locate us and on its fear of crossing rivers, streams, and broken areas in the terrain that we were watching.

We knew that as long as we stayed constantly on the move we were not in immediate danger. We were helped by the irregular nature of the terrain, which abounded in immense heights, formidable canyons, and slopes that were very difficult to climb, and which made an effective encirclement almost impossible. The enemy actually controlled only the best-known passes, which were just the ones we did not use.

For a long time the guerrillas and the soldiers played hide and seek, looking for each other and fighting brief engagements. If the guerrilla unit had remained faithful to the principle of mobility, of which it was perfectly capable, and had attempted to move far away toward other zones that were just as populated as where it was operating, it would have thwarted the army and survived.

But when a guerrilla thinks that he controls the terrain and is perfectly familiar with it, he begins unconsciously to fix himself to that area. And then he is lost, because not all of the information he has received is correct, and he does not have all of the information about his enemy that he ought to have.

By the end of 1965 the clashes had become unfavorable for the guerrillas, and on December 17 the unit was surprised by an army detachment at a place known as Tíncoj. Three comrades—one of them Edgardo Tello—died in that combat. The rest of the guerrillas were scattered, and, with a forest as dense and on ground as broken as the scene of our operations, it was impossible for us to find each other. We were not able to regroup in spite of all our efforts. Perhaps a larger unit would have been able to get over those difficult moments even though it had suffered heavy casualties, but there were very few of us and the loss of each man was a real blow.

With the guerrilla unit dispersed, its men were left to die one by one under the guns of their hunters.

Why did we not succeed? What was the cause of the Ayacucho failure?

The collapse and liquidation of the guerrilla band were certainly not due to lack of peasant support. As we have seen earlier, that support was shown in a number of ways. The area, with broken terrain unfamiliar to the army, was well chosen.

The roots of the failure must be sought in the guerrilla unit itself and in its leadership.

In this case as in others, a group of men, most of them from the city, tried to operate militarily in an unknown environment.

Lack of knowledge of the terrain is a disadvantage that can be quickly overcome if the group is alert and active. The guerrilla unit did in fact overcome this problem. But it did not always use its knowledge and often preferred the easier but much more dangerous way of moving, which was along known roads.

In doing this, the unit left a trail of information behind, which many peasants were not able to keep secret when they were tortured and murdered. The guerrilla band did not foresee, in practice, the severity of the repression to come.

The guerrillas made many friends, but they did not know how to take care of them. Everyone knew their supporters, and when the army came all it had to do was to shoot them in order to terrorize the rest of the population.

Despite friendship, language was always a barrier that separated the rebels from the natives. Peasants identify Spanish with the boss, especially in those places like Ayacucho that have a very large Quechua population. For the guerrillas to gain the trust of the peasantry they must be able to speak Quechua, and not just any Quechua, but the dialect spoken in the zone where they are operating (there are significant variations in the language from region to region in Peru).

Customs are another barrier. A high degree of discipline is required for a group of men to learn to respect, imitate, and *love* the ancient customs of the peasants and not hurt their feelings through clumsiness. Discipline, warm affection for the peasants, and modesty are not always characteristics of young students or of politicians filled with an intellectual self-sufficiency that offends simple people and which originates in daily habits that are often just the opposite of the way of life of country people.

In spite of the good will that they earned, the guerrillas lacked a deep understanding of local customs. That would have allowed them to distinguish the traitors from their friends with greater precision and to obtain better and more pertinent information concerning the enemy's movements.

Guerrilla tactics, when applied strictly—with their characteristics of mobility, evasion and secrecy, rapid attack and withdrawal—demand a high degree of physical fitness on the part of the combatants and a leadership with great military ability. The entire group must operate with iron discipline and perfect coordination. The E.L.N.'s guerrilla unit, like all the others operating that year, did not possess these qualities to the degree required to overcome the inevitable problems and face a large, well-trained enemy force. . . .

By the end of 1965 the guerrilla movement had been totally liquidated. The cadres who died in battle were the product of many years of struggle and possessed qualities of brilliant leadership for political persuasion; they were not, however, prepared to deal with the problems created by the revolutionary military movement at this point in Peruvian history.

City and Countryside

The 1965 actions took place almost entirely in the countryside. They didn't affect either the cities or Peru's long strip of coast where important production centers, several mines and oil centers, steel mills, and cane plantations with an agricultural proletariat having a long tradition of struggle are all located.

Two factors contributed to the failure of the urban centers of the coastal and mountain areas to act in support of the guerrillas. They were: (1) the guerrillas' conception of the war they were going to initiate and (2) the urban centers' lack of means.

Both for the M.I.R. and the E.L.N., the guerrilla war had to move from the countryside to the cities. In the first stage, its fundamental purpose was to win the support of the peasant masses and build a strong fighting vanguard, but this led not only to a neglect of the cities, but even to the issue of careful directives so that no premature action would be carried out there.

The goal was to establish a leadership in the countryside. It was feared that if an urban organization began to move too soon it would act on its own, thus creating problems of authority. But two factors worked against the guerrilla unit's retaining command of the movement.

First, one must realize how small both groups were. Opening four fronts in the mountains was already an effort beyond their capability. It was practically impossible at the same time to set up an organization that would operate in both rural and urban regions. Therefore, almost all of the cadres were in the countryside when the uprising began.

If we add to this the disagreement which existed in the rest of the Left, from the Trotskyists to the Communist Party, as to the timeliness of the insurrection, and the Left's moral "solidarity" but lack of practical help, we will realize why, toward the middle of 1965, the cities remained calm while fighting was going on in the interior. This calm was broken only by the activity of the repressive forces and by some isolated uprisings carried out by elements not under the command of either of the active organizations.

More generally, we must remember the characteristics of Peruvian social life. Our country, which still has not achieved total social, economic, and cultural integration, never reacts as a whole. Strong barriers separate the people who live in the countryside from the city dwellers, the workers from the peasants, those who live in the mountains from those who live on the coast, the north from the south. Powerful actions that take place in certain zones have no repercussions in the rest of the country. That is what has happened throughout our history, and that is what happened in 1965 when the bloody battles in the mountains had no effect on the coast, where the people remained indifferent and did not react to the guerrilla war as the guerrillas had expected them to.

It is true that the guerrillas shook the reactionaries and the oligarchy, since the latter saw quite clearly the danger our units represented to their stability, above all in a country with as explosive an economic situation as Peru's. But the people did not understand this because they lacked the same power of analysis. Nor did there exist a capable and active political leadership that could take advantage of what was happening for an effective propaganda campaign based on the example of the guerrillas. All the Left did was to publish a few timid messages in support of the guerrillas that did not reach beyond its own small sphere of influence.

However, it must be noted that through their actions the guerrillas in a few months created greater repercussions than had the Left in its entire history. But these repercussions did not include support actions by the people.

The mission that the combatants had given their few activists in the cities was to serve as point of liaison and coordination within our country and with the exterior. They were to supply men, arms, and equipment and to spread propaganda. These tasks were too great for such small groups, which soon lost all contact with the guerrillas when the latter were encircled.

Guerrillas and Peasants

The guerrillas were in a difficult position in regard to the peasant masses. For centuries there has been a tremendous imbalance in Peru between the urban middle and working classes, from which the guerrillas came, and the peasantry.

The man from the city discriminates against and feels superior to the man from the country, especially the Quechua peasant. And, conversely, the latter distrusts the man from the city. The peasant has always seen him as the exploiter, the man who has come to take away his land, the master.

A very large portion of our peasant population speaks only Quechua, and those who are bilingual prefer to speak their native language. They use Spanish only when they have to speak to the landowner. The division also exists in customs. The behavior of city dwellers often seems strange to the peasants and amuses or displeases them.

It is a question, then, of a social division which has deep historical roots in the colonial and republican periods and which can only be overcome by the efforts of the guerrillas themselves. . . .

There is a class factor at the bottom of all of this. The petty-bourgeois origin of the guerrillas gave them all the virtues and defects appropriate to this social sector of our country.

While they possess daring, imagination, and romanticism, these advanced groups of the petty bourgeoisie have always been susceptible to sectarianism, an excessive love of publicity, the desire to lead, and a tendency to underestimate the adversary. This is why, at the same time that they displayed abundant heroism in battling the enemy and audacity in throwing themselves into a dangerous fight, they were incapable of assimilating themselves in a short period of time into a peasantry that observed their sudden appearance with surprise and bewilderment.

There was another difference. The ideals proclaimed by the guerrillas necessarily appeared remote to the peasants, who were interested above all in their concrete and even local demands. Whereas the guerrillas advocated social revolution, the peasants wanted more tangible things—the realization of small demands that the revolutionaries were not always successful in incorporating into their program (in spite of the fact that these demands are the means for raising the people to a higher level of consciousness). The guerrillas' program was much more complicated and their goals much more distant.

During his entire existence the peasant is separated from the life of the nation and is unaware of the great national problems, even though he suffers their consequences. In general, there is no developed national consciousness in Peru. It has been systematically retarded by the ruling groups. Naturally, this consciousness does not exist in the countryside either. It is true that the peasants understand the meaning of the problems if they are explained in clear and simple language, but they do not feel them in their own flesh as immediate, pressing issues that would make them fight.

The key problem for us at this stage lies in moving toward the peasantry, in making their worries and desires our own in order then to carry the peasants on toward higher objectives, in making the most of all the issues that arise from the struggle for land and the defense against the large landowners. It is not a question of moving into a peasant zone and calling on the inhabitants to follow us. We must unite ourselves with them and with their leaders and stand by their side in every eventuality. Their immediate local objectives must be incorporated into the general and ultimate objectives of the revolution. . . .

The rebels must take into account the characteristics of the Peruvian peasantry. One is respect and obedience to communal authorities. The governor, representative, and mayor of the community represent the will of all its members, and their decisions are obeyed without any discussion. What effect does this have on the guerrillas? The members of the communities react collectively rather than individually, and the opinion of their authorities will determine to a great degree their attitude toward the revolutionaries. The guerrillas are not working with a simple mass but with an organism, a unity possessing its own power structure that must be respected if the outsiders are not to lose the people's trust or even come to be disliked by them. This will also allow the guerrillas, at certain times, to make use of a powerful collective force.

In 1965 the guerrillas were not able to make their methods one with those of the peasantry. The peasants and the guerrillas took separate paths because the guerrillas did not link themselves in time with the social upsurge that had been taking place in the countryside since 1965.

Summing up, we can say that the guerrillas must act and work not only for the distant objectives of the revolution, but also for the immediate ones of the peasants, and not only *for* the peasants, but *with* them.

Base and Leadership

The delay both in seeing all the factors that were operating against the guerrillas and in taking steps in time to correct them was due to the nature of many of the leading cadres.

It is true that the leaders were characterized by great honesty and revolutionary conviction, proved by the fact that they died fighting for their ideals. Nevertheless, they possessed too many other qualities and lacked too many needed ones to be able to deal adequately with the circumstances that arose.

We have already mentioned that the qualities of a party leader are not sufficient for the leader of an armed group. Physical adeptness, knowledge of the terrain, and skill in combat are all needed, and they are qualities that not all the leaders possessed in 1965. The decision to fight is not enough to make a man a guerrilla. Many comrades, who could have been excellent cadres in the urban resistance or in a liaison network, went to the countryside inspired by heroic determination but did not have the necessary stamina in spite of their iron wills. Without wanting to, they became a burden for their other, more physically fit, comrades and for the guerrilla unit as a whole. A more objective and pragmatic selection of the personnel would have secured better combat teams.

Meanwhile, hidden in the rank and file of the guerrillas and in the peasant masses were the cadres that a more careful process of selection would have raised to the positions of command that they would surely have earned in battle. But because the struggle was brief and violent, that process, which by its nature is long and slow, did not occur.

Survival and Expansion

It is possible, as has been demonstrated in several countries in Latin America, for militarily able cadres who are politically convinced of the correctness of their struggle to survive despite violent and repeated attacks by armies experienced in counter-guerrilla warfare. The guerrilla unit can survive even without adequate "subjective" conditions in the population among which it is operating.

The problem lies in whether the unit can develop to the point at which it really endangers the system and the stability of the regime as a whole. Given all of the social characteristics that we have noted repeatedly—disconnection, imbalances, isolation—it is possible for a guerrilla band to survive for many years without having any effect on the system's vital points.

Guerrilla warfare is not dangerous for the ruling classes so long as it does not exacerbate other social contradictions, giving rise to forms of action that will work in conjunction with it.

In order to initiate activity, it is necessary to break with rigid systems of thought and action. Clinging to a single plan of action is always dangerous because it leads revolutionaries to a struggle that is isolated and one-dimensional, exclusive and sectarian, closing off any possibilities of growth for the guerrilla unit.

We ought to add that dogmatism is more characteristic of those who carry out propaganda in favor of armed struggle than of those who engage in it.

Arms and Politics

Does armed struggle exclude politics? The answer has always been no, that there can be no contradiction between the two because, under the conditions that prevail in our countries, armed struggle *is* essentially a political struggle.

Our guerrillas must be able politicians at the same time that they are efficient soldiers, but they must not be the only politicians. While the armed struggle is developing in certain zones in the country, the political struggle must be carried throughout the nation in the most diversified forms.

What defines revolutionary conduct and distinguishes it from opportunism are its objectives and the consistent fashion in which they are pursued, and the subordination of all tactics to the only strategic objective a person who calls himself a revolutionary can have: the seizure of power. When an organization or a group of revolutionaries sets the seizure of power as its objective and does not lose sight of that goal, all forms of action are possible and none should be rejected.

Strikes, passive resistance, public demonstrations, and mass mobilizations all allow guerrilla actions to be felt in the rest of the country and serve to overcome the guerrillas' isolation. Armed struggle in the countryside ought not necessarily to be reflected in terrorist activities in the cities except when it is absolutely necessary, politically clear, explainable to the people, and when it corresponds to the level the masses have achieved in their own action.

The situation in the countryside is similar. If the guerrillas resign themselves only to carrying out armed actions, their position will be more difficult than if they combine them with organizing the peasants and encouraging them to wage mass struggle for clear and concrete objectives.

We should not forget that all the peasant actions recorded in the history of our country have been collective in nature and carried out in the peasants' own name with leaders who have emerged from those same oppressed masses. The guerrilla unit can offer a revolutionary perspective to the peasant struggle through its operations, but it cannot replace that struggle. The guerrilla unit is only part of the whole; it is not the totality of the struggle.

By its mobile nature, the guerrilla band is everywhere and nowhere. When it is not present, the masses must defend themselves by their own means against enemy repression by organizing around the most outstanding leaders of the peasant resistance.

When the guerrillas were liquidated in 1965, the people were left defenseless, completely at the mercy of the army. This was the logical outcome of only organizing the peasants around the guerrilla band, in order to provide it with food and men, without considering the possibility of a repression. The people were not prepared for this contingency because the guerrilla unit had not had time to prepare them nor had it even thought about the matter. In any case, it would not have been able to ready the people since it was still regarded as an alien body. The resistance must be organized by men who have emerged from the people themselves, the natives of that zone, accustomed to the kind of fight that did not take place here after the defeat of the guerrillas.

Mountains and Forests

It is essential to note that the geography of our country has forced the peasant population to concentrate itself in valleys and high zones, precisely where it is difficult and dangerous to carry on a guerrilla war of the kind known until now.

When we analyze the 1965 experience we see clearly how all of the guerrilla fronts were forced to withdraw into the forest zones of eastern Peru. They are the securest areas from the military point of view, but not from the political, because they have only a minimal population. The most densely populated zones are in the mountains and not the forest.

This is a problem that has still not been solved and that will appear again in future guerrilla actions. It will be overcome only when the guerrillas find ways of operating in the mountains and on the high, open plateaus. This is possible. Our country has a great guerrilla tradition, and the *montoneros* always operated in the Andes.

XIX.

War Comes to Long An

JEFFREY RACE

*Jeffrey Race, an American, was in the
military in Vietnam. In a book covering the
years 1954–1965, he analyzes how his
sector, that of Long An, was slowly lost to
the N.L.F. His is one of the very best
books written about the Vietnam war.*

. . . In looking back on the resistance period, one is not surprised that the government lost the countryside to the Vietminh.
The great difference between ruler and ruled in their perception
of the rural situation almost guaranteed that the steps the government took would be the wrong ones, because its understanding of
the rural situation was so badly flawed. To high officials, the
countryside was basically happy, and grievances were ipso facto
communist-inspired and thus to be ignored. Yet from the viewpoint of the peasantry, the rural situation was by no means
happy. How to reconcile these conflicting views? Perhaps the
official view of a contented countryside was once true in a sense,
with authoritative and respected village councils ruling locally,
and peasants quietly farming the lands and paying their rents
without complaint. But the reality behind this picture was well
expressed by a Vietnamese encountered in Long An: "If you are
a tenant farmer whose family has worked the same land for the
same landlord family for the past century, keeping just enough to
live and paying the rest to the landlord, and if you and your
father and his father had always been told that this was right, and
nothing had ever challenged this, then it is likely that you are

From Jeffrey Race, *War Comes to Long An: Revolutionary Conflict in a
Vietnamese Province* (Berkeley, Los Angeles, and London: University of California Press, 1972). Reprinted by permission of Marie Rodell–Frances Collin Liter-
ary Agency. Copyright 1972 by Jeffrey Race.

going to think like an obedient tenant farmer, and so are your sons." This fatalistic passive attitude of the peasantry was for a time a terrific stumbling block to the Vietminh; but one of their most enduring accomplishments in the South was the decisive destruction of this fatalism. It was as if they had given eyeglasses to a man nearsighted since birth. The peasantry had *seen* the landlords run, they had *seen* the village councils forced to sleep in outposts and to move in the countryside with armed escorts. As night fell in the countryside, the peasants saw where lay the power of the conflicting sides: the Vietminh slept with the people, the village councils slept with the soldiers in the outposts. The nine years of the resistance had destroyed the sense of inevitability which had kept the "contented peasants" quietly farming the fields.

Except for the midnight shots marking the execution of former resistance members, the period from 1954 to 1956 was one of relative peace for Long An. Doubtless the government had gained some credit for the removal of the French, and many followers of the Vietminh turned from communist leadership to cooperate with the regime in Saigon. There had also been a noticeable change in the composition of the village councils, a permanent consequence of the resistance. Traditional village notables now no longer wished to serve on the village council in such numbers as before. They generally explained this by saying that the posts—whether on the ban hoi te, the hoi dong huong chinh, or the appointed post-1956 councils—no longer retained their previous "prestige." . . .

Yet this modest improvement in the social composition of the government village councils was small compared to the enormous shift in the locus of local power effected by the Vietminh during the resistance. For in fact in Long An the overwhelming, immediate, and practical significance of the resistance had not been the elimination of the French presence, which had not been significant, but rather the overthrow of the power of the local elite, which the French had employed to carry out the functions of the central government in the countryside. In terms of actual impact on daily life, the resistance had meant an economic revolution to the peasant, and only incidentally was it anti-French. The genius of the Vietminh had been their skillful synthesis of these two aspects of the resistance. Indeed they described their movement as *phan de bai phong:* antiimperialist and antifeudal. One could not succeed without the other. By bringing an antifeudal revolution to the countryside, they motivated the peasantry to serve an antiimperialist revolution as well. The organizational key to their success had been the relative strength of their village organization: the chi bo. The absence of any comparable government organization to do battle on the crucial level of the village meant that much of the population went to the Vietminh almost by default.

Thus the return to the countryside of the exiled government village councils in 1954 under the Geneva Accords was regressive in its impact, as if the eyeglasses had suddenly been taken from the nearsighted man. The village councils always found themselves in the position of making demands on the population: for annoying paperwork, for taxes, for "volunteers" for the Dan Ve, for rents for the landlords. By 1956 they had no more resources than had the ban hoi te of the French, and they were now more than ever an instrument of the central government. Local government thus had no firmer foundation than a leaf floating on the ocean. The only thing that had changed since 1954 was that the ocean had temporarily abated its violent churning.

By 1956, then, it could not be said that anyone "controlled" Long An, politically or militarily. The mass of the peasantry felt no loyalty to the government-sponsored village councils; nor was the government strong enough to exercise unchallenged "control." Its forces were sufficient to deal with the local tipplers and hooligans, but the politically disaffected could always pick up and move a few miles to an area where government influence did not reach. The open areas in the Delta are too large to "control"; government opponents were simply driven out to where they could plot in secret. Neither did the Party exercise "control": its underground apparatus had been severely damaged, though in such a clumsy fashion that considerable resentment had been created even among those who had not fled or been imprisoned. The Party was retaining its vestigial military forces in absolute secrecy, well realizing that without an underground apparatus they were useless. In this situation the government appeared to have "control" only in default of overt violent opposition. Thus to say that the government later "lost control" is misleading, and any analysis which proposes to answer the question of why the government "lost control" or why there was an "erosion of mass support for established institutions" is addressing the wrong question.

By 1956 both the Party and the government had begun to develop their rival holds on the countryside. Both sides had advantages and disadvantages. The government's simple but immensely important advantage was that it could operate openly, whereas the Party's need for secrecy greatly hampered its work. Because it was the internationally recognized legal authority in the South, the Diem government was also free to use its military forces, as, for example, in the large sweeps of rural areas begun in 1956. The Party, however, was limited in this respect, because a resurgence of organized armed activity against the Diem authorities would clearly be identified with the regime in the North. The government was also in a position to draw openly upon extensive foreign resources, economic, technical, and military. Finally, the government, with the departure of the French, could claim itself a legitimate nationalist alternative to the Party. Thus the Party had lost a unifying symbol of first importance, although it was still able to draw on its nationalist reputation made during the resistance, especially in the rural areas where the majority of the population lived. Both the government and the Party, as we have seen, had the structure of a ruling organization, especially at the higher levels. The government had its system of village councils, district and province chiefs, and the regional delegate and central ministries leading up to the Presidency—all now theoretically invigorated by the reorganization of 1956. The Party retained its pre-1954 organization of hierarchical executive committees, stretching from the chi bo in each village up to the Central Committee, now established in Hanoi.

Yet the village structures of each were weak. The Party's once strong local organization had been smashed by the government, whereas the government's local organs had never been strong. It was here that the Party held its decisive advantage. In terms of actual composition and the interests it served, the government was a melange of urban middle-class and elite elements, landlords, and mandarin remnants, generally French educated if not actually with French citizenship, whose breadth of social vision was typified by the three former province chiefs quoted above. Although the technical skills of this group were considerable, its organizational skills at the local level had been poor compared to the Vietminh, and it had ruled in the rural areas through social elements whose interests were in practice hostile to the interests of the people they ruled. The Vietminh, however, had built up a strong local organization based on landless or land-poor elements; thus from its experience in the resistance the Party had both a better rural organization and more actual and potential sympathy. By dominating the villages, it had rendered the central government helpless. In the words of one former Vietminh cadre: "You have the central government, then the province, district, and village. But the lowest of the four is the level that lies with the people. If the village level is weak, then I guarantee you, no matter how strong the central government is, it won't be able to do a thing."

In 1956, then, the government "declared war" on the remaining elements of opposition in the countryside through a combination of efforts: tightening the administrative organization and extending it to the family level, increasing the efforts of its civilian programs to win over the uncommitted, and intensifying its military and police efforts to root out the opposition. The Party also decided to destroy the Diem regime and complete the revolution interrupted in 1954. It moved more quietly, simply keeping up a steady stream of antigovernment propaganda while secretly ordering the rebuilding of its Party structure. . . .

. . . [Here is] a quotation from a hamlet chief, in which he describes the situation in his village in 1959. . . .

The Vietcong were very smart. If they knew that Binh's family had been ill-treated by the government, they would work on that weak point. Perhaps Binh had had money extorted by an official—in his heart he had to feel resentment. So they would come by from time to time and say, "You see how bad the government is, it calls itself nationalist, but in the end it steals your money. . . . Are you just going to do nothing?" So, like fanning a flame, Binh's resentment would grow to anger, and his anger to hatred, and his hatred to revolt. Or maybe Xoai would be building a house. The Vietcong would come by and help him put it up, meanwhile talking about their life—no pay, living in the swamps, being shot at all the time. Naturally, Xoai would take pity on them, so the next time they came by and asked for a meal, he would invite them in. But when they took a meal it was not like our soldiers' way: burst in, demand food, sit around while it was being fixed, eat, and finally grab a couple of chickens and run off. Instead, the V.C. would go into the kitchen, clean the rice, and, while they were waiting for it to cook, they would sweep the house, wash the dishes, and set the table. When the meal was over, they would clean up, and then thank everyone politely. So the owner of the house would think, "The soldiers come in here as if they owned the place, but this other fellow is very polite and helps me out." Naturally, he let the Vietcong eat at his house all the time. That is how the Vietcong gained the people's support. They simply built on the opportunity we gave them.

. . . Le van Chan, the former deputy secretary of the Interprovince Committee for western Nam Bo, analyzed the situation this way:

During 1957 and 1958 the Party was able to recover its apparatus and its mass organizations, and it counted on contradictions within the government to produce a coup. Thus it emphasized troop proselytizing activities with the hope that in the event of a coup it could seize power. Because the Party judged that it had a sufficient chance to seize power in a coup through its mass organizations and its apparatus, it did not allow the armed forces it was still maintaining in the South to appear.

However, by 1959 the situation in the South had passed into a stage the communists considered the darkest in their lives: almost all their apparatus had been smashed, the population no longer dared to provide support, families no longer dared to communicate with their relatives in the movement, and village chapters which previously had had one or two hundred members were now reduced to five or ten who had to flee into the jungle. Because of this situation Party members were angry at the Central Committee, and demanded armed action. The southern branch of the Party demanded of the Central Committee a reasonable policy in dealing with the southern regime, in order to preserve its own existence. If not, it would be completely destroyed.

In the face of this situation the Central Committee saw that it was no longer possible to seize power in the South by means of a peaceful struggle line, since the southern regime, with American assistance, was becoming stronger and not collapsing as had been predicted. Not only had the southern regime not been destroyed, it was instead destroying the Party. Thus it was necessary to have an appropriate line to salvage the situation; if not, then it would lead to a situation which would not be salvageable. As a result, the Fifteenth

Conference of the Central Committee developed a decision permitting the southern organization, that is, the Nam Bo Regional Committee and Interzone 5 [a portion of central Vietnam lying below the 17th parallel] to develop armed forces with the mission of supporting the political struggle line. These forces were not to fight a conventional war, nor were they intended merely for a guerrilla conflict. Their mission was to sap the strength of the government's village and hamlet forces, or what they called the "tyrannical elements." They were only to attack such units as entered their own base areas, in order to preserve the existence of the apparatus and to develop forces for a new line which the Central Committee would develop. Only in November of 1959 did this policy reach the village level, and it was from this decision that the guerrilla movement and the current armed forces in the South sprang into existence. . . .

According to Party doctrine, the issue of land is an integral part of people's war. Thus, when the Party seizes an area, it considers that land reform is a strategic task which must be carried out regardless of cost, in order to produce an impact on the peasantry and in order to set the peasantry in opposition to the government and the landlords. At the same time this is a means of making the peasantry accept the need to pay taxes and to send its youth into the army. According to Party doctrine, the national democratic revolution has two missions: antiimperialism and antifeudalism. The one implies the other, because the landlords have conspired with the imperialists. It can be explained very simply to the peasants: if you want to keep your land, you must fight the imperialists, and if you want to fight the imperialists, your son must go into the army and you must pay taxes. That is the strategic line of the Party.

The Party's present land-reform program is basically the same as during the Resistance: to reduce land rents, to reduce interest, to reduce rental payments for farm tools and animals, and to confiscate the land of absentee landlords. The ownership of land and the right to collect rents of religious organizations is recognized, as well as that of landlords who remain in Party areas. Thus the land situation in the South is not the same as in the North, particularly in regard to denunciation meetings. This is for two reasons. First, in the South making a living is much easier since there is so much land. Second, the Party does not dare push the land issue so strongly as in the North, because from the time of the resistance so many of the Party members in the South have belonged to the landowning elements, the petty bourgeoisie, and the intelligentsia. Now the Party has reduced the numbers of such people, but it still does not dare push the land issue strongly because of the need to win over landed and

religious elements in the present stage of the national liberation
movement.

Party policy is to distribute land to the lowest elements in the
countryside, that is, the landless and poor peasants and certain
middle peasants. As for landlords, they are to be overthrown, just
as are the rich peasants, although this depends on the stage of the
revolution. At present the Party distinguishes various types of landlords: those to be destroyed are the ones who participate in the government; fence-sitters are temporarily permitted to retain their own
land, while patriotic landlords are permitted to collect land rents up
to a certain level and on a certain amount of land. With rich peasants the Party tries to educate them and persuade them to reduce
the rates they charge for interest and for rental of farm tools and
animals. During this period the Party never touches their land in the
South, but if they have much land and cannot work it themselves,
the Party persuades them to let it out at a very low rental.

Once it starts distributing land, what does the Party say to the
people? It never says that the land is theirs permanently—only that it is
theirs for ten years, fifteen years, perhaps their whole life, but still only
provisionally. This is a lesson drawn from the Resistance, when the
peasants got the impression the land was theirs permanently. In the
North after the war was over the government needed various areas for
industry, etc., but the peasants refused to return the land, demanding
compensation and making difficulties. Thus since 1960, when land re-
distribution began again, the Party has always said that the land is only
provisionally distributed, not permanently, because it plans after seizing the South to establish collective farms, industrial areas, etc. Despite what the Party says, the peasants feel that the land is permanently
theirs, and, should the Party succeed in taking over the South, it will
meet with no small opposition thereafter.

Nevertheless, once the peasants received land, their living standard increased tremendously. Formerly they had to pay rent to the
landlord and interest to the moneylender. Now for the first few
years they could keep the entire harvest, and thus their living was
comparatively easy, just as it had been in the Resistance. But as the
pace of the war increased, those who received land had to pay for
the war, for whenever the Party mentioned land it also mentioned
politics: the peasants now own the land, but the peasants are also
the main forces of the revolution. Only by sending their sons into
the army and paying taxes could the war be won, and only by winning the war could they keep their land. Thus land is a life and
death issue, inextricably tied to their own interests. Although sometimes their taxes to the Party are five or seven times those to the

government, they nevertheless pay them: in the time of the French, when their parents had no land, their life was extremely harsh. Now they have land, and they are willing to pay and to send their sons into the army to preserve it.

Chan also spoke of the extent to which assistance to the revolutionary movement was "forced" as opposed to "voluntary."

This is a subtle point. One cannot say that support is voluntary, and one cannot say it is not voluntary. Previously the peasantry felt that it was the most despised class, with no standing at all, particularly the landless and the poor peasants. For example, at a celebration they could just stand in a corner and look, not sit at the table like the village notables. Now the communists have returned and the peasants have power. The land has been taken from the landlords and turned over to the peasants, just as have all the local offices. Now the peasants can open their eyes and look up to the sky: they have prestige and social position. The landlords and other classes must fear them because they have power: most of the cadres are peasants, most of the Party members are peasants, most of the military commanders are peasants. Only now do the peasants feel that they have proper rights: materially they have land and are no longer oppressed by the landlords; spiritually they have a position in society, ruling the landlords instead of being ruled by them. This the peasants like. But if the communists were to go and the government to come back, the peasants would return to their former status as slaves. Consequently they must fight to preserve their interests and their lives, as well as their political power.

On the other hand, there are some, particularly the middle and rich peasants, who do not like the communists, because the communists hurt their interests: they are not permitted to charge interest and rentals as before, and if they want to hire laborers they are accused of exploitation. Thus they don't like the communists, but they don't dare oppose them, because, if they oppose the communists, they must go to live in a government area. But do they have enough money to go and live in Saigon? Probably not, and so they must be content to remain.

Thus there are those who willingly and voluntarily support the Party, and those who are forced, and to say that everyone is forced is mistaken. One must make distinctions between classes of people in order to understand the situation.

. . . The Party had not been inactive [while military preparations were underway]. Ideally, according to defectors, the Party would have called for its general uprising and final wave of attacks during the coup of November 1963. It had not done so, however, because of an insufficient development of its military forces. As a result, it called for a "general mobilization" on July 20, 1964, the tenth anniversary of the signing of the Geneva Accords. According to the terms of the order for mobilization, every male from eighteen to thirty was required to serve, but several defectors from Long An report that there was widespread evasion: perhaps only one-third of those eligible were actually inducted into military units. Another third fled to government areas, and the remaining third agreed only to dig up roads or to transport supplies, but not to carry weapons. Defectors report that at that time they had no authority to arrest those who declined service. . . .

[Lieutenant Colonel Edwin W. Chamberlain has written:]

> The foundation on which the V.C. activity in Long An province rested was the hardcore 506th V.C. battalion. Deprived of this base the local V.C. were little more than bandits and capable of being managed, in time, by the forces available to the province. Unfortunately the V.C. battalion proved itself to be an extremely effective combat unit which on three separate occasions succeeded in tactically defeating much larger government forces in the field. The A.R.V.N. did not conduct a ruthless campaign to hunt down and destroy this organization, thus dooming any real hope for the pacification of Long An province.[1]

By early 1965 revolutionary forces had gained victory in virtually all the rural areas of Long An, and they had the ability, based on the balance of forces within the province, to seize and hold the only remaining islands of government authority: the province capital and the six district towns. They held back because, to be successful, the attacks would have had to be simultaneous throughout the country to prevent a reinforcement of any one area, and elsewhere the Party had not quite yet achieved the victorious position it had already gained in Long An.

In conclusion, we may say that the combination of these factors—emphasis on class and local origin [in recruiting Party members], concentration of authority at low levels, institutional-

---

[1] Lieutenant Colonel Edwin W. Chamberlain, "Pacification," *Infantry*, LVIII: 6 (November-December 1968) pp.32–39.

ization of communications through enforced working principles, a continuous promotion chain—demonstrated clearly that political and military organization under the new society conformed to majority local interests, whereas the existing government organization was objectively the pawn of "outsiders"—both in the sense of place of birth and sympathy with the local area, and in the sense of following social life styles and economic interests different from those of the majority of the rural population.

As for status, certainly the government offered numerous positions, such as interfamily group chief, leader of youth and paramilitary organizations, etc. Why were these not status roles? The answer lies in the involuntarism that characterized membership in government organizations. For example, membership in government organizations such as the Republican Youth was universal and compulsory, whereas membership in revolutionary organizations during the entire period discussed thus far was largely voluntary—even, remarkably, after the "general mobilization" of July 20, 1964.

How could the revolutionary movement offer status roles which were voluntarily sought, while the government had to resort to coercion? Here we must return to the definition of status [as] a feeling of prestige obtained by occupying a role approved by one's peers. The comments of defectors that they joined the movement "for adventure" or "since I was tired of being treated like trash because I was poor" are examples of the status roles available to the rural poor through the revolutionary movement but not through the government. Why, after all, did so few people volunteer to join the government army "for adventure" or because they were "tired of being treated like trash?" To occupy roles in the revolutionary movement was perceived by major segments of the local population as defending its interests, while to occupy government roles was seen as being manipulated by outside forces in opposition to local interests—not to mention that it sometimes involved cooperation with and protection of criminal and corrupt elements within the government. Thus government roles were not regarded as giving status. . . .

XX. Our Strategy for Guerrilla War

NGUYEN VAN THIEU

*Nguyen Van Thieu lived in the maquis for
sixteen years during the two wars in
Vietnam. As an N.L.F. leader, he was in
charge of the relationship between the
towns and the countryside in the early
1960s and was a member of the N.L.F.'s
central committee.*

As far as we are concerned, revolutionary war is the people's
war. In other words, the role played by the population is not just
important: it is fundamental.

In 1954–1959, the Diem regime controlled the towns and even
the countryside—or was at least trying to. It had firm social backing within the towns and had managed to attract the support of
many religious sects. With the help of landlords and their agents,
it strived to control the villages. But it made one fatal error.
During the resistance against the French, nearly one million hec-
tares had been distributed to the peasantry; the regime took
these lands back. It began by doing away with everything the
revolution had brought the peasants, simply because those gains
had been the work of the Vietminh. But the peasants that had
been given the land put up strong resistance, in some cases even
assassinating the landlords that repossessed the fields. The class
struggle was very acute; peasants knew their interests were being
violated, and they nursed a lasting hatred for the Diem regime.

In order to control the villages, the Diem regime relied on the
Ac-on, its most cruel agents. Six to twelve were assigned to each
village. Each village was divided into groups of households that
were kept under regular surveillance. A board was posted in

From *Partisans,* special "Vietnam" edition (Paris: Librairie François Maspero), 1968.

front of each house, displaying the name, sex, and age of everybody who lived there. Sometimes the Ac-on ran checks at night. Any member of the household who was absent when they came was expected to produce a good explanation. The Ac-on were in fact more effective than the French administration and the old notables had ever been. No stranger could pass through without being reported.

After 1954 and the Geneva Accords, those of our revolutionary cadres who came from peasant backgrounds returned to work as peasants. The village is our basic unit. Most villages have about 2,500 to 5,000 inhabitants and are divided up into little hamlets. If they are not picked up by the forces of repression, our cadres influence the population through the daily contacts established when working.

Life was becoming much harder for the peasantry now that Diem had repossessed their lands. The cadres' task was to make the best use of the discontent created by the regime. For example, they might say, "What has the Diem regime ever done for us apart from taking our lands and increasing the cost of tenancy?" All our political propaganda was based on the peasants' everyday personal interests and on the general feeling of discontent, most pronounced among the very poor. *We absolutely had to have cadres who knew and understood the peasantry.* Fortunately about 85 percent of our cadres are of peasant origin.

We did not stress that we were fighting for freedom—that would come later. The overthrow of the regime was presented as a matter of immediate and direct personal interest. Big words are just so much hot air. What matters most is land. The first task is to liquidate the notables, the Ac-on, and the landlords. If the peasants are discontented, then their discontent can be elevated into positive hatred of the regime, and then they will join the struggle for a better life.

Not all our revolutionary cadres were based in villages. Many lived in the jungle, in the mountains, or in deserted areas. With nightfall, these cadres would try to enter the village—their own village—to maintain contacts. Generally the revolutionary cadres would stick to their village, where they knew the people and the lay of the land, where they had relatives. Some cadres lived like this for years, hiding out during the day, emerging only at night. A few even lost their eyesight as a result of never seeing daylight.

Life was hard under Diem. Everybody realized that conditions were unbearable, that something had to be done if we did not want death to be our only hope of respite.

Political struggles began to break out. The peasants would outline their grievances to the council of notables, but the usual result was more repression. Bit by bit the peasants began to realize that the only way out was to take up arms and that they alone could change things. The fewer conditions you as revolutionaries impose, the more the peasants will be able to act as conscious agents. Of course everything depends on the prevailing conditions, and you will no doubt have to rely largely on your own experience.

The main task is to make people aware of the need for armed struggle. Weapons can always be found. The insurrection began in 1959, in the Mekong delta, with hunting rifles. No munitions were en route from the North. The core of the peasant question is that it cannot be hurried. If the peasants do not understand the situation, it is dangerous and often useless for us to make a move by ourselves. The peasants themselves raised the issue of armed struggle in 1959.

In the Mekong delta, the first objective was to break the regime's stranglehold by liquidating the Ac-on. They were judged in open court. Once the villages had been liberated, we were able to intensify our propaganda effort.

Naturally the repressive forces usually reacted quickly and appeared on the scene in strength. The peasants would tell them, "Well-armed people come in the middle of the night and liquidated so-and-so. They told us not to leave the village and forced us to destroy the strategic hamlet's entire defensive system. They also hid things under those trees over there and warned us to keep away." Diem's men would not believe the last part of the story. Some would go to investigate and be blown to bits by mines. Another important propaganda effort is trying to convince the enemy's troops to desert. Some may be persuaded; others may simply become frightened as our strength increases.

To return to the problem of implanting yourself in the population; the main thing is to *stick to a village*. From 1954 to 1959 we lost many peasant cadres because Diem's men were well entrenched. But we held on, sometimes under very tough conditions. Sympathetic peasants dug holes to hide people in. The

Ac-on had metal spikes to find such hideaways, and often they did discover people. But the cadres managed to maintain their contacts with the peasantry and were often able to hold little meetings with seven or eight reliable people at night to discuss the local situation and divide up tasks. Each cadre had at least three hideouts in the village. The villagers themselves elected struggle committees composed of the most active and conscious peasants—those the others trusted.

One difficult but essential point is to ensure that the struggle becomes generalized rather than confined to only one region. There must be coordination and mutual aid between regions if we are not to be easily beaten, and this must in turn fit into a coherent overall plan that articulates to the greatest possible extent action in the village, the district, the province, the regions, and the country. Without patience you cannot make a revolution. Cadres who work at the village level must be stubborn and cautious at the same time. They also have to be highly mobile, since the enemy is constantly trying to find them. Peasant sympathizers will keep them supplied with rice, salt, and sometimes fish, which can be carried away to an underground hideout where the cadres will eat, sleep, and wait for nightfall, when they can begin to act. Sometimes the surveillance will relax such that sympathizers can put one of our people up for a while. In any case the peasants look after our cadres, providing them with shelters in several houses, in gardens, sometimes in wells. But the life is very hard; being a revolutionary is no simple matter. The peasant question is the most difficult and complex of all, but if it can be resolved then victory is sure; you can no longer be beaten. But just because the conditions are favorable does not mean you can simply grab a rifle and go out to tell the peasants that everything is going to change.

Since December 20, 1960, the Front has been leading the struggle, but it was the peasants that initiated it.

The problems of establishing yourself in the community are complex and various. You must study and know the local peasant mentality very well, especially anything concerning divisions within the peasantry. I do not mean only the land problem. In Africa there is the tribal problem. In Asia, for the most part, there are religious problems. Here, in Vietnam, religious sects account for 50 percent of the population. There are about

4,000,000 Buddhists, 1,800,000 Catholics, 1,000,000 Hoa-Hoa, and 1,000,000 Caodaists. And a great variety of problems arise in mobilizing these people.

We also have underpopulated areas, a fact which is all too often forgotten. Outside the Mekong delta, especially in the mountains, the population density is low and settlements are thinly scattered. Communication between people who live there is not easy to establish, but it is vital to do so. In addition to different religions, there are also various customs. In the Camau plain for example, where the peasants live in considerable isolation, their universe is restricted to their little plot of land, their family, and a few neighbors. The question is how to put these people in contact with other peasants. The cadres begin by bringing news of relatives who live elsewhere, perhaps 30 miles away, and leave having gathered news for the distant relatives. They go back and forth in this way for a while, and links gradually become established. It is a difficult process and requires patience, but it is very important. Gradually the peasants realize that they can move about, and, thanks to the cadres, they begin to see beyond their little plot of land. Then they start venturing out themselves, and the resulting increase in the number of travelers makes it easier for our cadres to go unnoticed. Of course all this is impossible if one lacks peasant cadres.

The peasant struggle naturally must be coordinated with the workers' struggle. The struggles are not separate; on the contrary, they are common and share a common goal. They must be fused into a single movement. The secret of the N.L.F. is simple: the Front has united the peasant problem, the workers' problem, the problem of the religious sects, and the problem of the national minorities.

This last point is very important. One thing I regretted about the O.L.A.S. conference[1] was the absence of any Indian elements, even though Indians form the majority in many Latin American countries. Here, in Hanoi, there are five of us on the committee, and one is a comrade from the national minorities.

To become accepted by the national minorities, our cadres have not only learned the language; they have pierced their ears or filed their teeth if that is the custom of the minority in ques-

[1] Held in Havana in 1967.

tion. They have lived like the minority, and that can be very hard. You must be patient, because these people are initially very suspicious of anyone from outside their own ethnic group. It is a delicate but decisive issue: obviously the ultimate aim is for cadres to come from the national minority itself. The reason we have been able to fight battles in which we had to commit up to an entire division is that our policy of forming alliances with the national minorities has been very successful: in the South, the minorities participate in the struggle.

I must admit that it is a very difficult task. You must study the language, the customs, and the mentality in order to win their trust; it is not easily won, but, once you have been accepted, you can rely on them absolutely. The Americans, like the French and the Japanese before them, have sought to divide us. But we have managed to establish ourselves. There are nationalities among whom we have been working five or even ten years in order to convince them to fight alongside us. If you want to make a revolution, you have to be prepared to make sacrifices and wage a long-term struggle.

The next phase is to articulate the town and the countryside. In our country, the working class has only recently emerged. Workers still have peasant relatives; their families still live in the villages. They go back there from time to time, and we use this movement between town and country to reinforce political links. Certain actions can be coordinated. For instance, when the enemy bombs and kills people all over the countryside, the peasants bring the bodies to the towns to put pressure on the regime and to show what is happening to the people; the workers support these demonstrations by going on strike. Correspondingly, the peasants support the workers when they strike. The coordination is complex, but it produces results.

We are not trying to lead isolated struggles of the population but to coordinate all forms of the revolutionary struggle—that is, the people's war—to overthrow the regime by cutting it off from all its bases, be they passive or active. Naturally, one may trigger the armed struggle before the political tasks are complete, but political work must follow the armed struggle very closely. The armed struggle helps break the regime's grip and opens the way for propaganda and political work. But political work is always necessary. Without it, there can be no victory.

If we did no political work, the peasants would not support us and we would probably be isolated. The enemy is always militarily stronger at first. When the enemy comes, you have to move and repression ensues, for which the peasants blame you, since you created the conditions that attracted the repression. You must explain the situation, and that demands political work. Our political cadres have remained, sticking desperately to their village despite the repression, in order to continue their political work, organize the population, and train more cadres in the village. We believe study and knowledge of the region in which one is establishing oneself to be quite fundamental. Areas exist where the regime and the landowners exert severe pressure and where the population is discontented yet does not know how to go about changing things. If the cadres understand how to establish themselves, they can create favorable conditions for political work and armed struggle. Every revolutionary movement needs to carry out this kind of painstaking study, because in the beginning what really matters is knowing how to create the most favorable conditions for the initiation and intensification of armed struggle.

You should never impose conditions on the peasantry; they must be helped to understand for themselves why armed struggle is necessary: they are already aware of their own interests. Above all, you should help elevate their political consciousness and their level of organization. We will never have more weapons, more tanks, more planes than the Americans. The real problem of revolutionary war is not primarily military. It is political. The secret of our success is that we strive to mobilize the people, resolve the peasant question, coordinate the town-countryside struggle, resolve the problem of the national minorities and religious sects, and elevate the level of organization and political consciousness. That is why we can stand up to the most powerful imperialism in the world.

XXI.   Urban Guerrilla Strategy

ABRAHAM GUILLEN

*An excellent theoretician, Abraham
Guillen was, among others, a "counselor"
to the Tupamaros in Uruguay. He
criticized the movement's strategy long
before its fall.*

To the credit of the Uruguayan guerrillas, they were the first to
operate in the cement jungles of a capitalist metropolis, to endure during the first phase of a revolutionary war thanks to an
efficient organization and tactics, and to confound the police and
armed forces for a considerable period. . . . With its failures as
well as successes, the Movement of National Liberation (Tupamaros) has contributed a model of urban guerrilla warfare that
has already made a mark on contemporary history—the scene of
a struggle between capitalism and socialism with its epicenter in
the great cities. The lessons that can be learned from the Tupamaros can be summarized in the following [seven] points.

1. *Fixed or Mobile Front?* When urban guerrillas lack widespread support because of revolutionary impatience or because
their actions do not directly represent popular demands, they
have to provide their own clandestine infrastructure by renting
houses and apartments. By tying themselves to a fixed terrain in
this way, the Tupamaros have lost both mobility and security:
two prerequisites of guerrilla strategy. In order to avoid encirclement and annihilation through house-to-house searches, the guerrillas can best survive not by establishing fixed urban bases but by
living apart and fighting together.

2. *Mobility and Security.* If urban guerrillas rent houses for

From Donald C. Hodges (ed.), *Philosophy of the Urban Guerrilla* (New York:
William Morrow, 1973). First appeared in Abraham Guillen, *Estrategia de la
guerrilla urbana* (c. 1971).

their commandos, they are in danger of leaving a trail that may be followed by the police who review monthly all registered rentals. Should most of their houses be loaned instead of leased, then the guerrillas should refrain as a general rule from building underground vaults or hideouts which would increase their dependence on the terrain. To retain their mobility and a high margin of security they must spread out among a favorable population. Guerrillas who fight together and then disperse throughout a great city are not easily detected by the police. When dragnets are applied to one neighborhood or zone, guerrillas without a fixed base can shift to another neighborhood. Such mobility is precluded by a reliance on rented houses or hideouts in the homes of sympathizers, heretofore a major strategical error of the Tupamaros.

3. *Heavy or Light Rear Guard?*   Urban guerrillas who develop a heavy infrastructure in many rented houses commit not only a military error, but also an economic and logistical one. For a heavy rear guard requires a comparatively large monthly budget in which economic and financial motives tend to overshadow political considerations. Lacking enough houses, the guerrillas tend to upgrade to positions of command those willing to lend their own. . . . Thus when promotion through the ranks is facilitated by owning a big house or a large farm or enterprise, the guerrillas become open to bourgeois tendencies. When guerrillas rely for cover not on a people in arms but on people of property, then urban guerrilla warfare becomes the business of an armed minority, which will never succeed in mobilizing in this manner the majority of the population.

4. *Logistical Infrastructure.*   Although a mobile front is preferable to a fixed one, there are circumstances in which a fixed front is unavoidable, for example, in the assembly, adjustment, and adaptation of arms. These fixed fronts, few and far between, must be concealed from the guerrillas themselves; they should be known only to the few who work there, preferably one person in each, in order to avoid discovery by the repressive forces. In the interest of security it is advisable not to manufacture arms, but to have the parts made separately by various legal establishments, after which they can be assembled in the secret workshops of the guerrillas.

It is dangerous to rely on a fixed front for housing, food,

medical supplies, and armaments. If the guerrillas are regularly employed, they should live as everybody else does; they should come together only at designated times and places. Houses that serve as barracks or hideouts tend to immobilize the guerrillas and to expose them to the possibility of encirclement and annihilation. Because the Tupamaros immobilized many of their commandos in fixed quarters, they were exposed in 1972 to mass detentions; they lost a large part of their armaments and related equipment and were compelled to transfer military supplies to the countryside for hiding.

To exercise control over their sympathizers and keep them under strict military discipline, the Tupamaros had to house them together. But they were seldom used in military operations at a single place or in several simultaneously, which indicates the absence of strategical preparation. If urban guerrillas cannot continually disappear and reappear among the population of a great city, then they lack the political prerequisites for making a revolution, for creating the conditions of a social crisis through the breakdown of "law and order." Despite their proficiency during the first hit-and-run phase of a revolutionary war, the Tupamaros have failed to escalate their operations by using larger units at more frequent intervals for the purpose of paralyzing the existing regime.

5. *Heroes, Martyrs, and Avengers.*   In revolutionary war any guerrilla action that needs explaining to the people is politically useless: it should be meaningful and convincing by itself. To kill an ordinary soldier in reprisal for the assassination of a guerrilla is to descend to the same political level as a reactionary army. Far better to create a martyr and thereby attract mass sympathy than to lose or neutralize popular support by senseless killings without an evident political goal. To be victorious in a people's war one has to act in conformity with the interests, sentiments, and will of the people. A military victory is worthless if it fails to be politically convincing.

In a country where the bourgeoisie has abolished the death penalty, it is self-defeating to condemn to death even the most hated enemies of the people. Oppressors, traitors, and informers have condemned themselves before the guerrillas; it is impolitic to make a public show of their crimes for the purpose of creating a climate of terror, insecurity, and disregard for basic human rights. A popular army that resorts to unnecessary violence, that is not a symbol of justice, equity, liberty, and security, cannot win popular support in the struggle against a dehumanized tyranny.

The Tupamaros' "prisons of the people" do more harm than good to the cause of national liberation. Taking hostages for the purpose of exchanging them for political prisoners has an immediate popular appeal, but informing the world of the existence of "people's prisons" is to focus unnecessarily on a parallel system of repression. No useful purpose can be served by such politically alienating language. Moreover, it is intolerable to keep anyone hostage for a long time. To achieve a political or propaganda victory through this kind of tactic, the ransom terms must be moderate and capable of being met; in no event should the guerrillas be pressed into executing a prisoner because their demands are excessive and accordingly rejected. A hostage may be usefully executed only when a government refuses to negotiate on any terms after popular pressure has been applied, for then it is evident to everyone that the government is ultimately responsible for the outcome.

So-called people's prisons are harmful for other reasons: they require several men to stand guard and care for the prisoners, they distract guerrillas from carrying out alternative actions more directly useful to the population, and they presuppose a fixed front and corresponding loss of mobility. At most it is convenient to have a secure place to detain for short periods a single hostage.

To establish people's prisons, to condemn to death various enemies of the people, to house the guerrillas in secret barracks or underground hideouts is to create an infrastructure supporting a miniature state rather than a revolutionary army. To win the support of the population, arms must be used directly on its behalf. Whoever uses violence against subordinates in the course of building a miniature counterstate should be removed from his command. Surely there is little point in defeating one despotism only to erect another in its place!

6. *Delegated Commands.*   In a professional army the leadership is recruited from the military academies within a hierarchical order of command. In a guerrilla organization the leaders emerge in actual revolutionary struggles, elected because of their capac-

ity, responsibility, combativity, initiative, political understanding, and deeds rather than words. However, at pain of forfeiting the democratic character of a revolutionary army and the function of authority as a delegated power, not even the best guerrilla commander can be allowed to remain long at the helm. . . . Epaminondas, the Theban general who defeated the Spartans, held a command that lasted only two years. Although the greatest strategist of his time, he became an ordinary soldier when his command expired. Only because of his extraordinary skill was he made a military adviser to the new commander-in-chief. Guerrillas can benefit by his example.

A delegated command is unlimited except for the time determining its delegation. The responsibility of subordinates is to discuss in advance each operation, to make recommendations, etc. But the discussion ends when the supreme command assumes responsibility for the outcome of a particular battle or engagement. If the commander is mistaken in his judgment, if the result is defeat rather than victory, his duty is to resign. Should he succeed in a vote of confidence he may retain his command, but two successive defeats should make his resignation irrevocable.

One of the most common errors of Latin American guerrillas is to make legends of their leaders as they did of Fidel Castro and Che Guevara. The resulting messianism conceals the incapacity of many guerrilla commanders who take their troops into the countryside—like the Tupamaros in 1972—without revising mistaken strategies. . . .

In their endeavor to create a state within the state through highly disciplined guerrilla columns, secret barracks, "prisons of the people," underground arsenals, and a heavy logistical infrastructure, the Tupamaros have become overly professionalized, militarized, and isolated from the urban masses. Their organization is closer to resembling a parallel power contesting the legally established one, a microstate, than a movement of the masses.

7. *Strategy, Tactics, and Politics.*   If the tactics adopted are successful but the corresponding strategy and politics mistaken, the guerrillas cannot win. Should a succession of tactical victories encourage a strategical objective that is impossible to attain, then a great tactical victory can culminate in an even greater strategical defeat.

The kidnappings of the Brazilian consul Días Gomide and the

C.I.A. agent Dan Mitrione are instances of tactical successes by the Tupamaros. But in demanding in exchange a hundred detained guerrillas, the Tupamaros found the Uruguayan government obstinate, in order not to lose face altogether. Here a successful tactic contributed to an impossible strategical objective. In having to execute Mitrione because the government failed to comply with their demands, the Tupamaros not only failed to accomplish a political objective, but also suffered a political reversal in their newly acquired role of assassins—the image they acquired through hostile mass media.

The Tupamaros would have done better by taping Mitrione's declarations and giving the story to the press. The population would have followed the incidents of his confession with more interest than the interminable serials. Mitrione's confessed links with the C.I.A. should have been fully documented and sent to Washington in care of Senator Fulbright. With this incident brought to the attention of Congress, the operation against the C.I.A. would have won world support for the Tupamaros. Once the Uruguayan government had lost prestige through this publicity, the Uruguayan press might be asked to publish a manifesto of the Tupamaros explaining their objectives in the Mitrione case. Afterward Mitrione's death sentence should have been commuted out of respect for his eight sons, but on condition that he leave the country. Such a solution to the government's refusal to negotiate with the guerrillas would have captured the sympathy of many in favor of the Tupamaros. Even more than conventional war, revolutionary war is a form of politics carried out by violent means.

With respect to Días Gomide, the Tupamaros lost an opportunity to embarrass politically the Brazilian government. They should never have allowed matters to reach the point at which his wife could appear as an international heroine of love and marital fidelity by collecting sums for his release. Every cruzeiro she collected was a vote against the Tupamaros and indirectly against the Brazilian guerrillas. In exchange for Días Gomide, a man of considerable importance to the military regime, the Tupamaros should have demanded the publication of a manifesto in the Brazilian press. Its contents might have covered the following items: a denunciation of the "death squad" as an informal instrument of the Brazilian dictatorship; a demand for free, secret, and direct elections; the legalization of all political parties dissolved by the military regime; the restitution of political rights to Brazil's former leaders and exiles including Quadros, Kubitschek, Brizola, Goulart, and even reactionaries like Lacerda; the denunciation of government censorship of the press; and a demand that popular priests be set free. With such a political response the revolutionary war might have been exported to Brazil. Guerrilla actions should not be narrowly circumscribed when they can have regional and international repercussions. . . .

XXII.　　　　　Al Fatah's Autocriticism

ABU IYAD

*Abu Iyad, Al Fatah's second in command,
attempts to evaluate the years 1967–1977.
He makes no mention of various
weaknesses of the Palestinian national
movement in general and of Al Fatah in
particular (notably in terms of
organization, politics, strategy, and an
overreliance on financial aid that enables
the Arab states to control the movement).
This autocriticism is, however, something
of a breakthrough, though we are still
waiting to see its consequences. Al Fatah is
the largest movement within the P.L.O.
and has played a key role in the revival of
Palestinian nationalism.*

It is time to draw up a balance sheet. The exodus of the Palestinian people occurred thirty years ago, and it is twenty years since Al Fatah was founded. I am forced to admit, with the deepest bitterness, that our situation today is far worse than the one we faced in 1958 that led us to launch our movement. I greatly fear that we may have to start again, from scratch. Naturally, I am not denying that we have had some successes. I am proud of my people and of the sacrifices we have been prepared to make that we might win victories on the battlefield against an enemy whose overwhelming might no one would now deny. I am pleased that the P.L.O. is a significant figure in the world scene. It is now recognized by most states as the sole legitimate representative of the Palestinian people and has finally won an observer's seat at

From Abu Iyad, *Palestinien sans patrie* (Paris: Editions Fayolle, 1979). Preface by Eric Rouleau. Reprinted by permission of Editions Fayolle.

the United Nations. All this notwithstanding, after twenty years of hard struggle the fate of my people remains grim. We still have no homeland, no identity. We have in fact lost ground; Israel now occupies all of Palestine, not just half. The United States, the guarantor of the Zionist enterprise, has extended and consolidated its hold over the Arab world. Egypt, the greatest and most powerful Arab country, was shipwrecked at Camp David. Arab oil, which could have been used as a formidable political weapon, is now no more than a commercial commodity. The Arab world has in recent years offered one-way concessions to Israel and is becoming weaker due to these shameful compromises. For the time being the Arab world is not politically ready to conclude an equitable and lasting peace; further, it lacks the force that would make such a peace possible.

It is true that we have shunned those mistakes committed by our predecessors, but our own errors, though less grave, have harmed us—perhaps irreparably. We have made what we considered to be strategic alliances with Arab nations, to discover to our great cost they were only provisional. This has caused us severe disappointment and unexpected reverses. We thought, for example, that Egypt would be forever at our side! That Syria would never—even briefly—supply arms that might be used against us by the Christian Right in Lebanon! Notwithstanding the divergent political views separating us and Iraq, we never imagined that country would assassinate our most eminent militants while they were traveling in foreign lands.

An error in strategy has compounded the problems caused by our mistaken understanding of the Arab world. Faced with political upheaval in an Arab country, we have usually tried to maintain relations with the regime in power, sacrificing our rapport with the downtrodden masses. We must in future follow the principle that should guide our actions, according to which the true source of our strength rests more in the popular sympathy we arouse than in the reluctant support governments proffer. It is of course true that we have occasionally maintained clandestine relations with opposition movements as well. But since the people were kept ignorant of our actions, they could only conclude that we were applying an opportunistic policy.

When we began actively to support governments, we came to be perceived more as politicians than as revolutionaries. This change in our public image has of course prejudiced the Arab masses against us; they expected us to act more honorably. And it has not guaranteed us the sympathy of Europeans and Americans. Unlike our Zionist enemies, we have neither means for nor experience in public relations. But the main cause of our failure has been our ignorance of western society and of the complex democratic mechanisms that operate there. More often than not, especially in the case of the United States, we fail to distinguish a government's imperialist policies from the psychological motivations—in themselves quite honorable—that shape people's attitude toward us. These misunderstandings lead us either to take action that can only further alienate western opinion or to seek refuge in despairing passivity.

We have also failed to unite the Palestinian movement or even to limit its fragmentation, although objective factors do prevent our achieving this goal. Al Fatah was originally conceived as a front that would bring together all Palestinians, irrespective of ideological or political differences. Without using force—which was quite out of the question—we could neither compel leaders like George Habash and Nayef Hawatmeh to join us nor prevent them from forming their own organizations. But we could easily have barred from the P.L.O. groups created by Arab regimes to serve as their political or military instruments. Given the present balance of forces, we cannot now insist they be dissolved or expelled. But we could have been much less conciliatory when they were first created, shortly after the June 1967 debacle; the recently vanquished and weakened Arab regimes would have been in no position to resist our initiative.

Those puppet Palestinian formations not only weaken our movement by reducing the cohesion and effectiveness of its actions; they can also play an actively negative role. Benefiting as they do from foreign support, they have constantly sought to raise the ideological stakes, launching provocative actions that have dragged us into adventures we would otherwise have avoided. The phenomenon is not unprecedented. In the domain of international relations, to take a well-known example, it is not unheard of for a small and in itself unimportant country to push a major allied power into adopting an unsuitable and harmful policy.

Our mistakes, weaknesses, and inconsistencies, however, should not be taken as the complete explanation of why our movement is in so delicate a position. It must be noted in our defense that the task we have shouldered is one of the most difficult history has ever seen. We lead a movement that, by its very nature, cannot enjoy a coherent base of support. The people we seek to mobilize and lead are geographically dispersed, psychologically heterogeneous, and of varying political beliefs. Palestinians live under different, sometimes contradictory, socio-economic regimes that inevitably influence them: they are subordinated to authoritarian systems within which dissidence is not tolerated, especially when differences or conflicts emerge between the state and the resistance movement. Under such conditions, our compatriots have little choice but to accept the official line, whether they like it or not, or to withdraw into a neutrality that at least protects them from official reprisals.

To spare Palestinians in such countries from reprisals, we are forced to treat their governments with kid gloves, to look the other way when they take hostile action we would otherwise certainly react against. Our freedom of action is decidedly limited.

XXIII. The Bargain War in Afghanistan

GÉRARD CHALIAND

The International Institute for Strategic Studies (London) asked Gérard Chaliand to write a report on the Afghan resistance. He visited the country in June and in October 1980. In the following pages, Chaliand analyzes the strengths and the weaknesses of the Afghan resistance.

June 1980

A recent visit of some weeks with the rebels in Afghanistan suggests two broad conclusions about the resistance movement. The first is that it is an extremely popular movement. It is not manpower that the guerrillas lack but weapons. The second is that in its leadership, organization, and coordination the Afghan movement is one of the weakest liberation struggles in the world today.

In most other national liberation movements and armed struggles in the Third World—in Vietnam, Cuba, Algeria, Guinea-Bissau, and elsewhere—the principal task of the revolutionary vanguard was to win the support of at least a part of the population, and to build an underground political organization. In Afghanistan the pattern was different: a few months after the coup that overthrew Mohammed Daoud's republic in April 1978, the Afghans joined in a spontaneous uprising against the new "socialist" government. The resistance grew steadily, although in a fragmented and uncoordinated way; even greater numbers

From Gérard Chaliand, "With the Afghan Rebels," *New York Review of Books,* XXVII, 15, October 9, 1980, and "Bargain War," *New York Review of Books,* XXVIII, 5, April 2, 1981 (both translated by Tamar Jacoby). Copyright 1980, 1981 by Gérard Chaliand.

joined the fight against the Soviet army and the regime it brought to power at the end of December 1979.

Today the resistance movement openly controls most of the countryside. The government and its Soviet military support hold the cities, the main roads, and military outposts scattered across the country. The rebels are mainly peasants, and their local leaders are tribal chiefs.

There are more than half a dozen different factions within the resistance movement, which is based in Peshawar, the Pakistani city near the Afghan border. They have no general strategy, no coordination, no organization other than traditional ties to tribe, region, and family. The resistance has scarcely any political or social program, and no vision of the future. Unlike virtually all of the guerrilla movements of Asia, Africa, or Latin America, the Afghan rebels have nothing new to show the visiting observer: no newly elected village committee, for example, no program for the integration of women into the struggle, no newly created people's stores or medical centers, no small workshops contributing to economic self-sufficiency of the sort one finds in guerrilla camps throughout the world. The Afghan rebels have undertaken no political experiments or social improvements.

In this respect, the Afghan movement resembles the insurrections of the Basmachis—the Muslims of the Boukhara emirate, now within the U.S.S.R., who resisted the Soviet takeover and the reforms that followed throughout the 1920s. Indeed many of the tribesmen in northern Afghanistan are sons and grandsons of Basmachis who fled across the border in the Twenties and Thirties, and they are traditionally anticommunist as well as anti-Soviet. Many rural Afghan tribes have also traditionally kept a distance from the central government of the country—whether the monarchy or the republic that replaced it in 1973. And issues of ethnic identity and autonomy have a long history in Afghanistan. The current Afghan resistance movement looks more like a traditional revolt of this kind than like modern guerrilla warfare.

But the fact is that the Afghan rebels violently reject the imposition of "socialism" by foreign tanks supporting a Marxist regime with no significant social base. Afghan nationalism has always been splintered by the ethnic loyalties of the different groups within the country—including Pashtuns, Tajiks, Hazaras, and Nuristanis, many of whom feel themselves more closely identified with their group than with Afghanistan. They have nevertheless come out in strength against foreign occupation and may well find the current struggle an occasion to cooperate more closely. Indeed this war may encourage the creation of a more unified Afghan nation—one that will owe less to a rational design than to a popular struggle against a common foreign enemy. The war in Afghanistan is a struggle for freedom and independence by groups that have traditionally resisted both the authority of the state and the rule of foreign invaders, whether British or Russian. The people I saw had no clearly stated aims; they were simply fighting spontaneously for freedom from what they felt to be an oppressive regime.

The organizations based in Peshawar cannot be said to constitute a true liberation front, although five of them have formed a loose coalition called the Islamic Alliance, while also competing for aid from the various Arab countries that support the rebellion. The leaders and most of the members of these factions are of Pushtan origin, but all the ethnic groups take some part in the struggle. And though the factions include secular liberals as well as conservative monarchists, all of the three most significant groups have connections with local Islamic leaders. The National Front for the Islamic Revolution of Afghanistan led by S. A. Gailani and the National Liberation Front led by H. S. Mojadidi both belong to the coalition. A third major faction, which has no part in the coalition, is the Islamic Party led by Gulbuddin Hekmatyar. Both Gailani and Mojadidi are from prominent families of Muslim leaders, and Gailani himself is a recognized member of the religious establishment. With the exception of the Hazaras, all the ethnic groups are Sunni Moslems, and although their religious leaders lack both the organization and the formal hierarchy of the Shiite Moslems in Iran, they have much prestige and have been important in focusing resentment against the secular leaders that have been in power since 1978. Insurgent leaders have said that the Afghans are a people fighting for their faith.[1]

[1] The other rebel factions are the Islamic Society of Afghanistan led by B. Rabani, the Islamic Revolutionary Movement led by N. N. Mohemedi, and the Islamic Party of Yunis Khalis, which is based in the Nangrahar province and whose leader, unlike the others, is fighting alongside his men. Finally, there is the Afghanistan Islamic and Nationalistic Revolutionary Council led by Z. K. Nassary, an American citizen born in Afghanistan.

All of these organizations compete with each other for support within Afghanistan and for international aid, especially from Egypt, Saudi Arabia, and Kuwait. Lacking a charismatic leader, the coalition is headed by Dr. Sayyef, a figure chosen less for his importance within the resistance than because he represented a compromise among the various groups. Gulbuddin is the only leader who refuses to join the coalition—more for personal reasons than ideological ones, although he is considerably more fundamentalist than both Gailani and Mojadidi, who tend to have fairly moderate views on questions of religion. The ideological differences among the groups are generally minor, certainly less divisive than the personal disputes among their leaders. But it is clear than many of the fighters inside Afghanistan are becoming impatient with these disputes and with the rifts between moderates and fundamentalists. This may eventually lead to further splits between the exiled leaders and the rebels fighting inside the country.

Most of the mujahidin, or freedom fighters, are based in provinces deep within Afghanistan and have little contact with the leaders in Peshawar. Arms and medicine are sent across the border, but there are no hit-and-run attacks by guerrillas based on the other side of the frontier—operations of a kind common in other liberation struggles throughout the world. For the most part, the war in Afghanistan is an internal struggle fought by local mujahidin who rarely leave their own provinces.

Traveling to Afghanistan from Pakistan, you have to cross half a dozen police barriers between Peshawar and the border. These barriers, which are intended to separate the "tribal areas" populated by Pakistan's Pathans from the rest of the country, cannot be crossed in either direction after seven o'clock in the evening. The rebel organizations ask foreign observers who want to enter Afghanistan to dress as Afghans so as to attract as little attention as possible. And although the Pakistani police sometimes stop journalists and send them back to Peshawar, most travelers have little difficulty getting through the barriers.

I spent the night in the small Pakistani city of Miramshah before crossing the border into the Paktia province with my guides from one of the resistance groups. We headed toward the cities of Tani, Khost, and Gardez, a round trip of about 120 miles on foot. At this time of the year, the humidity of the Pakistani monsoon season gives way to fresher mountain air as you approach the old British "Durand line" that marks the Afghan border. Unlike the Nangrahar and Kunar provinces, the hills in Paktia are still wooded. Caravans of camels, each carrying loads of four to six hundred pounds of wood, pass in the other direction on their way to Pakistan—a trek of some ten days across the mountains. There a load of wood bought in Afghanistan for 1500 afghanis can be sold for 4000 afghanis. Thus, little by little, the trees of Paktia are cut down and eventually erosion sets in, as it has elsewhere in the country.

The steep trails through this terrain look down on tiny streams of more or less drinkable water. You never feel alone on the march, since you constantly pass groups of mujahidin. Each wears a huge crested Pashtun turban, baggy trousers, and leather sandals with soles made out of car tires. A long bullet-studded bandolier, slung across the shoulder, holds in place the characteristic straight Pashtun dagger.

Most Afghans are good walkers, and the daily march can last up to ten hours. This leaves little time during the day to observe guerrilla activities at first hand. We occasionally stopped at small tea houses, called *chai khane,* that served green Chinese tea and black Indian tea—both sweetened with large quantities of sugar, which helps to relieve dehydration and loss of energy. In Afghanistan you rarely see extreme poverty of the kind found in Pakistan, but most Afghans live on very little. A typical meal would consist of tea and unleavened bread dipped in sauce. There are no vegetables or fruit, and meat is rare. Traveling with guides from the resistance groups, one usually spends the night in a camp built by the mujahidin or in a village. The fighters are generally treated hospitably by the local people, who serve them tea and buttermilk and what little food there is.

I observed only one military action during my stay, an attack on an outpost held by the Afghan army. The fighting began at about 8:30 in the evening, not far from the city of Khost, and it lasted for an hour and fifteen minutes. There was no clear outcome. Spectacular military action—the sort of fighting seen on television—is, of course, rare in guerrilla warfare. Decisive battles are even rarer. What I saw was an exercise in harassment, less effective as a military tactic than as a psychological one. The guerrillas' aim was to remind the government forces that they were trapped in an isolated outpost and incapable of controlling the surrounding countryside. As far as I could see, there were no casualties. The Russian Kalashnikov automatic rifles of the guerrillas were completely useless against both the outpost and the tanks, which made a brief foray from the fort in order to impress the rebels. But machine guns and cannons fired blindly from within the fort were ineffective against the guerrillas, who were well hidden in the rocky hills. It was impossible to get anywhere near the fort because of the minefield around it.

The arms used in this engagement provide a good example of the limited weapons the Afghan movement has at its disposal. Many of the fighters carried old-fashioned Lee Enfield rifles from World War Two, and some had automatic weapons made on the Kalashnikov model in Egypt. They had far too few heavy weapons. Throughout my stay, I saw only one heavy Chinese machine gun, one mortar, and two of the Soviet antitank weapons called RPG-2s. As a result, the mujahidin can undertake very little offensive action. Certainly they seem too weak to take over the government's military outposts, which are surrounded by minefields that were installed fairly recently. The main tactic left open to them is to sabotage the traffic on the roads; although their light weapons are useless against tanks and helicopters, they can be effective against truck convoys. The mujahidin tend to exaggerate their victories and enormous losses have been reported on both sides, but in fact the military situation is a standoff. On the one hand, the towns and outposts held by the Russians and the Afghan army are beyond the reach of the guerrillas. Government truck convoys are often intercepted, but troops in armored vehicles accompanied by helicopters travel freely throughout the countryside. On the other hand, the Afghan army cannot pursue the mujahidin into the hills and mountains they control.

Central to both the government and the opposition are the people of the Pashtun tribes, who make up about 40 percent of the population. They were directly involved in the creation of the Afghan state during the middle of the eighteenth century and have been able since then to gain control of most of the wealth in the country: the wheatfields in the north, the pastures in the central plains, and, most important, the state administration, army, and police.

The bureaucrats who have controlled the government since the coup against President Daoud in 1978 are also Pashtun, whether they come from the faction called Khalq, which largely controlled the regime until December 1979, or the one called Parcham, which the Russians have now brought to power. The members of the Khalq faction, which is wholly Pashtun, are poorly educated and politically unsophisticated. After they seized power in 1978, they tried to bring about rapid reforms but failed; their group was split by the rivalry between Nur Mohammed Taraki and his successor, Hafizullah Amin. The Parcham faction, which is more open to non-Pashtun groups, and more urbanized and better educated, also participated in the coup against Daoud's republic, but its members were soon pushed out of power and their leaders either arrested or sent into exile as ambassadors. Babrak Karmal, for example, was posted to Prague in July 1978, while the Khalq regime was receiving Soviet military aid. In recent weeks President Karmal has purged a number of Khalqs, who still account for two-thirds of the members of the ruling People's Democratic Party and many of the remaining officers of the army and air force.

Both groups are entirely secular. The shortsightedness of their regimes, the mechanistic way in which they have tried to "modernize" the economy, and their ignorance of conditions in the countryside have alienated them not only from rural Pashtuns but also from the other tribes that make up the population. There is, for example, widespread discontent amont the Tadjiks, who are Persian-speaking and make up some 35 percent of the Afghan population. Both the Nuristanis, who constitute about 3 percent, and the Shiite Hazaras, who account for 10 to 12 percent, are fighting to establish local bases of power and to avoid centralized control. The Turkish population—which is made up of the Uzbeck, Turkmen, and Khirgiz people living in the northern part of the country—has also joined the resistance.

Unlike in Iran, where the opposition to the Shah came principally from the cities, in Afghanistan the resistance is mostly rural and tribal, a response to the ill-conceived reforms of the Khalq regime. The agrarian reform instituted at the end of 1978 limited property holdings to 15 acres of fertile land and up to 180 acres if the land were less fertile. But in redistributing the land the regime neglected to redistribute seeds or to take into consideration the ownership and control of irrigation systems. This meant that large numbers of peasants found themselves in possession of land they could neither plant nor irrigate, and many of them were forced to ask their old landlords to exchange some of their new land for seeds.

Another unpopular decree banned the traditional dowries that many tribes relied upon to discourage husbands from seeking divorce—since the dowry had to be returned in an unsuccessful marriage. The regime also established education for girls as well as boys, but continued to hire only men as teachers. Many fathers would not allow their daughters to attend classes taught by men, and in some cases teachers were killed by villagers. In several instances the army retaliated, causing even more villagers to go over to the resistance. Following the putsch of 1978, the Stalinist measures of the Khalq regime only embittered the rural people traditionally hostile to outside leaders. Largely ignorant of conditions in the countryside, the new regime was unable to carry out reforms or impose a new system of law and order. And their policies soon led to economic failure and to growing resistance to the army throughout Afghanistan.

Neither the Soviet invasion nor the Parcham faction it brought to power has been able to solve these problems. However willing it may be to carry out reforms, the new regime has been too weak to do so, and because of its ties with the Soviet troops it has been unable to link its social policies with a nationalist program that would appeal to the rural populations. Of the 80,000 men serving in the army when the regime came to power, some 50,000 have either deserted or rallied to the cause of the resistance movement. In May 1980, an attempt to enlist young men from the cities ended in failure. And the fragmentary and uncoordinated nature of the resistance makes it considerably more difficult to control. The struggle between the government and the resistance is not restricted to the border regions but has spread throughout the provinces of Longar, Wardak, Ghazni, Parwan, and Badakhshan. Other provinces, like Hazarajat and Nuristan, are natural mountain fortresses, wholly inaccessible to regular government troops. There are also widespread reports of sabotage and other forms of resistance in the cities, particularly in Jalalabad and in the capital Kabul.

For the U.S.S.R., the situation is much more complicated than it seemed a few months ago. The Soviet invasion has rescued the "socialist" regime, and the remarkable brutality of the Amin government has been softened. (There is no basis for the accusations of "genocide" that some Afghans have made in the European press.) But the intervention has also made the regime even more unpopular in the countryside. The resistance has not been weakened, and it continues to attack the military outposts of the government. The guerrillas may lack an ample supply of arms, but they have strong morale, which remains the most vital resource of any army whether traditional or irregular.

Between the mid-1950s and 1973 much of Afghanistan's foreign aid came from the U.S.S.R. Soviet economic aid and military equipment and training cost approximately $2.5 billion before 1973, and then over $1 billion between the years 1973 and 1978. Now the cost is even higher. Suppressing the Afghan resistance will require more manpower and more money from the Soviet Union as well as considerably more time, especially if the resistance soon gets the weapons it seeks, including antitank weapons such as the British LAWS-66s and the Soviet RPG-2s. Up to now, financial support has come largely from Saudi Arabia and Kuwait, light weapons from Egypt. The U.S.S.R. can continue to create refugees by destroying homes and villages—a tactic which undermines the effectiveness of the mujahidin working in the provinces along the border—and by sending more troops into Afghanistan.

The refugees come from provinces where the fighting is heaviest, particularly the strategic provinces on the Pakistani border. When they cross the frontier they come under Pakistani control and are sometimes given tents and other supplies. The Pakistani regime is cooperative, but the aid the refugees receive is wholly inadequate. The U.N. High Commission for Refugees, which estimates that there are some 800,000 to 850,000 Afghans now in Pakistan, also contributes aid. But the commission has begun to receive complaints that part of that assistance is now going to Pakistanis rather than to the refugees it is intended for. When I was in Karachi, several boatloads of medicine had been sitting at the docks there for some two months, much of it undoubtedly spoiling in the heat. There is no work for the refugees in Pakistan, where unemployment is already high. And they live in appalling conditions, much worse, for example, than those of most Palestinian refugees. It is estimated that there are also some 50,000 Afghan refugees in Iran.

The most serious weakness of the Afghan resistance is its lack of decisive leadership. It has no modern leaders capable of organizing and coordinating the movement or creating a political hierarchy that could rival that of the government. It also needs skillful cadres to organize local fighting units. The resistance movement is a traditionalist revolt, not an expression of popular demand for economic and social change. Yet it represents a widely felt opposition to the brutal and mechanistic rule of the government—opposition that could in time produce a movement of a more modern kind. Assuming that the resistance receives the aid it needs to continue fighting, young leaders will eventually emerge from the struggle with their own demands for broader, more modern changes.

The Soviets are unlikely to withdraw for a long time. They would not have invaded in the first place if they had not intended to stay until they had guaranteed the survival of the regime, and they are still far from having accomplished this. The Russians seem to believe their strength in southwest Asia and elsewhere is based on the assumption that others see them as invincible. This is why withdrawal at this stage is unthinkable. The new Afghan war will go on. To believe it possible to return to a neutral Afghanistan is wishful thinking.

October 1980

How successful are the Soviet troops fighting in Afghanistan? During a second visit to the resistance forces, in late 1980, I found that in some respects the Russians were improving their tactics. For example, soon after I entered northeastern Pakistan with a group of five resistance fighters, one of my companions reached out abruptly to stop me from stepping on a mine that lay a few feet ahead on the mountain path. It was the size of a pack of playing cards and covered with green plastic which blended easily with the moss-covered ground. Walid, my translator and the leader of our group, took a photograph of the mine before he threw a rock and exploded it. These antipersonnel mines are scattered in the mountains by Soviet helicopters. They explode only when someone steps on them, and they can easily blow off your leg. They are relatively ineffective against insurgents traveling by day, but they prevent guerrillas from moving through the hills at night, particularly if they are accompanied by caravans of camels. By contrast, when I first visited the resistance groups last summer, we often traveled at night.

The Parcham faction now running the Afghan government which the Soviet Union brought to power in late 1979 has, moreover, been able to organize defense forces in the villages along the border, something the preceding Khalq regime was not able to do. Aside from ambushes on the roads, most of the skirmishes we observed followed a similar pattern: lightly armed guerrillas attacked mountain villages, forts, or military outposts held by the army, which then responded with heavy machine guns or, more often, mortars. The outcome in most cases was largely symbolic: there was no gain for either side, although such skirmishes can be unsettling for Afghan army soldiers, who feel isolated and vulnerable in these mountain outposts.

In other cases, however, the Russians won decisively. A band of some 300 resistance fighters was surrounded by Soviet troops between September 24 and 27, not far from the towns of Sao and Shal in Kunar province. After two days of artillery fire and bombing, Soviet "black beret" paratroopers were dropped from helicopters. "They were very fast," Walid told me, "faster than us, and good shots. When it got dark, they began to shoot flares from the hilltops, and the fighting went on throughout the night. For two days we had no food, no way to defend our position. It was raining, a hellish two days." There were few survivors among the resistance fighters. A similar operation took place in September in the Panjshir valley. Then in late November Soviet and Afghan troops began a campaign to drive the guerrillas not only from the Panjshir valley but also from the provinces of Baghlan, Parwan, Logar, Wardak, and the border region of Paktia. This continues today.

What have the Soviet troops achieved during the year that they have occupied Afghanistan? Until now their strategy has proven very effective, largely because they have avoided the mistakes made by the French in Algeria and the Americans in Vietnam:

they have not tried to overrun the country with an expeditionary force of some 500,000 men, and so have not been burdened with an enormous force of largely unneeded soldiers who would have been expensive to feed, and of whom only 10 to 15 percent would have been useful in fighting the resistance. Instead the Soviet Union has chosen, whether for political or economic reasons, to occupy Afghanistan with an army of only about 80,000 men— enough troops to assure control of the major cities and roads in the country. And for the most part, these troops are inconspicuous; they are rarely seen at all except in Kabul.

Since 1978, nearly half of the 80,000 men in the Afghan army have deserted to the resistance forces, often taking their arms and even their ammunition. But the soldiers who remain have been able to hold the government's positions on the Pakistani border, where the regime maintains a fairly dense line of invulnerable outposts. During the last year, mines have been planted around these camps; the resistance fighters, with their inadequate armies, have been unable to harass them effectively. The soldiers rarely leave the forts to pursue guerrillas into the surrounding countryside.

Soviet troops move in armored columns that are also largely invulnerable to guerrilla attacks. Most of the mines and other explosives the guerrillas have used until now have been of such poor quality that they are rarely able to damage a tank. The insurgents have few antitank guns, and Soviet losses have been very moderate. Soviet vehicles are also protected by armored helicopters, which intervene quickly whenever a tank is attacked. Airborne Soviet troops were not used until recently, and they remain rare even today. But if they prove effective, they may in the future be used more widely to prevent offensive attacks by Afghan resistance fighters.

The Soviet troops and the regime they installed in power have had some success in organizing the tribal people in the eastern mountains. In order to gain the allegiance of tribal chiefs who, for various reasons, were not sympathetic to the rebels, the Russians made payments to Moslem groups in Kunar, to the Shinwari tribe in the Nangarhar, and to the Mangal and Jaji tribes in Paktia. Not surprisingly these alliances have created difficulties for the resistance, particularly since Afghan traditions hold that no reconciliation is possible once blood has been shed.

But during this first year of occupation, Soviet activity has been concentrated in the cities, particularly in Kabul. The Soviets were concerned above all to impose order. To do so, they have tried to build up the administrative organization of the Parcham faction, which had been badly weakened by the rival Khalq faction the U.S.S.R. supported in 1978, after the coup against President Daoud. And they have replaced some Parcham functionaries with Soviet administrators. The Soviets have also improved transportation into Afghanistan and are setting up large numbers of economic projects that will help increase trade between Afghanistan and the U.S.S.R. In Kabul this summer special identity cards were distributed to merchants to help the Russians control travel into and out of the city. These measures also help prevent resistance fighters from infiltrating the bazaar.

And yet the regime still cannot count on much support among the people in the cities. It has not even been able to recruit enough young men to maintain an army of 40,000 fighters, although by Afghan standards army wages are considered good: a noncommissioned officer earns 6,000 afghanis, a militiaman 3,000 to 4,000 afghanis (i.e., between 90 and 120 dollars). The insurgents' networks in Kabul remain largely intact, and they claim to have supporters even in certain units of the Afghan army. On several occasions students have organized street demonstrations against the regime. Soldiers in Kabul are threatened by terrorist attacks, and last December, on the anniversary of the invasion, there were several riots which the government punished by arrests but not by mass killing. Some important administrators have also refused to collaborate with the regime, and many skilled and educated people have left the country—an erosion of the professional classes that has undermined the regime and the resistance alike.

But the cost of the Soviet strategy in Afghanistan has, until now, been very moderate. The Russians have lost little equipment, and the estimates of casualties announced to the Western press by the resistance and by "diplomatic sources" in New Delhi have been much exaggerated. Some reports have suggested that in September alone the Soviet army lost 1,500 men. From all I saw, this seems most unlikely. I suspect the Soviet army in Afghanistan has lost no more than two or three thousand soldiers during the past year.

Although at one time the Western press tended to overestimate the guerrilla forces, it has now become fashionable to take a more disparaging view. What is not said in these more skeptical accounts is that few resistance groups, whether Asian, African, or Latin American, have had to fight under such unequal conditions. Also unnoticed, and even more important now after a year of occupation, is that the morale of the Afghan resistance has not been broken. The insurgents have not yet suffered a fierce unrelenting attack like the antiguerrilla campaign in which General Challe destroyed the wilayas in Algeria in 1958 and 1959, or the "search and destroy" missions and Phoenix operation that the U.S. carried on in Vietnam in 1969 and 1970.

The outcome of the first year of fighting is thus uncertain. Although the resistance movement has not been broken, the insurgents are badly organized and much divided among themselves. They lack skilled technicians and effective local leaders. What heavy weapons they have are poorly distributed. Instead of being widely dispersed among a large number of insurgents as they are now, these weapons should be concentrated among a few small fighting bands that could be effective in sabotaging tanks. If the resistance is to be more effective, many of the guerrillas should be reassigned to more useful tasks such as producing food for other fighters, organizing food reserves, clearing mines, or gathering and spreading information.

For the most part, the peasants are thought to be favorable to the resistance, but, if they are to be used effectively, they too must be reorganized, either along tribal lines or in networks based on traditional patronage. Soviet and Afghan troops have already caused a large number of peasants to flee from their homes in the provinces along the border. A year ago there were approximately 400,000 Afghan refugees across the border in Pakistan. Today there are more than one million—some estimates run as high as 1.4 million—some of them driven from their land, others simply frightened by the fighting. As a result the guerrillas traveling through the border region often have trouble finding enough to eat. The antipersonnel mines that Soviet troops have scattered in the eastern border provinces create further difficulties. Until the various guerrilla factions can put aside their differences and better organize the rural populations, they will continue to have trouble defending themselves against the heavy weapons and armored vehicles of the Soviet troops.

Even today, the guerrillas cannot be said to be fighting for a clearly defined new government; they are united only by their rejection of Parcham's centralized authority. Local opposition to the land reform and literacy campaigns that were initiated by the Khalq regime originally produced the resistance movements, and they continue to oppose abrupt changes in their traditional tribal society. They reject the atheism of the Marxist-Leninist government, and they contest any extension of state bureaucracy. They also object, increasingly, to occupation by a foreign power—the first foreign occupation in Afghan history.

The goals of the six major resistance groups are often contradictory. The most extreme faction, the fundamentalist Islamic Party of H. Gulbuddin, uses torture and frequent purges to maintain a party line derived in part from the example of Khomeini's Iran. Gulbuddin opposes modernization and scorns Western liberal ideas. But he also opposes traditional spiritual figures like S.A. Gailani and S. Mojadidi, both leaders of rival resistance groups descended from prominent Moslem families within the Afghan religious establishment. Gulbuddin's commitment to revolutionary Islam leaves no room for the tribal allegiances and religious conservatism of Gailani and Mojadidi. He also disapproves of their Afghan nationalism, which is in fact inconsistent with the limited provincial nature of their support and the strength of their ties with local tribal chiefs. Gulbuddin's is the only major faction that does not belong to the loose coalition of resistance groups based across the border in Peshawar.

The largest insurgent group is the Islamic Revolutionary Movement led by N. Mohammadi, which despite its name rejects Islamic fundamentalism and is currently threatened by an internal schism. Several other small factions remain divided from the rest because they appeal exclusively to particular ethnic peoples such as the Nuristanis or Hazaras, notwithstanding agreements of cooperation that the Nuristani commander called "Anwar Khân" is reported to have made with leaders of both the Hazara and Kunar peoples.[2] The few groups that appeal to leftist ideologies are

[2] See the report by Mike Barry in *Le Nouvel Observateur*, January 26, 1981, pp. 64–65.

almost entirely without popular support. None of the factions has put forward a charismatic leader capable of overcoming the differences that divide the movement.

The fierce independence of the guerrilla fighters is at once the movement's most important strength and its greatest weakness. The rebels' determination has not softened during the past year of inconclusive skirmishes. They continue to fight in the flamboyant style of traditional tribal warriors—showing a kind of personal heroism that can be effective in isolated incidents but that also tends to work against the efficient military organization that the resistance movement so badly needs. In opposing the Marxism-Leninism of the regime, the insurgents have, for better or worse, much reinforced their own traditional values. Many resistance fighters in Kabul, for example, who took no part in organized religious practices only two years ago, now make some point of observing the Islamic schedule that calls for praying five times a day. The propaganda of both Khalq and Parcham points out that history and progress are on their side, whereas the resistance groups are said to represent reaction and obscurantism.

An even more pressing problem today is the rebels' lack of arms and ammunition. In this, there seems to have been no improvement between my first visit in June and my second in October 1980. The guerrillas are still fighting with British Lee-Enfield rifles left over from the Second World War and with Kalashnikov automatic weapons made in Egypt. Heavy artillery is still in short supply, as are the mines and other explosives the resistance needs to fight Soviet tanks and armored helicopters. The new American administration may undertake to supply them, perhaps clandestinely. Already there are rumors circulating in Peshawar that some Afghan insurgents are being trained to use S.A.M. ground-to-air missiles.

Until now the invasion of Afghanistan has had few serious repercussions for the Soviet government, whether internationally or at home. The reaction among Western countries has been extremely reserved: a limited boycott of the Olympic games; an American grain embargo without much consequence since other countries such as Argentina have continued to sell to the U.S.S.R.; a gradual reduction of American technological aid. Several Western European countries including France have denounced the invasion, while increasing their trade with the Soviet Union. Many Europeans also seem to accept the idea that the U.S.S.R. has a privileged interest in Afghanistan.

In explaining the intervention, people often refer to Soviet fears of a fundamentalist revolution among their own Islamic population. In fact, the U.S.S.R. does not fear Islam; that is a Western fantasy. The Soviet "empire" is in no danger of "exploding"; the invasion of Afghanistan may indeed have been welcomed by some Soviet Moslems as increasing the proportion of Moslems in territories controlled by the U.S.S.R.[3]

Even if the invasion is seen as a "defensive" measure designed to strengthen a floundering communist regime, it seems clear that Moscow was concerned above all with the kind of territorial aims that have always guided Russian policy in this region. The U.S.S.R. has strengthened itself by increasing its territorial margin of safety—a kind of defensive aggression that is familiar enough in Soviet history. Even if Pakistan and Iran are not today threatened by the Soviet presence in Afghanistan, the U.S.S.R. is now in a much stronger position to lean on either of these countries if the need arises, and also to counter what it sees as Chinese influence in Pakistan.

The U.S.S.R. has taken advantage of the regional instability caused by the fall of the Shah. In this global perspective, the Soviet stake in Afghanistan is secondary, but not unimportant. As for Pakistan, although it is a poor, weak country, it has recently been given a reprieve by the World Bank's decision to roll over its debt for the year 1980–1981, and by a $1.5 billion loan from the International Monetary Fund. This will, for the time being, put off financial crisis in the country that provides sanctuary for the Afghan resistance.

In early February, *The New York Times* reported rumors that Pakistan, under pressure from the U.S.S.R., might during the coming months enter into direct talks not with the Kabul government but with the Afghan People's Democratic Party—talks that would exclude the resistance groups. The report implied that the Pakistanis might be willing to make a deal by which the flow of weapons to the rebels would be cut off and the Soviet Union

---

[3] See Alexander Bennigsen's article, "Les musulmans de l'U. R. S. S. et la crise afghane " in *Politique étrangère*, June 1980.

would make a gesture of pulling out some of its troops—thus carrying Moscow closer to its goal of gaining international recognition of the regime it installed in Kabul. The report was vehemently denied by a Pakistani official, who reiterated his country's commitment to "total withdrawal" of Soviet forces.[4] The war could go on for a long time.

[4] See Bernard D. Nossiter's report in *The New York Times*, February 5, 1981, and the official denial published in *The New York Times* on February 11.

Annotated Bibliography

The following works, most of which are in English, will be of interest to the reader who wishes to pursue study of guerrilla warfare. Readers seeking additional material may refer to the bibliography in my *Stratégies de la guérilla: Anthologie historique de la Longue Marche à nos jours* (Mazarine, 1979), which includes some 250 titles in five different languages.

On Strategy

Edward Mead Earle, ed., *Makers of Modern Strategy: Military Thought from Machiavelli to Hitler* (Princeton, 1943).

Sun Tzu, *The Art of War,* translated with an introduction by S.B. Griffith (London, 1963).

Carl Von Clausewitz, *On War* (Harmondsworth, 1971).

On Guerrilla Warfare

Walter Laqueur, *The Guerrilla Reader* (New York, 1977) covers the eighteenth, nineteenth, and twentieth centuries and quotes more than forty authors. His *Guerrillas: A Historical and Critical Study* (London, 1977) is excellent, though not superior to John Ellis, *A Short History of Guerrilla Warfare* (London, 1975), which also covers guerrilla warfare from biblical times to the present. Robert B. Asprey, *War in the Shadows: The Guerrilla in History,* 2 volumes (New York, 1975), numbers more than 3,000 pages and is a truly monumental history of the guerrilla.

The pioneering work in terms of historical approach, written in

German, is Werner Hahlweg, *Guerrilla Krieg ohne Fronte* (Stuttgart, 1968).

A recent good reader is Sam S. Sarkissian, ed., *Revolutionary Guerrilla Warfare* (Chicago, 1975), which deals with contemporary problems.

Among the less recent readers that deserve consideration are: M.F. Osanka, ed., *Modern Guerrilla Warfare: Fighting Communist Guerrilla Movements, 1941–1961,* with an introduction by Samuel P. Huntington (New York, 1962) and Lt. Colonel T.N. Greene, *The Guerrilla and How to Fight Him, Selections from the Marine Corps Gazette* (New York, 1962), both of which are written in the spirit of the Cold War. For a more leftist perspective, see William Pomeroy, *Guerrilla Warfare and Terrorism* (New York, 1969), N. Miller and R. Aya, eds., *National Liberation in the Third World* (New York, 1971), and Eric R. Wolfe, *Peasant Wars in the Twentieth Century* (New York, 1969).

Many books on guerrilla warfare have a heavy emphasis on counterinsurgency. See, for example:

A.H. Nasution, *Fundamentals of Guerrilla Warfare* (New York, 1965), especially pp. 1–104.

David Galula, *Counter-Insurgency Warfare Theory and Practice* (New York, 1964).

Julian Paget, *Counter Insurgency Campaigning* (London, 1963) is a firsthand account of events in Malaya, Kenya, and Cyprus and is full of bright analysis.

Frank Kitson, in *Low Intensity Operations: Subversion, Insurgency, and Peace Keeping* (London, 1971) (especially chs. 6, 7, and 8), draws on his experiences in Malaya, Kenya, Cyprus, Oman, and Aden to offer a valuable book.

John McCuen, *The Art of Counterrevolutionary War* (London, 1966).

Robert Thompson, *Defeating Communist Insurgency, Malaya and Vietnam* (London, 1966) is a particularly remarkable work on the subject.

Robert Moss, *Urban Guerrillas* (London, 1971).

On Partisan Warfare during the Second World War

C.A. Dixon and O. Heilbrunn, *Communist Guerrilla Warfare* (New York, 1954).

O. Heilbrunn, *Partisan Warfare* (New York, 1962).

J.A. Armstrong, ed., *Soviet Partisans in World War Two* (Madison, Wis., 1964).

V. Dedijer, *Tito* (New York, 1953).

Leslie Gardiner, *The Eagle Spreads His Claws* (London and Edinburgh, 1966) is about Albania.

John Iatrides, *Revolt in Athens: The Greek Communist Second Round, 1944–1945* (Princeton, 1972).

First International Conference on the History of Resistance Movements, *European Resistance Movements, 1939–1945* (Oxford, 1960).

On China

Mao Tse-tung, *Military Writings* (Peking, 1963). In particular, see his works dated 1936 to 1938.

Edgar Snow, *Red Star Over China* (New York, 1938).

Agnes Smedley, *The Long Road* (New York, 1971).

Jack Belden, *China Shakes the World* (New York, 1973).

Chalmers Johnson, *Peasant Nationalism and Communist Power* (Palo Alto, Ca., 1962).

On Indonesia

G. Mc. T. Kahin, *Nationalism and Revolution in Indonesia* (Ithaca, N.Y., 1952).

A.H. Nasution, *Fundamentals of Guerrilla Warfare* (New York, 1965). See especially part 2.

On the Philippines

For the Huk perspective, see William J. Pomeroy, *The Forest: A Personal Record of the Huk Struggle in the Philippines* (New York, 1963) and L. Taruc, *He Who Rides the Tiger* (London, 1967), which is a biography of the leader of the Huks.

Valeriano and Bohannan, *Counter Guerrilla Operations: The Philippine Experience* (London, 1962) offers the counterrevolutionary point of view.

On Malaya

Anthony Short, *The Communist Insurgency in Malaya, 1948–1960* (London, 1975).

Richard Clutterbuck, *The Long Long War* (1968) offers a first-hand account of the counterinsurgency side.

On Vietnam

Paul Mus, *Vietnam, sociologie d'une guerre* (Paris, 1952) has been translated only in part and is in its entirety a key work. For the translation see John T. MacAlistair and Paul Mus, *The Vietnamese and their Revolution* (New York, 1970).

Bernard Fall contributed many excellent books on the war in Vietnam. *Street Without Joy* (New York, 1957) concerns the period of French involvement in that country (1946–1954), and *The Two Vietnams: A Political and Military Analysis* (New York, 1967) concerns the later U.S.-dominated years.

For a Vietnamese perspective, se Vô Nguyên Giap, *People's War, People's Army* (Hanoi, 1962) and *The Military Art of People's War* (New York, 1970).

Among the many books published on the U.S. intervention in Vietnam, for general background see:

J. Buttinger, *Vietnam: A Dragon Embattled*, 3 volumes (New York, 1967).

Senator Gravell, ed., *The Pentagon Papers*, 4 volumes (Boston, 1972) and N. Chomsky and H. Zinn, eds., *Critical Studies on the Pentagon Papers* together form a major document on the subject.

On village organization, see G. Hickey, *Village in Vietnam* (New Haven, 1964).

On the N.L.F. it is interesting to compare Douglas C. Pike, *The Vietcong: Organization and Techniques of the N.L.F. of South Vietnam* (Cambridge, Mass., 1966) with Wilfred Burchett, *Vietnam Will Win!* (New York, 1969).

Jeffrey Race, *War Comes to Long An* (Berkeley, 1972) is an outstanding treatment of U.S. presence in Vietnam.

William R. Carson has written an interesting critique of U.S. strategy: *The Betrayal* (New York, 1968).

Frances FitzGerald's *Fire in the Lake* (New York, 1972) makes the most successful attempt since Bernard Fall's books (above) to communicate the situation in Vietnam to the U.S. layman.

On the bombing in North Vietnam and the organization in the North to resist bombings, see Gérard Chaliand, *Peasants of North Vietnam* (Baltimore, Md., 1969).

On Algeria

Mohamed Harb, *Le F.L.N.: mirages et réalités* (Paris, 1980) is by far the best analysis of the Algerian struggle for national liberation from 1954 to 1962.

A worthwhile though more journalistic book in English is Alistair Van Horne, *A Savage War of Peace* (Harmondsworth, 1978).

On Cyprus

Charles Foley, *Island in Revolt* (London, 1962) is excellent.

Charles Foley and W. Scobic, *The Struggle for Cyprus* (Palo Alto, Ca., 1973).

George Grivas, *The Memoirs of General Grivas,* edited by Charles Foley (London, 1964).

On Aden and Oman

Julian Paget, *Last Port, Aden 1967–8* (London, 1968).

R. Fiennes, *Where Soldiers Fear to Tread* (London, 1971).

On the Kurds

On the Kurdish movement in Iraq see David Adamson, *The Kurdish War* (London, 1964) and Dana Adams Schmidt, *Journey Among Brave Men* (Boston, 1964).

On the Kurdish national question in the Middle East from 1918 to 1980 see Gérard Chaliand, ed., *People Without a Country: The Kurds and Kurdistan* (London, 1980).

On the Palestinians

Very few books have been written on the military aspect of the struggle. A good general introduction is given by William B. Quandt, F. Jabber, and A.M. Lesch, *The Politics of Palestinian Nationalism* (Berkeley, Ca., 1973).

Gérard Chaliand, *The Palestinian Resistance* (Harmondsworth, 1972).

For the Israeli side, see Gl. Y. Harkabi, *Palestinians and Israel* (Jerusalem, 1974).

On Latin America

For an interesting work on the 1960s see Vania Bambirra, ed., *Diez anos de insureccion en America Latina,* 2 volumes (Santiago, Chile, 1971).

Ernesto Che Guevara, *Guerrilla Warfare* (New York, 1963).

Ernesto Che Guevara, *Bolivian Diary* (New York, 1969).

A. Mercader, J. de Vega, *Tupamaros: Estretegia y accion* (Montevideo, Uruguay, 1969).

Alberto Bayo, *150 Questions to a Guerrilla* (Boulder, 1967).

Hector Béjar was the leader of a guerrilla group and has written an excellent analysis of its failure: *Notes on a Guerrilla Experience* (New York, 1971).

On Africa

Most of the writings of Amilcar Cabral will be of interest to those studying African liberation struggles.

On Kenya

J. Henderson and P. Goodheart, *The Hunt for Kimathi* (London, 1958), L.S.B. Leakey, *Defeating Mau Mau* (London, 1952), and Frank Kitson, *Gangs and Countergangs* (London, 1960) offer the perspective of the counterinsurgency.

D.L. Barnett and Karari Njama, expressing the Mau Mau point of view, have written *Mau Mau from Within* (New York, 1966).

On Guinea-Bissau

Gérard Chaliand, *Armed Struggle in Africa* (New York, 1969).

Basil Davidson, *Revolution in Guinea* (Harmondsworth, 1968).

Lars Rudebeck, *Guinea-Bissau* (Uppsala, 1974).

On Angola and Mozambique

John Marcum, *The Angolan Revolution: Exile Politics and Guerrilla Warfare (1962–1976)* (Cambridge, Mass., 1978) is the best book on the Angolan movements of liberation.

John Stockwell, *In Search of Enemies, A C.I.A. Story* (New York, 1978) examines U.S. policy from 1974 to 1975. To my knowledge there are no relevant works on Fremilo between 1964 and 1974.

On Chad

Robert Buijtenhuijs, *Le Frolinat et les révoltes populaires du Tchad, 1965–1976* (Paris, 1979).

On Western Sahara

John Mercer, *Spanish Sahara* (London, 1976) concentrates on the political and historical background of struggles in this region.

On Zimbabwe

Michael Raeburn, *Black Fire! Account of the Guerrilla War in Rhodesia* (London, 1978) contains fascinating accounts by both Z.A.N.U. and Z.A.P.U. fighters.

On Namibia

For information on S.W.A.P.O. see D. Mercer, ed., *Breaking Contract: The Story of Vinnia Ndadi* (Richmond, Va., 1974).

Designer: Eric Jungerman
Compositor: Huron Valley Graphics, Inc.
Printer: Vail-Ballou Press, Inc.
Binder: Vail-Ballou Press, Inc.
Text: 10/12 Times Roman
Display: Franklin Gothic